SCIENCE IN THE PUBLIC SPHERE

Science in the Public Sphere presents a broad yet detailed picture of the history of science popularisation from the Renaissance to the twenty-first century. Global in focus, it provides an original theoretical framework for analysing the political load of science as an instrument of cultural hegemony and giving a voice to expert and lay protagonists throughout history.

Organised into a series of thematic chapters spanning diverse periods and places, this book covers subjects such as the representations of science in print, the media, classrooms and museums, orthodox and heterodox practices, the intersection of the history of science with the history of technology, and the ways in which public opinion and scientific expertise have influenced and shaped one another across the centuries. It concludes by introducing the 'participatory turn' of the twenty-first century, a new paradigm of science popularisation and a new way of understanding the construction of knowledge.

Highly illustrated throughout and covering the recent historiographical scholarship on the subject, this book is valuable reading for students, historians, science communicators and all those interested in the history of science and its relationship with the public sphere.

Agustí Nieto-Galan is Associate Professor of History of Science and Director of the Centre d'Història de la Ciència at the Universitat Autònoma de Barcelona. He has written widely on the history of chemistry and natural dyestuffs, and on the history of science popularisation (eighteenth to twentieth centuries). His publications include *Barcelona: An urban history of science and modernity: 1888–1929* (co-editor, 2016) and *Popularizing Science and Technology in the European Periphery, 1800–2000* (co-editor, 2009).

SCIENCE IN THE PUBLIC SPHERE

A history of lay knowledge and expertise

Agustí Nieto-Galan

TRANSLATED BY FIONA KELSO

LONDON AND NEW YORK

Published in English in 2016
by Routledge
2 Park Square, Milton Park, Abingdon, Oxon OX14 4RN

and by Routledge
711 Third Avenue, New York, NY 10017

Routledge is an imprint of the Taylor & Francis Group, an informa business

© 2016 Agustí Nieto-Galan

Translated into English by Fiona Kelso

The right of Agustí Nieto-Galan to be identified as author of this work has been asserted by him in accordance with sections 77 and 78 of the Copyright, Designs and Patents Act 1988.

All rights reserved for the English edition. No part of this book may be reprinted or reproduced or utilised in any form or by any electronic, mechanical, or other means, now known or hereafter invented, including photocopying and recording, or in any information storage or retrieval system, without permission in writing from the publishers.

Trademark notice: Product or corporate names may be trademarks or registered trademarks, and are used only for identification and explanation without intent to infringe.

First published in Spanish in 2011 with the title *Los públicos de la ciencia: Expertos y profanos a través de la historia*

by Marcial Pons, Ediciones de Historia, S.A.
San Sotero, 6–28037 Madrid

British Library Cataloguing in Publication Data
A catalogue record for this book is available from the British Library

Library of Congress Cataloging-in-Publication Data
Names: Nieto-Galan, Agustí.
Title: Science in the public sphere : a history of lay knowledge and expertise / Agustí Nieto-Galan.
Other titles: Pâublicos de la ciencia. English
Description: Abingdon, Oxon : Routledge, 2016. | First published in Spanish in 2011 with the title: Los públicos de la ciencia : expertos y profanos a través de la historia (Madrid : Marcial Pons, Ediciones de Historia). | Includes bibliographical references and indexes.
Identifiers: LCCN 2015033056 | ISBN 9781138909519 (hardback : alk. paper) | ISBN 9781138909526 (pbk. : alk. paper) | ISBN 9781315640747 (ebook)
Subjects: LCSH: Communication in science. | Science—Social aspects. | Science news.
Classification: LCC Q223 .N4813 2016 | DDC 500—dc23
LC record available at http://lccn.loc.gov/2015033056

ISBN: 978-1-138-90951-9 (hbk)
ISBN: 978-1-138-90952-6 (pbk)
ISBN: 978-1-315-64074-7 (ebk)

Typeset in Bembo
by Apex CoVantage, LLC

Printed and bound in the United States of America by
Edwards Brothers Malloy on sustainably sourced paper

To the memory of Rosa Ambròs Barbany (1900–89), a wise lay woman

CONTENTS

List of figures	*ix*
Preface	*xi*

1	Introduction: the discontent of scientific culture	1
	1.1 The 'deficit model' legacy 3	
	1.2 The power of the publics 10	
	1.3 Lessons from the past 17	
2	Printed science	23
	2.1 The Scientific Revolution in print 25	
	2.2 Popular paradigms 34	
	2.3 The business of science publishing 38	
	2.4 Science and literature: common ground 41	
3	Spectacular science	52
	3.1 From curiosity to exhibition 53	
	3.2 Science museums 60	
	3.3 Theatrical science 68	
4	Heterodox science	81
	4.1 Alternative medicine 86	
	4.2 Professionals and amateurs 91	
	4.3 Popularisers and their public 99	
	4.4 Popular science and religion 104	
	4.5 Popularisation, distortion or simplification 108	

viii Contents

5 Classroom science 118
   5.1 Education and scientific culture 119
   5.2 Teachers and students 121
   5.3 Textbooks and notebooks 127
   5.4 Instruction, control and popularisation 133

6 Technological science 143
   6.1 Philosophers and artisans 145
   6.2 The publics of industrial culture 154
   6.3 Inventors, users and consumers 163

7 Media science 173
   7.1 Stars and planets 175
   7.2 Media molecules 178
   7.3 Our ancestors 182
   7.4 Cold fusion 186
   7.5 Climate change 190

8 Democratic science 197
   8.1 The participatory turn 198
   8.2 Health, resistance and appropriation 206
   8.3 Technoscience, risk and uncertainty 210

9 Conclusion 217

Bibliography 227
Index 261

FIGURES

2.1	The anatomy lesson of Andreas Vesalius and his audience (1543).	29
2.2	Bernard de Fontenelle explaining the plurality of worlds in his *Entretiens* (1686).	31
2.3	A phrenology head (1861).	37
2.4	Front cover of *Les merveilles de la science, ou description populaire des inventions modernes* by Louis Figuier.	42
2.5	Advertisement poster of Jules Verne's 'Extraordinary Journeys' (*Les voyages extraordinaires*) by Charles-Émile Matthis, 1886.	46
3.1	Levinus Vincent's *cabinet de curiosités* and its visitors in Haarlem, Holland (1705).	54
3.2	Visitors at the Great Exhibition of London in 1851.	57
3.3	Visitors in the Great Gallery of the Natural History Museum of Paris at the end of the nineteenth century.	62
3.4	The anatomy theatre of Leiden in an anonymous print from 1609.	69
3.5	A lecture in experimental physics by Jean-Antoine Nollet in the mid-eighteenth century.	70
3.6	Michael Faraday in a public lecture at the Royal Institution in London (1856).	73
4.1	Animal magnetism session in a Paris salon of the end of the eighteenth century.	82
4.2	A phrenologist in his consulting room.	84
4.3	Demonstration of anaesthesia using ether in Massachusetts General Hospital (1846).	89
4.4	Amateurs from the Barcelona Astronomical Society observing a solar eclipse in 1912.	95

x Figures

4.5	François Arago in the Académie des sciences, Paris, in 1839.	101
5.1	Joseph Black in a lesson on heat at the University of Glasgow circa 1760.	122
5.2	Students in the laboratory of Justus von Liebig in Giessen in the 1840s.	124
5.3	Henri Sainte-Claire Deville (1818–81) in a chemistry class with his colleagues and students circa 1890.	131
5.4	Linus Pauling teaching chemistry in the 1960s.	132
6.1	The death of Sophie Blanchard in an accident in 1819.	144
6.2	Public demonstration of the power of the air pump by Otto von Guericke (1654).	149
6.3	Artisan dyers in the Manufacture des Gobelins, Paris, 1772.	151
6.4	Public launch ceremony for a steam boat near Lyon, in 1783, invention of the marquis Jouffroy d'Abbans.	155
6.5	'Lab Technician Set for Girls', A.C. Gilbert Co. (1958).	165
7.1	Richard Leakey in 1977 with two skulls: *Australopithecus* in his right hand and *Homo habilis* in his left hand.	183
7.2	Stanley Pons and Martin Fleischmann announcing their results on cold fusion in the 23 March 1989 press conference.	187
8.1	Anti-GMO activists protesting in December 2005 in Hong Kong.	200
8.2	Environmental activists at the 'I Count Stop Climate Chaos' Rally, Trafalgar Square, London, 4 November 2006.	206

PREFACE

This book is the outcome of a long intellectual journey. It came into being in April 1994 in the Modern History Faculty at the University of Oxford, in a History of Science graduate seminar. There, at the heart of British academia, in the land of Isaac Newton, Charles Darwin and Michael Faraday, among other great names in Western science, I heard about 'popular science' and 'scientific culture' for the first time; I decided to revive and learn about not only the great luminaries from the past but also those who were lay, ignorant, forced aside from the epic struggle to explain the supposed truths of nature. At this informal gathering, someone mentioned an article published that same year by historians Roger Cooter and Stephen Pumphrey.[1] Despite the difficulty of reading it and the dense web of ideas it contained, the paper made a deep impact on me and led me to question the meaning of my work as a historian of science and to wonder about the ultimate reasons to ask certain questions of the past instead of others.

A few weeks later, my current colleague, Dr Xavier Roqué, who at that time held a post-doctoral position at the University of Cambridge, told me about the recent publication of a history of the science displayed at the nineteenth-century world's fairs, especially London's famous Great Exhibition held in 1851. It was a work by historian Robert Brain,[2] which contained amazing engravings of the Crystal Palace and some of the pavilions that housed machinery, inventions and scientific instruments in London, and also in Paris, Vienna, Chicago and Philadelphia.

Never before had I seriously considered the possibility of examining the history of science from the perspective of entertainment, fairs or popular culture, or from the plural perceptions of its multiple actors. Furthermore, back then I was particularly interested in the role of artisans, as crucial actors in the history of technology, but often forgotten in the romantic mythology of the great inventors, along with professional scientists and engineers working under the aegis of their academic institutions.

xii Preface

Some ideas need a long time to ripen, to slow-cook in the deepest recesses of our minds. Focusing on 'science in the public sphere' – I will return to this concept later – means to make old research topics useful and to dive into the abyss of a new field yet to be explored. So these first fascinating readings hibernated for ages in the messy drawer of disjointed musings, on the lists of good intentions that we all jot down in our notebooks during lulls in the maelstrom of everyday academic life.

In the summer of 2003, once I had finished my work on the craftsmanship skills of eighteenth- and nineteenth-century European dyers and printers, my seminal fascination for science in the public sphere resurged. It was during my stay at the Université de Paris X, Nanterre, when I spent many glorious days at the Bibliothèque nationale de France reading and rereading papers and books by authors that have become close friends in my teaching and research activities and who play a crucial role in the chapters of this book.

In the first decade of the twenty-first century, our group at the Universitat Autònoma de Barcelona worked intensively on the history of science popularisation in Spain. We took advantage of the numerous masters dissertations and doctoral theses from our History of Science graduate programme, whose results were presented at national and international conferences. After collecting new, unexplored case studies and developing some work at a comparative level, I personally decided to write in Spanish a sort of synthetic historical essay, a big picture of science popularisation, which could interest a great variety of readers particularly targeting the Spanish-speaking Latin American market. As a result, *Los públicos de la ciencia* appeared in 2011 published by Marcial Pons.

I am pleased to see how in the last four years the book has been well received and reviewed. It soon became a useful tool for history of science and science communication graduate teaching and a good starting point for those interested in science popularisation in a broad sense. I am indebted to my first reviewers – José Luis Peset, Jaume Navarro, Ana Simões, Jesús Galech and Oliver Hochadel for their critical, stimulating comments, but also to other friends and colleagues who encouraged me to try to produce an English version of the book, addressed to a global market of potential readers.[3] Thanks to Routledge's interest in the book (I am particularly indebted to Senior Editor (history), Eve Setch, to Editorial Assistant, Amy Welmers, and to the positive comments of five anonymous referees) an updated, revised English version, now titled *Science in the Public Sphere*, has luckily become a tangible reality. My indebtedness goes to Fiona Kelso for the translation and for her unfailing effort to adapt the Spanish syntax into a readable text in English.

In the present English version, some Spanish case studies have been substituted by other examples; the theoretical framework, which deals with difficult concepts such as 'popular science', 'public sphere', 'science as cultural hegemony', 'public participation in science', and 'co-production of knowledge', has been refined and polished to produce a more robust introduction and conclusion. Nevertheless, this new English version preserves the main spirit of the 2011 edition, which attempted to write a new big picture of the history of science popularisation, a historical essay which integrated the main works and authors of the secondary literature, but also provided a personal view of science as a genuine part of modern culture. The book uses a great variety of historical evidence to strengthen the analysis of the present-day participatory turn in science, which forms the core of debates on the ways in which scientific knowledge should be communicated and displayed in the early twentieth century. The book also attempts to reinforce the political dimension of science popularisation and refine its theoretical framework.

Many friends and colleagues were crucial in encouraging me to produce the Spanish version in 2011, and I expressed my deepest gratitude to all of them in the preface of the edition published by Marcial Pons. For the present English edition I am particularly grateful to José Ramón Bertomeu-Sánchez and Ana Simoes for their unfailing encouragement (in view of my early scepticism) to publish the book elsewhere in a new updated version for an international readership. My lectures, research seminars and conference papers in Lisbon, Valencia, Barcelona, Madrid, Mexico City, Berlin, Oxford, Paris, Athens, Corfú, St Andrews and Chicago have been extremely useful for the polishing of several aspects of this new edition. The ICREA-Acadèmia research prize, which I was awarded by the Catalan Government (2009–14), has also been of great help for the final success of the whole project. Research projects funded by the Spanish Ministerio de Economía y Competitividad, in particular (HAR2009–12918-C03–02), Science and Expertise in the Public Sphere: Barcelona (1888–1992) and (HAR2012–36204-C02–02), Scientific Authority in the Public Sphere in Twentieth-Century Spain, have also made a significant contribution.

As in the Spanish version, this book mainly uses nineteenth-century engravings from the works of the French science populariser Louis Figuier. It is a way, in my view, to pay tribute to one of the most outstanding figures of science popularisation in the past who still merits further historical investigation. It is also a useful way to reinforce the historical sensitivity, even when discussing present-day problems of science communication. I am therefore indebted to the Biblioteca de Catalunya (Barcelona) for allowing the consultation of Figuier's books and for its permission to reproduce the selected images.

Finally, my deepest indebtedness goes to Montserrat and Martí, who, as usual, have unconditionally supported my never-ending commitments and academic duties, and have given to me the patience and love to help me finish the book. I have no words to express what I feel for them.

★ ★ ★

This updated English version also entails complex ideas and concepts that can only be properly understood from a historical perspective, from specific cultural and geographic contexts. Words like 'popular', 'popularisation', 'public sphere', 'communication', 'instruction', 'curiosity', 'entertainment', 'demonstration' and 'show' have a history of their own, as historical actors used in the past. Even today they

xiv Preface

take on different meanings according to the cultural tradition we are examining. For example, in the Latin context the concept of 'vulgus', of vulgarisation or dissemination, has prevailed over 'populus', or the 'popular' or 'popularisation' from the English tradition. Furthermore, the word 'communication' has become the icon of different professional groups throughout the twentieth century (science journalists, science museum curators, science teachers, professional popularisers), but its use in other historical periods and cultural contexts is questionable at best.

When outlining the details of the specific historical cases, the book remains faithful to the nomenclature used by the main actors in each period and place: from the 'curious' science of the Renaissance to the 'domestic' science of the medical treatises from the Enlightenment, the 'recreational' science of nineteenth-century book series and, for example, the 'entertaining' science of twentieth-century interactive museums. The majority of these concepts have been shaped and reshaped over time through complex interactions between the issuers and receivers of discourses, between actors with diverse social statuses and levels of intellectual authority, yet ultimately actors who have been the meaningful protagonists of the fascinating process of constructing scientific knowledge.

In this morass of concepts and ideas, the publics (audiences) emerge as a diffuse and somewhat ambiguous category, often flexible and changing, yet with a unifying capacity throughout the book. Far from the rigid categories which are supposedly separated by a neat boundary between creators and receivers of knowledge, the publics of science refers to the constant feedback among the different actors involved at any given point in history; it refers to that process of constant exposition and debate of ideas for the legitimisation of scientific authority in Western societies, as a hallmark of our modernity.

Once the walls between those who know and those who do not have been shaken, we all at some point become active publics of science, as students, visitors, spectators, users or patients, but also as disseminators, amateurs and experts of a given corpus of knowledge. Even the leading world experts in subatomic particles or molecular biology, to cite just two emblematic examples from the latest frontiers of science, are also ignorant in other spheres of knowledge or other human skills. This dynamic view of the construction of knowledge is thus based on this flexible use of the idea of 'publics'. As the media theoretician Michael Warner recently noted, the concept of 'publics' (or 'audiences') is crucial to understanding our societies, yet at the same time it is very difficult to define. It is a kind of social space created through the reflective circulation of a given discourse, a relationship among different groups of individuals within a given historical context.[4]

Equally, 'science' refers throughout the book to an embracing, generalist concept of 'knowledge' in a broad sense, beyond strict academic, disciplinary boundaries. Despite the widespread processes of professionalisation and specialisation, historical research enables us to identify numerous sources that demonstrate how scientific knowledge has travelled and continues to travel through society today, and how the 'publics of science' have participated and still participate actively in this complex social web.

In spite of the growing interest shown by historians, and historians of science in particular, in popular science and science popularisation in recent decades, the majority of published studies limit themselves to certain national contexts, such as Victorian Britain,[5] France in the second half of the nineteenth century,[6] nineteenth-century Germany,[7] and unified Italy.[8] Others are the outcome of collective studies which combine examples from different periods and countries,[9] or alternatively they tend to focus on a given historical period.[10] Many contributions are primarily theoretical in nature.[11] Others strive to provide an overview of the issue, yet they still rely on certain examples and case studies within a given context.[12] Therefore, there is no overview that combines a variety of historical examples from different points in time and space in a balanced way within an up-to-date theoretical framework. Thus, this book aims to at least partly fill that lacuna.

This book is a big picture of science popularisation, from the Renaissance to the twentieth century. It attempts to go a step further in terms of the political load of popular science and its cultural role in contemporary societies as an instrument of hegemony and social control. It provides an alternative perspective on science popularisation, and gives a voice to the varied audiences of science in history. It is organised into a series of thematic chapters which become different layers not in an effort to be exhaustive; rather, when superimposed they help us to gradually construct the complete backdrop of the work. Actors, practices, spaces, objects and discourses intermingle throughout the text and provide us with a new, somewhat impressionistic, fresh look at the role of science in society in numerous contemporary cultural debates.

Chapters devoted to 'printed science', 'spectacular science', 'heterodox science', 'classroom science', 'technological science', 'media science' and 'democratic science' all shed light on new actors, all of them active to a greater or lesser degree in the making of scientific authority and the validation of knowledge. These historical actors span diverse periods and sites: printing presses, anatomy theatres and *cabinets de curiosités* from the sixteenth and seventeenth centuries; aristocratic salons, informal gatherings, workshops and public demonstrations from the eighteenth century; bookshops, libraries, exhibitions, factories and museums from the nineteenth century; mass media and its vast popularisation projects from the twentieth century; and the new venues of citizenship and digital participation at the dawn of the twenty-first century. While historical examples from different periods appear in the majority of chapters, albeit with a particular emphasis on the eighteenth and nineteenth centuries, 'media science' and 'democratic science' draw primarily from twentieth-century examples, and even more recent cases from the twenty-first century. Furthermore, they strive to connect the general discussion on the publics of science with issues much more closely linked to our world today.

From the Renaissance until the early twenty-first century (along with occasional allusions to our ancient and mediaeval scientific legacy), shared and yet distinct elements appear. Popularisation in the past usually evolved in constant tension between instruction and entertainment, took place in specific venues and openly affected the relationship between their different audiences and their credibility,

xvi Preface

defining the boundaries between orthodox and heterodox knowledge, between professionals and amateurs, in order to capture the interest of the different audiences.[13] During the Renaissance, in their bid to acquire knowledge, the practices of natural philosophers were not too distant from their displays and public strategies before heterogeneous audiences. At that time, the boundaries between knowledge, entertainment and usefulness, between the professional and the amateur, between expert and lay audiences, were fuzzy.[14] Science in the Enlightenment was an amalgam of multifaceted activities. It flourished in the period between the culture of curiosity – whose forerunners were the *cabinets de curiosités* and the automata of the seventeenth century – and the modern distinction between academic and popular science which gained ground over the course of the nineteenth century. The multiple cultures of science in the eighteenth century – public experiments and demonstrations, theatrical enactments, courses and lectures – created new spaces in the public sphere and stimulated a series of views of nature which competed with religion and traditional political notions.[15]

The professionalisation and gradual specialisation of science throughout the nineteenth century devised a widening gap between experts and laypeople. Curricula and popularisation programmes targeted certain audiences of science a priori which were increasingly regulated. In this context, a certain kind of 'popular' science could be found on the covers of numerous books as a strategy for attracting potential readers, yet at the same time they served as a kind of opposition to the professionals' scholarly science. That was also the time of the professional science popularisers being obsessed with finding the right language to convey knowledge to all emerging social sectors, including the lower classes.[16]

In the first few decades of the twentieth century, scientism and the growing authority of professional scientists further widened this gap. Scientific progress was based on the victory of expert knowledge (*episteme*) over public opinion (*doxa*), as set forth by French philosopher Gaston Bachelard (1884–1962) in *La formation de l'esprit scientifique* (1938).[17] After World War II, the successive waves of criticism regarding the ulterior motives of the scientific, military and industrial complex which emerged from the conflict, coupled with the rising mistrust of the value of science, led to new attempts to 'evangelise' the supposed ignorant, immersed in a purported epistemological abyss of intellectual inferiority. Despite the rising influence of the new media (film, radio, television) and the sweeping expansion of so-called 'science centres' or interactive science museums, the barriers did not seem to be blurred in societies that were also afflicted by a sense of mistrust in scientific progress. The last few decades of the twentieth century, however, seemed to reveal a new paradigm of citizen participation, albeit not without controversy of its own, in which scientific knowledge would be 'co-produced' in the blurred boundaries of science and society, by different actors actively involved in dynamic negotiation processes.[18]

This is a history of science that can inspire readers with widely disparate educational backgrounds. Perhaps by appealing to reflexivity, the book seeks new avenues of dialogue with audiences that until now have been unaccustomed to a critical discourse on science, often mediatised by a positivist legacy that still prevails in our contemporary societies. Although the book is intended for a wide readership, it is particularly useful for professional scientists, science communicators, science museum curators, science teachers and historians and philosophers. Conceived with high academic standards, it is nonetheless written in a way that might arouse the interest of an average reader with historical sensitivity and concern for contemporary cultural problems in Western societies.

In the guise of an essay, the book obviously benefits from the work of expert historians whose ideas I have striven to summarise and reference as faithfully as possible, although it has also been fed from my own research and that of the members of our team at the Centre d'Història de la Ciència (CEHIC) at the Universitat Autònoma de Barcelona. In any event, any error or omission is my own fault. Likewise, the book also draws from numerous intellectual traditions – the history of the book and reading, cultural history, literary studies, 'science, technology and society (STS)' – which unquestionably enrich the work of historians of science, but which also place them on stony ground where one often feels like a temporary visitor, like a member of the lay audience. Here, too, I take full responsibility for my interpretation of these diverse theoretical frameworks and their application to specific historical examples.

The initial hypothesis put forward here is the possibility that the major efforts to popularise science, especially throughout the second half of the twentieth century, have not yielded their desired results, and that we are still trapped in a certain discontent of scientific culture. Through a lengthy journey into the past, this book explores the possible reasons for this discontent and suggests possible solutions. In the turbulent yet enriching crossing of the oceans of history, the reader is gradually transported to a new paradigm of participation in science, which challenges traditional methods of science popularisation today.

I speak from my passion for history and my vocation as a historian of science, yet I am aware that history does not solve today's problems. Perhaps it can only help us to understand some of the hidden causes of our concerns and dissatisfactions, to diagnose our discontent and to think about possible remedies.

I sincerely hope that the reader finds some of these 'remedies' in the forthcoming pages.

Notes

1 Cooter, Pumphrey (1994).
2 Brain (1993).
3 For reviews of the Spanish edition, see *Dynamis*, 32 (2), 2012: 501–21; *Isis*, 103 (4), 2012, 772–3; *Host*, 6 (Fall), 2012; *Actes d'Història de la Ciència i de la Tècnica*, 5 (2012); *Asclepio*, 66, (1), 2014.
4 Warner (2002b).
5 Secord (2000); Topham (2000); Knight (2006); Fyfe, Lightman (2007).
6 Bensaude-Vincent, Rasmussen (1997).
7 Daum (1998).
8 Govoni (2002).

xviii Preface

9 Papanelopoulou, Nieto-Galan, Perdiguero (2009).
10 Bensaude-Vincent, Blondel (2008).
11 Shinn, Whitley (1985); Hilgartner (1990); Bensaude-Vincent (2000).
12 Raichvarg, Jacques (1991); Govoni (2002); Topham (2009b).
13 My thanks to Oliver Hochadel for his interest in finding unifying elements on the prob-lem of science popularisation in different historical periods.
14 Bensaude-Vincent, Blondel (2008).
15 Bensaude-Vincent, Blondel (2008: 1–10).
16 Raichvarg, Jacques (1991).
17 Bensaude-Vincent (2000).
18 Jasanoff (2004).

1

INTRODUCTION

The discontent of scientific culture

In 2003, philosopher Joseph Agassi perceived popular science as: 'vital for culture at large . . . to widen horizons and rationalize life . . . to break the isolation of science from rest of culture'.[1] But his optimism did not hide his concern about the role of science in our contemporary societies and the need to reassess its position. Despite many efforts in favour of its effective dissemination and its growing influence on major political and economic decisions, for many privileged observers, science would have been relegated, especially in the second half of the twentieth century, to a certain marginalisation and isolation in relation to 'culture'. In his famous book, *Das Unbehagen in der Kultur* (1930) – translated into English as *Civilization and Its Discontents* – Sigmund Freud (1856–1939) believed that modern science had failed to make the Enlightenment dream come true; a dream where the progress of natural philosophy had to yield to the progress of moral philosophy. Most scientific advances have only apparently affected human happiness. Once the euphoria of novelty had worn off, an inevitable hidden face would always appear. In Freud's own words:

> In the last generations, man has made extraordinary strides in knowledge of the natural sciences and technical application of them, and has established his dominion over nature in a way never before imagined . . . But men are beginning to perceive that all this newly-won power over space and time, this conquest of the forces of nature, this fulfilment of age-old longings, has not increased the amount of pleasure they can obtain in life, has not made them feel any happier. The valid conclusion from this is merely that power over nature is not the only condition of human happiness, just as it is not the only goal of civilization's efforts . . . If there were no railway to make light of distances, my child would never have left home, and I should not need the telephone to hear his voice . . . What is the use of reducing the

2 Introduction

> mortality of children, when it is precisely this reduction which imposes the greatest moderation on us in begetting them . . . And what do we gain by a long life when it is full of hardship and starved of joys and so wretched that we can only welcome death as our deliverer?[2]

This controversial Freudian diagnosis of our supposed unhappiness should be analysed in depth in its own historical context – a task that obviously goes beyond the scope of this book. But Freud's dissatisfaction with the results of scientific progress does not seem to have been completely eradicated in the present, and has become a passionate topic of debate, which certainly requires further analysis.

The positivist optimism that advocated a direct link leading from scientific to moral progress experienced a serious setback with the crisis in capitalism of the stock market crash in 1929, the same year that Freud began to write *Civilization and Its Discontents*. But this regression was only aggravated through the second half of the twentieth century, especially after the appalling consequences of World War II: the tragic end of the German scientific hegemony in 1945, which inspired Theodor Adorno (1903–69) and Max Horkheimer (1895–1973) in their famous *Dialectic of Enlightenment* (1947);[3] the start of the nuclear arms race and the Cold War; the persistence of poverty and hunger among much of the world's population; and rising concern over the environmental price of industrial growth.

Perhaps the American historian Leo Marx was right when he said that the second half of the twentieth century was the time of 'post-modern' pessimism, a period that witnessed the death blow to the old Enlightenment dream of progress. The horror of the Nazi military-industrial complex, which was capable of unleashing the Holocaust, the terrible deaths among civilians with the atomic bombs in Hiroshima and Nagasaki, and accidents such as Three Mile Island, Bhopal, the *Exxon Valdez* and Chernobyl were all combined with a worrying process of natural degradation, loss in biodiversity, air and water pollution, acid rain, deforestation and desertification, the greenhouse effect, a hole in the ozone layer and the threat of climate change.[4] Along similar lines, when analysing the role of science throughout the twentieth century, the prestigious historian Eric Hobsbawn stressed that:

> The progress of natural sciences took place against a background glow of suspicion and fear . . . fuelled by four feelings: that science was incomprehensible; that (both) its practical (and moral) consequences were unpredictable and probably catastrophic; and that it underlined the helplessness of the individual and undermined authority.[5]

That pessimism could be even partly quantified. In the 1990s, more than 6,000 scientific articles appearing in the British press between 1946 and 1990 were analysed and classified. Among other striking results of the study, in around 1960 there emerged a kind of natural split between two contrasting views of science. In the preceding period, despite the horrors of the two world wars, the start of the Cold War and the arms race, the press still mainly disseminated a positive image of science as beneficial for humanity, and one that deserved to be celebrated by reporting on the major events in the lives and deaths of the great scientists and their discoveries. However, articles dating from post-1960 generally showed a much more negative, critical image filled with risks and dangers, albeit without delving too deeply into the underlying causes.[6]

As Harry Collins discussed in his recent book on scientific expertise, we have moved from a heroic image of science to a new scientific culture of everyday life in which things are crowded and complicated, full of uncertainties and risks that weaken the authority of the experts.[7] The following section is an attempt to analyse the possible causes of this shift.

1.1. The 'deficit model' legacy

In view of this negative image, which questioned the underlying values of Western societies, voices came to the fore that attributed dissatisfaction to the supposed scientific ignorance of the public at large, to a growing distance between contemporary societies and their expert elites.[8] In the 1980s, the 'deficit model' became popular in the English-speaking world through a movement called the 'Public Understanding of Science' (PUS), which assumed a considerable epistemological inferiority between experts and receivers of a scientific discourse. PUS stressed the chasm separating both camps and reinforced the role of scientists. It legitimised new professionals, science communicators, who were supposed to act as mediators to effectively and faithfully transmit 'official' knowledge to lay audiences, the latter receiving information acritically and supposedly passively via simple accumulation. This was the only way to improve the public image of science, which had been considerably damaged.[9]

The supposed public deficit justified a kind of scientific 'crusade', one that was vertical and one way, top-down, which legitimised an alliance between scientists' professional interests and political and corporate power, which was more concerned with justifying science than with it being effectively understood among large audiences. In theory, PUS was supposed to bring benefits to science itself and to the economy, the nation, the individual and the democratisation of society as a whole, along with moral, aesthetic and intellectual benefits. It would also act as an antidote to 'anti-science' movements which promoted pseudo-scientific practices that had always caused consternation among contemporary science popularisers and professional scientists.[10]

PUS was largely justified by the professional scientists' own discomfort with the supposed ignorance of the public, with hopes that better information would ultimately lead to greater social acceptance of science. In 1989, an article entitled 'The Public Understanding of Science', which appeared in the prestigious journal *Nature*, concluded that, based on several surveys conducted in the United Kingdom and the United States, the public had a very low level of scientific

4 Introduction

understanding. Citing the example of Isaac Asimov (1920–92), one of the top science writers of the twentieth century, the authors of the study stressed that in order to eradicate the mistrust caused by disinformation, PUS's popularisation efforts should build a new image of respect and admiration for science. Science popularisation therefore became a prime weapon, the ideal antidote to combat this discontent in scientific culture which had moved large swaths of the population to scepticism, often tinged with parascientific influences regarded as irrational. In its conclusions, however, the article displayed a certain degree of optimism:

> Finally, there is the question of the relationship between public understanding and public support for science . . . Preliminary analysis of results on these measures indicates that there are important relationships between public understanding and public attitudes, with a tendency for better-informed respondents to have a more positive general attitude towards science and scientists . . . The results we have provided indicate that although the public is largely uninformed, it is also largely interested in science.[11]

The problem, however, seems more complex than a certain ingenuous optimism about PUS indicates at first glance, and it dates from decades earlier. Back in the 1960s, numerous intellectuals criticised the populations of Western countries for blithely approving billions of dollars for scientific research through their votes, despite being incapable of understanding the meaning of this research. Unable to organise a political response, the new users of 'black boxes', unaware of their mechanisms and explanations, more or less explicitly mistrusted contemporary science. Its complexity and hyperspecialisation accentuated scepticism and ultimately led to a gradual expert–lay distancing.[12] Despite its qualitative and quantitative exponential growth, along with its intense process of specialisation, professionalisation and institutionalisation over the past two centuries, the social 'conquest' of science had never been fully accomplished. Traditional, popular wisdom had probably prevailed in the most stable communities and among the least adaptable individuals. In spite of the optimism of PUS campaigns, familiar beliefs and practices and a varied set of strategies of resistance would have remained.[13]

In 1965, the American historian Oscar Handlin claimed that the public had learned to tolerate science but not to assimilate it; it had tended to accept science as a useful 'truth' but one that was disconnected from their everyday beliefs or habits. This was top-down science, a science that had not truly changed the ancient beliefs in nature and morality and which had led to the coexistence or juxtaposition of two different kinds of knowledge that were supposedly disconnected from each other. In his unquestioning defence of expert science, Handlin contrasted academic knowledge with a vague, messy set of beliefs that he wished to eradicate. However, their very existence revealed that something had gone awry in the experts' popularisation plans.[14]

Along similar lines, in 1976 the prestigious American physicist Gerald Holton, who had a keen intellectual interest in the history and philosophy of science, was concerned about the poor public image of science in contemporary Western societies despite the vast efforts invested in reporting on it.[15] Holton expressed a certain unease regarding the spectacular growth in educational projects, science museums and audiovisual products whose results were questioned then and still are today. His book *Science and Its Public* (1976) was primarily a reaction to the virulent criticisms against science in the nuclear age and the Cold War.[16] Ultimately, Holton sought to use public debate to forge new alliances between science and society; new mechanisms of communication in a context of rejection and criticism.

However, communication problems also emerged within expert circles. As the literary critic Lionel Trilling (1905–75) bemoaned in his 1972 essay 'Mind in the Modern World',[17] the core of modern scientific knowledge was not shared by many people in the world of the humanities and social sciences. In other words, Trilling was reviving the old debate from the 1950s unleashed upon the publication of the famous book by British scientist Charles Pierce Snow (1905–72), which criticised the increasing gulf between humanistic culture and scientific culture in Western societies. Snow signalled a gradual impoverishment and isolation of the different expert groups who were unable to engage in fluid, open dialogue, which in the long term would affect their ability to communicate.[18]

Some of these problems, which showed symptoms of a Braudelian 'longue durée',[19] seemed even to have survived the wave of PUS in the 1980s. In 1994, the exhibition 'Science in American Life' opened at the Smithsonian Institution's Museum of American History in Washington, DC, sponsored by the American Chemical Society, the powerful association of professional chemists in the United States.[20] The exhibition comprised five thematic areas: 1. 'Laboratory science comes to America', which explained the synthesis of saccharine as a sweetener and the changes this brought about in the diet of everyday citizens; 2. 'Science for progress', which described the technological advances from 1930 to 1940 as they were presented at the 1939 New York World's Fair; 3. 'Mobilising science for war', which discussed the atom bomb and the Manhattan project, along with the discovery and application of penicillin; 4. 'Better than nature', which presented the benefits of DDT (despite the old controversies from the 1970s which came in the wake of the famous book by Rachel Carson, *Silent Spring* [1962]), plastics and contraceptive pills; and 5. 'Science in the public eye', which examined the latest advances in genetics and superconducting.

Despite these clearly positive and constructive titles, not to mention the rhetorical separation between scholarly science and its subsequent applications, the exhibition contained critical notes on the role of science in society – the marginalisation of social minorities from the practice of science, ethical and environmental problems and the close relationship between science and war – which caused significant upheaval in American public opinion and placed the American

6 Introduction

Chemical Society in an awkward position as the promoter of the exhibition. The press debate spurred by 'Science in American Life' regarding the worth or shortcomings of the public image of science deserves specific, in-depth examination of its own. However, what is relevant here is the very existence of this controversy, the resistance by many actors in contemporary science to accepting a minimally critical vision of science, its social immersion and its consequences in the everyday lives of citizens. What was the source of this unease? Why is the dialogue between scientific experts and lay citizens still so complex and rough at the edges at the dawn of a new millennium? Why, in short, is scientific progress perceived with mistrust by much of society, while at the same time the leading scientists, entrenched in their shells as the unquestionable authority, often discard lay opinions?

In the recent past, science popularisation has been perceived as a route of legitimisation and social acceptance of science's own status. But there have also been warnings against the dangers of oversimplification and even distortion of supposed 'truths', or even caution about a doorway open to the 'dangerous' pseudo-sciences. The statistics in France largely fuel this concern. In 1995, in the country that was the cradle of the Enlightenment and positivism, 50,000 citizens defined their profession on the income tax declaration form as astrologers, mediums or healers, while only 36,000 defined themselves as Catholic clergy and 6,000 as psychiatrists. Recent surveys confirm a notable rise in the followers of witchcraft and parapsychology. And as a backlash to biomedicine, which deconstructs human nature down to its tiniest particles, France is also the country that consumes and produces the most homeopathic medicine.[21]

To the minds of many scientists, opening the doorways of their palaces of knowledge too wide entails the not negligible risk of comparing science to any other corpus of beliefs and values, in a kind of alarming epistemological symmetry tinged with relativism which has caused a great deal of unease among many professionals in recent decades. Most of them were trained in the epistemological superiority of scientism, so they tend to scorn relativism which upholds a plurality of contingent, local rationalities.[22] This was the case, for instance, of the famous 'science wars', which have had many emblematic episodes, including the major scandal caused by physicist Alan Sokal. In 1996, with the specific intention of discrediting this rising relativism, Sokal managed to bypass the peer-review system and publish an article brimming with falsehoods in the journal *Social Text*.[23] With this 'experiment' he sought to demonstrate the depths to which some humanists and social scientists had reached with their interest in the study of science yet imprisoned by their own ignorance.[24] The consequences were bitter and rancorous, and once again questioned the problem of scientific authority and the limits of expertise.[25] The conflict had probably begun in 1994 with the publication of a controversial book by biologist Paul Gross and mathematician Norman Levitt as a reaction to the criticism proffered against science by the 'academic left' which, in their opinion, was seriously contaminating scientific research.[26] The book by Sokal and Jean Bricmont on what they considered 'intellectual impostures' appeared in 1998 at the height of the science experts' fury towards the supposedly relativist or simply fraudulent new interpretations.[27]

Indeed, from the 1980s onwards, the supposed excessive influence of the social sciences and humanities in public opinion has become one of the 'demons' in the scientific community. Their bid to analyse science as a topic of study has often been regarded as overly radical. From the perspective of the established expertise these positions place too much emphasis on the relationship between science and power and attack this naïve yet effective image of an objective, neutral science as an unquestionable servant to the progress of humanity.[28] As noted by the British thinker Jerôme R. Ravetz, the public perception of science had changed considerably.[29] In a short time, science went from being considered a neutral, objective method of studying nature or discovering the 'truth' to being viewed as a phenomenon that is socially conditioned by factors such as values, beliefs, professional interests, personal ambitions or property rights.[30] Thus, the current criticism of science often expresses itself publicly and grounds its opinions on science's lack of social robustness; that is, on science's inability to engage itself in sincere dialogue with society.[31] This nostalgia for pure science can be seen in France, for example, with the frequent protests by professional researchers (around 150,000 in the entire country) against the hierarchisation of the science system and the reduction and control of the public sector. The primacy of academic research with independent cognitive purpose is giving way to a new regime of knowledge in which, within a new techno-scientific paradigm, the distinction between basic and applied research and the supposed idealised independence of the scientist from society is becoming blurred.[32]

If modernity is based on values such as the prestige of academic science and its ability to shape technology, the new era has produced, as we shall see in several chapters of this book, the hegemony of technology and the crisis of scientific expertise, the crisis of the traditional disciplines as they gradually converge in a new corpus of knowledge in constant negotiation with social actors.[33] For authors like Helge Nowotny and Dominique Pestre, science can no longer base its authority on claims of its special relationship with truth or its role as a mouthpiece for nature itself. Both claims have lost strength and meaning and have been replaced by other more instrumental values. What truly matters today are relations with industry and the markets to produce complex technical gadgets and tangible benefits for society.[34] Along similar lines, in the 1980s the French philosopher François Lyotard (1924–98) heralded a view of knowledge in which traditional academic science gradually lost legitimacy. This was mainly due to a crisis in science's role as an emancipating agent, the weakness of a big picture for the sake of unbridled specialisation and the accelerated fragmentation and plurality of discourse.[35]

Still framed within the deficit model, Western science and its experts are increasingly concerned with their public image, and their possible loss of influence and social acceptance. Hence the repeated attempts in expert circles

8 Introduction

(professional scientists, public administrators and private managers) to boost the public interest, understanding and even complicity with science — yet another symptom of the discontent of scientific culture which is clearly visible today.[36]

These are just impressionistic and by no means exhaustive glimpses of our inherited discontent. This is probably due largely to the negative consequences of what could be described as a 'traditional' view of science popularisation which must have subtly filtered through our world views and values through the twentieth century. Many authors concur in asserting the legacy of overly biased, vertical, textual, ahistorical scientific knowledge.[37] From this angle, scientists and scientific institutions are the indisputable authorities when deciding what is and what is not science, between what should be transmitted to society and what should remain within the restricted expert sphere.[38] Expert authority would also be attributable to any historical period with no distinctions or nuances. Moreover, the supposed lay audiences would, in scientific terms, be a desert of ignorance and epistemological passivity; they would have practically no say, nor could they question the experts' superior and more reliable knowledge. In some cases, they may express their satisfaction or dissatisfaction as the spectators of a given public display of science (lectures, museums, films, etc.), but they could never question the content. Literary or even artistic criticism, which is deeply rooted in the public sphere in the West, could not be extrapolated to science, since knowledge of the latter would always travel one way: from the expert knowledge creators to the ignorant audiences.

In this tradition, scientific knowledge mainly lies in texts. It reinforces experts' authority as the 'legislators' of knowledge, as the authors of the written norms to distinguish a rigorously 'scientific' explanation from a more or less superficial account of a given phenomenon. So, in the popularisation process, these texts would be simplified and often distorted or degraded, and knowledge would lose its pristine state of purity once it was modified to be explained to those who are not in the know. Obviously, each scientific speciality would develop its own language (literary, mathematical, symbolic) and choose its own canonical reference texts. However, other ways of expressing scientific knowledge (drawings, photographs, models, scale models, diagrams, laboratory objects, etc.) would have secondary consideration that was more subsidiary or complementary to the essence of written or printed knowledge.

In this traditional view, science popularisation tends to be considered politically neutral. The very formal separation between science and technology in many public discourses would feed into this idea, such that the intellectual creation of pure, rational and objective science would be liberated from the purported miseries of the quotidian, from any ethical responsibility for its applications. This would justify the need to spread science to lay audiences, to prevent them from falling into the boggy terrain of pseudo-science or into the subjectivity of ideology or personal opinions. In fact, all of this stems from the issuers' self-satisfaction and ethical and epistemological superiority, based on the supposed victory of the expert's *episteme* over the lay *doxa* or public opinion. In 1990, historian of science Steven Shapin largely summarised the spirit of the traditional view of science popularisation in the following terms:

> Where science . . . was once influenced by or interfered with the public and other institutions, the scientific community controls its own proceedings, stipulates the nature of proper relations between itself and the public, and even extends its influence importantly into the arena of public affairs.[39]

More or less consciously, the inherited image of modern science is too centred on a very small elite who create fascinating theories, experiments and machines. For decades, the standard accounts of the great figures, the history of the science of luminaries such as Copernicus, Galileo, Newton, Darwin and Einstein and of their outstanding works has distanced us from scientific discourse closely tied to the context in which they were born, grew and developed. They have fostered instead a gulf between the great actors in history and the supposedly ignorant passive masses. This is an apparent paradox, yet one that is extremely important in the construction of Western culture. If at first increasingly large audiences consumed scientific discourses, especially from the nineteenth century, and contributed to the construction of new and more fluid channels of lay–expert communication, precisely the opposite seems to have occurred. The authority of the scientific elites has been legitimised through an almost esoteric gulf between science creators and science consumers. It has constructed a public image of an optimistic, neutral, objective, useful science in which audiences always play second fiddle.[40] From this perspective, modern science would have been erected based precisely on its distance from public opinion, preventing itself from being influenced or contaminated by it. It would have been forged in the great pro-science crusade of the twentieth century which largely sought to redeem science's poor image after the two world wars, or in its victory over the supposedly depraved opinions of irrationalism and superstition.[41]

The now-famous article published by Stephen Hilgartner in 1990 in the journal *Social Studies of Science* accurately describes the stages in the traditional model of science popularisation.[42] First, from their supposed position of considerable autonomy from the rest of society, professional scientists develop new knowledge in their laboratories and research centres, which are closed to the public. In the second phase, the scientists themselves, who are often science popularisers as well, spread new versions of this knowledge to society at large. However, Hilgartner criticised the way scientists and experts use this popularisation strategy to make their own definition of how science should be interpreted by lay audiences, and to thus maintain their privileged social status. This is a 'dominant view of popularisation', with appropriation and control over the contents of the simplified discourses. This dominant view would give scientists something akin to the epistemic value of the right to mint coins. Even in cases where experts could demonstrate that the popularisers had made mistakes when disseminating

10 Introduction

science to the public, this would likewise reinforce their authority as the exclusive repositories of knowledge.[43]

Other authors have followed Hilgartner's critical thinking towards the traditional view of scientific popularisation and the deficit model. In 2000, David Dickson, the news editor of *Nature* and a brilliant science writer, assessed several aspects of a report by the British House of Lords on the relationships between science and society at the end of the millennium.[44] Dickson rejected the image of a hierarchical transmission of science (largely legitimised by PUS).[45] He expressed it with the claim 'The public is not stupid', which perhaps overly succinctly yet powerfully summarises much of the spirit of this book.[46] In other words, our science audiences in the broad sense do not remain passive. They have a variety of intellectual tools at their disposal to more or less critically examine the addresses from the experts, institutions and media. According to Dickson, years ago publications like MIT's *Technology Review* and *New Scientist* managed to develop a discourse that was sensitive to the complex epistemology of their readers, but this communication style had lost force and influence in recent decades. Dickson advocated stimulating a constructive dialogue between the issuers and receivers; an epistemological strengthening of the public, ultimately through a controversial yet necessary process of gradually democratising contemporary science.

1.2. The power of the publics

A good number of the case studies appearing in this book have been researched and analysed in the last decades under the banner of the social and cultural history of science. The old critique against a history of the great figures and ideas; the relevance of any kind of historical actors for the sake of a more symmetrical approach to the past; the importance of everyday practices, objects, tacit knowledge, as well as the crucial role that the seduction of specific audiences plays for the legitimation of theories and experiments, all are firm reasons for historiographical renewal.[47] In 1990 Steven Shapin published 'Science and Its Publics',[48] a canonical paper on a revisited history of science popularisation, which remains today a reference text to be cited as an introduction. Moreover, in tune with the 'strong programme' of the Edinburgh School of the 1980s, Shapin wrote a critical approach to the Scientific Revolution, a 'social history of truth'.[49] Together with Simon Schaffer, he described how the distinguished publics shaped the authority of Robert Boyle's experiment with the air pump at the Royal Society, and contributed to a serious revision of the nature of science in the sixteenth and seventeenth centuries.[50]

Nevertheless, as one of the paradoxes of our intellectual adventure, a good part of the critical revision of the deficit model has found its inspiration in thinkers such as Ludwik Fleck (1896–1961) and his 'esoteric-exoteric' circles, Antonio Gramsci (1891–1937) and his concept of 'cultural hegemony', and Jürgen Habermas (1929–) and his description of the 'public sphere'. It is therefore possible to describe a new participatory model through some of their proposals, and link them to later, more contemporary re-elaborations (from Terry Shinn's and Richard Whitley's precious concept of 'expository science' to Michel Callon's models of 'lay participation in science'). In fact, the research presented in this book is a combination of old and new theoretical patterns, a sort of intellectual 'bricolage', an eclectic approach. Details of the life and work of Fleck, Gramsci and Habermas below will help to frame the discussion.

Ludwik Fleck studied medicine at the University of Lwów or Lviv (now in Ukraine), after which he gave biology classes at the same institution. He later worked at a hospital and a bacteriology laboratory in Lwów. He was of Jewish descent and was deported with his entire family during the Nazi invasion to different concentration camps where he was subjected to forced medical research projects. The liberation of 1945 finally took him to Warsaw where he continued his scientific career. In 1954 he was elected a member of the Polish Academy of Science. In 1956 he emigrated to Israel to work at the Israel Institute for Biological Research. He died in 1961.[51]

Fleck studied the discovery of a serological test for syphilis which had been developed at the beginning of the twentieth century by the German doctor August von Wassermann (1866–1925). This historical example inspired him to reconsider the concept of illness and think of it as a combination of material and cultural elements: clinical symptoms, responses to therapy, laboratory results and social impact.[52] It was no coincidence, then, that in 1935, the same year he published his major contributions to the problem of syphilis, his *Entstehung und Entwicklung einer wissenschaftlichen Tatsache* (*Genesis and Development of a Scientific Fact*) appeared. This canonical work, which was only translated and published in English almost half a century later, in 1979, set out fundamental ideas relating to the importance of audiences and processes of negotiation and the acquisition and legitimation of the authority of experts, later to inspire some of the leading thinking in sociology.[53] Fleck was convinced of the social nature of scientific knowledge and that it was produced under certain conditions of collective thought (*Denkkollectiv*), which in turn produced a particular style of thinking (*Denkstil*). Day-to-day scientific practice, tacit knowledge and the capacity for sharing certain activities constituted a fundamental part of group cohesion. For Fleck a scientific experiment or piece of work carried out in a certain local context could only take on a universal quality when the collective thought was transferred to other contexts and successfully exposed to society as a whole.[54]

However, in the 1930s Fleck was considered an amateur in his philosophical and sociological reflections on science, far removed from the pedigree and prestige of the great names in logical positivism of the famous Vienna Circle (Karl Popper, Rudolph Carnap, etc.) or the Frankfurt School (Adorno and Horkheimer). For decades his thinking about science and the scientific fact was thought of as marginal, distant and even opposed to the positivist tradition, which rejected any association of scientific thought with sociological factors and has only recently attracted renewed interest. From his position of academic isolation, despite coming up against strong opposition and criticism, his thinking remains a magnificent

12 Introduction

source of inspiration and reinterpretation today. Removed from the supposed stability of Thomas Kuhn's 'normal science',[55] that oasis of knowledge which from Kuhn's point of view reflected the consensus of the experts in textbooks, Fleck's style of thinking was the result of multiple, dynamic interactions between experts and laypeople.

From a position that could be considered critical of the traditional view of science popularisation, Fleck stated that each member of a *Denkkollectiv* was simultaneously a member of many other groups both 'inside' and 'outside' science. Each person played a different part in the groups (for example, as a member of a university department, an amateur science society or a neighbourhood librarian) and that meant that each carried out their own particular synthesis of the knowledge which in the long run moulds certain styles of thinking. The different social roles of each individual, whether as expert or layperson, are a significant factor in the construction of scientific knowledge itself.[56]

Fleck divided his collective scientific thinking into four concentric circles: the two inner circles known as 'esoteric' and the two outer ones 'exoteric'. The first, central circle contained a small group of top research experts surrounded in the second circle by professionals. The third circle contained a large group of scientific laypeople and the fourth, outer circle was reserved for the general public.[57] For a better understanding of the different circles, each of them can be attributed to a certain kind of publication: the research journal might assimilate the central nucleus of esoteric knowledge: the vade mecum the second circle of professionals; the textbook would represent the third, exoteric, circle; while popular science books as tools for an introduction to scientific knowledge for the general public would represent the outer circle. Under this scheme an individual could only move from the exoteric to the esoteric circles after receiving a science education. Also, for Fleck, the most important element in the operation of this system was the democratic exchange of ideas and experiences, from esoteric to exoteric and back again. Only through these ideas and the arrival of conveniently appropriated, filtered and re-sent information could the resulting intellectual work be consolidated into a scientific 'fact'.[58]

This analysis as a system of collective thought meant that, for Fleck, there was no clear boundary between the esoteric and the exoteric, and the general public was a fundamental agent in the process of feedback between the circles – a basic requirement for the consolidation and acceptance of scientific theories. In the absence of such feedback, according to Fleck, the same thing would happen as often does with religion: the esoteric elites would exert an abusive and dictatorial influence over the public. Fleck's work was therefore clearly an important starting point in the 1930s which, apart from inspiring ideas that have developed strongly in recent decades, advocated the first crack in the expert–lay boundary and highlighted the need for feedback among the members of all four circles. In other words, a scientific theory could only be properly established and agreed on in a certain place and time if the details of its content had previously circulated from the elites of basic research to the anonymous person in the street.

Introduction **13**

This kind of feedback mechanism between the esoteric and exoteric circles also took place more subtly and sometimes rather 'irrationally', through common places, metaphors and more or less explicit elements of popular exoteric culture to which the experts reacted and continually defined within the continual network of information that gradually made up the *Denkkollectiv*.[59]

Curiously enough, in 1992 the Society for Social Studies of Science, one of the main academic mouthpieces for the new social and cultural history of science, introduced the Ludwik Fleck Prize for the best annual research. It was a late, but clearly well-deserved homage to his pioneering and brilliant ideas.

Perhaps younger readers will not have heard references to the Italian thinker **Antonio Gramsci**, and older people probably consider him to be out of fashion. Gramsci has sometimes been superficially associated with Marxist thought seen as something of a homogeneous monolithic block which, like the Berlin Wall, was pulled down at the end of the twentieth century, leaving progressive thought empty of ideas and incapable of building a sufficiently attractive alternative to liberal conservative thought. However, from a somewhat more optimistic position, I have attempted to rescue some of Gramsci's ideas as a potential source of inspiration when it comes to analysing again the problem of expert and lay scientific knowledge. Reading some of his texts has been a tremendously moving experience and one which certainly merits sharing with my readers.[60]

The son of a modest civil servant, Antonio Gramsci was born in 1891 in the small Sardinian town of Ales. In 1911, once he had finished his secondary education, he was awarded a scholarship to the Faculty of Arts of the University of Turin, where he began to publish political articles inspired by socialism. On the rise to power of the dictator Benito Mussolini (1883–1945) in 1922, Gramsci was exiled to the Soviet Union. In 1924 he was elected to the Chamber of Deputies to represent the Italian Communist Party, which he had helped to found in 1921 as a breakaway from the Socialist Party. He returned to Italy and was very active in politics until 1926 when, despite his parliamentary immunity, he was arrested by Mussolini's police and sentenced to 20 years in prison. If Gramsci was already an activist and tireless writer of short journalistic articles, this point represented the start of a dramatic period in his personal life of extraordinary creativity. From his isolation he produced 32 notebooks of more than 3,000 handwritten pages famously known as the *Quaderni del carcere* (*The Prison Notebooks*). When they were finally published after World War II, they had an enormous impact in Italy and later all over the world.

The dramatic circumstances in which they were produced, the epic story of Gramsci's life, his sharpness and depth, and his ability to express his thinking with sensitivity towards the particular characteristics of Western civil society, gave Gramsci a unique standing in the history of Western political thought. However, similar to the case of Fleck, the assimilation of his thought in the English-speaking academic world did not occur until well into the 1970s. The somewhat chaotic and disordered texts of the *Quaderni* contained a range of remarkably sharp and sensitive reflections on culture, politics, education, power

14 Introduction

and history. Among many other ideas the concepts of *hegemony*, or the problem of *intellectuals*, continue to capture the interest of many readers from multiple perspectives today.[61]

Hegemony was one of Gramsci's leading ideas.[62] The control of the elites at a certain moment in history through the state (the so-called political society), through laws, the police, the army (in other words, basically through the application of force) was, for Gramsci, insufficient to understand the stability of our societies. For him, it was necessary to take into account the role of civil society, where institutions such as school, family, church and even the multitude of everyday practices contribute to the continual production of meaning and value that maintain a more or less spontaneous consent and acceptance of a certain status quo.[63] But hegemony is not simply the crude defence of dominant opinion, or a simple top-down manipulation. It is much more than that, covering the whole of our experience, habits and hopes; it is our full perception of reality.[64]

In his *Quaderni*, Gramsci showed an interest in popular literature, folklore and social groups, which he referred to as subalterns. Gramsci tried to understand their identity and values as a starting point for constructing a new, largely utopian counterhegemony that could substitute the dominant values in early twentieth-century Italy. But Gramsci also dedicated a considerable number of pages to the protagonists of hegemony: the *intellectuals*. Whereas in the rural, pre-industrial and feudal world of the ancien régime it was the clergy who had monopolised the construction of a certain hegemony, in the capitalist industrial world of the contemporary nation-states, others had taken over: judges, senior civil servants, professors and scientists – all of them at the service of the elites.

For Gramsci, every emerging social group that played an important role in the world of economic production organically created for itself one or more levels of intellectuals that provided homogeneity to the group and controlled its function in the social and political sphere.[65] Here, the close relationship between knowledge and power inspired by Foucault transcends a structural, anonymous and poor historicist analysis to put names to the main figures in their role as intellectuals in well-defined historical contexts. Consequently, experts and laypeople could be thought of as 'organic intellectual' representatives of different interests who clashed and continue to clash. They struggle to obtain cultural hegemony, scientific authority, institutional control, social prestige and academic power. The strategies of many of the figures who appear in this book probably respond to a similar kind of logic. What better way to prevent excessively ingenuous interpretations of scientific popularisation than Gramsci's concept of hegemony and the analysis of the role of experts and laypeople as organic intellectuals? And what better example than Gramsci's legacy to analyse with an appropriate critical distance phenomena such as popular science, science teaching, spectacular science and the tensions between entertainment, instruction and control, apparent in places such as theatres, museums and exhibitions?

In this context, all the actors play an epistemologically active role, albeit with different intensity. The question is rather more complex than the simple diagnosis of the deficit model by PUS. The plurality of meanings of scientific activity, along with its practices, rituals, spaces, images and representations invite a reflection on the intellectual dignity of all its leading figures, their resistance and appropriation mechanisms. Under the inspiration of Gramsci's hegemony and intellectuals, a finer analysis can be made of the reasons and interests often hidden in the continuous exchanges of knowledge that have occurred throughout history.[66] Numerous examples show the enormous difficulty in trying to draw a clear line between experts and laypeople, or to present an independent history of scientific knowledge restricted to experts, even during historical periods that seem remote from our accelerated contemporaneity. The Gramscian framework helps to consider scientific popularisation, not as an activity that is peripheral or marginal to scientific knowledge, not as something inferior or subaltern, but completely integrated at all levels of daily scientific practice, on the front line of the battle for hegemony, authority and power.

Jürgen Habermas, one of the most prominent philosophers of the second half of the twentieth century, was born in 1929 in Düsseldorf to a middle-class family. He studied philosophy under Adorno and Horkheimer two key figures of cultural Marxism from the Institute for Social Research, known as the Frankfurt School.[67] In 1962, he was offered the position of 'extraordinary professor' of philosophy at the University of Heidelberg, at the same time as he gained huge reputation for his habilitation work entitled *Strukturwandel der Öffentlichkeit; Untersuchungen zu einer Kategorie der Bürgerlichen Gesellschaft* (published later in English in 1989 as *The Structural Transformation of the Public Sphere: An Inquiry into a Category of Bourgeois Society*).[68] In 1964, he took over Horkheimer's chair in philosophy and sociology in Frankfurt. Habermas's thought has been mainly inscribed in critical theory, which since the 1920s had tried to analyse social and cultural structures of domination. In that context, any form of knowledge could be used as a powerful tool of social control, so any uncritical approach to progress should be taken with caution.

Even though it is even further afield from science studies, one important notion which has provided solid arguments to criticise the traditional view of science popularisation is the idea of the 'public sphere' formulated in 1962. Habermas explained the emergence of democracy in the West since the eighteenth century through a series of new cultural phenomena: the proliferation of books, newspapers and magazines and their circulation; the advent of new institutions that mediated between the state and the individual; the rise of criticism and public discussion; and the growing importance of rational critical discourse. In short, the public sphere is an urban, bourgeois phenomenon that lies at the very base of Western modernity. The bourgeois milieu that is capable of integrating discussion, criticism and controversy gradually emerged from the private family sphere, to civil society and the public sphere of the state. From the perspective of science, the printing press, the crisis of hermeticism and alchemy, the authority of experimentation and public speech, debate and controversy are all significant new developments of the culture of the Enlightenment,[69] the roots of

16 Introduction

which can even be traced back to the Renaissance, but also extrapolated much later in the nineteenth and twentieth centuries.

Habermas's idea of the 'public sphere' has provided consistent arguments for a critical approach to the deficit model legacy.[70] In his reflections on the mechanisms of communication in modern societies, Habermas stressed that to overcome the tensions between the rigid, vertical, normative discourse of the state and the discourse stemming from civil society, new spaces for deliberation and decision making were needed.[71] Therefore, a democratic society requires varied, constant interactions among multiple spheres in which civil society and political institutions intersect. The key to understanding the subtle power relationship between experts and lay actors in history lies mainly in the complexity of communicative acts in the public sphere.[72] To Habermas, the increasing inclusion of more participants in a discussion in any sphere of knowledge can degrade or distort the quality of the discourse, but the requirements of democracy and the characteristics of our societies now make it impossible to revert back to a restricted, elitist sphere. In other words, we can no longer avoid the debate on the 'democratic' nature of scientific knowledge.[73]

Habermas's concept of the public sphere has been criticised for not including the lower, working classes, in spite of his Marxist background at the Frankfurt School,[74] or a perspective of gender.[75] Criticisms have also appeared for not taking into account the crucial importance of the public sphere in the twentieth-century mass media society, and even for not including science in his model. In spite of all those potential weaknesses, the public sphere has become a very useful, illuminating concept. Historians of science have used it when approaching, for instance, the uses of experiment in seventeenth-century England, the spaces of sociability of Newtonianism or the public dimension of the chemical revolution in the eighteenth century.[76] It has become a very useful tool to assess how knowledge (and public knowledge in particular) did lead to effective power in specific historical contexts.[77]

London, for example, had 3,000 coffee houses in the early eighteenth century. In France, private salons opened their doors to merge a literary aristocratic public sphere with a new bourgeois political public sphere. In Germany, table societies brought together academics and other kinds of publics.[78] As discussed by Thomas Broman in the context of the Enlightenment: 'It was the evolution of the public sphere that gave to the new philosophy its widespread cultural authority in the eighteenth century, an authority that it has never surrendered'. And more important, it is mainly in the public sphere where the process of science professionalisation and scientific expertise of the following centuries in practice took place.[79] In addition, the Habermasian civil society, and its influence in the public sphere, has played in the past and probably still plays today a crucial role in the making of scientific authority, in the way in which science has been transformed into public knowledge.[80] It was probably the printing revolution together with the new experimental science that reshaped the views of 'reason and public opinion that made possible the liberal model of the public sphere'.[81]

The Habermasian public sphere has become a very useful tool to re-examine the public nature of scientific activity, the meaning of public knowledge and the way in which it is constructed and legitimised in specific local settings and before particular audiences.[82] This is precisely the main aim of this book.

1.3. Lessons from the past

The chapters of this book are organised based on Habermas's public sphere, understood in its broad sense. With the aim of critically surveying the deficit model legacy, and approaching new trends towards the participatory turn in science in the early twenty-first century, each chapter brings the reader closer to active issuers and receivers of scientific knowledge in certain times and places in history.

'Printed science' has its point of departure in the Renaissance, at the advent of the printing press and its role in the circulation of scientific knowledge in new books and their readers. Later it addresses issues such as the culture of Newtonianism, encyclopaedias and other practices of disseminating printed knowledge. The chapter then shifts towards the printed culture in the nineteenth-century industrial world, where such select paradigms as Darwinism or such controversial ones as phrenology would appear with unexpected vitality in books, articles, pamphlets and newspapers. Moreover, it analyses how the perceptions of health and illness historically stepped beyond the strict boundaries of university medicine to permeate society as a whole with books on domestic medicine and popular pharmacopoeias. It also explores the common places and mutual feedback that science and literature shared. Through the circuit of the printed book, authors, publishers and readers unexpectedly take centre stage as audiences of science, so much so that their mutual influences become important factors when analysing what lies behind knowledge in the making. What better source than an encyclopaedia to capture the state of a given field of knowledge at a particular point in time, or to determine how certain popular books exerted such a significant influence on the very configuration of scientific disciplines or research policies?

'Spectacular science' presents important aspects in the material culture of science, framed in the visual turn and related to objects, representations, rituals, fascination and fairs. Hence the importance of the *cabinets de curiosités* until well into the eighteenth century, along with world's fairs, science museums in their different forms and complexity, but also the public shows of science capable of filling theatres and cinemas with audiences eager for entertainment and fun. These are ideal cases to transcend the hegemony of the textual – so deeply rooted in the traditional view of science popularisation – and to turn the limelight onto an entire series of cultural expressions with a huge mediating capacity. While anatomy theatres opened the doors to varied audiences, fascinated by the new dissection rituals and interactions with the human body, later other theatres were filled with curious people enthusiastically waiting to view spectacular physics or

18 Introduction

chemistry experiments. Machines, instruments and diverse objects displayed in public in machinery halls and science pavilions thrilled thousands of visitors with spectacular, bombastic rituals with a host of intentions and reactions. In constant tension between instruction and entertainment, science has gradually been administered a significant dose of theatricality in the public sphere. Strategies to create dialogue with the audience are therefore often more important than the content of the knowledge to be communicated in itself.

'Heterodox science' discusses expert–lay bridges of dialogue and antagonism. Major issues regarding professional legitimisation or corporate interests, specialisation and scientific authority are often resolved in the public sphere and require constant negotiation and consensus. Scientific authorities in each period despised heterodox practices (such as animal magnetism, homeopathy and phrenology) but the public spectacularly legitimised them, judging by the queues of patients eager to submit to these strange treatments. Even well into the nineteenth and much of the twentieth century, the amateur factor, at the outer limits of orthodoxy, played a more prominent role than might be imagined at first glance. In astronomy or natural history, amateur societies, discussion groups and networks of personal contacts became crucial for measuring and observing, as well as for spreading information.

However, the bridges from amateur science can also be extended to science popularisers, who became particularly important in the nineteenth century, albeit with a somewhat ambiguous and ill-defined status. University professors often became popularisers, yet others gradually gained a new professional status of their own which enabled them to earn a living from the sales of their science books written for lay audiences. Their role was neither ingenuous nor neutral. Science popularisers have interests and political ideologies just like any other professional, but their role as mediators and their ability to cross boundaries and connect social classes and thematic areas is particularly significant. Similarly, the struggle between professional science, associated with experts and orthodoxy, and amateur science, associated with laypeople and heterodoxy, was, and continues to be, aired in the public sphere at different levels in a constant struggle for cultural hegemony, which also comprises religion.

'Classroom science' focuses on students – one of the major audiences of science from both a qualitative and quantitative standpoint. Students are all too often presented as a captive audience that passively receives the consensus of a given period in the guise of normal Kuhnian science, packaged in the form of curricula and school or university textbooks. However, students can be seen as active agents in the construction of scientific knowledge. A more critical look at education in general, and science education in particular, leads to the controversial issue of the role of science teaching as a tool for social control and discipline. Within a Foucauldian framework, it counterbalances tacit optimism with positivist roots that lie behind numerous discourses on the progress of science and its perennial consequences for the benefit of humanity. Here what is asserted is the intellectual creativity of the act of teaching, the need for a rigorous reconstruction of classroom practices, an ethnography and archaeology of learning in which objects and sources have been until now barely considered. Students' notes, scientific instruments, exams and teachers' class preparations take centre stage. Furthermore, in a context where the boundaries between science popularisation and formal education are especially diluted, this chapter does not turn its back on the existence of an array of informal education practices, ranging from university extension movements to the educational projects of working-class athenaeums.

'Technological science' addresses the eternal tension between thinking and doing, between the hand and the brain, and it restores artisans and industrial workers as historical actors, who have dialectically constructed much of the scientific culture of Western societies, to a position alongside scholars and engineers. Just as the Scientific Revolution of the sixteenth and seventeenth centuries cannot be understood without taking into account a largely unknown set of printed texts, so it is impossible to approach the scientific culture from this period without the active participation of artisans and instrument makers. This chapter avoids any essentialist discussion on the boundaries between science and technology and places itself in the shoes of the main actors in every historical period. It shows the plurality of holders of specific technological skills, both pre-industrial and industrial. Artisans, industrial workers, engineers, specialised technicians and users are all audiences of technology, each group with its own values and its own peculiar relationship with the object and the machine. That is how the old guild cultures survived throughout the centuries, even in the midst of industrialisation, and this would explain the major movements against technological change that have arisen throughout the nineteenth and twentieth centuries. In more recent times, users have emerged as prime actors, often related to consumers, the key agents in our mass production industrial societies. Users' attitudes towards machines, their purchasing decisions and their perceptions of technology largely shape objects themselves in the long term. Beyond the theoretical or academic legitimisation of each of the machines that accompany our day-to-day lives, their role is crucial in understanding fundamental aspects of our present world.

'Media science' suggests that, at least in the second half of the twentieth century, the presence of certain scientific topics in the media (the press, radio, television, internet) may not simply be the outcome of a simplification of previously conducted research for the audience at large but a part and parcel of the very process of knowledge construction. Examples like the Gaia theory, the public face of biochemistry, human evolution, cold fusion and climate change show that the analysis of each of these topics entails significant media participation, together with the experts' involvement in them. It also points out the consequences that the publication of certain results in the media might have on future avenues of research. If experts' knowledge, including their points of contention, reaches the public without prior consensus, the experts' authority suffers considerably, yet nonetheless the legitimisation of certain theories requires the blessing of the

20 Introduction

media and public opinion at large. This is one of the paradoxes of the 'media' personality of science today.

Finally, 'Democratic science' identifies some changes that have taken place in recent years which seem to reveal a more prominent role for the public, lately morphed into an active citizenry. This is a participative model that today is progressively replacing the old deficit model. Concerned active patients, consumer or user associations, ecology groups, anti-nuclear activists or groups speaking out against genetically modified organisms, the new ethical concerns regarding the limits of molecular biology and other issues are examples that inspire optimism, antidotes that can effectively combat the discontent of our scientific culture which has befouled the entire twentieth century to a greater or lesser extent. New patient groups, which are particularly active and vocal, may even have managed to shape certain avenues of medical research, and their witnesses may have at least returned, some say, a voice to the ill, beyond the rigidity of the traditional medical processes. This democratic impetus can at least serve as inspiration for broadly outlining the desirable features of a new scientific culture that is unquestionably being forged in our post-industrial societies today. It is from the complexity of the participatory trends in our present that this book provides a historical reflection on different publics of the past which can be particularly illuminating.

★ ★ ★

Both in the past and now, in the third millennium, the existence of well-defined expert–lay boundaries, along with mediators that automatically put them in touch with each other, may initially appear as an overly ingenuous idea. All actors have their own interests and negotiate their legitimisation and status with regard to others in any given historical time and place. Fleck, Gramsci and Habermas help us provide an alternative perspective on the traditional view of science popularisation, in which the voice of the varied publics of science must be heard throughout history. Amid the debris of the past, different sources will reveal what historical actors knew. They will also help us to reconstruct their own particular strategies to actively appropriate knowledge. It is the only way the arguments needed for a new scientific culture can become clear and perhaps contribute to palliating the subtle discontent described in this introduction.

Notes

1 Agassi (2003: vii–viii).
2 Freud (1930: 31–2).
3 Adorno, Horkheimer (2002).
4 Marx (1992); Smith, Marx (1994).
5 Hobsbawn (1994: 530).
6 Gregory, Miller (1998: 118).
7 Collins (2014).
8 In the 1960s, in a study on scientific communities, John Ziman defined science as 'public knowledge', Ziman (1968); Lewenstein (1992b).

Introduction **21**

9 Gregory, Miller (1998: 18); Wynne (1995).
10 Durant, Evans, Thomas (1989); Holton (1992).
11 Durant, Evans, Thomas (1989: 14).
12 Handlin (1965: 184).
13 Wynne (1995); Broks (2006).
14 Handlin (1965: 191).
15 Holton, Blanpied (1976: ix).
16 *Science and Its Public* was published in conjunction with William A. Blanpied, who that same year had been hired by the US National Science Foundation as Program Manager for Ethics and Human Values in Science and Technology. Holton, Banpied (1976).
17 Cited by Holton (1993).
18 Snow (1959).
19 I am referring to that 'slow' historical time, that 'longue durée' defined by historian Fernand Braudel, which subtly permeates a given culture over the course of generations and is distinguished from other 'quicker" historical times associated with revolutions or radical transformations.
20 Gregory, Miller (1998: 214–19); Friedman (1995).
21 Ramsey (1999: 316–17).
22 For a history of the scientific spirit, see Olson (2008).
23 Sokal (1996a, 1996b); Hilgartner (1997).
24 Kleinman (2000: 2).
25 Hilgartner (1997).
26 Gross, Levitt (1994).
27 Kleinman (2000: 3); Sokal, Bricmont (1999).
28 Gregory, Miller (1998: 56–7). Worth bearing in mind is the work of Stanley Aronowitz, Sandra Harding, Judi Waicman and Rachel Carson.
29 Ravetz (1990).
30 Steven Shapin, Harry Collins, Bruno Latour and Simon Schaffer, among others, have fanned the academic debate on science in recent decades. Golinski (1998, 2005); Ashmore, Richards (1996).
31 Nowotny et al. (2005: 1–27).
32 Pestre (2003a, 2003b, 2013).
33 Bensaude-Vincent (2009b: 19, 34).
34 Nowotny et al. (2005: 193).
35 Lyotard (1984); Michael (1992).
36 Weingart (2007).
37 For representative texts of the traditional view of science popularisation, see for example *Royal Society of London* (1985), cited by Myers (2003); see also Grundmann, Cavaillé (2000).
38 Gieryn (1983).
39 Shapin (1990: 999).
40 Broks (1996: 52).
41 Bensaude-Vincent (2000: 135).
42 Hilgartner (1990).
43 Hilgartner (1990: 534).
44 Dickson (2000).
45 '[A]n effective science journalism is that one allows individuals to challenge the way that decisions about the development and applications of science are made'. Dickson (2000: 921).
46 Dickson (2000: 920).
47 For an overview of the new social and cultural history of science see Golinski (1998, 2005).
48 Shapin (1990).
49 Shapin, (1994).
50 Shapin, Schaffer (1985, 2011).
51 Harwood (1986); Hedfors (2007).
52 Golinski (1998: 34).
53 Fleck (1979); Harwood (1987); Hedfors (2007); Golinski (1998).

22 Introduction

54 Golinski (1998: 32–5).
55 Kuhn (1962); Stuckey, Heering (2015).
56 Harwood (1986: 179).
57 Ibid., 160–1.
58 'The most characteristic operational feature is a democratic exchange of ideas and experience, going outward from the esoteric circle, permeating the exoteric circle, and then feeding back upon the esoteric circle. The work of the mind thus conveyed undergoes a process of social consolidation and becomes thereby a scientific fact'. Fleck (1979: 161).
59 Harwood (1986: 182).
60 Nieto-Galan (2011a).
61 Forgacs (2000).
62 Burke (2005).
63 Holub (1992: 6).
64 Cooter (1984: 193); Williams (1977).
65 Forgacs (2000: 301).
66 Cooter, Pumphrey (1994: 249).
67 Calhoun (1992); White (1995).
68 Habermas (1962, 1989).
69 Withers (1998: 47–50); Habermas (1962, 1989); Golinski (1992).
70 Habermas (1968); Calhoun (1992).
71 Nyhart and Broman 2002; Mah (2000).
72 White (1995: 13).
73 Calhoun (1992: 3); Broman (1998); Mah (2000); Nyhart and Broman (2002).
74 Calhoun (1992); Withers (1998).
75 Fraser (1990).
76 Shapin and Schaffer (1985, 2011); Stewart (1992); Golinski (1998).
77 Calhoun (1992: 3).
78 Calhoun (1992: 12).
79 Broman (1998: 125).
80 Broman (2002: 1).
81 Calhoun (1992: 226).
82 Golinski (1992).

2

PRINTED SCIENCE

In his famous book *The Cheese and the Worms* (1979), historian Carlo Ginzburg reconstructed the life of Domenico Scandella, also known as Menocchio, who was a miller from the region of Friuli in the north of Italy and possessed a series of intellectual interests that were very unusual among people of his kind at the end of the sixteenth century. Menocchio had access to books such as *The Decameron*, *The Bible* in the vernacular and *Il Fioretto della Bibbia* (a translation of medieval Catalan chronicles).[1] He produced his own cosmology, an unorthodox story in which the role of God in the creation was questioned much to the discomfort of the ecclesiastical authorities at the height of the Counter-Reformation. Menocchio declared before the Inquisition that at the beginning there was chaos; the four Aristotelian elements (earth, water, air and fire) were uniformly mixed so that just as cheese is made from milk, from the original mass of the cosmos worms appeared embodied in the angels and in God himself. This was a highly heterodox and provocative view of the cosmos with shades of materialism that appeared not to fit in either with the old natural Aristotelian philosophy adapted to Christianity throughout the Middle Ages, or with the modern science that was emerging during that time.

Before Nicolaus Copernicus (1473–1543), father of heliocentric theory, Andreas Vesalius (1514–64), the famous anatomist, and humanists such as Erasmus of Rotterdam (1466–1536) and Thomas More (1478–1535), Menocchio was an unexpected historical actor. His story shows the different, conflicting views of the cosmos that coexisted during the same period, the fragile mechanisms of authority and the blurred boundaries between orthodox and unorthodox knowledge. It raises questions, not only about the cultural gap that existed in the sixteenth century between the humble miller and the most refined intellectual groups, but also on the common spaces that both could have shared.

24 Printed science

Perhaps Menocchio was an exception, a curious anecdote, a microhistorical blip that cannot be extrapolated. But in the light of the evidence of lay knowledge in the sixteenth century, the supposed isolation, autonomy and unquestionable superiority of the Renaissance natural philosophers and humanists, whose authority goes back to the medieval university professors, should be questioned.[2] In fact, recent studies have shown that the Inquisition was more concerned with controlling and repressing the less educated potential readers than the intellectual elite. In one way or another, the latter had certain alliances and agreements with the Church, once the initial moments of tension had been overcome. Urban readers with a middling or low level of culture, free readers, women, non-university educated young people were the subjects of greater control.[3] Menocchio's apparently exceptional case brings to the fore the need to review the mechanisms by which knowledge, and scientific knowledge in particular, circulated in an age where the old manuscript culture was being replaced by the new print culture.

It is usually assumed that, from the fifteenth century to the end of the twentieth century, printed texts, associated with the discovery and spread of the printing press, acted as the main vehicle for setting out and later disseminating scientific knowledge. Influenced by the work of Thomas S. Kuhn (1922–96), the great paradigms of science are generally associated with iconic printed texts such as: Claudius Ptolemy's *Almagest* and the Renaissance compilation of geocentrism; *De Revolutionibus Orbis Celestis* by Copernicus and the birth of heliocentrism and 'modern' science; the *Principia Mathematica Philosophia Naturalis* by Isaac Newton (1643–1727) and the height of the Scientific Revolution; Antoine-Laurent Lavoisier's (1743–94) *Traité élémentaire de chimie* and the chemical revolution at the end of the eighteenth century; the *Origin of Species* by Charles Darwin (1809–82) and the rejection of creationism in favour of the new evolutionary paradigm; texts by Albert Einstein (1879–1955), printed and published from 1905 as symbols of the new revolution in physics in the twentieth century.[4] So Western science would, to a great extent, be condensed in these masterpieces of writing, in these sublime texts, which time and again had to be saved from the recurrent imaginary flames at the Library of Alexandria.

There is no question that these, and many other printed works, belong to our scientific heritage and should be preserved and analysed critically by historians. However, we run the risk of turning the history of science into a magnificent photograph album of iconic and unrepeatable moments, while masking the complex circulation of these paradigms and their printed versions in particular contexts. Years ago, historian Robert Darnton described the cycle of the book: messages pass from authors to editors, printers, distributors, bookshops or book sellers, finally reaching the readers and, depending on their reactions, returning to authors and editors, to begin a new cycle in a process of continual feedback. Authors themselves write texts after multiple interactions with other people, starting during their period of training right up to their full practice as experts in their social environment. In other words, authors have been readers and their intellectual production can only be understood within this complex circuit. Consequently, rather than fixed and immobile products, printed texts become cultural objects with a life of their own.[5]

Until recently scholars agreed that printed books, and science books as a case in point, acted as elements for fixing classical knowledge. Once they had been recovered, translated into the vernacular languages and effectively 'stabilised' in the new printed culture, they enabled scholars to begin to question the authority of the ancient texts.[6] However, the recent historiography of reading practices invites a distancing from this apparent stability. It brings us to a history in which books become vehicles for permanent negotiation among authors, editors and readers as active audiences of science. A first point of analysis should therefore be printed science in the time of Menocchio followed by a closer look at the cultural dynamism of subsequent centuries.[7]

2.1. The Scientific Revolution in print

At the end of the fifteenth century, the printing press had not only overcome the limitations of the manuscript culture but had also made a decisive contribution to public knowledge, and thousands of copies of the ancient natural philosophies and also emerging ideas accelerated their circulation.[8] Vesalius published his *De Humani Corporis Fabrica* in 1543, the same year that *De Revolutionibus* by Copernicus appeared. These two great works reinforced the 'annus mirabilis' as the beginning of the Scientific Revolution of the sixteenth and seventeenth centuries, which progressively cemented heliocentrism, together with mechanical and corpuscular natural philosophy, mathematical language and a new experimental culture. The completion of the Scientific Revolution is attributed to Newton with his *Principia* (1687) and *Opticks* (1704). In fact, the Scientific Revolution is probably one of the subjects that has most written about in recent decades.[9] While in the mid-twentieth century some considered it to be a milestone in terms of Western culture, comparable only with Christianity,[10] the end of the twentieth century saw more critical interpretations, which even disputed its existence as a historical period.[11] Beyond debates about change and continuity, a new approach to scientific culture during that period revisited the old standard accounts that had been dominant until recently.

The great works of that period obviously had their readers, but other, lesser-known texts, also made their mark on knowledge transfer outside the reduced circles of experts. In 1543, Vesalius published his *Epitome*, a kind of appendix that summarised the content of his main work. It was conceived to give students and other readers greater access to his fascinating anatomical project. Dissection became a substantial element in the new experimental medicine that questioned major aspects of the Hippocratic and Galenic legacy.[12] Along the same lines, in 1551 Erasmus Reinhold (1511–53), Professor of Astronomy at the University of Wittenberg and a disciple of Copernicus, drew up a set of tables which, although based on the work of the latter, opened up the new astronomy to a much larger number of readers.[13] Just a few decades later, Danish astronomer Tycho Brahe

26 Printed science

(1546–1601) appropriated all these data through the printed versions that would influence his future observations.[14]

Other publications escaped the academic circles. The so-called *books of secrets* typified a major transition from the medieval esoteric tradition to a new, more popular, utilitarian natural philosophy that was closer to craft traditions and the so-called *magia naturalis*. The books of secrets contributed to the new Baconian style of modern experimentation. Authors of these books, such as Alessio Piemontese, Giovanni Ventura Rossetti, Girolamo Ruscelli, Isabella Cortere, Leonardo Fioravanti and Giambattista della Porta, among others, became 'teachers of secrets' and dedicated themselves entirely to this new occupation. They produced a new public science, written and printed in the vernacular and distributed through apothecaries, craft workshops, academies, courts and town squares. They provided readers with knowledge about metallurgy, practical alchemy, medicines, dyestuffs, medical prescriptions and domestic advice. As for the more 'official' sciences with a greater theoretical content, such as astronomy, optics, mechanics and medicine, the texts were more accessible to craftsmen, laymen and non-academics.[15]

Piemontese's *Secreti*, initially published in 1555, had reached more than a hundred editions in different languages by the end of the seventeenth century.[16] Although it was based on complicated alchemical and astrological assumptions, Della Porta's *Magia naturalis* (1558) provided practical advice for traders: plant and animal care and female beauty, cooking recipes, transmutation of metals, distillation and precious stones.[17] Detailed studies by historian William Eamon show that the teachers of secrets generally held little faith in theory. However, they did inherit a coherent view of the natural world and they carried out their research within a shared intellectual framework with the majority of their readers. This can be the only explanation for their successful sales. From the common places of empirical recipes and daily life, the philosophical basis of the printed secrets provided rational explanations to the hidden forces of nature, which could be imitated, improved and exploited.[18]

This kind of literature was completed with academic knowledge from universities on mining practices and the direct experience of artisans and their tacit knowledge of certain processes. Although sometimes ambiguous with respect to alchemical practices, open criticism of alchemy gave these books significant prestige and a large readership, not only for natural philosophy but also for the utility of their practical recipes. In the early sixteenth century, German Central European booklets on mining and metallurgy known as *Probierenbüchlein* became popular. Some decades later, other books by prestigious authors appeared, such as *De la Pirotechnia* (1520) by mine inspector Vannoccio Biringuccio (1480–c. 1539), the famous *De Re Metallica* (1556) by physician and humanist Georg Bauer (1494–1555), also known as Georgius Agricola, and *Beschreibung* (1574)[19] by metallurgy assayer Lazarus Ercker (1530–94), a former student at Wittenberg, like Reinhold. Each of these authors aimed their work at a different readership. Agricola wrote for humanists and educated elites, although he would soon become more famous for his magnificent engravings. He did not ignore practical recipes but he was more interested in theoretical explanations of the nature of metals and the way they reacted in Earth's interior. Biringuccio and Ercker were concerned mainly with mine owners and traders with specific economic interests in mining and metallurgy. They prioritised practical recipes over theoretical speculation.[20]

Books of secrets and alchemical prints (the latter also containing practical recipes for metal purification and distillation) provided a whole set of subtle intersections between the recipe culture and the new, hitherto little-known experiments.[21] These books suggest that any discussion about the foundations of the Scientific Revolution should go much further than the life and works of the great luminaries of the time.[22]

In the sixteenth century, books 'circulated' through communities of readers, reviews in periodicals, sermons, lectures, informal gatherings and correspondence. There was not always a clear distinction between the popular and the informed, oral and written, lay and expert, Menocchio and Copernicus. The lack of a strict definition of ownership allowed for several layers of appropriation through different reading practices.[23] The custom of reading aloud contributed to overcoming the apparently impassable barrier of illiteracy. Obviously orality did not disappear with books and neither would it in the following centuries.[24]

In fifteenth- and sixteenth-century markets in European towns and cities, knowledge was spread through calendars, almanacs and forecasts, and treatises of astrology, construction, medicine and health, metallurgy and dyeing. Alchemy leaflets contained a selection of texts in large folders consisting of eight pages, with tales of knights and religious writings, but also almanacs and practical texts similar to the books of secrets. The so-called *occasionnels* were published as religious propaganda against the Counter-Reformation and had abundant descriptions of natural catastrophes making them yet another source of scientific content available to a large public.[25] As Menocchio's case demonstrates, this world of active reading was more complex than expected. Moreover, printed books with handwritten notes in the margins, pamphlets and translations enabled new levels of appropriation of knowledge.

In societies where disease was rife, with few medical resources and a weak and irregular medical profession, books on medicine and health flourished. They aimed to tell ordinary readers how to look after their own bodies, either in the absence of or as a supplement to professional medical care.[26] Since the introduction of the printing press books of medical advice, secrets and recipes had been made for the general public.[27] From 1490 to 1520, the *Fasciculo di Medicina* (1493), a kind of anthology of university texts, enjoyed considerable success with numerous reprints and translations. Leaflets and flyers showing male and female anatomies were available not only to students but also to surgeons' apprentices, barbers, healers and a broad general public.[28] The books of secrets also contained curing recipes, often enhanced with magical or alchemical components. In the seventeenth-century Christian charity of the Counter-Reformation, some of the first self-help books appeared in the form of charitable handbooks.[29]

28 Printed science

Printed images became a powerful means of spreading knowledge. Vesalius's *De Humani Corporis Fabrica* (1543), with its magnificent anatomical illustrations almost certainly made by followers of the great painter Titian, was printed by the Swiss publisher Johann Oporinus (1507–68) (see Figure 2.1). Vesalius made prints of both the inside and outside of the human body. They showed the skin lifted back to display muscle structure and through the different muscle layers readers could appreciate the bones and internal organs.[30] Similarly, the famous *Micrographia* (1665) by Robert Hooke (1635–1703) contained a spectacular set of images of tiny creatures, never before seen, observed under a microscope.[31] While thousands of printed images had become a major source of religious propaganda, now the details of a fly's wing seen through a microscope, patiently drawn, etched and finally printed, spread the power of the new experimental philosophy, and legitimated the authority of the microscope. Printed words circulated freely, but so did images with an unprecedented impact. The first thousand copies of *Micrographia*, which was to become a reference for microscopic observations throughout the seventeenth and eighteenth centuries, extended practical scientific information far beyond the reduced audiences of the prestigious Royal Society of London. Private experimentation became public knowledge.[32]

Vesalius's and Hooke's engravings are just a small sample of the visual revolution of printed science in the sixteenth and seventeenth centuries. As discussed in the introduction of this book, the inherited view of science popularisation gave great weight to texts as depositories of 'truths', while the image, the illustration, played a secondary and even subsidiary role. However, from the readers' perspective, or even from the illiterate public's point of view, looking at images of an experiment, a mining process or an exotic plant with medicinal properties became a hitherto unknown means of spreading scientific knowledge, which merits further historical examination.

Isaac Newton largely represents the height of the Scientific Revolution, as the father of universal gravitation, the laws of mechanics which lasted throughout the twentieth century and the diffraction of light into its constituent colours. This book is obviously not the place for a full description and analysis of Newtonian physics but rather an opportunity to focus on the cultural dimension of Newtonianism.[33] In fact, anyone interested in the history of science will have leafed through the original 1687 Latin edition of the *Principia* at some time, but few will have read the whole text in detail. Newton's geometrical demonstrations are hard to follow and account for the huge distance between the mathematical language of the seventeenth century and our own. But that problem was also experienced by many of Newton's contemporaries, who read numerous works 'translating' the almost esoteric Newtonian world to more popular sensibilities.[34]

It is worth mentioning best sellers such as *Astronomical Dialogues between a Gentleman and a Lady* (1719) by John Harris (1666–1719), who also wrote the well-known seventeenth-century scientific dictionary, the *Lexicon Technicum* (1704–10), or *The Young Gentleman and Lady's Philosophy* (1759) by instrument maker Benjamin Martin (1705–82). In France, Pierre-Louis de Maupertuis

FIGURE 2.1 The anatomy lesson of Andreas Vesalius and his audience (1543). Andreas Vesalius (1997) *De humani corporis fabrica* (facsimile edition). Madrid: Doce Calles. Reproduced with permission of the Biblioteca de Catalunya (Barcelona).

30 Printed science

(1698–1759) published *Discourse sur les différentes figures des astres* (1732), which could be read by a much broader audience than a paper presented at the Académie des sciences in Paris.[35] Another famous title aimed at a specific readership was *The Newtonian System of Philosophy, Adapted to the Capacities of Young Gentlemen and Ladies* (1761) by John Newbery (1713–67) (also known as Tom Telescope), which explained the basic concepts of Newtonianism through everyday objects and examples. The book was aimed at children aged 12 to 15 and had sold 30,000 copies by the end of the eighteenth century.[36]

The culture of Newtonianism deeply pervaded European society in the eighteenth century. Despite its great mathematical difficulty, industrialists, traders, craftsmen, women, young people and children came into contact with different aspects of Newton's work. So Newtonianism went far beyond Newton's individual genius. His critics, promoters, readers, propagandists and commentators filled the salons, while the number of scientific expeditions to corroborate some of the theories in situ multiplied.[37] Faced with the difficulty of Newtonian language, his supporters gained public attention with utilitarian and theological arguments. In Britain the new laws of heavenly and terrestrial bodies, which were then fully unified, were forecast to bring enormous benefits in navigation, trade and construction, while the mathematical harmony of the cosmos turned out to be a powerful argument for the existence of God and the marvellous design of His creation. In 1725, one of the biggest promoters of Newtonianism, John-Théophile Desaguliers (1683–1744), stressed that, even with no training in mathematics, anyone should be able to understand the natural phenomena that had been discovered through geometrical principles and experimentation.[38]

One of the most successful books, *Newtonianismo per le dame* (1737) by Francesco Algarotti (1712–65), appealed directly to a female readership. Émile du Châtelet's (1706–49) publication *Institutions de physique* (1740), followed a few years later by the first French translation of Newton's *Principia*, reached aristocratic circles. In the salons, Mme de La Fayette, Mme de Sévigné, Mme de Sabre, the Duke de La Rochefoucauld and readers of these works would gather to discuss natural philosophy, Cartesianism or Newtonian physics. Their members, mainly women, became one of the principal audiences for the science of the Enlightenment. The spoken word and conversation were the ultimate complement to Newtonian printed science.[39]

In 1686, just one year before the publication of the *Principia*, Louis-Bernard de Fontenelle (1657–1757), the future perpetual secretary of the Académie des sciences and one of the best-known critics of Newtonian natural philosophy, published *Entretiens sur la pluralité des mondes*,[40] a book that was republished until well into the nineteenth century. It was set in the aristocratic culture of salons, and in the form of a conversation between a Cartesian natural philosopher and a non-expert but intelligent lady. Fontenelle described the systems of Ptolemy, Copernicus, Brahe, the planets, satellites and stars, while mooting the possibility that there were other inhabited worlds (see Figure 2.2). Whereas he had initially

FIGURE 2.2 Bernard de Fontenelle explaining the plurality of worlds in his *Entretiens* (1686). B. Fontenelle, *Entretiens sur la pluralité des mondes. Nouvelle édition, avec des remarques & des figures en taille-douce de M. Bode*. Imprimerie de L.P. Wegener. Berlin, 1783. Reproduced with permission of the Biblioteca de Catalunya (Barcelona).

32 Printed science

aimed the book at select circles of the educated Parisian aristocracy, capable of switching conversation topics from poetry to philosophy and astronomy, successful sales persuaded Fontenelle to revise both the preface and the main text. He even advised on the most appropriate levels of readership of *Entretiens* according to social class. In his own words:

> I should warn those that have some knowledge of natural philosophy, that I do not suppose this book capable of giving them any information; it will merely afford them some amusement, but presenting in a lively manner what they have already become acquainted with by dint of study. I would also inform those who are ignorant of these subjects that it has been my design to amuse and instruct them at the same time: the former will counteract my intention if they here expect improvement, and the latter, if they here only seek for entertainment.[41]

Some decades later, Antoine-Noël Pluche's (1688–1761) *Spectacle de la nature* (1732–50) offered lengthy explanations and plates that caught the attention of thousands of readers.[42] All eight volumes were written in the form of a cultured and witty conversation, typical of an Enlightenment salon, and covered topics such as natural history, physics, economy, the arts and manufactured products. In France, it appeared in more than 50 editions and was translated into English (1735), Italian (1737), Dutch (1737), German (1746) and Spanish (1752).[43] Pluche was keen to stimulate the curiosity of young aristocrats and he inculcated in them religious piety and an enthusiasm for experimental natural philosophy. Inspired in Newtonian natural theology, readers were introduced to the wisdom of the Creator through gravitation, light diffraction, the formation of rivers and oceans, earthquakes, breathing, the nature of fire and air as well as a detailed description of many experiments. Translations of the *Spectacle* were also, however, adapted to the cultural particularities of each country, making the work even more successful on a European level.[44]

But the printed science of the time also appeared in other formats. In the context of eighteenth-century medical pluralism, a plethora of self-help manuals filled the market. Catalogues of curative remedies often included the motto 'everyone shall become their own doctor'. At the same time and throughout the eighteenth century, magical elements progressively faded away and the popular texts became a powerful defence against superstition. They aimed, more or less explicitly, to ensure that the medical profession prevailed over the numerous charlatans and healers competing for the same area of practice.[45] 'Domestic' medical books such as those by Scottish doctor William Buchan (1729–1805) and Swiss physician Samuel-André Tissot (1728–97), promoted self-knowledge about the human body,[46] deeming concepts such as hygiene and preventative habits more worthy than aggressive treatments. Reluctant to over-inform their patients, other doctors were in favour of providing some information to lay people, but limiting it to hygiene, preventative measures and first aid. They underlined the dangers of 'popular mistakes', without entering into the ultimate causes of the constitution and functions of the human body.[47]

Domestic Medicine or *A Treatise on the Prevention and Cure of Diseases by Regimen and Simple Medicines* was first published in Edinburgh in 1769. In the book Buchan positioned himself against excessive elitism in the medical profession and advocated public access to medical secrets. However, it was not his intention that every patient should become a doctor or that his book should substitute the task of the expert doctor. From his point of view, if half of humanity could not even afford to visit the doctor, given the dangers of falling into the hands of charlatans or healers, or being taken in by a variety of therapeutic superstitions, then his book could be highly useful. Buchan stressed that important aspects of medical knowledge should be a substantial part of an individual's general education. It should protect patients against charlatans but also help them to take better care of their children at home. Buchan also believed that this kind of popular printed medicine would improve the expert–lay relationship. In a similar vein, *Lectures on Diet and Regime* (1799) by Anthony F. M. Willich, gave advice on hygiene in people's daily lives. In a puritan context which favoured control over one's body, and adopting some neo-Hippocratic reminiscences, his book covered balneology, cosmetics, prevention, physical exercise, diet and pharmacy. Making preventative habits popular was more frequent and accessible than therapeutics. The book also drew a line between medical expertise and patients' skills, to prepare the latter for more effective future visits to the doctor.[48]

Astronomy, natural history, medicine and the natural philosophy of the Enlightenement in its broad sense were also spread through encylopaedias. This was the case, for instance, of the *Dictionnaire universel des arts et sciences* (1690–4) by Antoine Furetière, the *Cyclopaedia* (1728) by Ephraim Chambers, the *Encyclopédie ou dictionnaire raisonné des sciences, arts et métiers* (1751–72) by Denis Diderot and Jean D'Alembert and the *Cyclopedia* by Abraham Ress (1800). Encyclopaedia reconsidered the classificaction of knowledge – as in the famous 'Discourse préliminaire' of Diderot's and D'Alembert's *Encyclopédie*. Expert voices described knowledge boundaries at all times, as well as new disciplines. In some cases, they even included original research. In their sales strategies each new encylopaedia gave a rigorous description of emerging fields and a review of the concepts that had appeared in previous editions. In other words, these were by no means static views of knowledge. Readers frequently demanded easy access to these new sciences and their organisation, and publishers had to progressively adapt their products to potential new customers.[49]

In the eighteenth century, the content of encyclopaedias and dictionaries was not considered to be inferior to any other source. It had a lasting value for its readers, who used it to approach a specific field or to gain a greater appreciation of the connections between different topics in the map of knowledge.[50] Encyclopaedias therefore became privileged sources for assessing the scientific culture of a particular time and place, and in many cases also for analysing the state of the art of different subjects.[51] Readers of encyclopaedias became customers,

34 Printed science

subscribers and correspondents with the publishing houses. Between 1751 and 1772 the Diderot's and D'Alembert's *Encyclopédie* became big business for the dissemination of knowledge: 17 volumes of text, over 70,000 written voices by more than 130 authors, more than 2,500 plates in 11 volumes and some 25,000 subscribers.[52]

Robert Darnton's *The Business of the Enlightenment* (1979) appeared as a result of finding the publisher's archive of Diderot and D'Alembert's *Encyclopédie* in Neuchâtel, Switzerland. This finding was of paramount importance for obtaining first-hand information about the readers of the *Encyclopédie*, and identifying the preferences for that publication among the aristocratic classes of the Ancien Régime and the mercantile and bourgeois classes for reconstructing a 'sociology' of readings of these controversial texts and their magnificent engravings. Just within the fringes of legality, publishers such as Charles-Joseph Panckoucke (1736–98) exploited the *Encyclopédie* as a commodity through the Société typografique in Neuchâtel. The relationship between publisher and potential readers (or subscribers) became a subject of special interest and completed the above-mentioned circuit of the book. Despite the subversive and threatening messages from the establishment and subtle strategies to overcome official censorship, the Neuchâtel archives show that the readership of the *Encyclopédie* was basically the elite of the Ancien Régime, including aristocrats, the clergy and professionals (doctors, lawyers and academics). It was only the format in quarto and octavo that allowed the printed texts to reach readers from the Third Estate. Subscriptions in mercantile and industrial cities, with their emerging bourgeois and capitalist culture, were paradoxically very low. So it was mainly the elites of the Ancien Régime, including the most conservative paradigms of the established order, who became its main readers. Panckoucke's publication of the *Encyclopédie Méthodique*, on the eve of the French Revolution, neutralised the political weight of the voices that had previously appeared. Again, this is significant proof of the importance of the different actors in the circuit of a book.

Moving away from the traditional distinction between popular and elite culture and showing how intellectuals and ordinary people often share the same problems reinforces the point that printed science, from the Renaissance to the Enlightenment, contributed to the circulation of scientific knowledge and its validation between the different social groups, thereby breaking down the intellectual barriers between the Menocchios and the Newtons.[53]

2.2. Popular paradigms

The story of Charles Darwin, his biography, background, defenders and detractors, is well known, and especially the impact of his famous book *Origin of Species*, published in 1859, which would soon become one of the best-known titles in Western culture. It was a synthesis of the evolutionary paradigm which would gradually substitute the ancient creationist theories.[54] However, another book, the *Vestiges of the Natural History of Creation*, about the origin and evolution of the earth, was of great interest to large sectors of British society, but is much less well known. As historian James Secord has shown, *Vestiges* was published anonymously in 1844, preceding the *Origin of Species* by 15 years.[55] The first edition contained information about astronomy, geology, moral philosophy and even some predictions for the future. It covered some of the most profound questions of existence and discussed more than a dozen different sciences but, to the surprise of the readers, there was no identifiable author. Some read it as a true science book and others criticised it and rejected it as the product of an amateur or hobbyist.

The narrative was dominated by an image of progress and dynamism capable of provoking accusations of materialism and evolutionism or an unacceptable departure from theology. In fact, at the beginning of the book, the role of God as creator was taken for granted, but later on the narrative progressively extrapolated the laws of astronomical and geological progress of living beings, civilisation and the destiny of the human race. This dynamic view was articulated in paragraphs such as the following:

> the formation of bodies in space is still and at present in progress. We live at a time when many have been formed, and many are still forming. Our own solar system is to be regarded as completed, supposing its perfection to consist in the formation of a series of planets, for there are mathematical reasons for concluding that Mercury is the nearest planet to the sun, which can, according to the laws of the system, exist. But there are other solar systems within our astral system, which are as yet in a less advanced state, and even some quantities of nebulous matter which have scarcely begun to advance towards the stellar form.[56]

Similarly, the dynamism of the solar system could be extrapolated to the lives of the different species on Earth, confirming that the study of plant and animal development on the planet was a clear advance towards new and higher forms of organisation.[57] More than 100,000 copies of the *Vestiges* made an impression on readers and basically laid the foundation for the evolutionary culture that would be taken up by Darwin from 1859. Some of the readers' reactions are particularly significant. In 1845 the following comments appeared in the personal diary of politician Sir John Hobhouse:

> I have read this week − *Vestiges of the Natural History of Creation* − a most remarkable work − which has made a great noise . . . In spite of the allusions to the creative will of God the cosmogony is atheistic − at least the introduction of an author of all things seems very like a formality for the sake of saving appearances − it is not a necessary part of the scheme.[58]

The Reverend Adam Sedgwick (1785–1873), Professor of Geology at Trinity College, Cambridge, had considered some months previously that *Vestiges* was

36 Printed science

not a work worthy of men of science and was pure materialism.[59] Even the workers' leader Joseph Barker in Leeds ridiculed the book in the weekly *The People*:

> Suppose we admit the theory contended for by the author of the work entitled *Vestiges of the Natural History of Creation*, namely that mankind sprang from an inferior order of animals, such as the monkey or the orangoutang . . . how should it happen, that monkey parents produce offspring so widely from themselves – so vastly superior to themselves in so many respects, yet so greatly inferior to themselves in so many respects . . . The theory of the author of *Vestiges* is incredible.[60]

Others considered that the author of *Vestiges* may have been mistaken in his conjectures, but that he deserved the praise of all those who thought that stimulating research and debate was the way towards progress and that the book had contributed more to that end than any other of its time.[61] In fact, after 1859, largely thanks to that context, Darwin's work quickly gained a place with a much broader public readership who constructed multiple and sometime contradictory readings of its social implications. Forty years later, in 1884, the name of the author of *Vestiges* was finally unveiled. Most of the public debate had been carried out in the context of an anonymous work. Up to 60 possible authors had been suggested but the writer finally turned out to be Robert Chambers (1802–71), a Scottish journalist, publisher, amateur scientist, a liberal with deist religious inclinations. In the 40 years since the appearance of the first edition printing techniques had changed considerably, making it possible to produce smaller, cheaper editions that significantly eased the circulation of *Vestiges*.

The attraction of the book among the readers was unprecedented. *Vestiges* was 'dissected' at scientific meetings, condemned in the pulpits and conference halls, loaned to infinity in itinerant popular libraries and, above all, repeatedly read so that the evolutionary ideas became a regular topic of conversation.[62] Its success did not come from the marginal sectors of society, as was thought until recently. Exhaustive research by James Secord has shown that *Vestiges* and its success hailed from the very heart of the new industrial order in Victorian Britain. It is undeniable that, more than establishing a new paradigm, Darwin and his *Origin* epitomised a peak in the controversy about evolution that had begun long before. It was in the realm of the living debate in the public arena that the culture of evolutionism grew, and *Vestiges* played an important part in that.[63]

If there was one scientific topic that the publishing market could take issue with in *Vestiges*, it was phrenology. Today, phrenology may sound like an exotic term with no clear meaning, but throughout the nineteenth century it acquired considerable public acclaim. Phrenology compared the cranial protuberances to physical and moral qualities in individuals.[64] Its origin lies in studies undertaken by the German doctor Franz-Joseph Gall (1758–1828),[65] who identified 27 organs in the human brain, 19 of which corresponded to animal faculties and eight to moral and intellectual ones. Given that the skull ossifies around the brain during its formation, its external analysis (craneoscopic examination) provided the method for diagnosing mental states (Figure 2.3). In 1813, Johann Kaspar Spurzheim (1776–1832), a follower of Gall, set off for Britain to promote the new science, which also spread to the east coast of the United States. Gradually Gall's system became both a moral and social philosophy.[66]

In 1828, the *Constitution of Man Considered in Relation to External Objects* by Georges Combe (1788–1858), a follower of Spurzheim, became one of the best sellers of the nineteenth century. From 1828 to 1899 more than 100 publishers issued the *Constitution of Man*. It was a lay manual of natural philosophy which, despite opposition from ecclesiastical and conservative sectors, reinforced natural laws and the need to abide by them.[67] It was a true constitution for the regulation of social and individual behaviour and it assured happiness by following a series of moral actions in accordance with the law of phrenology. Combe

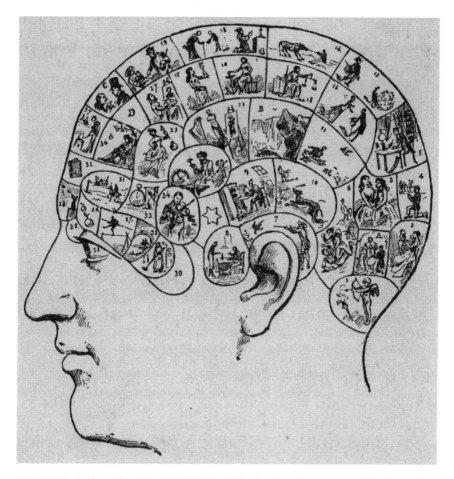

FIGURE 2.3 A phrenology head (1861). Louis Figuier, *Conócete a ti mismo. Tratado popular de fisiología humana*. 2 vols. Herederos de Pablo Riera. 1881, I, p. 389. Reproduced with permission of the Biblioteca de Catalunya (Barcelona).

38 Printed science

played a crucial role in the transformation of phrenology from its original status as an obscure theory of the brain and personality to a respectable science which had the potential of improving social life in the mid-nineteenth century.[68] Combe's treatise sold some 330,000 copies with reprints made until 1899. Its popularity can be compared only with that of *Vestiges*, John Bunyan's *Pilgrim's Progress* (a British literary classic inspired by Protestantism) and Darwin's *Origin*. While by 1847 Combe's text had sold 80,500, almost 20 years later sales of Darwin's *Origin* stood at only 50,000.[69]

Although it was met by a good deal of suspicion in other countries, the success of phrenology in Britain was considerable. In France, a popular treatise on human physiology from the 1880s saw it as inferior, since it had been overridden by consistent anatomical and physiological arguments: 'however, there is another opinion about this matter in England and America, countries that give great weight to phrenology. It is taught in public university courses and legal practice uses it for investigation of crimes, vices and the aptitudes of supposed criminals'.[70] Phrenology pervaded deeply in Western societies in the mid-nineteenth century. Thousands of Combe's readers and those of many other phrenology-related books, articles, pamphlets and printed images played a major role in the legitimation of a specific scientific practice that overcame the frequent suspicions and official restrictions.[71]

Although at the end of the century the phrenological phenomena seemed to gradually burn out and disappear, printed phrenology managed to attract the interest of very broad audiences. As in the case of *Vestiges*, even its detractors (university doctors, representatives of the medical profession, people who feared that these practices would weaken their authority, the clergy and ecclesiastical authorities, sceptical of what the phrenological code might mean for their traditional moral monopoly) felt they needed to speak out, albeit to discredit it. Among its defenders and followers were the urban middle classes and working classes, whose interests ranged from pure curiosity and entertainment to the possibility of including a secular moral code in their behaviour and ideology.[72]

Far beyond strict academic circles, very broad audiences legitimated evolutionism and phrenology. All of that gave way to spectacular publishing deals in direct competition with the great literary authors. In spite of frequent controversies, both topics had a constant impact in the public arena. They would influence thousands of people who had their say on scientific authority and expertise. In practice, both paradigms, apparently restricted to small expert circles, became part of the popular culture.

2.3. The business of science publishing

Vestiges and *Constitution* are just two major examples of a much greater circulation of printed science. While in the eighteenth century, expert and lay actors shared an open experimental philosophy from their diverse social positions, the professionalisation of science throughout the nineteenth century restricted the

Printed science **39**

notion of discovery and experiment and defined more rigid criteria in terms of experts and disciplines.[73] This process ran parallel to a new popularisation to serve the new professional scientist, in a context in which the business of publishing was undergoing great changes.[74] Small-scale publications gradually gave way to mechanised composition processes and publishing houses were adopting new marketing strategies. Railways afforded a faster and more efficient distribution of the new books. The old printer-booksellers became the new publishers, able to put authors, printers, distributors and readers in close contact. New authors, new formats and layouts alongside a more precise identification of potential customers and marketing shaped a new way of publishing that targeted new kinds of readers. In Britain, general interest periodicals such as the *Gentleman's Magazine* and the *Edinburgh Review* included scientific topics for the interest of the new urban middle classes.[75]

Other sources of communication also gained ground: new encyclopaedias, dictionaries, scientific articles and reviews in generalist popular science and leaflets.[76] This was the age of the new periodicals devoted to science popularisation: *Die Natur*, founded in 1852, can be considered a pioneer of this new genre. It aimed to attract an educated readership from the middle and professional classes, who had mainly been readers of literary texts, and to introduce them to the world of science and industry. A few years later, in 1869, *Nature* appeared in Britain, followed by *La nature* in France (1873), and its Italian version *Natura* (1883). Other big titles of nineteenth-century popular science periodicals were *Scientific American* (1845), *Cosmos* (1852), *La science pour tous* (1856), *La science populaire* (1880) and *L'astronomie* (1880).[77]

Most of these periodicals appeared in highly-illustrated, small formats, accessible to large numbers of readers. Despite some complaints, they often contained extracts of articles published elsewhere as well as reviews of recent books. Among the authors and editors were professional scientists, but also emerging science writers and populatisers. The readership ranged from the upper, educated circles to the urban middle class with an interest in science, and even to the culturally inspired working class. Readers usually found articles halfway between expert and popular knowledge. They could therefore take scientific periodicals either as curiosities and entertainment or as a source of inspiration for their own intellectual work. Comparing, for instance, the periodicals that appeared in Britain and France during the nineteenth century, it is easy to see that in Darwin's country publishers tended to have quite different interests and professional profiles and most of the authors were amateurs, albeit specialised in a certain field. All of this was under the banner of a Baconian rhetoric that stressed equal capabilities for assimilating any scientific content. In France, however, a more professional group of authors emerged. From the perspective of the professional *savant*, they aimed to develop a scientific discourse that could be understood by lay audiences.[78]

Scientific news and articles also made their way into the daily press, especially from the last few decades of the nineteenth century. Most newspapers with a reasonably large circulation tended to include science news covering a wide

40 Printed science

range of topics: natural disasters (earthquakes, volcanic eruptions), technological accidents (explosions, train crashes), medical advice for public health, homage to great scientists and inventors, or simply an enormous number of adverts selling all sorts of lotions, balsams and pills for any ailment, usually under the certification of a professional who accredited their scientific authenticity.[79] In some cases scientific news in the press appeared in regular 'science sections', commissioned to science popularisers. In Britain, in the early twentieth century, newspapers like *The Times* and *Guardian* published regular columns with scientific news mainly devoted to natural history, astronomy and technology, but also reporting on prominent public lectures, scientific controversies and commemorative practices.[80] Topics varied considerably, depending on the ideology of the newspaper, with expert voices having a greater presence in the more conservative publications, while the more liberal and even the left-wing socialist press tended to portray a more empirical image of science to be adapted to the readers' needs. In any case, thanks to the daily press the scientific culture grew and spread spectacularly.

As active science audiences and producers of consumer goods, publishing houses enjoyed a heightened status throughout the nineteenth century. Under different names (popular science, science for all, educational, entertaining, recreational science), the popular science book became a valuable object for business and an essential complement to daily press and periodicals. To cite just one example, in 1865 publisher Louis Hachette (1800–64) embarked on a project known as *Bibliothèque des merveilles*, which was made up of small two-franc volumes covering all aspects of nature and accessible to all kinds of readers. The first number was commissioned to the young Camille Flammarion (1842–1925) to write about celestial marvels. Flammarion would become one of the great science popularisers of the century. He wrote the text in a month, was paid 1,000 francs without royalties and 5,500 copies were printed. In 1912 more than 60,000 copies had been sold in different editions, proving that printed science for all was a profitable business.[81] By 1880 Flammarion had published his *Astronomie populaire* (1880), but this ambitious project on astronomy and meteorology had begun years before with the 1862 publication of *La pluralité des mondes habités*, which largely took up Fontenelle's ideas and was already in its 26th edition by 1880. Later came other best sellers such as *Les mondes imaginaires et les mondes réels* (1865), *Dieu dans la nature* (1869), and *L'atmosphère* (1871). In 1882, Flammarion began to work on the publication of *L'astronomie* and by the end of the century the journal had sold 100,000 copies.[82]

The cheap, popular science series of the late nineteenth century targeted a broad market for scientific readership to compete with readers of literature and even with the textbook market. They offered a fluent relationship with readers and subscribers, whose comments were taken into account when modifying the texts for future editions (see Figure 2.4). Readers of *Recréations scientifiques* (Popular Scientific Recreations) (1880) were particularly vocal. This highly successful book was the work of the French science populariser Gaston Tissandier (1843–99), founder of *La nature*. He borrowed most of the entertaining experiments that appeared in the book from a large group of experts, to be later tested by amateurs, young people, children and lay readers in general. Tissandier himself described the process in the preface to the 1883 English edition like this:

> Another kind of recreation, both intelligent and useful, consists in collecting ingenious inventions which are constantly being supplied to our requirements by the applied sciences, and learning how to use them. We have collected a number of mechanical inventions and appliances, with which most ingenious and skilful people will wish to supply themselves, from Edison's electric pen, or the chromatography, which will produce a large number of copies of a letter, drawing, etc., to the more complicated but not less valuable contrivances, for making science useful in the house.[83]

University lecturers often combined their academic teaching and research work with contributions to popular science books with academic and popular content. These tasks not only contributed to augmenting the professors' salary, but also to increasing their social prestige beyond the closed academic circles. In fact, from research articles to textbooks and popular leaflets available to all intellectual levels, university scholars produced a wide range of publications which traversed different literary genres and catered for a varied readership

Peter Bowler has recently shown how early twentieth-century Britain became a golden age for science writers. Very much influenced by the publishers, practising scientists were very actively writing about their work for a general readership without any particular hostility from their peers. From the 1960s onwards, with the increasing figures of students in colleges and universities, the interests of professional scientists in popularisation decreased slightly,[84] and the myth of the isolated professional was not tenable anymore. Scientific topics such as atomic physics, cosmology, relativity, evolution, human origins, medicine, and more practical knowledge such as science and industry, electricity and radio, amateur astronomy, and observation of nature became good business and had considerable financial benefits for science writers.

Printed science spread widely in society through books, periodicals, magazines, encyclopaedias, popular libraries, and bookshops. It was available in different registers and was appropriated in different ways by a plural readership. It also shared pages, texts or paragraphs with other genres and disciplines. As the boundaries of printed science had become blurred in society, so they had in its content, as shall be seen in the next section on the crossover between two supposedly distant worlds: science and literature.

2.4. Science and literature: common ground

The long-standing split between the humanities and the sciences has meant that it is hard to conceive of a common ground between science and literature;

FIGURE 2.4 Front cover of *Les merveilles de la science, ou description populaire des inventions modernes* by Louis Figuier. 4 vols. Fourne, Jouvet et Cie, editeurs. Paris 1867. Reproduced with permission of the Biblioteca de Catalunya (Barcelona).

common ideas or expressions that may be shared in a novel and in a scientific text.[85] However, science and literature have a lot more common values, conceptual frameworks and cultural aspects than expected. To a greater or lesser extent, both are subject to public reactions.[86] Similarly, some scientific concepts require metaphors and other literary devices to make them more easily understood. A large range of texts combine artistic and scientific language in a complementary and non-exclusive manner, meaning that scientific culture can subtly reach readers of literature or that writers of literature can include aspects of scientific knowledge in their creations. Perhaps some examples from the past can give us a better idea of scientific texts from a literary perspective, but they can also help to analyse the scientific content in many works of fiction.

In the past, telescopes and microscopes greatly stimulated the literary imagination and had a significant impact on the general public. Telescopes provided two possible ways of spreading astronomical knowledge: the first through mathematics and physics, and the second through the description and use of instruments that not only became effective ways of popularising astronomy to those who were not familiar with the laws of physics, but also acted as a source of imagination for literary creation.[87] In Victorian Britain, for instance, scientific theories, new discoveries and wild hypotheses caught the attention of writers, who often cited prestigious scientists in their literary texts.[88] Similarly, generalist publications often included scientific content.[89] Concepts such as evolution, entropy, unity of physical forces, and the struggle for survival appeared frequently in the nineteenth century in both scientific and literary works – sometimes as generally agreed definitions among the experts and sometimes as metaphors or allegories of social or moral problems.[90] These common places can easily travel from one context to another, from a scientific to a literary discourse. They play a fundamental role in the circulation of scientific knowledge and often become useful agents for science popularisation. Even the names of the great scientists can be identified as common places: Maxwell's Demon, Darwin's survival of the fittest, Einstein's relativity and Heisenberg's uncertainty principle.[91]

Science and literature also fed into mutual methodological inspiration. Émile Zola (1840–1902), for instance, adapted the observations on laboratory medicine by Claude Bernard (1813–78) in *Le roman experimental* (The Experimental Novel) (1880) to justify his own literary style in the following terms:

> I really only need to adapt, for the experimental method has been established with strength and marvellous clearness by Claude Bernard in his 'Introduction à l'étude de la medécine expérimentale'. This work, but he savant whose authority is unquestionable, will serve me as a solid foundation . . . It will often be but necessary for me to replace the word 'doctor' by the word 'novelist' to make my meaning clear and to give it the rigidity of scientific thought . . . I am going to try and prove for my part that, if the experimental method leads to the knowledge of physical life, it should also

44 Printed science

lead to the knowledge of the passionate and intellectual life. It is but a question of degree in the same path which runs from chemistry to physiology, then from physiology to anthropology and to sociology. The experimental novel is the goal.[92]

Zola's appealing ideas about the gradual move from experimental science to the novel suggest that there were no clear demarcations between a work of pure literary fiction and a science book, but only a *continuum* sown from multiple common grounds.[93] This is especially useful when approaching popular science texts, and also for science fiction, a new genre that was finding considerable success throughout the nineteenth century. Despite its controversial origins, Mary Shelly's *Frankenstein* (1818) can be considered the first milestone in which science fiction aimed to create a literary narrative of the sublime without resorting to traditional magical, mystical or supernatural phenomena.[94] *Frankenstein* was a work of fiction but one that was based on major scientific elements in the early nineteenth century: hidden forces such as electricity and magnetism were closely linked to health and life so the creature could only overcome death through massive electrical charges. *Frankenstein*'s readers could subtly learn about aspects of the scientific culture of their time, as described in the following paragraph:

> The event on which this fiction is founded has been supposed, by Dr. Darwin, and some of the physiological writers of Germany, as not of impossible occurrence. I shall not be supposed as according the remotest degree of serious faith to such an imagination; yet, in assuming it as the basis of a work of fancy, I have not considered myself as merely weaving a series of supernatural terrors. The event on which the interest of the story depends is exempt from the disadvantages of a mere tale of spectres or enchantment. It was recommended by the novelty of the situations which it developes; and, however impossible as a physical fact, affords a point of view to the imagination for the delineating of human passions more comprehensive and commanding than any which the ordinary relations of existing events can yield.[95]

The narrative described the effects of a nightmare, but it also based those effects on factors that did not depend on supernatural elements. The new genre was a result of the convergence of a number of previous traditions: fantastic journeys, utopian literature, philiosophical–moral tales, the Gothic novel, social, technological and biological foresight.[96] Some of the recurring themes, at least in the nineteenth century, reflected aspects of scientific knowledge embedded in the readers' culture. A good number of the novels described transport systems by land, sea and air, and conceived of utopian cities or imagined future megalopolises. They discussed evolution, astronomy and geology, and speculations about the age and the history of the earth.[97] Added to the utopian tradition and the technological and social predictions in science fiction were dystopias resulting from technological pessimism and the growing discontent that would gain ground in the West following the Second World War, but which had its roots in the First.

The success of novels by Jules Verne, Albert Robida and H. G. Wells provides further proof of the growing interest in science at that time. Verne's novels were read by thousands and widely translated (Figure 2.5). They included descriptions of hot air balloons, giant cannons, chemical products, climate speculations and futuristic transport systems. All that gave readers a solid scientific culture, albeit at different levels, which often complemented what they had learnt at school. Here, for example, is an extract describing a real physics class in *From the Earth to the Moon* (1865):

> 'Is it possible to transmit a projectile up to the moon?' – Yes; provided it possess an initial velocity of 1,200 yards per second; calculations prove that to be sufficient. In proportion as we recede from the Earth the action of gravitation diminishes in the inverse ratio of the square of the distance; that is to say, at three times a given distance the action is nine times less. Consequently, the weight of a shot will decrease, and will become reduced to zero at the instant that the attraction of the moon exactly counterpoises that of the earth; that is to say at 47/52 of its passage. At that instant the projectile will have no weight whatever; and, if it passes that point, it will fall into the moon by the sole effect of the lunar attraction. The theoretical possibility of the experiment is therefore absolutely demonstrated; its *success* must depend upon the power of the engine employed.[98]

There is no doubt that science fiction belongs to our contemporary scientific culture. It fascinates young people, university students and society at large.[99] Science fiction novels have both optimistic and pessimistic, technophile and technophobic discourses that transport readers towards a moral dialogue of the pros and cons of modern science and whether it can provide significant advances for humanity or whether it will be the final destruction.[100] Take for instance Isaac Asimov (1920–92), a prolific writer of science fiction and science populariser, with more than 500 titles published. In spite of his scientific training (PhD in Biochemistry from the University of Columbia in 1948) Asimov soon turned to writing literature. Of particular interest are his stories about robots: *I, Robot* (1950) and *The Rest of the Robots* (1964), which were subsequently taken to the big screen. With his famous laws of robotics, the conflict between humans and machines is taken to its limit. Between 1951 and 1953 he published the *Foundation* trilogy composed of *Foundation* (1951), *Foundation and Empire* (1952) and *The Second Foundation* (1953), where the new hybrid science of 'psychohistory' was able to forecast the future behaviour of the masses. In fact, Asimov's novels, as well as those of many other science fiction writers, provide excellent primary sources for studying the different images of scientists

FIGURE 2.5 Advertisement poster of Jules Verne's 'Extraordinary Journeys' (*Les voyages extraordinaires*) by Charles-Émile Matthis, 1886. Reproduced with permission of the Bibliothèque nationale de France.

Printed science **47**

throughout the ages, as well as analysing the ambivalences of the public perception of science. They are helpful for gaining a deeper understanding of the popular scientific culture, which sometimes views professional scientists as magicians or efficient experts; in other words, as ambiguous demiurges or heroes for human progress.

Through the analysis of some popular science books it is possible to see that the differences in comparison with science fiction books were not that obvious, especially in the nineteenth century. In an attempt to attract broader public interest, Flammarion's books, for instance, were full of allegories, metaphors and fictional elements. In 1889, combining autobiographical data, utopian ideas and feminist stances, Flammarion published the novel *Urania*. It described the universe through the series of adventures of a young man (Flammarion himself) who was transported in space by the beautiful, young Urania, the muse of astronomy. His own words give us an idea of the difficulty of limiting his narrative to a single, well-defined genre:

> Then I saw the Earth sinking down into the yawning depths of immensity; the cupolas of the observatory, Paris with its lights, were rapidly fading away. Although feeling as if I were motionless, I had the same sensation which one experiences on rising in a balloon and seeing the earth descend. I went up, up, in a magic flight toward the inaccessible zenith. Urania was with me, a little higher up, looking at me kindly and pointing out the kingdoms below . . . As we passed through the -Moon's neighborhood I had noticed our satellite's hilly landscapes, the mountain crests radiant with light, deep valleys filled with shadows, and I should have liked to stop for a nearer study of the surroundings; but Urania did not deign to bestow so much as a passing glance at it, and drew me on in a rapid flight toward the sidereal regions.[101]

Urania, *Lumen* and *Stella* are the three Flammarion novels. They differ only partially from the style of his popular science pieces in books, periodicals and newspapers. Flammarion was convinced that astronomy transmitted a message of peace through the spectacle of the sky, which enabled a natural harmony to be extrapolated to social harmony and thereby create new common places for science and literature. The contemplation of the heavens became a social leveller, and acted as a sort of social 'lubricant' between the upper and lower classes, in the same way that popular science, science fiction and scientific novels bridged humanistic and scientific cultures.[102] In addition to the astronomy tradition, scientific literature for children also became an important common ground. In the nineteenth century all sorts of writers presented new scientific discoveries to young readers in fairy tales, nursery classics and other fictional accounts which bound fantasy to science through a rich circulation of ideas, practices and objects.[103] Equally, in Victorian Britain, novels by Charles Dickens, among other contemporary writers, frequently included serious concerns about

48 Printed science

child psychology and psychiatry, as another example of the complex intersections between science and literature.[104]

★ ★ ★

These are just some examples that show how literary sources can be extremely useful for the history of science, many of which are still being explored. They are further evidence to that in the previous sections of this chapter, and clearly demonstrate how printed science, in all its genres, can help us to access the fundamental aspects of the scientific culture at a certain period. From the first printing presses to twentieth-century publications for mass consumption, the examples examined precisely demonstrate how printed science was not the exclusive reserve of restricted circles of actors but that the readers and publishers themselves played an important role in shaping knowledge in the past and continue to do so today. The book circuit, described years ago by Darnton, is still important despite the competition that printed science has been subjected to since the advent of the new audiovisual media.[105]

And herein lie the lessons of history. Books of secrets were sold beyond the essentialist debates of natural philosophy in the sixteenth century, and many people admired the engravings from *Micrographia* or the illustrations of the books on Newtonianism, even though they were unfamiliar with the details of the force of gravity or experiments in optics. Others embraced the discourses of the phrenologists, attended their demonstrations and bought and read their books by the thousands, while evolutionary ideas were printed in an anonymous book that seemed more famous than Darwin himself. Science for all, libraries of wonders, science fiction novels and real and imaginary worlds occupied pages and pages of books and magazines, which many sectors of the population could afford. While the professors of secrets ousted Copernicus in the world of the book, they would have to do the same to Verne, Flammarion and Asimov, in all cases dignifying the authority of the readers and publishers as active audiences of science.

Notes

1 During the first Inquisition process that Menocchio was subjected to, the following books were mentioned: *La Bibbia, Il Fioretto della Bibbia, Il Lucidario della Madona, Il Lucendario de santi, Historia del Giudicio, Il cavallier Zuanne de Mandavilla, Il sogno dil Caravia*. In the second the following were added: *Il Supplimento delle cronache, Lunario al modo di Italia, Il Decameron*, plus a supposed Italian translation of the *Quran*. Ginzburg (1980: 35–6).
2 Le Goff (1993).
3 Pardo-Tomás (2003–4: 17).
4 Kuhn (1962).
5 Darnton (1982); Topham (2000: 568).
6 Eisenstein (1979).
7 Frasca-Spada, Jardine (2000: 3); Johns (1998).
8 Burke (2000).
9 For a review of the historiography of the Scientific Revolution, see Cohen, F. (1994).

Printed science **49**

10 Butterfield (1949).
11 Two opposite views of the problem can be seen in Hall (1954) and Shapin (1996).
12 Kusukawa, Maclean (2006).
13 Hoskin (1997).
14 Pyenson, Sheets-Pyenson (1999: 216–17).
15 Eamon (1994).
16 *I Secreti del reverendo donno Alessio Piemontese*. Venezia 1555. Eamon (1994: 140, 252).
17 Eamon (1994).
18 Ibid., 194.
19 *Beschreibung aller fürnemisten mineralischen Ertzt und Bergwercksartten* (Prague 1574) (Description of the principal processes of ore extraction and mining methods).
20 Long (1991).
21 Eamon (1994); Zilsel (1941–2); Rossi (1996).
22 'I do not mean to suggest that the Scientific Revolution was a "revolution from below". But I do believe that any discussion of the "foundations" of the Scientific Revolution must consider a much broader base for it than historians of science have so far attempted'. Eamon (1994: 11).
23 Chartier (1995).
24 Waquet (2003).
25 Daston (1991).
26 Porter (1992).
27 Porter (1992:1–2).
28 Pardo-Tomás, Martínez-Vidal (2005).
29 Rey (1991: 142).
30 Gillispie (1959: xxiii).
31 Hankins (1995); Wise (2006).
32 Aaron Dennis (1989); Rossi (1996).
33 For a biography of Newton see, for example, Westfall (1980, 1993). One of the most pioneering books for the dissemination of Newton's ideas in Great Britain is Stewart (1992).
34 Stewart (1992).
35 Terral (2000).
36 Secord (1985).
37 Hankins (1985).
38 Stewart (1992).
39 According to historian Benedetta Craveri: 'in the eighteenth century men and women from the elegant classes collected minerals and fossils and mounted chemical cabinets and astronomical laboratories in their houses; they followed the experiments of Mesmer passionately and applauded the first hot air balloon'. Craveri (2005: 271); Waquet (2003).
40 Fontenelle (1724).
41 Fontenelle (1803: xii).
42 The full title of the French version was: *Le spectacle de la nature, ou Entretiens sur les particularités de l'histoire naturelle, qui ont paru les plus propres à rendre les jeunes-gens curieux, et à former l'esprit.*
43 Serrano (2012).
44 Serrano (2012, 2013).
45 Rey (1991: 413).
46 Perdiguero (1992: 173).
47 Perdiguero (1992).
48 Blake (1977: 12).
49 Yeo (1991: 43–9).
50 Yeo (2001: 76); Kafker (1981, 1994).
51 Just as the *Encyclopédie* is an excellent source for identifying the ideological conflicts of the second half of the eighteenth century, the British encyclopaedias of the first decades of the nineteenth century give detailed information about the competing transport

50 Printed science

techniques of the time (animal-pulled carts, navigable canals, railways), with their positive and negative aspects, and show the complexity of technical changes which were full of coexistences, resistances and apparent contradictions. Evans (1997).

52 Darnton (1979); Chapter 6 will return to the analysis of the visual factor in arts and manufactured products through prints.
53 Darnton (1985: 6).
54 Browne (2010).
55 Secord (2000).
56 Secord (1994: 21).
57 'In pursuing the progress of the development of both plants and animals upon the globe, we have seen an advance in both cases, along the line leading to the higher forms of organization'. Chambers (1844, 1994); Secord (1994: 148).
58 Cited by Secord (2000: 176).
59 Secord (2000: 234).
60 Cited by Secord (2000: 319–20).
61 Secord (2000: 481).
62 Secord (2007).
63 Secord (2002).
64 Cooter (2001: xv).
65 Van Wyhe (2004a, 2007).
66 Cooter (2001).
67 Cooter (1984).
68 Cooter (1984: 101).
69 Cooter (1984: 120).
70 Figuier (1879: 386).
71 Cited by Yeo (2001: 76); van Wye (2007).
72 Cooter (1984).
73 Bensaude-Vincent (2000); Bensaude-Vincent, Blondel (2008).
74 Topham (2000: 560); Apple, Downey, Vaughn (2012).
75 Pyenson, Sheets-Pyenson (1999: 226–7).
76 Sheets-Pyenson (1985: 550).
77 Bensaude-Vincent, Rasmussen (1997).
78 Sheets-Pyenson (1985).
79 González-Silva, Herrán (2009); Papanelopoulou, Kjærgaard (2009); Secord (2014).
80 Bowler (2009: 196–202).
81 Flammarion (1912).
82 Cotardière, Fuentes (1994); Bensaude-Vincent (1989).
83 Gaston Tissandier's *Recreations scientifiques* (1877) was translated into Spanish, English, German, Italian, Swedish, Nowegian, Danish and Russian. Tissandier (1883: vi).
84 Bowler (2009).
85 Shuttleworth (2010); Sleigh (2011); Willis (2014); Keene (2015).
86 Levine (1987: vii); Naumann (2005); Gieryn (1983); Jordanova (1986); Myers (1985).
87 Nicolson (1956: v–viii).
88 Chapple (1986: 4).
89 Beer (1990: 787).
90 For more information about nineteenth-century thermodynamics as a common space between science and literature, see Myers (1985); Pohl (2009). For Darwinism, see Bowler (1993).
91 Myers (1985).
92 Zola (1893: 1).
93 Myers (2003).
94 Alkon (1994: 2).
95 Shelley (1818: preface).

96 'Writing a story that preserves something like the effects of a disturbing dream, while grounding those effects in plots that do not depend on supernatural events', Alkon (1994: 5).
97 Alkon (1994: 18–20).
98 Verne (1867: chapter iv).
99 Suvin (1979: vii).
100 Alkon (1994); Landon, Brooks (2002).
101 Flammarion (1890: 19).
102 Nieto-Galan (2009).
103 Keene (2015).
104 Shuttleworth (2010).
105 Darnton (1982).

3

SPECTACULAR SCIENCE

Spectacle, wonderment and enjoyment were common words at the heart of the Enlightenment. In France, the 'electric kiss' was one of the most famous public experiments by Jean-Antoine Nollet (1700–70),[1] but in 1746, he also proceeded to electrify 180 of Louis XV's guards and 200 Carthusian monks who, to their absolute amazement, shared the electrical charge by holding hands.[2] The success of these demonstrations was not so much to evidence the nature of electricity in experiments, but to show its most spectacular side to the audience. The natural philosophy of the Enlightenment therefore became a kind of ritual to make dramatic, stunning properties emerge from inert matter. The paradox was clear. The public needed to have almost irrational feelings if they were to be convinced of the truth behind fairly rational questions from the scientific perspective of that time.[3] Natural philosophers were variously seen by the public as magicians, beings capable of triggering rain and storms, traders and even as members of religious sects who used electricity as a source of spiritual seduction. Everything seemed to hang between superstition and enthusiasm.

In the nineteenth century, the so-called 'philosophy of demonstration' formed part of a business that extended from the theatres to the popular galleries of practical science, where the limits of what was real were often challenged using magic lanterns, optical illusions, dioramas and panoramas.[4] For the sake of the dialogue with the public, that natural philosophy became part of the culture of entertainment and spectacle.[5] In that world of the spectacular, objects were paramount: vacuum pumps, electric machines, ivory balls, mirrors, automata, planetary systems, machine models, human bodies, molecular structures, graphs, diagrams, tables, illustrations, prints, collections of natural (and sometimes artificial) objects,[6] a set of 'things' charged with multiple cultural meanings.[7] The use of drawings, photographs, advertising material and exhibitions gave rise to a new common place between experts and lay actors. The rigid line between images and scientific texts began to blur, as did the clear distinction between exhibitors and visitors, demonstrators and spectators.[8]

This 'visual turn' offers a closer view of new scientific knowledge and new protagonists who, until recently, have received little attention.[9] Creators of images and objects, exhibitors, their materials and techniques and audiences – visitors and spectators – must occupy as important a position as that of the writers, publishers and readers of books, whose vicissitudes were described in Chapter 2. According to historian Norton Wise, dichotomies that traditionally differentiated art and science, museums and laboratories, geometric and algebraic methods, have hindered a deeper approach to the visual factor. However, it is precisely at the intersection of those dichotomies where the most creative part of scientific work often occurs.[10] In the spectacular science of demonstration, exhibition and theatre, the visual factor plays a fundamental role. Without overlooking the power of the spoken word, the natural philosopher's ability to persuade audiences or even the written explanation that accompanied the exhibition of objects, images became a more accessible language which further reduced the lay–expert distance, and opened up Fleck's esoteric circles of knowledge with their specialised terminology to a much broader public. The following sections will present some examples to illustrate that point.

3.1. From curiosity to exhibition

From the sixteenth until well into the eighteenth century, physicians, apothecaries, university professors, aristocrats, princes and monarchs put a lot of energy into collecting things; accumulating natural and artificial objects, organising them in special places and showing them off to select visitors. The exhibition of rare, valuable and curious objects were testimony to their owners' power and magnificence. From the aforementioned collections emerged the Renaissance museums, *cabinets de curiosités*, or *Wundernkammern*. They aimed to recreate nature, even in its most exotic and monstrous dimensions.[11] This kind of comprehensive accumulation spread through a European network of 'cabinets', which became obligatory stops for distinguished travellers to visit these early palaces of science.[12]

In 1567, the cabinet of Italian naturalist Ulisse Aldrovandi (1522–1605) displayed more than 9,000 *cose diverse*. They included plants, minerals, fossils, stuffed animals, painted figures, woodcuts, marbles, sculptures, clocks, instruments and globes. Other collections worth mentioning were those of Francesco Calzolari in Verona (c. 1622), Ferrante Imperato in Naples (c. 1590), Ole Worm in Copenhagen (1655) and Ferdinando Cospi in Rome (1677).[13] The Dutch collector Levinus Vincent (1658–1727) published magnificent illustrations from cabinets in his 1719 catalogue (Figure 3.1).[14] Splendid pieces of furniture, including sumptuous wardrobes, dressers, walls and ceilings full of objects that provided great fascination for visitors, were all habitual findings. They were

FIGURE 3.1 Levinus Vincent's *cabinet de curiosités* and its visitors in Haarlem, Holland (1705). Engraving c.1719. Dutch School. Bibliothèque des arts décoratifs. Paris. Archives Charmet. Reproduced with permission of the Bridgeman Art Library.

organised in ways which did not correspond to systematic classifications, at least until well into the eighteenth century, and included a wide range of diverse objects known as *artificialia*.

In seventeenth-century England, the *curiosi* were aristocrats, gentlemen or aspiring gentlemen, mainly landowners but also clergy, lawyers, academics, doctors, traders and apothecaries. The curiosity was considered a gentleman's virtue and involved a fascination and admiration for anything strange, new and surprising. The 'grand tour' of the Continent formed part of the education of these young aristocrats, who returned home weighed down with 'curious' objects and left written testimony to their adventures in the form of travel journals.[15] This was the case, for instance, of traveller John Evelyn (1620–1706), who described in his notebooks his visits to numerous cabinets throughout Europe. During his stay in Paris in 1644, Evelyn alluded to Noah's Ark, a market stall close to the Isle du Palais selling all kinds of natural and artificial curiosities: mollusc shells, ivory, porcelain, stuffed creatures, insects, birds, drawings and 'exotic extravaganza'.[16] In 1651, Evelyn visited the gardens of one Mr Morine in London, with all their natural rarities: coral, minerals, Red Sea crabs, more than a thousand types of sea shell, an insect collection; a butterfly that looked like a bird and a supposed rhinoceros bird featured as monstrosities, all of them accompanied by numerous paintings of flowers and plants.[17]

At the beginning of the seventeenth century, the collection of Nicholas Grollier de Servière in Lyon contained the most precious curiosities of the time. After a brilliant military career in the service of King Henry IV of France, Servière put all his efforts into organising a house that contained the most original objects, filling entire galleries with machines, clocks and other rarities. An early eighteenth-century description of Servière's cabinet alluded to: 'several inimitable pieces worked in ivory . . . extraordinary clocks, different kinds of machine for elevating water, bridge constructions and, in short, anything that could be useful and convenient for the public and individuals'.[18] In a similar context, the medical museum of Pierre Borel in Castres contained *artificialia* from the chemical and mechanical arts, as well as a wide collection of *naturalia*, which largely represented the extremes of nature from the abnormal and monstrous to the exaggerated. It was the contrast between unusual objects and those seen in everyday life that attracted the interest of the visitors and afforded the corresponding social prestige to the owner of the collection.[19]

Both collectors and visitors were active in the construction of the collection. In order to acquire new pieces the collector had to be part of an international network for the exchange of objects. That involved drawing up inventories, lists and desiderata as well as correspondence. Since the possession of a curiosity or marvel was a matter of social prestige, the attraction of new visitors, aristocrats and nobility had to commission experts (naturalists, draughtsmen, painters, sculptors, etc.) to maintain and improve their collections. Select new visitors usually brought objects as courtesy presents to expand the collection and, along with travellers and correspondents, they contributed to a wide circulation of the *naturalia* and *artificialia*. In addition, collectors shared a moral economy which led to them putting their results on public display and opening the doors to potential visitors according to a certain set of rules.[20]

At the end of the eighteenth century, the cabinets gradually lost visitors and their objects were reorganised and transferred to the new scientific institutions of the Enlightenment (cabinets of machines, natural history, physics and scientific instruments) or to university collections. This meant that they lost a lot of their original identity, which was only preserved in cases where the transfer was ineffective or incomplete due to specific historical circumstances.[21] A reconstruction of the sixteenth- and seventeenth-century contexts offers an understanding of the subtle mechanisms of communication operating in these strange places of knowledge and a demonstration of how, in that world, there were no clear distinctions between the natural and the artificial, between the collector, visitor and correspondent, between knowledge of nature and social prestige or between monstrosity and the marvel of divine creation.

In publications of the period referring to the different cabinets, the word 'museum' was often used in the sense of a temple of muses or repository of knowledge, similar to the way it was used to define the Classical Greek and

56 Spectacular science

Roman collections. Cases in point are the *Wormianum Museum* (1655) in Copenhagen, the *Cospiano Museum* (1677) in Rome and the *Museographia* (1727) of Caspar Friedrich Nickelius in Leipzig. Added to these are the collections of seventeenth-century mechanical models such as Jacques de Vaucanson's automata (1709–82),[22] and the foundation of new institutions with a clear expository function such as the British Royal Society of Arts in 1754, which aimed to show visitors its collection of objects, inventions and machines,[23] Benjamin Franklin's private collection of mechanical models in Philadelphia and the cabinet of machines in the Conservatoire nationale des arts et métiers in Paris. The latter was a collection designed specifically for technological education and students (an audience that will feature in more detail in Chapter 5). In 1794, Henri Grégoire (1750–1831) presented a new project to the Conservatoire in which he highlighted once more the fascination of visitors for the machines and objects on display.[24]

Although the organisation, content and significance would differ substantially, this early culture of curiosity contained some of the signs of identity that would mark the science museums of the future. Curiosities, their exhibition and exchange with the visitors would become a way of seeing and learning science, in a distinct setting from the printed texts and the academic circles in universities, and it did not always coincide with the activities of scientific societies.[25] Cabinets of machines and scientific instruments exhibited locally and nationally gained ground in the public sphere during the first decades of the nineteenth century. The culture of exotic curiosities had not completely disappeared, but it had certainly lost its force when set against the new industrial objects that were being increasingly exhibited in public and achieving major international status from the mid-nineteenth century onwards.

The Great Exhibition of London in 1851 attracted 6 million visitors and was an unprecedented success. The majestic Crystal Palace, built from more than 300,000 pieces of glass and iron, the 14,000 exhibitors (half of them non-British) and the more than 100,000 articles presented gave the event an exceptionalness that established its status as a pioneering example throughout the second half of the century. At the 1889 Paris Exhibition, 32 million visitors marvelled at the Eiffel Tower and 11 years later, in 1900, the same city managed to attract 42 million people.[26]

The venues and rituals that accompanied these universal exhibitions were rich and complex. The distribution of space and the definition of the pavilions set out a kind of topography of the knowledge of the time: from the machinery pavilions and the science and industrial palaces to the pavilions of nations and the most powerful brand names. Once classified, the objects were exhibited in sections according to the juries that had been assigned to them, normally made up of academic and industrial experts. Their job was to select the best pieces, the inventors of which were awarded prizes in pompous public ceremonies in the presence of the political and economic elite. A medal from the exhibition signified the ultimate prestige for the brand or inventor and a great opportunity to launch a promotional campaign for the product.[27]

The decisions of the juries were sometimes controversial but they always insisted on the need for standardising measuring systems as a strategy for mass consumption and homogenisation by the new manufacturers. The aim was clear: to elevate the good taste of the middle classes, improve scientific culture, educate the business classes and offer a moral education to the working classes, all within a combination of entertainment, fun and education. The public exhibition of machines and industrial processes influenced the way in which visitors perceived the scientific culture of the time.[28]

The 1851 exhibition in London was a clear reflection of the height of the British Empire (Figure 3.2), but it also responded to the obsession of the elite for social stability as a reaction to the revolutions that had swept Europe in 1848. Equally, the 1889 Paris Exhibition was a celebration of the centenary of the French Revolution, but in a period when France was losing political and industrial supremacy.[29] In 1893, Chicago celebrated the 400th anniversary of the discovery of America, but its exhibition also symbolised the emergence of the new transatlantic potential. Without abandoning either imperialism or nationalism,

FIGURE 3.2 Visitors at the Great Exhibition of London in 1851. Piccadilly Circus. George Cruikshank (1792–1878). The Stapleton Collection. Reproduced with permission of the Bridgeman Art Library.

58 Spectacular science

each country constructed a rhetoric of universality and cosmopolitanism.[30] Strengthened by the capitalist economy and opposition to the socialists and communists, who were calling for radical changes in the model of production and substantial improvements in living conditions for the working class, the exhibitions propounded an interclass rhetoric, a harmonious society, full of 'peace and goodwill', which was the slogan of the crowds travelling from Piccadilly Circus to the Exhibition in 1851. The representation of this utopia required new spaces in the form of machine halls and palaces for science and industry, where, far from the miseries of daily life experienced by most of the visitors, the supposed virtues of the factory could be idealised.

But beyond the rhetorical proclamations and the plans of the elite in the design and dissemination of the exhibitions, public testimonies in a broad sense are worthy of special note. Like the *flâneurs*, who took in all the galleries of the Crystal Palace and invaded Hyde Park on the opening day full of admiration and fascination, entire families went to the Great Exhibition looking for amusement and entertainment. The press, foreign visitors and the general public all reacted fairly unanimously to these new buildings and the quantity and quality of the objects displayed within them. They were keen to see the machines hall that everyone was talking about with such great enthusiasm. Texts from the period offer descriptions such as the following: '[the visitor] . . . was anxious to see the machinery room, which everybody spoke of with such enthusiasm. There was the monster pump, with its two mouths, pouring out its river of water, – he wanted to see the steam printing-press, and the carding and spinning-machines, and the power-looms, of which he had heard such marvels'.[31] The strength of the steam engines at full power, with their spectacular movements and noise, seemed to transport the visitors to a state of unconditional admiration.

Some years later, the mechanical elements that had caused the greatest fascination with machines shifted to electricity. In the 1867 Paris Exhibition, the telegraph had a particularly great impact, along with the transatlantic cable which had come into operation the previous year, after a long and costly installation period. The 1878 exhibition showcased the telephone, the phonograph, the Wheatstone bridge for the Morse telegraph system and the first plans for electrical lighting. In 1881, also in Paris, a new exhibition dedicated exclusively to electricity welcomed no fewer than 900,000 visitors. The 'telephonic earphones', which transmitted the sound of opera performances from the stage, were received with particularly great enthusiasm and awe. There were different designs for incandescent lamps, and Gramme, Siemens, Edison and Graham Bell soon became popular heroes and household names with the visitors, regardless of their social origins.[32]

The exhibitions were also expressions of the internationalism of the second half of the nineteenth century. This ran in parallel to international scientific conferences and international language movements such as Esperanto were invented. But the trend towards internationalism sat side by side in permanent tension with the growing rivalry of the nation-states. Telegraphs, telephones, the railway and steam shipping could put people in contact over very long distances, but the trend for cooperation did not bode well with that of fierce competition. Most of the visitors went down the famous 'street of nations', in which each individual country proudly showed off its own pavilion.

Documents left to us by the political, economic and scientific elites echoed national and international voices about the supposed virtues of the universal exhibitions. They highlighted the exhibitions' capacity to elevate the status of labour, their stimulus of social harmony and their strengthening of an image of progress. However, the so-called 'civilising' programmes were, for some visitors, simple propaganda and manipulation.[33] Critical voices with different arguments could be heard. The exhibitions were potentially a dangerous attack on healthy national protectionism. In Britain, frequent comments declared that the country had nothing to learn from its foreign neighbours. Celebrated visitors William Morris (1834–96) and John Ruskin (1819–1900) criticised the ugliness of the industrial products and the dehumanisation of work through the mechanisation process that was so revered in the machinery halls.[34] Russian writer Fiodor Dostoyevsky (1821–81) perceived them as pagan deities, far removed from religious values – a question that also perturbed the Anglican Church. Workers' movements criticised the enormous investment in economic resources and urban reforms that only seemed to benefit the entrepreneurial classes, although they also saw the exhibitions as opportunities to reinforce workers' internationalism among the visitors.[35]

Despite the public rhetoric of inviting the ordinary people, they were marginalised from some of the events, which were reserved for the elite. In the main, the lower classes perceived the 'shilling days' at the Great Exhibition, which provided greatly reduced entrance tickets, as a denigration of their social condition. Even though workers were the undisputed protagonists of the construction of most of the machines on display, many of them considered that their efforts had not received the public recognition that they deserved. Growing consumerism, hailed as a means of reducing conflict, clashed with the strong trade union culture of the working classes, which refused to consent with the public rhetoric of the official addresses.[36] From the perspective of the working class, it was common to find critical comments against the exhibitions' latest objectives and interests. They saw fancy objects, bourgeois parties, luxury goods and prizes for entrepreneurs as a kind of alienation that perpetuated the hegemony of the ruling elites, and they denounced the marginal role of the main protagonists who made the machines, fireworks and electric wonders.

The radical critics of international exhibitions are useful to remind us that even in the twentieth century, the megalomaniac, propagandistic aspects of scientific culture did not disappear. In spite of the elites' supposed agenda for improving the scientific and technological knowledge of their visitors, the results of the international exhibitions did not seem to reflect that. The entertainment and fun factor took priority over the educational capacity and promotion of the scientific spirit.

60 Spectacular science

3.2. Science museums

The short-term spectacle of the exhibitions was in stark contrast to the growth of new permanent sites for scientific display. In early nineteenth-century Britain some hospitals included small, limited-access museums. During the 1820s a number of natural history museums appeared in provincial cities, aiming to attract members of the local scientific community. Then came the anatomical spectacles for which admission required an entrance ticket instead of the membership of a scientific institution. A large number of temporary industrial arts exhibitions were organised and permanent private collections were set up in universities. Many of the efforts put into the universal exhibitions also resulted in a series of permanent collections open to the public.[37]

The Conservatoire nationale des arts et métiers in Paris is considered to be the 'first' science museum. Although the claim itself is somewhat dubious (chambers of marvels, cabinets, exhibitions and museums all form a densely branched tree from the past and not a simple linear evolution), the case of the Conservatoire nationale is particularly relevant. It foregrounded a vocation for teaching and learning as well as the opportunity to inform provincial craftsmen, who were regular visitors, using the machines themselves. In fact, the educational objective of the collections of machines and instruments lay in the origin of the new science museums that emerged in the latter decades of the nineteenth century. In 1856, for instance, at the height of the industrial revolution, Georges Wilson, a professor of 'technology' at the University of Edinburgh, addressed a select audience at the Philosophical Institution with the following words:

> An industrial museum is intended to be a repository for all the objects of useful art, including the raw materials with which each art deals, the finished products into which it converts them, drawings and diagrams explanatory of the processes through which it puts those materials, models or examples of the machinery with which it prepares and fashions them, and the tools which specially belong to it, as particular craft. Such a museum should also include illustrations of the progress of each industrial art form age to age; . . . of its relation to good morals, and the service which it can render the State by employing the needy, increasing the comforts of the poor, advancing the civilization of all classes, adding to the material, intellectual, and moral prosperity of the whole nation, and, through it, more or less to the entire world.[38]

It was precisely under this utilitarian rhetoric of progress that science museums grew in the second half of the nineteenth century. They attempted to identify the public with the new values of industrial culture, and to legitimate industrial processes. The South Kensington Museum in London, for example, originated from the Great Exhibition itself, as a political decision to dedicate some of the spaces of the 1851 infrastructure as permanent exhibition sites.[39] It opened its doors in 1857 as a museum of industrial arts and crafts and would soon subsume scientific objects. Aiming to popularise industrial arts and crafts, and science, Bennet Woodcroft (1803–79), head of the patents office and an active figure in the Great Exhibition, displayed machines and included the original designs for steam engines and locomotives. In 1874, as a result of a report by the Royal Commission on Scientific Instruction and the Advancement of Science, the instruments and machines collections expanded and finally led to an exhibition in 1876. From then on, despite changes in the premises and transfers to different buildings (in 1909 the museum was divided in two to become the Science Museum and the Victoria and Albert Museum), industrial-related technology was to dominate the content. Gradually, the old university collections gave way to these new spaces, to the new legitimating temples of industrial culture.[40]

But the permanent exhibitions of scientific objects went beyond the displays of instruments and machines. Throughout the nineteenth century, most European cities had a natural history museum presenting the three kingdoms of nature: animal, vegetable and mineral, in their different forms. They were housed in fine buildings, often designed in the neoclassical style, and they became true 'temples' of science. The crisis of the old cabinets meant that *naturalia* was destined to be exhibited according to pre-planned itineraries.[41] Cases with stuffed animals, reconstructed skeletons, herbaria, the ever-problematic fossils of extinct species, and the inclusion of new colonial species from then became accessible to the urban middle classes. Some of these new museums were based on the old university collections, such as the Ashmolean in Oxford, or originated from mining practices, such as the Museum of Practical Geology in London; others were built as new icons of urban culture: the Natural History Museums in London and Oxford, with their magnificent Victorian neo-gothic architecture, the Musée d'histoire naturelle in Paris at the Jardin des plantes (Figure 3.3), and the Natural History Museum of New York, built just next to Central Park – the ultimate space for urban recreation.[42]

The spatial organisation of the museum interiors and their location in the city at a certain time in history raise new aspects that are, perhaps, not obvious in the history of science.[43] Focused on technology and industry, the central location of science museums in the city reflects the importance of science, its public image and its relationship with culture, institutions and power in certain societies. Some science museums acted as a complement to academic life, while others were situated next to public recreational spaces, and sometimes even shared a pre-eminence with buildings of economic or political power.

Inside the museums, the rooms and exhibition itineraries spoke for themselves, conditioning the visitor's physical and mental journey. The distribution of the Natural History Museum in London was the result of different perceptions of nature, in a society that was tinctured with natural theology (the marvels of the natural kingdom intended to reinforce the marvellous divine creation), but at the same time shaped by the birth of Darwinism and scientific naturalism. So, a simple analysis of the architectural design of the spaces, the organisation and

FIGURE 3.3 Visitors in the Great Gallery of the Natural History Museum of Paris at the end of the nineteenth century. French School. Bibliothèque des arts décoratifs, Paris. Archives Charmet. Reproduced with permission of the Bridgeman Art Library.

exhibition of the collections designed by the different museum directors, offers a good indication of the different conceptions of nature embodied by the museum itself.[44]

At the end of the nineteenth century, William Henry Flower (1831–99), Director of the London Natural History Museum, split the collections to separate research material from the educational and exhibition items. The former were to be preserved and studied in private, while the latter would be used to offer the public general knowledge about the three kingdoms of nature. But the tension that arose between preservation, study and exhibition was inevitable. Flower's proposal was imposed over that of his predecessor, Richard Owen, who conceived the collections in a more integrated manner.[45] Some of these tensions were reflected in the voices of the visitors. The differing views on the exhibition of an old-style natural history, closer to an antiques collection, can be counterbalanced by the presentation of new life sciences that included recent discoveries with a more dynamic and evolutionary discourse about nature. In fact, the science museums (and in particular the natural history museums) served two types of visitor: the small, select groups of scholars and academics (the Whipple Museum of the History of Science at the University of Cambridge still maintains this criterion today), and a broader, non-specialist audience. This probably remains one of the unresolved tensions in the history of science museums, from the nineteenth century to the present day.

For the sake of their own legitimisation, natural history museums tended to be located in parks or open spaces, which often contained botanical gardens and zoos; they became a kind of highly popular open-air museum and privileged place for science where certain reconstructions of nature could be exhibited using living species. Of course, the tradition of the botanical gardens went back to the sixteenth century. After the pioneering *hortus botanicus* in Padua, Leiden, Montpellier, Paris, Uppsala and Oxford, other gardens such as Kew, Buitenzorg and the Jardin du Roi in Paris became models to imitate in Europe and the colonies. The first gardens were created next to the faculties of medicine to complete the education of future doctors in the Hippocratic-Galenic tradition. However, they were soon to become depositories for storing and distributing new plants in exchange centres of a broad international network.[46] In industrial cities, botanical gardens lost their original Baconian function as collections, and soon became recreational public spaces. Visitors could come into contact with lost nature, while experts, like in the science museums, could study and investigate the different species.[47]

At the end of the nineteenth century, a network of more than 200 botanical gardens extended throughout the metropolises and the colonies. They would soon become laboratories for experimenting with new species, places for discussing new names and taxonomies, but also living museums open to the public for the contemplation of exotic nature often beyond the realm of the plant kingdom.[48] For different reasons, the botanical gardens acted (not always successfully) as agents of acclimatisation for tropical plants in European continental climates. Exoticism and the artistic beauty of these distant species were of primary interest. The introduction of natural spaces in the urban conglomeration was in the interests of hygiene and public health, as a revival of the ancient environmentalist tradition for the improvement of air in the industrial city.[49]

Despite the problems, acclimatisation of plants extended gradually to animals. Unlike the *ménageries* of the Ancien Régime, or private collections of live animals for their owners' prestige, in the nineteenth century public zoological parks paralleled the growth of zoological societies.[50] In the context of the natural history reform movement, which lauded the study of living animals over dead ones (skeletons and stuffed creatures) and their use in teaching the public, there were several attempts to build new zoological parks. As with the universal exhibitions, entertainment of the masses took priority over scientific instruction. The zoo became a public space where exotic animals often lived together in complexes that included restaurants and family entertainment areas, very similar to the fun fairs and amusement parks.

Distanced from university debates among experts, most of the directors of the zoological parks practised a pragmatic, applied natural history.[51] They focused on empirical descriptions of the behaviour of living creatures to improve farming, husbandry and even fish farming. In the zoos, animals became hybrid objects, natural in their origin but disciplined in their routines and confined in artificial spaces. The cages were not much different to shop windows, and they tended to

64 Spectacular science

imitate some of the aesthetic elements of the universal exhibitions. The domestication of animal habits often disappointed visitors, who frequently expected to find in these artificial spaces a reproduction of nature in the wild, and the Darwinian fight for survival of the fittest.[52]

Apes, for instance, were the central objects of discussion, and seeing them in the zoos confronted the visitors with their own human behaviour. Anatomical dissections of dead animals following short periods in captivity steered debate about the differences between apes and humans. In around 1900, apes appeared in all types of public spectacles and provoked a variety of reactions by visitors, with the question of human origin closely linked to the question of race.[53] Just like the science museums and the universal exhibitions, zoological parks became spaces where animal habits were controlled, but also those of the visitors. As part of the agenda of applied natural history, there was a particular interest in establishing new ways of presenting nature for the moral education of the general public.

At the end of the nineteenth century, Germany had approximately 150 natural history museums, Great Britain had 250, France had 300 and the United States had 250. In the US, the biggest were the American Museum of Natural History in New York and the National Museum, as part of the Smithsonian Institution in Washington, the latter resulting from donations received after the International Exhibition of Philadelphia in 1876.[54] In the early twentieth century, the exhibition style in these museums began to change. Animals and plants were placed in spaces that mimicked their natural environments. The old glass showcases seemed outdated in the light of new public demands.

The first few decades of the twentieth century marked a progressive transition among the museums with major collections and heritage that once again had connections with the universal exhibitions' programme of instruction, entertainment and discipline for the agents of industrialisation. They moved towards a new model of science museum that placed the visitor at the centre of a set of objects that largely lacked historical connotations. In 1936 the Museum of Science and Industry opened in the Rockefeller Centre, New York, with changes that would be adopted internationally over the next few decades. It aimed to reach not only the industrial workers of the previous century but also a new kind of average citizen, described in the following terms:

> They have come from all parts of the United States and from every corner of the World, impelled by the universal human desire to see what makes the wheels of everyday life go around. These are the people – the man in the street, the women in the home, the child in the school, vitally interested in the marvellous achievements of modern science and eager to understand where these fit into the pattern of their own daily routine – for whom the Museum was primarily designed.[55]

In 1937, the Palais de la découverte opened in Paris as part of the Exposition internationale des arts et des techniques dans la vie moderne. Under the direction of leading scientists such as Jean Perrin (1870–1942) and Paul Langevin (1872–1946), the Palais was designed as a legitimating strategy for French science just one year before the foundation of the Centre national de la reserche scientifique – the main French research institution, and Leon Blum's (1872–1950) Popular Front public investment in science education. It also took advantage of the third centenary of the publication of *Discourse de la méthode* (1637) by René Descartes, a milestone in the development of science and modern rationalism in France. However, Descartes was one of the few historical references in the new museum, which presented science as a corpus of indisputable knowledge. Experimentation and demonstration, interactive to a certain extent, gained prominence over theory and historical objects. The Palais attracted over 2 million visitors and its temporary exhibition would later become permanent.[56]

Although the public image of science presented in the Palais should be understood in the context of the 1930s, its philosophy appeared to suggest a new way of offering science to visitors. It would later become fully developed in the English-speaking world after the Second World War, and spread internationally throughout the second half of the twentieth century. With the appearance of the so-called science centres, or interactive museums, educational models were gradually imposed on scientific heritage. Directors of historical collections lost ground to a new professional figure: the 'science communicator'.[57] This was not someone who would demonstrate or comment on an antique microscope from some dusty university laboratory, or a steam engine donated by an industrialist (such as those that continue to give such a thrill to the visitors of the London Science Museum). The communicator's job was to use abstract and interactive models and mock-ups to represent certain scientific concepts.[58]

The San Francisco Exploratorium, founded in 1969, is a good example of these new interactive science 'palaces'. It was Franck Oppenheimer (1912–85), brother of the famous physicist Robert Oppenheimer, who initiated the project in the midst of the Cold War. The new space was designed for experimentation, play, entertainment and the intersection between art, science and spectacle; an amusing, playful science that would be imitated worldwide. Far removed from the old galleries and static, ordered glass cases of the traditional science museums, it opened up the possibility of creating new informal and flexible spaces. The three volumes, titled *Exploratorium Cookbooks*, provided a standardised model for these new interactive spaces. They contained 'recipes' for 201 thematic exhibitions on topics such as light, sound, electricity, magnetism, colour, mechanics, temperature, neurophysics, animal behaviour and mathematics.[59]

Since the 1980s, strong links to the Public Understanding of Science (PUS) movement have meant that science centres have welcomed millions of visitors, seduced by unproblematic shows, with the blessing of governments and private companies. In the 1990s there were around 40 science centres in the United Kingdom and over 300 in the US.[60] In 1986, the foundation of the Cité des sciences et de l'industrie in Paris was a kind of symbolic 'burial' of the old Palais de la découverte; what appeared in 1930 as a project that broke with the museum

66 Spectacular science

traditions of the nineteenth century had been left behind as a relic of the past just half a century later.[61]

Despite their spectacular expansion, the science centres today face a more critical period with respect to scientific progress, watered down by a subtle discontent. They exist at a time when, as will be seen in detail later on, the mechanisms that are able to confer scientific authority are increasingly complex.[62] Behind a more or less philanthropic objective for the visitors' 'instruction', science centres have gradually become useful tools for the social legitimation of scientific experts, and they have therefore reinforced the dominant view of science popularisation already discussed in the introduction.[63] Exhibitions tend to lack a clear authorship and are often presented as an indisputable product of experts aimed at lay audiences, with no symmetrical accounts that can describe the position of different social groups on a specific scientific problem.[64] They have therefore become artificial spaces where scientific principles are plucked out of the natural and the social world.[65] Although visitor figures are measured in their millions and they compete almost directly with prestigious art museums, science centres transmit an undisputed image of an autonomous, neutral, politically correct scientific knowledge. Exhibitions on subjects which break down the borders between expert and lay knowledge, between scientific and social and cultural factors, are usually scarce.[66]

Both in the case of science centres and, retrospectively, the universal exhibitions, botanical gardens, zoos and science museums in the nineteenth century, the objects displayed are subject to the same kind of questions that we might ask about the biography of a certain scientist: origin, life story in the context of a collection and a specific site, as well as audiences' perceptions.[67] The meaning of objects changes over time and space, but also according to those who are looking at them. A museum object is related to the other objects that form the collection, to collectors and curators, but also to visitors, who are the main historical references here.[68]

The Philadelphia International Exhibition of 1876 is mainly remembered in the official catalogues for its impressive steam engines, but at that time most of the visitors remained blissfully unaware of the telephone or some of the incandescent lamps on display. Bombarded with information, resulting in inevitable fatigue, visitors often learned very little and would have absorbed only a few items by the time they reached the exit door. Visits generally became an emotional and motivating experience that had little to do with scientific knowledge in itself.[69]

Visitors do not leave their culture and identity in the coatroom nor do they respond passively to the exhibits, but rather they interpret them through their own previous experiences and culturally acquired beliefs, values and perceptual skills.[70] This question has been studied in detail in relation to the visitors' attitudes to natural science museums, and in particular their reactions to exhibitions about human evolution. Despite deep-rooted expert debates and controversies over the different branches that have led to *Homo sapiens* (Chapter 8 will show that there is a fragile expert consensus about the number of species and their positioning on the human genealogical tree), visitors tend to approach an exhibition of this kind with a linear and hierarchical conception of the problem, in which everything seems to have evolved from the simplest to the most complex.[71] Similarly, visitors tend to accept a linear unproblematic narrative of scientific progress. In their family outings to science centres they seek entertainment and fun, especially for the youngest, a specific audience for which much of the displays have been adapted.

For some social theorists, from the nineteenth century onwards, science museums have become spaces not only for entertainment and instruction, but also for discipline and control of certain behaviours, with major parallels to exhibitions, commercial shopping centres, amusement parks, botanical gardens and zoos. They have become places for standardised representation (this is especially true of the science centres),[72] where official and popular culture, expert and lay culture, meet, and not always on an even footing, since a certain cultural hegemony is imposed by the elites.[73] In that sense, controversial questions such as war, immigration, pollution, pseudo-sciences and questions of class or gender rarely appear.

Paradoxically, where large numbers of visitors have been consulted before the content of an exhibition is decided, a consensus is extremely difficult to reach. A particularly well-known example is that of the Smithsonian National Air and Space Museum exhibition for the 50th anniversary of the atomic bombs dropped on Hiroshima and Nagasaki in August 1945. In the face of disagreement among the various parties (professional historians, war veterans, the Japanese government, public opinion expressed in the media, etc.) agreement over what content should be used to narrate the Enola Gay story 50 years later was initially pushed through, but ultimately broke down after two years of bitter controversy from 1993 to 1995.[74] The war veterans in particular, a very special kind of audience, highlighted the tension between academic experts in World War II and the memory of those who were involved. The former legitimated the attack in an effort to force Japan to surrender and save more human lives in the long term. For them, however, any public revision of the events, exposed as they were in the prestigious Smithsonian Institution, was perceived as a mockery of their personal sacrifice on the Pacific front.[75]

Returning to the present, the Science Museum of London has a somewhat ambivalent existence between the old industrial museum model, where instruments and machines play a very important role in a historical context, and the new interactive culture of science centres, to the point that the work of the Department of Conservation and the Learning Department (commissioned to design the interactive exhibitions) is increasingly divided. In fact, the role of the old curators in designing the content of new exhibitions vetted by government or private companies is of diminishing importance.[76] Science museums have gradually substituted a promiscuous perception of the ancient culture of curiosity for a new, regulated view that has turned them into more reasoned and

68 Spectacular science

distant places of observation.[77] Standardisation of the exhibition sites, visitors' guides and catalogues, the growing marginalisation of historical discourse and scientific heritage, an emphasis on an educational and interactive agenda and the obsession for entertainment and fun have all contributed to a certain alienation of museum audiences.[78] This may be another underlying cause of the subtle discontent of scientific culture described at the beginning of this book. But there are other dimensions of spectacular science to consider in the following section.

3.3. Theatrical science

In spite of their educational nature (they initially belonged to the faculties of medicine), from the sixteenth until well into the nineteenth century anatomy theatres transcended the university classrooms to enter the public sphere of Western societies. The famous engraving by Andreas Vesalius, *De humani corporis fabrica* (1543), which showed the professor of anatomy dissecting a body in front of a large audience, is a good example of how these theatres and their book plates offered a new public image of medicine (see Figure 2.1). Vesalius portrayed himself in the centre of the theatre, surrounded by 165 onlookers ordered hierarchically from the front rows reserved for faculty members, students, the clergy, artists and aristocratic women.[79] Some of them flaunted their presence in the theatre while others looked on unseen from discreet openings in the balcony of the amphitheatre. Until then the *lectio* had been the only activity of professors in the Hippocratic-Galenic tradition of the medieval universities, with direct intervention on the body left to barbers and surgeons of low professional status. However, the event gradually became unified before the public with the *ostentio* and the *dissectio*, as entangled practices of the anatomy lesson.[80]

Although preceded by temporary installations, designed for the same purpose, the anatomy theatre of the University of Padua is considered to be the oldest of its kind to have survived intact today. It was built in 1595 by Hieronymus Fabricius (1533–1619), a professor at the same university and a disciple of Vesalius. Also from the University of Padua, Alessandro Benedetti (c. 1450–1512) in his *Historia corporis humani, sive Anatomice* (1502) described details of the body to be dissected and the most appropriate architectural design in which to hold that public event.[81] The body had to be a recently executed prisoner, a plebeian without any local family or friends; the theatre had to be temporary and made of wood, the site well ventilated to avoid the stink of putrefaction (dissections only took place during the winter months). The ideal body had to be large enough for the public to see every detail. It was placed on a well-lit table in the centre of the rows of seating (Figure 3.4).

English traveller John Evelyn recorded his personal experience of a visit to Padua in 1646 in his diary: 'I went to Padua, to be present at the famous anatomy lecture, celebrated here with extraordinary apparatus, lasting almost a whole

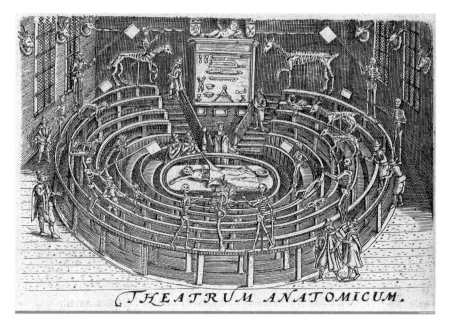

FIGURE 3.4 The anatomy theatre of Leiden in an anonymous print from 1609. Reproduced with permission of the Wellcome Library, London.

month. During this time, I saw a woman, a child, and a man dissected with all the manual operations of the surgeon on the human body.'[82]

There were slight differences in the way each theatre operated but the main objectives of the representation were common to all of them. The crude exhibition of the body before a large audience reinforced the acceptance of death while showing the perfection of divine creation. Also, dissection was seen as the result of the prehensile skills of the dissector; an indisputable symbol of human intelligence granted by God. The anatomy theatres and their seating stalls accommodated the presence of all kinds of spectators, united by curiosity, fascination and also by the need to overcome their anthropological fear of death. Like any other building, the theatre itself represented a certain power relationship between expert and lay audiences, and shaped the order, classification and functions of the public. Similarly, the rows of seating, walls, boxes, openings to look through but not be seen offer the possibility of reconstructing rituals between science and the public, to understand the subtleties of the struggle for scientific authority in a certain place and time. Theatres, chambers of marvels, backrooms, salons, cafés, machinery cabinets, botanical gardens, astronomical observatories, amphitheatres and manufacturers: all of these spaces had a significant effect on the relationship between experts and lay audiences. The topography of each of them in an urban setting frequently indicates the hierarchy of scientific practices in a given society.[83]

Throughout the eighteenth century, anatomy theatres became public spaces for other kinds of activity apart from dissections. Experiments in pneumatic chemistry and electricity and literary sessions were also open to the public. Students and professors discussed specific medical topics, but also the new and emerging sciences of the end of the Enlightenment. In that sense, the dissections gradually closed their doors to become the exclusive domain of the professors and students of the faculties of medicine. The huge success of the 'Bodies' exhibition and the controversial comments that it has recently provoked in the media and in current public opinion would possibly explain a certain nostalgia for that familiarity with the corpse that the theatres of anatomy provided for centuries and which has been irreversibly lost today.[84]

As seen at the beginning of this chapter, at the height of the Enlightenment, Nollet was convinced that natural philosophy should become a theatrical reproduction of the 'drama' of nature. Jean-Jacques Rousseau (1712–78) described Nollet's *cabinet de physique* as a magic laboratory where one could see a collection of 'miracles'.[85] In spite of that, Nollet was fully dedicated to offering spectacular courses in experimental physics as well as making and selling scientific instruments (Figure 3.5). Among his distinguished spectators were Antoine-Laurent

FIGURE 3.5 A lecture in experimental physics by Jean-Antoine Nollet in the mid-eighteenth century. Louis Figuier, *Les merveilles de la science,* I, p. 561. Reproduced with permission of the Biblioteca de Catalunya (Barcelona).

Lavoisier (1743–94), the central figure of the chemical revolution at the end of the eighteenth century, and Charles-Augustin Coulomb (1736–1806), who made a decisive contribution to living the Newtonian dream by calculating the electrostatic forces of attraction and repulsion along with their torsion balance, which expressed a mathematical function similar to that of universal gravitation.[86]

The newspaper *Les affiches de Paris* made regular announcements of conferences in the city covering mathematics, physics, natural history, geometry, chemistry and pharmacy.[87] The travelling shows of François Bienvenue, professor of physics and inventor and manufacturer of scientific instruments, filled theatres all over Europe to present his numerous experiments on pneumatics, hydraulics, electricity and galvanism to the public. Until the outbreak of the French Revolution, Bienvenue had aimed his experiments at a wealthy aristocratic clientele, but new market demands meant that he became a travelling professor in search of audiences throughout Europe.[88] In the summer of 1797, Bienvenue settled in Spain, presenting himself as an international expert in instruments of experimental physics. A year later he could be found in Valencia with an entertaining programme of physics and chemistry demonstrations, accompanied by mathematical games and fireworks of his own invention. In 1808, he carried out physics experiments and demonstrations in a theatre in Vienna. In 1811, his show in the Grand Theatre in Rotterdam became famous for its hydrogen explosions.

Far from limiting himself to entertaining spectacles, Bienvenue's public experiments also contributed to the international dissemination of the new chemistry. But the chemical revolution at the end of the eighteenth century went far beyond Lavoisier's genius and his circle – with the theory of combustion, acidity, the leading role of the new oxygen theory and the new nomenclature associated with it. The new chemistry captivated large audiences across the continent through talks, publications and debates. So, while Lavoisier was making very expensive instruments (balances, calorimeters and gasometers), which initially only reinforced his authority in small circles of experts, on the other side of the Channel, Joseph Priestly (1733–1804) was using simple instruments in his public presentations for experiments which his audiences could also carry out effectively. Priestly's chemistry resisted Lavoisier's new nomenclature for oxygen until his death, but his experiments were largely validated by the support of his audiences.[89]

It was at that time that chemistry became public culture. Its definitive approval would have required sophisticated, mainly private, experiments carried out by Lavoisier, Priestley's more accessible instruments, the reports held in prestigious scientific societies such as the Académie des sciences in Paris and the Royal Society in London, and also the kind of public experiments conducted by Bienvenue in theatres all over Europe. Just like in the culture of Newtonianism, the theatricality of experimental physics and the new chemistry attracted utilitarian interest, sparked a fascination for the wonders of nature, or simply a desire to be entertained, but integrating debates about the composition and properties of matter.[90]

72 Spectacular science

In England, the Royal Institution (RI) presented some of the most prestigious public lectures of the nineteenth century. Since its opening in 1799, the theatre of science saw such great figures as Humphrey Davy (1778–1829), Thomas Brande (1788–1866), Michael Faraday (1791–1867), William Henry Bragg (1862–1942) and John Tyndall (1820–93) in action. The Friday Evening Discourses, Christmas Lectures for Young People and the articles that appeared in journals such as the *Literary Gazette*, the *Atheneum*, and later the *Proceedings of the Royal Institution* itself, offer a good insight into its public impact.[91] Competing with London's West End theatres, the RI offered fascinating experiments again combined with varied doses of natural theology and utilitarianism. This can be seen in the transcripts of several famous lectures, such as Faraday's talks on the 'The Chemical History of a Candle' or Thomas Huxley's 'On a Piece of Chalk'.[92] The speakers created new styles of communication to attract prestigious audiences, but that did not mean they were prepared to reject the entertaining aspect of their presentations.[93]

In 1860, Faraday's address to a young audience about the combustion of a candle included the following statement:

> And, before proceeding, let me say this also: that, though our subject be so great, and our intention that of treating it honestly, seriously, and philosophically, yet I mean to pass away from all those who are seniors among us. I claim the privilege of speaking to juveniles as a juvenile myself. I have done so on former occasions, and, if you please, I shall do so again. And, though I stand here with the knowledge of having the words I utter given to the world, yet that shall not deter me from speaking in the same familiar way to those whom I esteem nearest to me on this occasion . . . And now, my boys and girls, I must first tell you of what candles are made.[94]

Although Faraday started out as a laboratory technician, he soon discovered that the key to success was in these public lectures (Figure 3.6). He believed that the theatre should be small with seating placed close to the speaker and the platform where the experiments took place; lighting should preferably be natural and there should be sufficient ventilation to get rid of the fumes given off in the chemistry experiments as quickly as possible. Faraday invited journalists to his public lectures, sending them free tickets with ample notice. In doing so, he guaranteed press reviews of his experiments, which were published side by side with literary critiques of the latest novels by Charles Dickens or George Eliot, plays and concerts. This was just a small sign of the heterogeneity and growing importance of science at the heart of Victorian culture.[95]

Parallel to the activity of the RI, the Royal Polytechnic Institution became another popular place for science in London. It too had a lecture theatre, together with a laboratory and a major collection of instruments and machines. Its famous Great Hall held public exhibitions of curious objects such as the diving suit, the oxyhydrogen microscope, electrical machines and model ships floating in a long

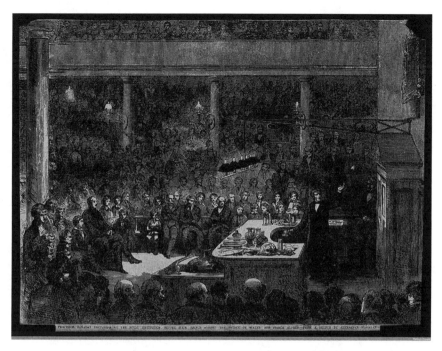

FIGURE 3.6 Michael Faraday in a public lecture at the Royal Institution in London (1856). Wood engraving by Alexander Blaikley (1816–1903). Reproduced with permission of the Wellcome Library, London.

channel of water. Another popular show was that of John H. Pepper, with his optical illusions and phantasmagorical experiments, often criticised in the press for their excessive theatricality.[96]

Given these large doses of spectacle and performance, some historians have suspected hidden intentions that are not made explicit in the presenters' rhetoric or apparent from the reaction of the public. Perhaps the success of the RI can only be understood by analysing science as just one more system of values in the industrial world of the nineteenth and also a good part of the twentieth century; as one more strategy to cope with the contradictions and tensions in those societies.[97] From that perspective, science would become an instrument of order and social stability (a point that will be covered later). This is a more critical analysis of the audience's supposed naïve fascination. In that industrial culture, the theatre show with its electrical sparks, magnets and stinking gases was perhaps not an innocent entertainment of the elites. Again, as in the international exhibitions and science museums, the dilemma between instruction and entertainment, and even the arguments on the ultimate goals of these practices often re-emerges. In fact, the use of spectacle and theatricality seemed to be intrinsically linked to public shows. In 1896, in the Urania theatre in Berlin there were public demonstrations of x-rays. In six months, more than 60,000 visitors enthusiastically

74 Spectacular science

received a mixture of solid information and entertainment. Like in London, that kind of science museum was at the core of the city's cultural activities alongside concerts, plays, operas, circuses, lectures and art exhibitions.[98]

There were other attempts at providing shows and theatricality. At the end of the 1880s, after a full 25 years' dedication to science popularisation, Louis Figuier (1819–94) decided to bring to the stage the life and works of great scientists and inventors.[99] He had already found fame in 1851 with his printed *Feuilletons scientifiques*, *L'Année scientifique et industrielle* and 23 popular science books. His wife, Juliette Buscaren, organised a salon with scientists, artists and journalists. Attracted by the science fiction novels of Jules Verne (although still a defender of the genuine, non-fiction character of his own genre) Figuier was inspired in *Le tour du monde en 80 jours* (1874) to write his own first scientific play, *Les six parties du monde* (1877). He then continued with the lives of the great men of science: Kepler, Jussieu, Papin, Guthenberg, among others. These were followed by titles such as: *Le mariage de Franklin*, *Miss Telegraph* and *La femme avant le deluge* – stories that Figuier had written about in his popularisation works.

Figuier's strategy was based on the heroic, romantic nature of the greatest minds, the great drama of the inventor, and on the romantic comedies, adventures and misfortunes of his main characters. However, his plays were fairly naïve, weak works in terms of literary quality, requiring overcomplicated sets. The educational aims were far outweighed by the elements of adventure, fiction and entertainment. The press reviews were blunt and to the point: 'it lacks spectacle' and 'it is all too naive, austere, simple and rudimentary'. From 1877 until his death in 1894, Figuier fought for the success of his scientific theatre, but in the end it was a complete failure that brought him economic ruin. Again, science, fiction, spectacle, entertainment and instruction converged uneasily on the stage. But despite academic controversies and commercial success or failure, that spectacular scientific culture seemed to firmly conquer nineteenth-century bourgeois cities.

Equally, that theatricality would take the form of other kinds of spectacle in the twentieth century. From plates in printed books, paintings and photographs, the invention of cinematography by the Lumière brothers in 1985 can be considered a new form of theatricality; a new stage of the visual turn. Taking cinema as a step further from optics, photography, chemistry and scientific instrumentation would make it another fascinating new chapter in the history of science. But the most interesting aspect to analyse here is how, from the end of the nineteenth century, cinema would become a cultural mass phenomenon to be later appropriated by television in the middle of the twentieth century. Films are excellent popularising tools, since their images and messages encode the main elements of the scientific culture of a certain period. Despite their multiple possible readings and interpretations, just like any other work of art, films play an important role in the subtle indoctrination of the population, again in constant tension between educational persuasiveness, or simple entertainment.[100]

Commercial films are important agents of science popularisation in contemporary societies, especially considering their circulation on television and more recently via the internet. It is precisely their capacity to reach millions of spectators that shapes the public image of science. Although their scientific content is often highly superficial, films provide biographies in the form of 'biopicture' or 'biopics', discoveries, controversies, places of scientific practice (hospitals, laboratories, universities, etc.),[101] moral dilemmas and attitudes towards science in certain societies and at certain periods.[102] Twentieth-century audiences usually encounter the lives of scientists as consumers of audiovisual productions. Biopics are simply contemporary versions of a long biographical tradition that has marked the public image of science over different periods of history. They are not so far removed from the old tradition of scientific obituaries in academies or the profiles of well-known nineteenth-century scientists and inventors (more about this topic later on), or the more 'traditional' biographies of great personalities in politics and art.

A large part of the population forms its own conception of modern science through our popular contemporary culture (film, television, radio, press, internet). Scientific knowledge of the average citizen probably comes more from the visual culture of film than from school education or the systematic reading of printed science. Throughout the twentieth century, cinema created stereotyped images of the role of scientists in society: the romantic, eccentric, idealist, elitist adventurer, combined with stereotyped images of science itself: mysterious, incomprehensible, dangerous, true and fun. It permeates the viewer's subconscious and moulds the role of science in contemporary societies through the prism of certain political, economic and media interests. Recent studies of the image of chemists as professional scientists in twentieth-century cinema have shown that, despite numerous attempts by professional associations and corporate industrial groups to offer a friendlier and more positive public image, beyond the stereotype of producers of pollution, explosive experiments and obscure alchemical traditions, their image as 'mad scientists' in popular culture still remains.[103]

Documentary cinema has expanded the public image of science. The first scientific documentaries, which reported nature in wild and often exotic settings, or described natural disasters, were shown in cinemas as an additional option to fictional films. Natural sciences and the television format of 'science in the field' have become some of the most successful genres of science popularisation in recent decades, possibly competing only with the medical fiction series.[104] The human body and nature, with immense possibilities for visual representation, are the great scientific topics on TV.[105] In Britain, for instance, science documentaries played an important role throughout the twentieth century (and particularly in the second half through shows produced by the BBC and Channel 4).[106] After a fairly amateur start, they became useful propaganda machines during the Second World War in the interests of public legitimation of war machines, public health and agriculture.

76 Spectacular science

From esoteric topics to entertaining narratives, science on TV has also contributed to constructing the authority of professional scientists in the public sphere.[107]

As elements of propaganda and political control, documentaries are also identified fairly readily with totalitarian regimes. Science and technology (the space race, new technologies, public health issues) played a crucial role in political and nationalist campaigns in Nazi Germany, Mussolini's Italy and Stalin's Soviet Union.[108] After the launching of the Sputnik in 1957, the space race, its heroes, projects and promethean dreams of conquering the galaxy were shared by Soviet and American audiences, even beyond ideological barriers.[109] The NoDo documentaries during General Franco's regime in Spain reported on the opening of hospitals and other health centres to fight against illnesses such as tuberculosis and gave great importance to hygiene campaigns and health propaganda. They showed large empty spaces, without people, as culturally sterilised, technical works, intended to demobilise public opinion, reinforcing the authoritarian character of the regime, emphasising the rupture with the democratic past and strengthening the militarisation of screen space. It was only from the 1950s on, with the opening up of the regime internationally and its repositioning in the light of the Cold War, that NoDo presented reports on nuclear energy, universal exhibitions and surgical operations. As in other times and places, the visual factor of science was charged with political intentions.[110]

From the start, film has been not only an instrument for scientific research, documentation and science popularisation, but also an experimental narrative in constant evolution. It has presented different and often conflicting images of science and its central agents. Cinema gathered essential elements of nineteenth-century science fiction in an audiovisual format aimed at twentieth-century mass audiences: utopias and dystopias, exotic and strange worlds, from *Gulliver's Travels* to *Frankenstein*, from futuristic cities to the space ships that conquer other planets. Mary Shelly's *Frankenstein* was first screened in 1910. The novels of Verne and Wells also reached the big screen during the twentieth century. Millions of readers of science-based adventure stories were now accompanied by huge numbers of viewers.

Throughout the twentieth century, films brought science closer to the people, especially during the nuclear escalation of the Cold War in the second half of the century. An approach to 'big science' in general and nuclear technology in particular can be found, for example, in the work of Stanley Kubrick (1928–99). In a series of fixed and dispassioned long shots, Kubrick offers the viewer a rigid and distant image of science itself. The HAL computer rebels against the astronauts of the spacecraft in *2001: A Space Odyssey* (1968), an idea that is also present in *Dr. Strangelove*, and which would be taken up again by Steven Spielberg, inspired by Michael Crichton's novel *Jurassic Park* (1991), in the negative but spectacular results of biotechnology. Spielberg also addressed our inability to control climate change in *Artificial Intelligence: A.I.* (2001), a topic that was taken up again in documentary form in *An Inconvenient Truth* (2006): broadly distributed by Al Gore as part of his campaign against global warming and its consequences, it highlights the role of scientists' authority in the public arena.[111]

Analysing the design and production of Spielberg's *Jurassic Park* in more detail reveals significant elements about the public image of science at the end of the twentieth century. This film is an excellent vehicle for ensuring that scientific knowledge on topics such as palaeontology, molecular biology, computing and hot issues such as evolution, chaos theory, the genome project and DNA synthesis reach millions of viewers. These issues appear in documentary format in the film, in other words as simplified explanations for the benefit of both the characters and the cinema audiences. Children also play an important role as lay public, in the context of the commercialisation of science where much of the cutting-edge knowledge is used not only to recreate the huge extinct dinosaurs as a spectacle but also for the private revenues of Jurassic Park's promoters.

In the twentieth century, urban and industrial cinema contributed to transforming modern science into a true spectacle and a commodity of entertainment and fascination beyond the scope of the content itself. Adorno and Horkheimer already considered film as a tool for manipulating passive audiences, and their thesis permeated cultural studies in the 1960s.[112] The enormous power of cinema in contemporary mass societies must be taken into account seriously when analysing the role of its millions of spectators in the huge theatre of scientific culture of our time.[113] *2001: A Space Odyssey* (1968), *Planet of the Apes* (1968) and *Soylent Green* (1973) discussed evolution, reproduction, biomedical experimentation, artificial intelligence, genetic engineering and nuclear technology among other issues related to future-world scientific advancements.[114]

The history of the twentieth century is in part the history of the public display of moving pictures, and the history of science in the same period is therefore the history of the images in motion related to laboratories, experiments, discoveries, hospitals and public works. Making films, their public exhibition and the viewers' feedback are fundamental to any assessment of our contemporary scientific culture.[115]

★ ★ ★

Collections of natural and artificial marvels, enormous steam engines spitting out smoke and noise, theatres packed with audiences keen to witness the dissection of bodies, spectacular controversial experiments, the fascinating technological reconstruction of the Cold War and the fictional worlds of film are just some examples of the spectacularity of science through history and its role in the relation between expert and lay audiences. In permanent tension between entertainment and instruction, the rational and the emotional, fiction and reality, the spectacle has pervaded our scientific culture. It supposedly makes science accessible to millions, but at the same time it trivialises versions and reproductions of the experts' academic knowledge, as unique artists.[116] It is a difficult dilemma. Hilgartner was almost certainly right in his canonical article on the dominant view of science popularisation. The borders between reasonable simplification and distortion are always changing and are once again subject to continuous expert–lay negotiations: between the stars of the show and their respective audiences; between the rituals of public fascination and their rationality, through a

78 Spectacular science

plurality of voices. Perhaps, far from supposed objectivities and timeless truths, the deep cultural, controversial, dynamic character of science lies precisely in its spectacular nature.[117]

Notes

1 '[Nollet] hung the boy from the ceiling by silk cords and electrified him by means of an electrical machine ... Frequently he encouraged a young girl to touch the electrified boy or, better yet, to give him a kiss. He dimmed the lights of the room and the boy and the girl, facing each other, would move close enough for sparks to pass from one to another ... This "electric kiss" was quite popular, especially, contemporaries claimed, among the ladies', Lynn (2006: 31). Lynn refers to J.A. Nollet (1746), *Essai sur l'électricité des corps* (5th edn), Paris: Guérin.
2 Lynn (2006: 29–32).
3 Schaffer (1983: 1).
4 Morus (2007); Lightman (2007b).
5 Morus (1996). More recently Aileen Fyfe and Bernard Lightman have insisted on the idea that science and its teaching was yet another object for consumption in the market. Fyfe, Lightman (2007).
6 Mazzolini (1993: viii–xix).
7 Daston (2004).
8 Myers (2003); Wise (2006).
9 Wise (2006).
10 Wise (2006: 75).
11 Olmi (1992); Impey, MacGregor (1985).
12 Olmi (1992); Pardo-Tomás (2014).
13 Olmi (1992); Benedict (2001).
14 Vincent (1719).
15 Whitaker (1996: 75).
16 Smith, Findlen (2002: 299).
17 Evelyn (1901).
18 Tissandier (1883); Grollier de Servière (1719).
19 Pyenson, Sheets-Pyenson (1999: 126–8).
20 Kohler (2007).
21 This is for instance the case of the Salvador cabinet de curiosités in Barcelona, Pardo-Tomás (2014).
22 Schaffer (1999).
23 Lightman (2007a).
24 Grégoire (1794: 8).
25 Pickstone (2000).
26 Schroeder-Gudehus, Rasmussen (1992).
27 Brain (1993).
28 Greenhalgh (1988: 18–19).
29 Fox (2012).
30 'Fairs were held around the world, in cities ranging from Saint Petersburg and Brussels to Rio de Janeiro and Hanoi. These fairs were linked to imperialist expansion in Asia, Africa and Latin America, and to the massive industrial developments in the Western World'. Rydell (1984: 8). See also Schroeder-Gudehus, Rasmussen (1992), with a descriptive list of the most important exhibitions.
31 Mayhew (1851: 149).
32 Carre (1989: 38).
33 Greenhalgh (1988: 22); Mackenzie (1986).
34 Parry (1996); Goldman (2005).

35 Brain (1993).
36 Gurney (2001).
37 Alberti (2007, 2011).
38 Quoted by Anderson (1992: 170); Craveri (2005).
39 Ferguson (1965).
40 Morris (2007: 289–300).
41 Pickstone (2000).
42 Yanni (1996).
43 Forgan, Gooday (1996); Forgan (2005); O'Connor (2007).
44 Yanni (1996).
45 Pyenson, Sheets-Pyenson (1999: 132–3).
46 Cunningham (1996: 51–2).
47 Pyenson, Sheets-Pyenson (1999: 158–9).
48 Findlen (1994: 256–61).
49 Osborne (1994).
50 Pyenson, Sheets-Pyenson (1999: 169).
51 Nyhart (2009).
52 Wessely (2008).
53 Hochadel (2010).
54 Pyenson, Sheets-Pyenson (1999: 134–5).
55 *New York Museum of Science and Industry* (1938). *Science in Action.* Philadelphia. Published by Ruth Murray Miller, p. 1. Sastre-Juan (2013).
56 Eidelman (1985, 1992: 70).
57 Bennett, J. (1995).
58 Taub (1998).
59 Pandora, Rader (2008: 357–60).
60 Gregory, Miller (1998: chapter 8).
61 Fox (2006).
62 Schroeder-Gudehus, Rasmussen, Bolenz (1992: introduction).
63 Hilgartner (1990).
64 MacDonald, Silverstone (1992).
65 MacDonald (1996); Moranta, Guggenheim, Gisler, Pohl (2003: 155).
66 Bensaude-Vincent (2009b).
67 Daston (2004).
68 Alberti (2005: 569).
69 Gregory, Miller (1998: 210–14).
70 Scott (2005: 3).
71 Scott, Giusti (2006).
72 Bennett, T. (1995: 5–6, 2007); Fara (1995).
73 Bennett, T. (1995); 'linked to the well-acknowledged fact that museums were places for civilizing the working classes by diverting restless minds into acceptable forms of learning and encouraging a reverential frame of mind at the magnificence of a God-created world', Forgan (2005: 581).
74 Gieryn (1998).
75 Goldberg (1999).
76 Peter Morris specifically studied the chemistry halls of the Science Museum in 1906, 1926, 1977 and 1999. Morris (2007, 2010).
77 Alberti (2007: 393).
78 Shiele, Koster (1998).
79 Hug, Cunningham (1994); Kusukawa (2012).
80 Rippa Bonati, Pardo-Tomás (2004); Pardo-Tomás, Martínez-Vidal (2005).
81 Pardo-Tomás, Martínez-Vidal (2005).
82 Evelyn (1901: I, 214).
83 Livingstone (2003); Forgan (2005).

80 Spectacular science

84 For more details about 'Bodies', see Bodies. The Exhibition, http://www.premierexhibitions.com/exhibitions/4/4/bodies-exhibition (accessed 15 June 2015).
85 Lynn (2006: 32).
86 Blondel, Dörries (1994).
87 Lynn (2006: 8).
88 Bret (2004).
89 Golinski (1992).
90 Golinski (2008: 118).
91 James (2002); Knight (2002).
92 Faraday (2011).
93 In 1801, given the success of Davy's public lectures, and the avalanche of carriages arriving at Albemarle Street, which led to the RI, it became the first one-way street in London. James (2002).
94 Faraday (1865: lecture I, 2).
95 James (2002: 226–7); Faraday (1865, 2011).
96 Lightman (2007b).
97 Berman (1978).
98 Hessenbruch (2000). On science popularisation in Germany, see Daum (1998, 2002).
99 Cardot (1989); Nieto-Galan (2012b).
100 Apple and Apple (1993); Florensa, Hochadel, Tabernero (2014).
101 Shortland (1987); Reingold (1985).
102 Dickson (1986).
103 Weingart (2007); Kirby (2011).
104 Kuklick, Kohler (1996).
105 Gregory, Miller (1998: 121–4); La Follette (2012); Florensa, Hochadel, Tabernero (2014).
106 Boon (2015).
107 Boon (2008); Gregory, Miller (1998: 121–4).
108 For Nazi propaganda films see Michalczyk (1994); for the political role of science popularisation in the Soviet Union, see Andrews (2003).
109 Andrews, Siddiqi (2011).
110 Medina-Domènech, Menéndez Navarro (2005).
111 Stern (2004).
112 Adorno, Horkheimer (2002).
113 Friedman (2004); Boon (2008).
114 Amy Chambers (2015), 'From Star Child to Star Wars: American Science (Fiction), Film, and Religion, 1967–1977' (unpublished paper).
115 Boon (2008).
116 Benjamin (1969).
117 Hilgartner (1990).

4

HETERODOX SCIENCE

In 1778, Viennese physician Franz Anton Mesmer (1734–1815) opened a consultancy in Paris with the intention of administering a mysterious new fluid to his patients; a fluid that supposedly had great healing qualities and passed through healthy bodies filling them with vitality. Mesmer thought that sickness was the consequence of the obstruction of this fluid and that magnetic rods should be applied to patients to stimulate their animal magnetism and help to restore their wellbeing. He held group therapy sessions, mainly with aristocratic women. Once they had held hands they experienced trances and convulsions, supposedly as a result of the efficiency of his method and its capacity to cure.

Despite radical opposition from members of the Académie des sciences in Paris, and an aggressive public campaign to blacken his name, Mesmer's patients continued to knock on his door and the waiting lists did not stop growing. The so-called mesmerism gained support and patients vouched for his authority to the stupor of 'official' science. Was Mesmer really a mad charlatan or a genius of his time, whose natural philosophy was not so very far from the general consensus among experts of the Enlightenment? Some of the keys to the interpretation of this historic event are described below.

During the 1780s, animal magnetism was grouped with other imponderable fluids that were in 'circulation' in Europe in the eighteenth century (electricity, phlogiston, vital force, caloric). Their quantification and measurement materialised the famous 'Newtonian dream', which attempted to extrapolate mathematical physics from the universal gravitation in all of these phenomena. Just as in the time when Voltaire (1694–1778) was preaching Newtonian gravity, Benjamin Franklin (1706–90) was applying the properties of electricity to lightning rods, and the Montgolfier brothers were causing a storm in Europe with their flights into the atmosphere, Mesmer's fluid did not seem quite as miraculous. References to very similar fluids that appeared in articles of Diderot and

82 Heterodox science

FIGURE 4.1 Animal magnetism session in a Paris salon of the end of the eighteenth century. Louis Figuier, *Les merveilles de la science*, II, p. 633. Reproduced with permission of the Biblioteca de Catalunya (Barcelona).

D'Alembert's *Encyclopédie* were described as 'fire' or 'electricity'.[1] Contemporary experiments of animal electricity, electrified people or the famous Leyden jar were not so very different to Mesmer's practices (Figure 4.1). All of them took place in a context where both the vitalist and mechanist explanations in relation to the human body revealed their limitations, and the four Aristotelian elements (earth, water, air and fire) had entered an irreversible crisis, steering the speculation and proliferation of cosmologies, amid popular enthusiasm and curiosity for finding out the ultimate causes of natural phenomena.

Publications about mesmeric practices were everywhere. His experiments were present in academic debates, salons, police investigations, and even in the theatres and the Mozart opera *Così fan tutte*. Pamphlets, advertisements and comments on mesmerism were about as common in the public sphere as the political slogans.[2] For example, it is calculated that 8,000 people were magnetised in the first few months of 1784.[3] It was quite normal to find popular songs dedicated to Mesmer, such as the following:

> That the charlatan Mesmer,/With another confrere/Should cure many a female;/That he should turn their heads,/In touching them I know not where,/It's crazy/Very crazy/And I don't believe in it at all/Old ones, young ones, ugly ones, beauties,/All love the doctor,/And all are faithful to him.[4]

In a letter, the lawyer A.J.M. Servan, who was a friend of Voltaire and D'Alembert, expressed his enthusiasm for mesmerism and for an electric machine that he had in the following words:

> Never have the effects of magnetism struck me so: if anything should confirm for me the existence of a universal fluid, unique agent in its modifications of so many diverse phenomena, it will be my electric machine. It speaks to me in Mesmer's language about nature, and I listen to it with ravishment.[5]

However, despite Mesmer's undeniable success and the praise of his patients, dignified members of the Académie des sciences such as Lavoisier and the anatomist Félix Vicq d'Azyr (1746–94) began an energetic campaign to discredit the 'charlatan'. They declared in public that any therapeutic property of this fluid was due to the imagination of the poor and the ignorant. The marquis de Condorcet also made a worried appeal to the authority of doctors to judge the universal fluid.[6] But the effect of the campaign was minimal. The doctor and revolutionary Jean-Paul Marat (1743–93) had also had problems with the authority of the Académie as a result of his interest in imponderable fluids. This is yet one more piece of evidence of the coherence of Mesmer's animal magnetism in scientific culture at the end of the eighteenth century, and not one that is necessarily concordant with the criteria of official science.[7]

Something similar happened with phrenology (see Figure 4.2). As seen in Chapter 2, in the mid-nineteenth century the mechanisms of permeability in this controversial science were spectacular on every social level. All these supposedly heterodox practices spread through itinerant lectures, and to a large extent they shaped the definition of the expert and the acceptance of certain healing methods.[8] The public conferred great authority on phrenology. How could a theory or practice be discredited while thousands of people enthusiastically followed the explanations of phrenologists on the physical and

84 Heterodox science

FIGURE 4.2 A phrenologist in his consulting room. Coloured etching by George Cruikshank (1826). Reproduced with permission of the Wellcome Library.

moral consequences of our cerebral topography? Phrenology public lectures were advertised widely in the daily press, lunches and informal meetings with the speakers, visits to local institutions and comments and reviews following the event. They became genuine and wide-reaching cultural phenomena,[9] using recently extracted brains, skulls, busts, models, diagrams in an ambitious programme of visual culture. Also, as mentioned above, some of the courses or series of talks were successfully published in book form, the most well known probably being Combe's *Constitution of Man* (1828).

Much has been written about the case of Mesmer and animal magnetism and about the success of phrenology, homeopathy and other controversial medical practices. Although each case should be studied in its specific historical context, the queues of patients (or clients) at the doors of the practitioners' consulting rooms, questioned by the experts, raise the issue of the epistemological status of the public and its credibility at any given time.[10] However, in any historical time, the boundaries between science and pseudo-science, between orthodox and heterodox practices are the result of a complex contention among the actors involved.[11] Nowadays, Hippocratic-Galenic medicine, alchemy, astrology, natural magic, animal magnetism, phlogiston theory, phrenology and the Romantic-inspired *Naturphilosphie* are perceived of as extinct branches of scientific thinking. Nonetheless, all of these natural philosophies had a large number of followers, and they were seldom placed outside the boundaries of orthodox knowledge. The main figures in each period engaged in intricate contentions to form their own ideas about what was considered orthodox and heterodox, the difference between expert and lay actors, professionals and amateurs, the rational and the irrational. Despite their efforts, they never managed to achieve a definitive and unquestionable demarcation of these intellectual boundaries.[12]

It is perhaps too easily acknowledged that the professionalisation of science throughout the nineteenth century was responsible for gradually reinforcing the line between the supposedly amateur or heterodox street shows and the 'rigorous' displays in the universal exhibitions or within the museum walls; the circus acts and the zoological parks; the medicine of charlatans and that of reliable and academically trained practitioners; the overexcited masses and the educated and disciplined visitors. However, the idea that there existed well-defined groups of experts and laypeople is oversimplified. The so-called amateurs, enthusiasts, science popularisers, promoters, the professionals or experts and the supposed laypeople are all dynamic and changing agents in their task of constructing knowledge boundaries and the making of scientific authority. Often, popularisation has contributed precisely to justifying the monopoly of the experts in certain areas of the public sphere and adjusting it to the lay expectations, reinforcing a particular kind of orthodoxy to the detriment of other worldviews.[13]

Consequently, the essentialist debates about who holds or does not hold scientific 'truth' should be avoided. Each actor should be analysed according to their training, payment, practices, experiments, publications and other social strategies.[14] That is largely the aim of this chapter. It will focus on the criteria for defining the limits of knowledge and the inevitable 'heterodox' component (be it simplification, distortion or rejection of the orthodox) which requires the extension of scientific knowledge beyond small circles of experts. This is where the subtle mechanisms of domination and scientific and institutional hegemony, which leaked into the public sphere and even the

86 Heterodox science

debates between science and religion during the nineteenth and twentieth centuries, are most apparent.[15]

4.1. Alternative medicine

As seen previously, the struggle for the scientific authority of mesmerism was largely repeated in phrenology and could also be extrapolated to other therapeutic practices. In the early nineteenth century German doctor Samuel Hahnemann (1755–1843), the founder of homeopathy, demonstrated his hatred of the arrogance of his professional colleagues. From the end of the eighteenth century he began to set up an alternative system based on the principle of similitude and the law of infinitesimals. Under his system, illnesses were treated with medicines that caused the same pathological symptoms, but always in extremely small doses. Despite heavy criticism from official medicine, and even public ridicule, homeopathy attracted thousands of new patients throughout the nineteenth century.[16] Compared with the terrible blood-lettings, the painful purges and other Hippocratic-Galenic methods, these tiny homeopathic balls had no secondary effects and could be successfully administered to children. Women soon became adept at homeopathy and went on to become experts in this new medical culture in their own homes.[17]

During that time, in the United States, Dr Samuel Thomson (1769–1843) recovered certain aspects of ancient medical tradition using plant extracts. Thomson was convinced that health was closely related to body temperature and that *Lobelia inflata*, an emetic plant used by the Native Americans, contributed to re-establishing normal body temperature. Up until 1830, some 3 million Americans adopted his system, which was described in the extensive *New Guide of Health or Botanic Family Physician* (1822), including a description of the plants and their preparation as therapeutic remedies. His motto was: 'Every man his own doctor',[18] in line with the new citizens' desire for freedom and their attempts to liberate themselves from the influence of the clergy, lawyers and doctors. It also gave women considerable medical independence.

Another heterodox option was hydropathy, which did not use any type of medicine, either mineral or vegetable, in large or small doses. Recovering elements of the ancient Hippocratic-Galenic corpus, hydropaths based their therapies on fresh air, sunlight, exercise, a vegetarian diet and, above all, water in all its possible applications. For some of its followers, hydropathy was intended to make patients their own doctors. This is evident from the letters of thanks and support for the suggested therapies that readers sent to the 1845 US publication *Water-Cure Journal*.[19]

Despite the fact that the professional medical elites of the nineteenth century were able to suppress manifestations of these alternative practices, publications of this kind and their readership grew spectacularly. In France, the prestigious *Gazette de santé* was an official medical journal but it was aimed at a very wide readership which included patients. Largely along the lines of the domestic medical tradition of the previous centuries, titles like 'Medicine without Doctors', 'Health Manual' and 'Popular Almanac' were the norm and were widely read. In most cases these works transmitted a hegemonic version of the official view of medicine, of which topics could be covered and how it should be done. However, some cases did not fit in with this trend.

In the middle of the century, French doctor François-Vincent Raspail (1794–1878) tried to break with this dominant view of medical popularisation.[20] Raspail came from a modest provincial family and his scientific training had always been heterodox. Although he contributed to topics related to organic chemistry, cell theory, microscopy and parasitology, he never obtained a university degree.[21] His domestic pharmacopoeias, which invited patients to prepare their own medicines, were a great publishing success. Between 1847 and 1849 he published the *Revue élémentaire de médecine et de pharmacie domestiques*, which was clearly aimed at a broad public and critical of official medicine. His famous health almanac, the *Manuel annuaire de la santé*, sold some 10,000 copies annually and appeared for almost a century from 1845 to 1935. In 1913, one of the new boulevards in Paris was named after Raspail and soon afterwards a statue was erected in his honour in the Place Denfert-Rochereau – further proof of his great prestige and popularity. Raspail died in 1878, curiously the same year as Claude Bernard, one of the great figures of academic and experimental medicine, and his funeral became a public event comparable to that of Louis Pasteur (1822–95) a few years later in 1888.

For Raspail, any medical practice that was not based on an idea accessible to simple people was considered an irrational practice. He also thought that illnesses could be cured more quickly if medicine were less elitist and closer to popular wisdom. The transcription of Raspail's famous trials, in which he was repeatedly denounced by the medical authorities for professional untruism, faithfully reflected his defence of significant autonomy on the part of the patient. In his health manual and his popular pharmacopeia, a set of case studies justified the need to apply Raspail's medical criteria rather than those of official medicine.[22]

Among his cases, one that particularly stands out is that of 1846 when he was accused of 'illegal medical practice' by Mateu Orfila (1787–1853),[23] who was then Dean at the Faculty of Medicine in Paris. Raspail defended his position in the courts in no uncertain terms:

> Not only have I not usurped the title of doctor of medicine, but I have always been careful to show the public that I have nothing in common with those who hold the title; to prove this, I am happy to read you a single passage from my *Manual of Health*, from this little work that has spread like wildfire among all classes of the French population and all over the globe, I venture to say, to the great satisfaction not of the doctors but of the patients . . . Ah! Allow me, gentlemen, in my humble but decent and honourable condition . . . Do I need qualifications? What would I do with

them? What would I gain by accepting them? And if I refused them, what would I lose? Ah! 30 years ago they produced the same repugnance for me as they do today.[24]

The law courts came to have a central place in the public sphere of medicine. Independently of the sanctions and the individual outcomes of each of Raspail's trials, the impact of this kind of controversy on the public only went to strengthen his popularity and increase his book sales and numbers of patients.[25] Raspail thought that official medical authority was weighed down in exaggerated tradition and specialisation; when it came to dealing with the illness, the unity of the patient had broken down, popular wisdom had been pushed aside and there was too much faith in written texts. He saw the need for a more empirical, descriptive and classifying medicine based on family tradition and true to popular observations of nature and the human body, and one which respected the ancient nomenclature that was more accessible to the lay population.

Raspail's radical republicanism and his active participation in the revolutions of 1830 and 1848 led to his arrest and exile, but they also gave him a somewhat heroic status which, despite the controversy that he had provoked, placed his name firmly in the Parisian public sphere. Raspail promoted a certain kind of 'democratic' medicine where patients, especially from the lower classes, retained considerable dignity and protagonism. For Raspail, popular wisdom had to be dignified and contributed to raising the cultural level of the masses and their social and moral progress. It was not a question of a top-down science popularisation, from the academic circles of experts, but to place a value on a different type of knowledge that had been overlooked until then by the monarchic powers of the time. Medical reform became political reform and a supposedly liberating option for the patient who could regain their self-confidence independently of medical authority. Patients therefore became the central figures of a new medical doctrine that only made sense with the integration of their own experiences in the so-called 'Raspail system'. This programme, in France at least, enjoyed more success among the petit bourgeoisie in the liberal professions, the middle classes and the working class elites than with the aristocrats and the lower classes.[26]

Strict regulation of official medicine in France paradoxically produced a large number of 'alternative' medicines. Just as 'official' state medicine was gradually established throughout the nineteenth century, 'alternative' medicine emerged in opposition, covering a wide range of practices under different names: unorthodox, irregular, frontier, vernacular, popular, unconventional, unofficial, complementary, non-standard, counterhegemonic.[27] Strategies for challenging official medicine did not differ greatly from those used by Raspail. In the boundaries of an alternative conception of the human body and health, they questioned the monopoly, privileges and methods of the professionals and promoted underground treatments.[28] Consequently, it is difficult to draw a clear line between expert and lay practitioners competing in the public market for medicine in the nineteenth century.[29]

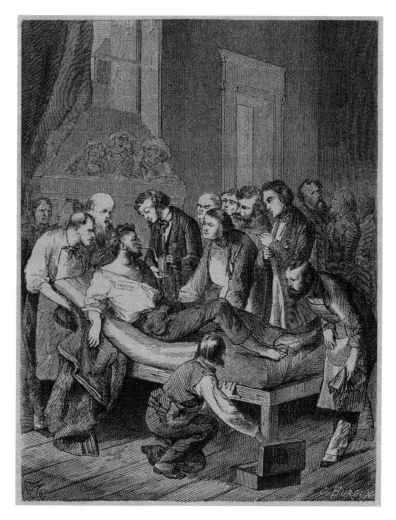

FIGURE 4.3 Demonstration of anaesthesia using ether in Massachusetts General Hospital (1846). Louis Figuier, *Les merveilles de la science,* II, p. 653. Reproduced with permission of the Biblioteca de Catalunya (Barcelona).

It is well known, for instance, that around 1840 mesmeric practices and ether were competing for use as anaesthetics (Figure 4.3). Both methods were fairly effective in relieving pain (mesmeric practices took the patient into a hypnotic state). However, the surgeons' corporate influence on the use of ether gradually gained ground over the relatively marginal position of the mesmerists.[30] Similarly, the priority given to British surgeon Joseph Lister's (1827–1912) successful antiseptic treatment over the alternatives of his contemporaries can be explained in the context of Victorian society and its concept of physical and moral cleanliness.[31] In the case of homeopathy, some historians have given more weight

90 Heterodox science

to the intentions and interests of certain users of the therapy and the reactions of their opponents than to any strictly scientific discrepancies. For example, in the mid-nineteenth century the exclusion of homeopathy from professional recognition was the result of a deliberate corporate move by professional doctors, but it was not based on the analysis of the treatment itself.[32]

Like Mesmer, practitioners of alternative therapies continued to use them as long as they had patients. Evidence of this can be found in hygiene and popular therapies which included several medical systems by well-known doctors such as Raspail, Leroy, Morrison and Holloway, and summed up homeopathic principles.[33] Louis Leroy was the author of *Curative Medicine*, a bestselling volume that propounded the use of purges as a universal remedy for all kinds of ailment. Frank E. Morrison published a considerable number of popular health treatises which were continually republished until well into the twentieth century. Holloway's case probably refers to the British millionaire Thomas Holloway, whose pills were advertised widely in the press during the 1860s and claimed to be able to cure almost all ailments.[34]

A similar situation occurred in the United States during the first half of the nineteenth century. Mesmerists, dentists and other kinds of healers, all of them itinerant, travelled from the cities to rural areas to offer their services, since professional doctors considered such activity to be inconvenient and badly paid. It was only when communications improved that certain medicines, such as quinine, became used extensively, but even then perceptions by the lay practitioners of its healing capacity was far removed from professional medical counsel.[35]

There are many other examples where, despite the supposed heterodoxy of a certain therapeutic theory or practice, it was justified in business terms and the numbers of patients/clients even increased its prestige in the public sphere. In 1919, the German company 'Dr. Madaus and Co.' was set up and sold medicinal herbs and homeopathic medicines, despite not having a licence. As a result of its success the company not only sold medicines but also ended up publishing books and magazines to promote alternative therapies and even took part in some major public health debates in Germany in the 1920s and 1930s. Its activity culminated in the 1938 publication of a manual of healing methods designed to sit alongside the official pharmacopoeias in the bookshops.[36] Several private initiatives during the same period manufactured drugs with great commercial success but dubious scientific orthodoxy.[37] Against an intricate background of medical pluralism, the hegemony of certain practices over others was not always guaranteed.

The examples above show that throughout the nineteenth century the path towards an experimental medicine with a strong clinical content was slow. The influence of the ancient medical systems, the plurality of the Hippocratic–Galenic tradition, refashioned by novelties such as homeopathy, phrenology and hydrotherapy, played a considerable role. It was further strengthened by the flourishing of a popular medicine based on folklore that would persist right up to the twentieth century. It was often linked to the idea that human beings experienced multiple connections with plants, animals, minerals and the planets. The limits of expert authority continued to be debated in the public sphere.[38]

4.2. Professionals and amateurs

The nineteenth century has often been described as a triumphal march towards professionalisation and specialisation. However, these are problematic concepts which historians of science continue to battle with generation after generation. In what terms can professional scientists be defined? If we accept the 1830 definition of 'scientist' by English philosopher William Whewell (1794–1866) should we talk of amateur science in the periods prior to that date? Should we necessarily associate professionalisation with scientific progress when names such as Lavoisier, Faraday and even Darwin himself could be considered amateurs? The meaning of words and concepts changes over time. It is difficult to talk about amateurs in the nineteenth century outside the framework of the professionalisation of science, growing specialisation and increasing institutionalisation of scientific disciplines, destined to standardise the expert and the layperson, the orthodox and the heterodox. It is very difficult to free ourselves from our contemporary conception of professionalisation of science when analysing the past.[39]

The professionalisation of science has been presented as one of the great achievements of the nineteenth century, as a progressive victory of the academic world of the new universities, specialised scientific societies, and the Comtian disciplines of positivist rationality, over amateurism, superstition and heterodoxy. However, a firm distinction between experts, amateurs or dilettantes and the general public seems dubious. There are many examples in history where the role of amateurs has been particularly significant; where they have been capable of participating both in academic and popular culture and contributing to the democratisation of knowledge.[40] Between the scientific publications aimed at the general public and the specialised research journals there was a scientific literature aimed at amateurs. Similarly, scientific societies often represented a space where amateurs and professionals could meet, and the biographical profile of many scientists – at least until well into the nineteenth century – shows how their practices were not always easy to demarcate.

Throughout the nineteenth century, the new professional scientists also existed side by side and sometimes shared important aspects supposedly associated with amateur culture: the pleasure of learning, aesthetic emotions and metaphysical speculations. Despite their frequent distancing from what was strictly orthodox or official, amateurs largely appropriated these values without renouncing their role as providers of data for the professionals.[41] The spread of scientific knowledge among the public would give amateurs sufficient authority, and that probably explains their obsession with public lectures and demonstrations, exhibitions, articles in the daily press and the publication of popular science books and journals. Amateurs and popularisers therefore became inseparable and complementary categories, in many cases.[42]

92 Heterodox science

Under the leadership of the French populariser Camille Flammarion, the network of astronomical amateur societies around 1900 describes a fluid, quite symmetrical arrangement for sharing and circulating astronomical knowledge, but also for exchanges of individuals, teams and instruments across Europe. Regardless of being in Manchester or in Barcelona, amateur astronomers shared the same status, perhaps only feeling peripheral compared with their local professional astronomers. To this thesis, it should also be added that, in contexts of weak professionalisation and a lack of great names in science at an international level, amateur astronomers often played a more important role than in well-established scientific communities.[43]

Amateur astronomers acted therefore as a bridge between experts and lay-people and often blurred rigid boundaries of elite and popular culture.[44] A huge range of practitioners used scientific instruments and read widely distributed 'popular astronomy' books. In spite of some amateur 'subaltern' practices such as astronomical observations and collection of meteorological data which served the professionals' interests, amateurs claimed scientific authority and public recognition. They also often became active science popularisers and that counterbalanced their secondary position in academia with a growing prestige in the public sphere.

In the urban context, amateur science popularisation provided flexible paths for a more or less heterodox education, and contributed greatly in the long term to the establishment of a genuine scientific culture.[45] Michael Faraday (1791–1867) entered the Royal Institution as an assistant in 1813, but he did not dedicate himself fully to research until 1862, and even then the Institution did not even have sufficient funding for research until the end of the nineteenth century.[46] That meant that one of the great geniuses of Western science, the father of electromagnetism, would have acquired a good part of his knowledge and carried out his experiments in a rather peculiar manner, distanced from the professional university profile. That was the norm, especially in Britain, but could be extrapolated to other Western countries in subjects such as astronomy and natural history.[47]

In the case of astronomy and its development as a modern science over the last two centuries, the professionals never gained complete control and amateurs frequently became an institution within the discipline.[48] In 1830, Auguste Comte (1789–1857) – the father of the positivist doctrine – was especially interested in popularising astronomy to the general public and he even founded a new association for popular teaching. In 1836, the second volume of the *Cours de philosophie positive* contained 16 lessons on astronomy and physics. Simply presented and with a low mathematical content, for Comte astronomy became the ideal example of how to initiate the public in the positivist spirit. It was also an excellent example of the unchanging nature of natural laws and the history of their understanding – from ancient mythology to Newtonian physics. This was an ideal strategy for explaining to the public the historical process which, according to Comte, human knowledge had experienced before reaching maturity and the stages in which it did so: theological, metaphysical, 'positive'. To that end he deliberately chose astronomy, the 'first' empirical science, in his classification, placed just after the most abstract science, mathematics, and above physics, chemistry, biology and sociology or social physics.[49] Faced with the impossibility of being accepted in the professional scientific circles of Paris, Comte hoisted the flag of amateur science as a reaction against the establishment.[50]

Some decades later, Flammarion developed a flexible astronomical research programme which allowed for mutually beneficial cooperation between amateurs and professionals. His international conferences and meetings promoted numerous astronomical societies whose statutes reflected a great sensibility for amateur astronomy. This encouraged the creation of new astronomical groups, popular observatories, prizes, courses and public talks, at which amateurs occupied common places between expert and lay astronomy: they were both audiences of science and science popularisers.[51]

Amateur astronomers were proud of their status. They formed networks, shared instruments, discussed the results of specific observations of stars and planets, according to their interests; they read literature by the likes of Flammarion, and studied photographs and astronomical drawings; sometimes sculptures were even used to give detailed descriptions of protuberances observed on the surface of the planets. The opening up of boundaries between creativity, tacit knowledge in daily practice, and supposedly objective observations, strengthened the fluid circulation of scientific knowledge throughout the nineteenth century.[52] The numerous books on popular astronomy that were bought and read by amateurs frequently included advertising and practical advice on the use of simple astronomical instruments by a large but non-professional audience. For example, the books by T. W. Webb on telescopes enjoyed considerable success among amateur astronomers. There were regular publications that gave instructions on how to build a simple telescope, giving lay users sufficient autonomy and minimum quality for their observations.[53]

Meteorology was another of the fields taken up by amateurs, whose influence on the collection of data has been largely maintained up to the present day. In fact, practices for measuring and collecting meteorological data go back further than the age of professional science. For example, at the end of the seventeenth century, the British wealthy classes often acquired barometers, thermometers, hygrometers and rain gauges, which they installed in their homes, thus contributing to a certain 'domestication' of atmospheric phenomena such as storms. These new instruments complemented a meteorological knowledge rooted in popular wisdom and the neo-Hippocratic environmentalist. The British elites therefore became Enlightenment amateurs in the field of meteorology.[54]

Photographs of meteorological phenomena and the measurement of temperatures, atmospheric pressure and precipitation provided by small weather stations have been very valuable both in scientific research and for information and popularisation in the media. Meteorology is also associated with older, more heterodox popular traditions. It is linked to tacit knowledge based on empirical

94 Heterodox science

daily observations and passed down through the generations. Although for many experts this has a clear place in the field of superstition, the popular observations have been useful throughout history. Equally, from the Lisbon earthquake in 1755 onwards, seismology has relied on lay observers, and has become very much dependent on the help of non-geologists.[55]

It is worth mentioning here the works of Catalan engineer and folklorist Cels Gomis (1841–1915), who focused his interests on lower-class culture, in particular on the 'popular science' of his time. As part of his folklorist agenda, he interviewed thousands of local villagers in all the towns he worked in for the railways companies,[56] ending up accumulating an enormous amount of data on astronomy, meteorology and botany.[57] One of Gomis's most popular books was *La lluna segons lo poble* (The Moon according to the People) (1884), in which he collected popular proverbs on our satellite and its influence on the weather, health, etc. Gomis's folklorist agenda did however have a clear political purpose. With regard to the popular knowledge he collected about the Moon, he described his main purpose in the following terms:

> We should recover all popular concerns, not to perpetuate them, as some believe, but to destroy them, only keeping some written records to allow people in the future to assess their state of progress as well as the backwardness of their ancestors.[58]

In practice Gomis became a *mediator* between his elite culture on civil engineering and his popular experiences in small towns. His impressive empirical, folklorist work prevented him from becoming a simple bridge for the transmission of the elite culture. In Gramsci's terms, Gomis acted as an 'organic intellectual' of the lower classes. In the struggle for cultural hegemony, his science was closer to the subaltern cultures of the Catalan peasants and craftsmen whom he regularly interviewed.

Using his own articles from *La nature*, French populariser Gaston Tissandier published his *Récréations scientifiques* in 1877, to considerable success (*Popular Scientific Recreations in Natural Philosophy, Astronomy, Geology, Chemistry* [1883]).[59] It placed special emphasis on day-to-day science and the aspect of play. Aimed at young students and lay readers in general, it boasted the capacity to diffuse scientific knowledge through the use of everyday objects and games. Illustrated by the author's brother, Albert, it was widely republished and translated.[60] Largely inspired by the old cabinets of curiosities and the tradition of collecting, the chapter entitled 'Science at home' proposed a set of machines and objects that could be contained in any amateur home. Among other things they included the so-called 'writing machine', the electric pen, the camphylometer, the chromograph, the 'mysterious' clocks, a new calculating dial and the pedometer. These objects were aimed specifically at amateurs, although their teaching application was not ignored.

The tradition of amateur astronomy was largely maintained during the twentieth century. Local astronomy societies still exist in large numbers; telescopes are an object of great commercial interest from children's toy versions to adaptations that meet the wants and needs of amateurs. Solar and lunar eclipses (just like in Flammarion's time) continue to captivate public and media interest.[61] Summer observations of the night sky in remote places far from the light pollution of the cities, or from the planetarium of a science museum continue to fascinate amateurs and the general public. They are bewitched by the magic of the universe to which Flammarion had so strongly appealed.

There is even evidence of the active participation of amateurs in the emergence of new specialities. Their ability to develop certain practices that were considered risky or controversial at the time opened up new paths for research. In the case of astrophysics, the use of photography, spectroscopy and reflection telescopes by amateurs allowed extremely useful sets of data to be collected. Although some were members of the same societies and shared honours with professional astronomers, amateurs acted with greater freedom and less pressure when it came to introducing new heterodox practices (Figure 4.4).[62]

But there were other dimensions to amateur science. In the first few decades of the nineteenth century in Britain, amateur naturalists were much more

FIGURE 4.4 Amateurs from the Barcelona Astronomical Society observing a solar eclipse in 1912. *Boletín de la Sociedad Astronómica de Barcelona*, 18, 1912, 23. Reproduced with permission of the Biblioteca de Catalunya (Barcelona).

96 Heterodox science

than simple collectors and providers of species for professional botanists, whose institutional position was relatively weak. At the end of days spent exploring, observing and collecting species, the amateurs would meet in pubs to discuss their results, turning these popular leisure-time establishments into unlikely places of scientific practice.[63] For example, Richard Buxton (1786–1865), a cobbler's apprentice from Ancoats, was self-taught in botany through the collection of herbs that would be useful for preparing infusions. Concerned about which names he should give the plants, having taught himself to read and write at the age of sixteen, Buxton bought several books about plant collections from which he gradually adopted the nomenclature set out by Carl von Linné (1707–78). He came into contact with other amateur botanists and they organised regular Sunday meetings which eventually became occasional get togethers in the pub to exchange species and books, and generally ended up with a round of pints and a few songs.[64] On the other side of the Channel, during the French Revolution, natural history was considered an equalitarian and democratic science, easily accessible to the new free citizen. So, while the Revolution saw the closing of the Académie des sciences because of its close ties with the aristocracy of the Ancien Régime, in 1793 the new Muséum d'histoire naturelle opened with the aim of extending knowledge of the three kingdoms of nature to ordinary people.[65]

An interest in flower growing, the garden and nature drawing drew not only aristocratic women but also the lower classes and the general public towards an interest in botany. The process of professionalisation of science throughout the nineteenth century, however, relegated women to a basically amateur status, dedicated mainly to the collection and identification of certain species of plants.[66] Growing amateur interest in gardens was reflected in popular encyclopaedias on horticulture, popular books and, at least in Britain, an increase in horticulture societies, which, among other things, covered the hybridisation of different popular flower varieties such as hyacinths, tulips and anemones.[67]

The zoological and botanical societies of London admitted women and the scientific societies in the provinces also opened their doors to 'ladies' until 1870, although membership of either of them was unusual at the height of the Victorian era.[68] Female attendance at the itinerant meetings of the British Association for the Advancement of Science (BAAS) was significant, to the point that ladies did not conform passively with the overriding male hegemony. Although only a minority of women gave talks of their own, their presence at academic sessions, scientific excursions and informal meetings, lunches and public events was visible in all the cities visited by the BAAS. They contributed to defining the border between science and its audiences and forged necessary alliances with the local elites to reinforce the scientific authority of the professionals. They acted as a kind of mediator between expert and popular science,[69] and to an extent they were not excluded from the circles of experts, playing a similar role to the numerous male amateurs in astronomy and natural history, and even in the popularisation of science. Take the case of Mary Somerville (1780–1872) and her *Mechanism of the Heavens* (1831), a popular version of the physics of Pierre-Simon Laplace (1749–1827). In 1834, with the help of John Herschell (1791–1891), Somerville published *On the Connection of the Physical Heavens*, selling more than 15,000 copies. However, she was never admitted as a member of the Royal Society.[70]

Natural history appears to be a picturesque, bucolic, useful and accessible science. Unlike what happens in the physics and chemistry laboratories, natural science seems to belong to everyone. However, since the field of study extends across the whole planet, professional naturalists (especially from the nineteenth century onwards) have always needed volunteers to collect plants and minerals and to observe animals. This cooperation has not always been harmonious. Whereas at the beginning of the century the term 'amateur' referred in a positive sense to someone knowledgeable about certain species or phenomena, close to the expert, by the end of the century it had come to mean a dilettante, unreliable, heterodox and lacking scientific rigour.[71]

Laboratories and experimental stations gradually became exclusive spaces of scientific practice where there was no room for amateurs. The perceived dominant view by the professionals was as custodians of a certain popular botany that was unacceptably heterodox. However, like astronomy, natural history has kept a certain amateur spirit up to the present. Gilbert White's famous book *The Natural History of Selborne* (1789), which has been published in more than 200 editions and was still being published in the 1970s bears this out. The *Souvenirs entomologiques* by French naturalist and populariser Jean-Henri Fabre (1823–1915) is still being published today, a century after its first edition.[72]

It is also significant that many of the academic debates about the animal kingdom were influenced by contributions from secondary actors. Taxidermists, fossil collectors and zookeepers all played a part at different times and places in the knowledge about certain species: anatomical and physiological studies, and their classification and position on the evolutionary tree. Darwin himself was a regular visitor to zoological parks, which he used as a source of inspiration for his own theory. However, he never held a university post and his intellectual training was fairly eclectic. It was his condition as a gentleman that gave his work considerable prestige, a common occurrence in Victorian Britain, although he was never clearly defined as a professional scientist. It is surprising, then, that during a century of professionalisation, in the 'age of science', someone of Darwin's standing should be considered an amateur.[73]

Some taxidermists were authors of important scientific works in applied natural history. Popular perceptions of evolution were shaped by talks and books such as *Vestiges* and *Origins*, but also in exhibitions of certain types of apes in zoos by amateur keepers with profound knowledge of their behaviour, who were able to provide the academic experts with extremely valuable etiological data. Gorillas are a case in point, exhibited in fairs and zoos and represented

98 Heterodox science

by artists, illustrators and photographers (as natural history amateurs). They contributed not only to public but also academic debate about the evolutionary 'missing link'.[74]

Similarly, in natural history museums, academics had to negotiate with curators and artists (supposedly amateurs in science) when it came to setting up exhibitions. Their rooms were full of objects that could be interpreted in different ways by different groups, from the strictest professionals to the most inexpert lay public, with the curators and artists falling somewhere inbetween. However, the objects were also robust enough to be successfully displayed side by side in the same room.[75]

Recreation was one of the main driving forces for amateurs. Thousands of inventors in the Victorian era did not necessarily expect economic or social success from their engines, but enjoyed their creative activity as a hobby. This recreational spirit of science also reached out to children and young people as major audiences, something that had not been studied until now. Mechanical games, chemistry sets, mineral collections, toy microscopes and telescopes, dolls for studying anatomy, card collections and illustrations all formed part of an important tradition of children and young people's science and technology which fit in with nineteenth-century recreational science.[76]

In the case of journals, amateur contributions were common in Britain throughout the nineteenth century. These publications offered a fluid dialogue between like-minded amateurs and gave them a forum for expression that was often vetoed in academic publications. Editors tended not to subject the drafts to strict quality controls and the pages were filled with advertising for scientific instruments and events organised by the numerous scientific societies with avid amateur members. In the Baconian tradition, the main priority was an empirical attitude and rigorous observation that was, nonetheless, open to non-professionals, while theory was often perceived of as excessive speculation. The gradual accumulation of modest observations could therefore provide amateur culture with valuable and stimulating information. The *Intellectual Observer* highlighted the huge increase in microscope and telescope sales which had a place in many homes, alongside other objects that were inseparable from amateurs and the recreational nature of science popularisation.[77]

The inertia of amateur science permeated well into the twentieth century. From July 1957 to December 1958, the International Year of Geophysics brought thousands of professional scientists from more than 60 countries together to share research into geodesy, geophysics, atmospheric science and oceanography. The event contributed to more extensive exploration of the Antarctic and a better understanding of tectonic plates.[78] Despite the fact that, until recently, only the biggest names associated with the event were known, it is now clear that thousands of amateurs from around the world took part, especially in the Moonwatch satellite observation programme coordinated by the Smithsonian Astronomical Observatory in Cambridge, Massachusetts.[79]

Heterodox science **99**

One of the consequences is that the boundaries between experts and lay public have remained blurred.

4.3. Popularisers and their public

Perhaps because their professional status has undergone a number of changes over time, science popularisers tend to be thought of as having philanthropic qualities, with an interest in educating and extending expert–lay bridges to help society understand the great changes that were occurring in science. But that is too simple an image, and one with little historical foundation that could be considered debatable today. This section aims to convince the reader that in both past and present, popularisers are not exempt from the corporate struggle for professionalisation and scientific authority, and they clearly do not lack ideologies, values and interests.

The process of professionalising science throughout the nineteenth century steered the growing emergence of science popularisers who would gradually become professionals following more or less orthodox paths. The demand for scientific knowledge emerged from a broad range of audiences with equally broad interests: politics, education, a utilitarian ideology frequently associated with businessmen and industrialists, and professional scientists keen to define the expert–lay boundaries of the new university disciplines. Popularisers themselves had the role of new mediators in the professionalisation process and sought a lighter and more entertaining image of science that would be attractive to large sectors of the population and satisfy their publishers.[80]

Throughout the nineteenth century, popularisers with a greater or lesser degree of professionalisation wove into the dense fabric of relations between experts, laypeople and amateurs; in other words, between the orthodox and the heterodox. They worked with a variety of intentions and programmes according to the cultural context in which they carried out their activities, but there were common elements among them. A closer look at the similarities reveals a profile of an initial scientific training, and even some research activity, and the subsequent decision to pursue popularisation activities.[81] Their political positions, values and perceptions of expert and lay science, however, did not fit into a single pattern.

In France, the foundation of the *Cercle de la presse scientifique* in 1856 marked a turning point. It was seen as a pioneering professional organisation for scientific journalism which held at the centre of its foundational discourse a rejection of the supposed intellectual 'aristocracy' of academic science. At the same time, the Cercle stressed the beat of the new popularisers to act independently of the academy.[82] The multiple arguments extolling the virtues of popularisation and the intention to offer a science for all, in France at least, concealed two broad images of science: the first orthodox, academic, standardised, mathematised, professional, with textbooks, elites and *grandes écoles*; the second heterodox, exhibited, explained, imagined, invested with noble aims and somewhat mystical

100 Heterodox science

and utopian.[83] Comte himself had been involved in this debate some years earlier, probably influenced by the fact that he was never accepted in professional academic circles. He often criticised the exaggerated academy of official science as being one of the problems in transmitting its new positive spirit to the public. Curiously enough, from that perspective, the success of popularisation lay to a large extent in its distance from orthodox science rather than to its proximity. Comte's positivist philosophy necessarily relied on a popular and supposedly more democratic, empirical science than the official, aristocratic and mathematised version. It was up to the experts to become popularisers, mediators and communicators, but it was also part of their duty.[84]

François Arago (1786–1853) achieved scientific prestige in Paris with his contributions to electricity, magnetism and light, as Director of the Paris Astronomical Observatory from 1813 to 1846, and especially as the perpetual secretary of the Académie des sciences from 1830 until his death. Arago was also very active in French politics and, as a republican, made a notable contribution to educational reform to bring knowledge closer to the lower classes. He gave his full support to freedom of the press and was a passionate defender of scientific progress. Like Comte, his *Astronomie populaire* was the result of his public courses, in this case at the Paris Observatory, where from 1813 he gave a series of lectures on astronomy that later made him famous. A brilliant speaker, capable of captivating audiences, his lectures were a popular social event that attracted large sectors of Parisian society, including women, children and dignitaries. Arago gave these lectures over a period of 30 years until 1846 (Figure 4.5).[85]

His objectives as a populariser were not that different from Comte's. Arago believed in the popularisation of science – partly because of the intellectual influence Alexander von Humboldt (1769–1859) had on him, but mainly because of his deep republican conviction of the democratisation of knowledge. He was a 'militant scientist' who believed that science would lead to greater political emancipation and the progressive democratisation of society. A climate of free and open debate would allow advancement towards a less aristocratic and more meritocratic society where the best would be judged by the public sphere and not from inbred circles of power.

Opening up the Académie sessions to the press led to a harsh confrontation with many of Arago's colleagues. For example, Jean-Baptiste Biot (1774–1862) criticised him for watering down the knowledge of the experts to a simplified (or distorted) version of topics that were difficult to understand, such as the wave theory of light, animal chemistry or spontaneous generation, to mention just some of the subjects being discussed at that time. In 1840, Italian mathematician Giuglielmo Libri (1802–69) published an article in the *Revue des deux mondes* where he set out his reasons against opening the doors of the Académie. Echoing some of the arguments of Arago's opponents, Libri believed that public political opinion was a real threat to orthodox science and could have too great an influence on professional scientists. In his view, the public could never understand the details of high-level research or rigorous mathematical language

FIGURE 4.5 François Arago in the Académie des sciences, Paris, in 1839. Louis Figuier, *Les merveilles de la science*, III, p. 41. Reproduced with permission of the Biblioteca de Catalunya (Barcelona).

and he endorsed an elitist 'Republic of Letters'.[86] Despite these hurdles, Arago contributed to the popularisation of science before a wide range of audiences: from the young people and children who came to his courses at the Observatory to professional astronomers interested in his communication strategies and scientific contributions. From his perspective, it was not a question of closing doors, as Biot had claimed, but allowing scientific knowledge to circulate freely in the French society of the mid-nineteenth century.

Professional scientists also became 'amateur' populariser. They would use it to complement their university salaries, together with any income they earned from the publication of manuals for their subjects or translations of foreign manuals. Similarly, many engineers were authors of books available to a large readership on electricity, mechanics and transport. However, there were other, more heterodox popularisers; authors without a solid scientific training, journalists,

102 Heterodox science

science writers, who were sometimes considered dilettantes or re-writers. They nevertheless played a very important role in nineteenth-century cultural life.

There were also other reasons for popularising. Humboldt's great intellectual work *Kosmos* from the first few decades of the nineteenth century was part of his obsession with giving the public an image of romantic fascination for the unity between man and nature that went beyond simple empirical descriptions; an image of a nature capable of purifying and pacifying the spirit. However, those values would change radically over the century and Humboldt's style soon disappeared. The heterodox view of a unifying nature was overtaken by the growing specialisation and professionalisation of science, which defined new and changing boundaries between experts and amateurs. Popularisation became a powerful weapon in a public sphere plagued by arguments and interests that did not always coincide.[87]

In France, the popularisers who managed to become professionals shared some common traits: a scientific training, journal editing, prolific writing, active speakers at public talks and exhibitions, frequent appearances in the daily press, an interest in education and promotion of libraries.[88] Despite his solid scientific training in chemistry, medicine and pharmacy, the weight of orthodox science fell heavily on Louis Figuier in 1856 when he was discredited in public as a result of an argument with Claude Bernard over the post-mortem secretion of sugar in the liver. This was a crucial turning point in Figuier's career and one that led him to dedicate himself fully to popularisation as a weapon against the esoteric nature of specialised scientific language. In 1856, he began publishing the *Année scientifique et industrielle*, a kind of almanac for the year's scientific advances, which would become a highly successful periodical across Europe. After that came the *Vies des savants illustres* (1866), *Les merveilles de la science* (1867), *Les merveilles de l'industrie* (1873), *Connais-toi toi-même: notions de physiologie* (1879), and the *Feuilletons scientifiques* in the press.[89]

In 1862, at the age of 20, Flammarion published the highly successful book *La pluralité des mondes habités*, emulating the old tradition of Fontanelle's *Entretiens*. But his initial attempts to combine his academic training in astronomy at the Paris Observatory with his popularisation activity seemed destined to failure. In 1866 the director of the observatory and Arago's successor, Urban Le Verrier (1811–77), brought the authority of orthodox science down on Flammarion and expelled him from that particular temple of science with the famous words: 'Monsieur, vous n'êtes pas savant mais poète' [Sir, you are not a scientist but a poet]. However, his publishing success continued unabated. Popular astronomy was a regular topic in his talks, evening classes, books, journal articles, periodicals and novels.[90]

Popularisers such as Flammarion were also operating in the grey area of pseudo-science and left the door wide open to spiritist and occultist practices. His popular success once again raised the issue of how to draw the line with orthodox science. The ensuing controversy is another good example of how scientific culture went yet again beyond the strict limits set out by the official science expert.

The simple hypothetic relationship with the dead through a medium was seen as a challenge to ecclesiastical authority, on the one hand, and to academic science, on the other.[91] It is interesting that some of the translations of Flammarion's work eliminated all references to spiritism from the text given the hostility that this doctrine attracted. Again, the publics of science carried significant weight when it came to legitimising or dismissing certain scientific practices.

In peripheral contexts of science, popularisation was often considered a useful and even priority strategy by many to bring the country into the new century. 'Science for all' could stimulate new callings in young people and lay down the foundations for the subsequent development of a solid scientific culture.[92] Even in leading countries like Germany, distinguished scientists such as Hermann von Helmholtz (1821–94) and Justus von Liebig (1803–73) would soon appreciate the importance of popularisation as a strategy for the social legitimation of the new, emerging experimental sciences. They demanded greater intellectual prestige and respect, especially in universities where they competed directly with the humanities and liberal arts.[93]

The corporate use of popularisation as a strategy for professional improvement also concealed the dissemination of some controversial and heterodox topics that were of great public interest. In fact, speculation about the possible existence of life on other planets came from the tradition of Fontenelle in the seventeenth century and was taken up again by Flammarion two centuries later. Other questionable topics were used to support arguments for or against professional science. The case of spontaneous generation, refuted by the late nineteenth-century science professional *par excellence*, Louis Pasteur, was used as an example by many major popularisers such as Victor Meunier (1817–1903), in his defence of Félix Pouchet (1800–72), who had confronted the all-powerful Pasteur from a much weaker position.[94]

Even Figuier speculated on the future of the soul. Meanwhile, as mentioned previously, others were discussing communication with the dead and spiritism, and all of them enjoyed considerable commercial success and large audiences in their frequent public lectures.[95] The popularisation of heterodox science largely succeeded in reinforcing its authority in the public sphere. This has been seen in detail in the case of astronomy but it can also be seen in phrenology, some aspects of romantic science (occult forces, holistic visions, emotions and inspiration in nature, anti-Newtonianism), medical questions related to animal magnetism and homeopathy. Recognition and social acceptance of heterodox scientists was inevitably linked to their ability to capture clients and gain an active public prepared to defend their methods, even though these clashed with those of the professionals.

Others attacked the orthodox science of their time head on for different reasons. Victor Meunier was convinced of the scientific aptitude of the public and systematically rejected any mediation between the experts and the supposedly ignorant masses.[96] A socialist militant and defender of a model of popularisation of science that did not necessarily depend on experts, Meunier stood for an

104 Heterodox science

independent journalism from the Académie, with a certain intellectual autonomy. These ideas were reflected in his *Science et démocratie* (1865), the result of several years of publishing in the daily press.[97] On a similar line to Arago's, and with a fervour worthy of Raspail, Meunier caricatured academic science in his *Scènes et types du monde savant* (1889) and advocated a new style of scientific article in the press. It would be more heterodox, more in accordance with utilitarian and philanthropic science that could make work easier, increase wealth or multiply communication, and be capable of speaking for the illiterate. It would educate them beyond simple entertainment, stimulating intellectual curiosity in readers who were otherwise considered ignorant by the academic elites. He made his position clear in the introduction to his *Essais scientifiques* from 1857:

> Yes, people, it is science that will bring you happiness. Do not listen to those who tell you it is difficult to access, high-flying, pretentious; they are imposters. Science is good, simple, human; science is divine beauty and eternal youth just like yours. If they try to distance you from it it is because they know very well that the generation that will born from your union with science will not be a pack of dogs but a nest of eagles.[98]

4.4. Popular science and religion

In the light of the growing influence of science in the public sphere in the nineteenth century, and its increasing rivalry with religion, many popularisers took very different stands. Victorian scientific naturalism, for instance, represented the English version of a general cult of science during the second half of the century, associated with scientific materialism.[99] This was a doctrine based on a mechanistic view of nature and a devout disciple of the Darwinian evolution. It was a worldview that clearly separated God from nature, subordinated spirit to matter and questioned religious orthodoxy at its very root.[100] Its defenders used evolutionism, atomism and energy conservation as the instruments to oppose the dominant clerical culture; a missile to fire against religion and a strategy to reinforce professional scientists based on naturalist principles.[101]

It was within that context in Britain that the BAAS played a moderating role for the controversies and disagreements among the clergy themselves in the face of the growing influence of scientific naturalism.[102] Every author approached evolutionism, or the account of the history of life and the cosmos, in their own way. It was a very popular subject, as seen previously in *Vestiges*. Authors like Samuel Butler, Richard Proctor and Thomas Huxley gave some very good examples in their analyses of how to negotiate scientific authority through popularisation. Other lesser-known names with a clear amateur status clung to Anglican natural theology or used the press and the many popular science magazines to stake their place in the public sphere of Victorian science.[103]

Heterodox science **105**

From an anticlerical position, Darwinism also acted as a strong stimulus for the popularisation of the natural sciences. The case of Odón de Buen (1863–1945) is well known. His vocation to become a populariser was largely a result of his being temporarily suspended as professor at the University of Barcelona in 1895, precisely as a result of his Darwinian teachings. In the preface of his *Historia natural popular*, he responded with comments such as: 'I have published this popular edition, which I have been preparing for a long time, quickly as a response to the urgent pressure I have received from the public, keen to see the work anathematized by the Catholic Church ... to make positive science to reach the heart of the people'.[104] Similarly, the popularisers of Darwinism in unified Italy at the end of the nineteenth century are worth noting. Tensions between Antonio Stoppani (1824–91), a clergyman and geologist, and Paolo Mantegazza (1831–1910), freemason, anti-cleric and follower of Darwin, or the publications of Giovanni Canestrini (1835–1900), translator and populariser of Darwin for the bourgeois elite, followed a similar pattern. Unlike de Buen, Mantegazza managed to become a professional full-time populariser of science, while the former kept on his professorship in addition to his hugely important work as a populariser, imbued, as in Arago's and Meunier's cases, with a profound political commitment.[105]

Despite the growing polarisation, some still praised the compatibility between science, or the natural philosophy of the time, and the dominant cultural values of religion.[106] The *Bridgewater Treatises* case is iconic in this regard.[107] The full title itself is already a good guide as to its contents: *The Bridgewater Treatises on the Power, Wisdom and Goodness of God as Manifested in the Creation under the Auspices of the Earl of Bridgewater and Written by Seven Leading Men of Science, Together with One Prominent Theological Commentator*.[108] This was a set of very popular books published between 1833 and 1836; widely distributed it probably made up for the lack of textbooks in Britain at the time, presenting an image of science acceptable to the professional middle classes. Its combination of natural theology and popular science attracted a large number of readers, even reaching the working classes through public comments and talks. There were several editions with more than 60,000 copies printed in 1850 and hundreds of reviews in newspapers and magazines.[109] In the context of natural theology, religious evangelisation through scientific 'evangelisation', which showed the wonders of the world and their divine creation, seemed to form part of a single strategy. It sought a compromise between orthodoxy and heterodoxy from both a religious and a scientific perspective.

In another attempt to moderate and integrate these opposing views, Flammarion rejected the materialism of the *philosophes*, but also criticised the radicalism of the Catholic Church. For him, the scientists of the time believed neither in God nor the soul, but only in chemical combinations of matter, while the burden of ancient dogmas distanced the Catholic Church from society. Flammarion hoped to develop a 'religion by science', a positive philosophy that included aspects of natural theology, and allowed contemporary materialism to be rejected from a midpoint between atheism and religious fanaticism.

106 Heterodox science

Flammarion's popular astronomy therefore became a kind of effective balm for soothing the tensions between science and religion in a rhetorical argument that extended to other works of science.[110] It justified the genre as an efficient means of diffusing the wonders of nature in society and indirectly reinforcing and dignifying the act of divine creation. Flammarion dealt with a popular astronomy with its own epistemology. He considered the topic beyond a simple literary adaptation of the experts' discourse and as dignified as physical-mathematical astronomy.[111] In his opinion, popular wisdom about the stars was not rigidly deposited among the people and separated from the experts and professionals, but astronomical observations and data circulated freely through all the different social classes.

Growing interest in heterodox practices such as spiritism and somnambulism, mediums and ghosts, also responded to the attempt to reconcile science and religion, something that scientific naturalism and the anticlerical reactions in numerous public addresses had called seriously into question.[112] So at a time when science popularisation had contributed to strengthening the 'wonders' of modern science through the works of Figuier and Flammarion, at an age when physics, physiology and psychology were gaining considerable ground and when there was a strong re-emergence of romantic influences, occult practices found a comfortable space to develop and become public.[113]

Social, political and reformist tensions stimulated the publication of popular science magazines to provide readers with 'interesting' information and distract them from other, more dangerous, politically subversive and often anticlerical texts. The British magazine *The Penny Mechanic*, for example, confirmed that the study of physical and natural science tended to improve moral and intellectual behaviour, calm the spirit and reduce tensions and the inability to control passions.[114]

In Spain, scientists, intellectuals and politicians used the book *Teorías modernas de la física* [Modern Theories in Physics] in their articles, textbooks and public lectures. It was written by scientist, and Nobel Prize of Literature winner, José Echegaray (1832–1916), who was one of Spain's great intellectuals at the end of the nineteenth century. Echegaray tried to offer a simple and entertaining explanation of the new scientific theories of light and electricity, from a conception of mechanics and the unity of material forces but together with the figure of God the creator. Several Catholic leaders coincided with Echegaray in the need to shun heterodoxy and the dangers of scientific materialism in thermodynamics.[115] Echegaray's book, however, existed alongside texts that criticised religion and defended materialist views of nature. This was the case with *Kraft und Stoff* (*Force and Matter*) (1868) by the German physician Ludwig Büchner (1824–99),[116] or the articles by Irish populariser John Tyndall (1820–93),[117] which took the conservation of energy as proof of a universe ruled exclusively by natural laws, without the need for the existence of a god as creator. A large number of these texts, which were markedly anticlerical in tone, were used and diffused by republicans, socialists and anarchists.

Heterodox science **107**

In a context that was hostile to scientific materialism and faced with the growing threat to workers' movements, a significant number of popularisers used religion as an instrument for social order and control. One of the strategies consisted in seeking some kind of compatibility between popularised science and dominant cultural values, and resulted in the need to avoid materialism and restore the idea of God. Not only did thermodynamics present a potential materialist danger, it also offered the chance to scientifically demonstrate the existence of God and the immortality of the soul.[118]

It was common to find scientific publications making great celebration of the religious appropriation of a scientific fact. For example, in France, the *Encyclopédie theólogique* by Jacques-Paul Migne (1800–75), known as Abbé Migne, tried to adapt and popularise science for a faithful and safe audience of Catholic clerics. Aware of their lack of scientific background, they sought a training that would be compatible with their Christian faith. The text of the *Encyclopédie theólogique* reveals a certain fear among the clerics given their ignorance of science and their personal distancing from it. In fact, none of the authors of the articles in that *Encyclopédie* were professional scientists willing to pass on the result of their own research to a world of Christian believers. For Migne the aim of the publication was clear: the religion of the time was not one of science and the science of the time was not religious. So they had to work both ways: to bring Catholic thinking as close as possible to modern science, and at the same time analyse scientific concepts to try to identify in them a latent Catholicism, in a kind of positive, and possibly utopian, feedback between science and religion. The purposes of the *Encyclopédie* were, among others, an exaltation of papal power, the fight against Masonic secret societies and the defence of miracles and traditions, combined with an interest in other supernatural phenomena, not to mention the fight against Protestantism, the physical-chemical reductionism of life, atomism, scientific materialism and the idea of a modern science associated with the secular values of the French Revolution. All in all it was a true battle for cultural hegemony in the public sphere.[119]

The potential for emancipation that experimental science presented was obviously a concern for the Church authorities and their popularisers, hence the attempts to appropriate scientific ideas and deliver them to the public according to their own interests. That, for instance, was one of the strategies of the Jesuits. During the opening decades of the twentieth century a considerable number of its members received advanced scientific training which they could later use to contribute to research, teaching and also popularisation. Jesuit scientific journals such as *Brotéria* in Portugal and *Ibérica* in Spain played a crucial role in developing a new synthesis between Catholicism and modernisation (modern science) in the struggle for cultural hegemony. In spite of its popular, didactic character, *Brotéria* contributed substantially to current knowledge on zoology, botany, biochemistry and molecular genetics in Portugal, but it also became an excellent strategy for restoring the Jesuits reputation in Portugal throughout the nineteenth and twentieth centuries. *Ibérica* was founded in 1914 by a group of Jesuits

108 Heterodox science

in the Observatori de l'Ebre, in Catalonia. Its combination of popular science and basic research led to a weekly circulation of about 10,000 copies in the 1920s, and became a very useful material for the introduction of scientific subjects in Jesuit curricula. Popular science was aimed at reinforcing scientific training in the numerous Jesuit teaching institutions, while offering an image of science that was coherent with Catholic dogma.[120] A positive rather than problematic image of science emerged. Once again, winning over the public was directly related to certain interests and ideological positions, such as the desire to draw a line between the orthodox from the heterodox from a specific viewpoint.

4.5. Popularisation, distortion or simplification

Is it possible to justify certain heterodox practices which aim to seduce their respective audiences, even if they lie outside the orthodox science at a certain time and place? Is it possible to popularise scientific knowledge without distorting or simplifying it? As some of the previous examples, mainly from the nineteenth century, have shown, these are difficult and controversial questions. Observing the profiles and discourses of the well-known science popularisers throughout the twentieth century presents the dilemma of where simplification ends and distortion begins; where the popularisers' complicity ends and their mistrust in orthodox science begins.

In the last century a large group of science popularisers with different training and backgrounds gradually established important areas of influence. Detailed analysis of some of them clearly identifies multiple overlaps between the orthodox and the heterodox, from their initial training to their discourses and popularisation strategies. The use of new mass media communication would seem to be a conclusive reason for separating these authors from their past counterparts. However, from further analysis of their popularisation programmes, Hilgartner's dominant view re-emerges. It shows the complexity of the popularisers' intentions and their relationship to professional scientists. Below are some examples.

In 1894 the Austrian engineer Hanns Hoerbiger (1860–1931) forwarded a heterodox theory (*Welteislehre*) which suggested that a large part of the universe was made of ice. Hoerbiger had combined his training as an engineer with his interest in astronomy and, like the amateurs in many European societies, he used a small telescope to observe the heavenly bodies in his spare time, especially the Moon, whose bright surface particularly caught his eye and formed the basis of his hypothesis about the existence of ice. In his book *Glazial-Kosmogonie*, Hoerbiger described how a collision of stars would have produced a large explosion. The smallest fragments would have been expelled into interstellar space and the water would have condensed to form giant blocks of ice. These would have formed the origin of the solar system, including our own, which would have undergone a long process of evolution. Although it was harshly criticised at the time by a large part of the scientific community, who considered it an absurd idea promoted by a charlatan, *Welteislehre* enjoyed great success in the public sphere from 1920 to 1930 and was even used as propaganda by the Nazis as an example of 'pure' German science. Hoerbiger used maps, schemes, graphs and tables to spread his theory and give it 'objective facts' which, together with the illustrations, drawings and photographs, presented the science as a spectacular field of fantasy and visual sensations.[121]

There are other examples of this kind of 'objectivity of fiction', capable of fascinating readers and spectators. It could be considered heterodox in the context of the academic science of its time but it often contributed to reinforce the public authority of the experts. This was for example the case of writer Edgar Rice Burroughs (1875–1950), the creator of Tarzan and author of the famous work of fiction *The Land that Time Forgot* (1918), which borrowed inspiration from Sir Arthur Conan Doyle's *The Lost World* (1912) and Jules Verne's *The Mysterious Island* (1874) and *Journey to the Center of the Earth* (1864). By the 1910s, *Tarzan of the Apes* had sold millions of copies. Meanwhile the director of the American Museum of Natural History, Henry Osborn (1857–1935), carried out a massive reconstruction of the struggle for survival of the ancient dinosaurs, including Brontosaurus and Tyrannosaurus Rex. He was assisted by painters such as *National Geographic* illustrator Charles Knight. Osborn was also an indefatigable traveller who collected rare specimens and fossils for his museum. Knight's illustrations in the museum inspired Burroughs to write his novel *The Land That Time Forgot*, later taken to the big screen and television, which described in a wealth of detail fictional creatures in a permanent struggle for survival. With certain heterodoxy and a good deal of imagination, he presented animals and humans of the past, but maintained a conservative position that tacitly assumed the superiority of the Caucasian race. Its public success was indisputable.[122]

The controversy among contemporaries of Albert Einstein (1879–1955) over whether his theory of relativity could be made accessible to the public at large is well known. Unlike Einstein himself, and claiming as their argument the extreme difficulty in understanding his postulates, some considered that any attempt to simplify Einstein's work was useless, while others emphasised some aspects that were not strictly scientific and which would in time represent his forceful public image. While the great figures of science such as Einstein were seen as pure and exceptional individuals, separated from other mortals in their ivory towers, as a counterbalance to the public's inevitable ignorance, the new quantum and relativist physics were viewed by many as a heterodox attack on common sense and intuition.

The 1930 *Encyclopédie française* described the problem from a historical perspective, arguing that in the eighteenth century there had simply been a difference in style between expert and lay knowledge. In the nineteenth century this became a difference in language, but by the twentieth, two incommensurable and irreconcilable worlds had been constructed. In France, the historian Hélène Metzger (1889–1944) claimed that all knowledge that could not be expressed in a single language and was not accessible to everyone should be considered

110 Heterodox science

superfluous. Émile Meyerson (1859–1933) used the theory of relativity as an iconic example of the impossibility of explaining scientific concepts through day-to-day experiences and common sense as an obvious example of the victory of the *episteme* over the *doxa*, an argument that would be taken up some years later by Bachelard.[123]

There was no consensus over this question. The fact that Einstein was awarded the Nobel Prize for Physics in 1921 for his discovery of the law of the photo-electric effect was good enough proof of the resistance to the theory of relativity within the Nobel jury itself.[124] However, Einstein, Paul Langevin (1872–1946), Louis de Broglie (1892–1987) and other eminent physicists opted decisively to explain their new theories to a broader public.[125] From the *annus mirabilis* of 1905 to the general theory of relativity in 1915, Einstein had gone through a process of complex intellectual maturation which did not exclude the diffusion of his ideas to lay audiences during the process of their creation. In fact, Metzger was convinced that any kind of simple explanation designed for the general public could not be considered heterodox since it contained useful ideas for the work of the experts.

The need to wipe the slate clean of Newtonian physics to present his new theory brought Einstein closer to the popular language. His popular texts were largely written in parallel to his intellectual work. The 1917 text was republished 14 times and widely translated between 1917 and 1923. But it was his article 'My Theory', which appeared in *The Times* on 28 November 1919, that catapulted him to fame worldwide. He would receive the Nobel Prize just two years later. Also in 1919, the astronomer Frank Dyson (1868–1939) made a series of observations during an eclipse in an attempt to demonstrate the phenomenon of the curvature of light when it passes through a black body. The result had a resounding impact in the media, especially *The Times* and the *New York Times*, which took the opportunity to celebrate with their readers Einstein's triumph over Newton. However, historians of science have since reconstructed Dyson's astronomical observations and concluded they were not as clearly in favour of Einstein's relativity as the press had made out.[126]

When Einstein visited Paris in the spring of 1922 the controversies about his theory of relativity inundated the public arena. Four different positions were identified in the city: active enthusiasm and support as a result of the new physics; sceptical neutrality; active ignorance which claimed that the theory was not at all necessary; and direct hostility. Curiously, the more radical positions of support and enthusiasm and total rejection were expressed loudest in public while the more watered-down views were held in discreet silence. The debate attracted large sectors of Parisian society, but the gossip that emerged as a result of the visit eclipsed a rigorous discussion of the light and shadows of the new physics.[127]

Dyson's observations, the positions of the French popularisers and the impact of his visits are just small examples of Einstein's public persona throughout the twentieth century; an impact that undoubtedly transcended the strict content of his physical theories. Behind the famous $E=mc^2$ were intense arguments about the limits, if there were any, of the popularisation of science, the criteria by which to draw the line between simplification and distortion and the continuity or discontinuity between the epistemology of the elite (or the geniuses) and popular wisdom.

During the peak of Einstein's popularity, James Gerald Crowther (1899–1983) was a pioneering supporter of the emergence of professional scientific journalism in Britain. With little interest in pure mathematics, he had left Cambridge without obtaining his degree and became a secondary school teacher, as well as a regular speaker on scientific matters and a publishing consultant. In 1928 he was appointed as a science writer for the *Manchester Guardian*, an important new position in British journalism at that time. In the 1930s Crowther gained a great reputation, to the point where many professional scientists became keen readers of his columns and new science audiences, interested in the future of other specialist areas on which they did not consider themselves to be experts. He published works of popularisation to great success, such as *An Outline of the Universe* (1931) and *The ABC of Chemistry* (1932). Influenced by Marxist thinking and a close collaborator with prestigious historians of British science who embraced the same ideology such as John Bernal and Joseph Needham,[128] Crowther formulated his own ideology and its relation to science in the book *The Social Relations of Science* (1941). As Director of the British Council, he made a significant contribution to bringing German scientists fleeing the Nazi regime to Britain. After the Second World War his influence declined but he never abandoned his ideology or his criticism of the use of science in capitalist countries.

Crowther also contributed to the circulation of scientific information among different groups of experts. He spread an image of science that was far from neutral politically speaking and its supposed 'autonomy' with regard to society (a key point in the traditional view of science popularisation). However, from their obsession to define clear boundaries of scientific authority, others turned popularisation into a weapon against heterodox science and pseudo-science. This was the case of Carl Sagan (1934–96), a physicist with a PhD in astronomy and astrophysics, who combined his academic work with space projects in NASA (Mariner, Apollo, Pioneer, Voyager), while remaining a militant pacifist and environmentalist, albeit from a strong scientific standing as his work *The Demon-Haunted World: Science as a Candle in the Dark* (1995) demonstrates. In his attempt to explain the scientific method to laypeople, Sagan strongly emphasised the sharp distinction between valid science and pseudo-science, which had to be tested by rigorous thinking and questioning. Following his initial success in popularisation, such as *The Dragons of Eden* (1978), in 1979 he embarked on a groundbreaking project for the popularisation of astronomy on television. The 'Cosmos' series was watched by over 500 million people in 60 countries. He also continued to write science fiction.[129]

Other popularisers, such as John Emsley, remained closer to orthodox science in an attempt to gain public legitimation. Emsley taught chemistry at King's College, London, until he began a career as a populariser, frequently appearing in

112 Heterodox science

the press and on radio and television. He eventually became a professional science populariser and an associate of the Department of Chemistry at Cambridge University. In his books, he continually attempts to connect important aspects of scientific knowledge, chemistry in particular, to elements of daily life and in doing so improve its public image, which had been so badly damaged during the second half of the twentieth century.[130] *Molecules of Murder* (2008) is a chemical account of the great poisoning cases in history; *Better Looking, Better Living, Better Loving* (2007) offers a simple description of products that can improve our health, eating habits and material wellbeing. *The Consumer's Good Chemical Guide* (1994), winner of the Rhone Poulenc Science Book Prize in 1995, gives details of perfumes, sweeteners, fats, fibres, dioxins and plastics in an attempt to shake off the misconceptions that many members of the public have about these products and thereby legitimate the work of professional scientists, especially in industry. *The Elements* (1998) takes up the icon of the periodical table as a key topic for the public image of chemistry in society today. It includes a meticulous description of the properties, history, applications and anecdotes of each element in a similar line to previous attempts at popularisation, such as that of Isaac Asimov. Also along the same line is *Nature's Building Blocks: An A–Z Guide to the Elements* (2011), which continues to sell in the 'Popular Science' collection of Oxford University Press.[131]

Far from the old traditions of natural theology, popularisation of evolution contributed greatly to the opposition to religious orthodoxy and repeated attempts to return to creationism in the twentieth century. Richard Dawkins, who teaches 'Public Understanding of Science' at Oxford University, shot to fame following his 1976 publication *The Selfish Gene*, which offered a wide readership a new view of evolution centred on genetics, while maintaining his own academic contributions on the subject. Dawkins had been a staunch opponent of intelligent design, especially in his book *The Blind Watchmaker* (1986), where, in an analogy of the ancient Platonic visionary who supposedly created the world, the watchmaker's blindness makes him a minor character by force of fate, mutations and natural selection. His most recent book, *The God Delusion* (2006), follows a similar line and has become one of the biggest best sellers in popularisation of our time. The English version has sold more than 1.5 million copies and has been translated into more than 30 languages.[132]

Similarly, despite the importance of his academic texts and his expert profile (he contributed to the evolutionary theory of 'punctuated equilibrium' as opposed to phyletic gradualism), some of the main ideas of Stephen Jay Gould (1942–2002) on evolution were originally published in popularisation articles. Gould provided a friendly open door to evolutionary theories for the millions of people allowing them to understand and appreciate the work of Darwin and his followers. Gould studied geology at the University of Columbia and in 1967 he was appointed Curator of the Invertebrate Palaeontology at the Harvard Museum of Comparative Zoology and would later go on to become Professor of Geology at the same university.[133]

★ ★ ★

All these cases highlight aspects that can be described as the popular scientific culture in the twentieth century. These are authors and works that go beyond the old printed science or spectacular science, now diffused through a range of media and in diverse formats to reach millions of readers, viewers, listeners and internet users. Protected to a greater or lesser extent by the academic umbrella and by their original scientific training, they forged alliances with both the public and the private sectors to extend their discourses throughout the public sphere, often with very different ideologies and working programmes: the crusade against the supposed dangers of the so-called pseudo-science and heterodox science (which form part of the cultural discontent of the twentieth century that is dealt with in this book); the rejection of creationism and religious orthodoxy (with echoes of the secular and anticlerical programmes of some of the nineteenth-century popularisers); the passionate defence of the environment and criticism of the abuses and risks of our scientific development; and the public softening of chemistry as a strategy to clean up its image as a science all too frequently associated with contamination and aloofness from nature.

Far from a supposed philanthropy and naïve generosity, the popularisation projects of the nineteenth century (and also those of the twentieth) adhered to ideological, moral and religious positions, specific economic and corporate interests, and bitter struggles for cultural hegemony. With a fresh appeal to the flexibility of the definition of 'public', this is a good time to recall that each of us has an accumulation of both expert but also lay attitudes and beliefs, both the professionals and the amateurs. Or perhaps we are simply curious, an attitude that is fundamental for audiences receptive to the great discourses of popularisation, but at the same time critical and capable of making interesting objections on any topic. If the public is never stupid, then we are all heterodox amateurs to a greater or lesser extent. History also teaches us how Lavoisier the aristocrat, Darwin the traveller, Faraday the lecturer and Einstein the poor student, among many others, navigated the turbulent waters of ambiguous orthodoxy back in their day.

It may seem paradoxical that in offering the public detailed and apparently interesting and accessible information on a wide range of scientific topics the professional status of academic science is subtly reinforced, as are the boundaries between the orthodox and the heterodox. This is, perhaps, one of the hidden causes of the persistent discontent of scientific culture, despite these enterprises' vast capacity for popularisation. Perhaps overcoming this discontent entails, among other things, a revision of the heterodox and a new permeability between boundaries and categories which, until now, have been too watertight.[134]

Notes

1 Darnton (1968: 21).
2 Darnton (1968).
3 Figuier (1881: 334).

114 Heterodox science

4 'Que le charlatan Mesmer/Avec un autre frater/Guérisse mainte femelle/Qu'il en tourne la cervelle/En les tâtant ne sais où/C'est fou/Très fous/Et je n'y crois pas du tout/Vieilles, jeunes, laides, belles/Toutes aiment le docteur/Et toutes lui sont fidèles'. Cited by Darnton (1968: 58).

5 'Jamais les effets du magnétisme ne m'ont autant frappé; si quelque chose achève de me confirmer l'existence d'un fluide universel, agent unique par les diverses modifications de tant de phénomènes divers, ce sera ma machine électrique. Elle me parle le même langage que Mesmer sur la nature, et je l'écoute avec ravissement'. Cited by Darnton (1968: 60).

6 'Les seuls témoins qu'on doive croire sur les faits extraordinaires sont deux qui en sont les juges compétents. Il [existe], dit-on, un fluide universel dont les effets s'étendent depuis les astres les plus éloignés jusqu'à la terre. Eh bien, je n'y puis croire que sur l'autorité des physiciens ... parce que je dois me défier alors de l'imagination et l'imposture. Ce fluide guérit les malades sans les toucher ou en les touchant, alors j'ai besoin que les médecins m'attestent la maladie et la guérison', Condorcet, 'Raisons qui m'ont empêché jusqu'ici de croire au magnétisme animal', Institut de France, ms 883, fol. 231–47 (1784–5). Cited by Darnton (1968: 199–200).

7 Gillispie (1980).

8 Winter (1994: 317).

9 van Wyhe (2007).

10 Dinges (2002).

11 Debus (1987); Wallis (1979).

12 Gieryn (1983).

13 Jasanoff (2005).

14 Cohen, Drouin (1989: 7–10).

15 Berman (1975); Desmond (2001).

16 Jütte, Risse, Woodward (1998); Haller (2009).

17 Numbers (1977: 56–62).

18 Numbers (1977: 55).

19 Numbers (1977: 62–8).

20 Poirier, Langlois (1992: 10).

21 Among the important scientific works published during his first period are *Essai de chimie microscopique* (1830); *Nouveau système de chimie organique* (1833); *Nouveau système de physiologie végétale* (1837).

22 Raspail (1847).

23 Bertomeu-Sánchez, Nieto-Galan (2006).

24 Raspail (1876: 30, 35). Translated from the Spanish edition.

25 Raspail (1847); Bertomeu-Sánchez (2014).

26 Poirier, Langlois (1992: 40).

27 Ramsey (1999: 287–8).

28 Ramsey (1999: 290).

29 '[I]t has often been hard to draw a clear external boundary between professionals and laity battling it out in the medical marketplace ... Official medicine is a social and cultural construction ... within the public sphere', Ramsey (1999: 289).

30 Winter (1991).

31 Fox (1988).

32 Nicholls (1988, 2001).

33 See for instance the Spanish book: (1857) *Los cuatro métodos curativos, o sea Manual de higiene y de medicina popular que comprende los sistemas de Raspail, Leroy, Morrison y Holloway, acompañados de un resumen de homeopatia*, Barcelona: Luis Tasso.

34 Ibid.

35 Cassedy (1977: 42).

36 Timmermann (2001).

37 Gaudillière, Hess (2013).

38 Andries (1992).

39 Lenoir (1997).
40 Cooter, Pumphrey (1994: 251).
41 Nieto-Galan (2009); Bigg (2010).
42 Ruiz-Castell (2008); Nieto-Galan (2009).
43 Perhaps with the exception of Victorian Britain, this statement can be generalised. Chapman (1998).
44 As Anne Secord argued convincingly some years ago, at least in early nineteenth-century Britain, artisans were more than mere providers of specimens to elite botanists. Secord (1994: 299).
45 Kargon (1977: 11).
46 James (2002: 251).
47 Sheets-Pyenson (1985).
48 Lankford (1981a, b).
49 Nieto-Galan (2009).
50 Bensaude-Vincent (1991: 58–9).
51 Nieto-Galan (2009); Chapman (1998).
52 Myers (2003).
53 Chapman (1998).
54 Golinski (1999).
55 Coen (2013).
56 Gomis (1987).
57 Among his works, it is worth mentioning: *Lo llamp y'ls temporals* (1884); *Meteorologia y agricultura populars ab gran nombre de confrontacions* (1888); *Botànica popular* (1891); *Rudimentos de agricultura española* (1900); *Zoologia popular catalana* (1910); *La lluna segons lo poble* (1912). The latter had already been published in 1884 in short articles in the periodical *L'Avens*.
58 Gomis (1884: 15). Translated from the Catalan edition.
59 Tissandier (1883: 747–56).
60 Tissandier (1883).
61 Ruiz-Castell (2008).
62 Lankford (1981a).
63 Secord (1994).
64 Secord (1996: 380).
65 Drouin, Bensaude-Vincent (1996).
66 Shteir (1996, 1997).
67 Pyenson, Sheets-Pyenson (1999: 159).
68 Ibid., 336.
69 Higgitt, Withers (2008).
70 Pyenson, Sheets-Pyenson (1999: 337, 347–9).
71 Drouin, Bensaude-Vincent (1996: 417–18).
72 Ibid.
73 For information about taxidermists see, for example, Nyhart (2009).
74 Hochadel (2010).
75 Star, Griesemer (1989). For more on boundary objects see Gieryn (1983).
76 See for example Taylor (2009).
77 Pyenson, Sheets-Pyenson (1999: 227–8).
78 It also coincided with the time of the launch of the first artificial satellite, the Soviet *Sputnik* in October 1957.
79 McCray (2006).
80 Bensaude-Vincent, Rasmussen (1997: 17).
81 Béguet (1990); Daum (1998).
82 For more on French popularisers, see Benedic (1994).
83 Bensaude-Vincent (1989: 3–6).
84 Petit (1989).

116 Heterodox science

85 Dörries (2000: 47); Nieto-Galan (2009).
86 Dörries (2000).
87 Bayertz (1985); Daum (1998); Hilgartner (1990).
88 Béguet (1990: 35).
89 Béguet (1990).
90 Bensaude-Vincent (1989: 94).
91 Treitel (2000: 128).
92 Nieto-Galan (2009).
93 Bayertz (1985); Daum (1998).
94 Latour (1988).
95 Fox (1988).
96 Bensaude-Vincent (1989).
97 Glaser (1989).
98 'Oui, peuple, c'est la science qui te conduira au bonheur. N'écoute pas ceux qui te la représentent comme étant d'un accès difficile, hautaine, prétentieuse, ce sont des imposteurs. La science et bonne, simple, humaine; la science est belle d'une beauté divine et comme la tienne sa jeunesse est éternelle. Et s'ils essaient de t'en éloigner, c'est qu'ils savent bien que la génération qui naîtra de ton union avec elle ne sera pas une portée des chiens, mais une nichée d'aigles'. Cited by Glaser (1989: 32).
99 'Victorian scientific naturalism represented the English version of a general cult of science that swept across Europe during the second half of the century and that was associated with the names of Renan, Taine, Bernard, Büchner, and Haeckel, as well as with various forms of scientific materialism and scientific socialism'. Turner (1974: 13).
100 Turner (1974: 15).
101 Turner (1980: 591).
102 'The particular genius of the BAAS lay in its ability to serve as an instrument of public order and social cohesion while at the same time smoothing over the contradictions and internal tensions that characterized scientific clergy'. Morrell, Thackray (1981: 20).
103 Lightman (2007a).
104 De Buen (1896: xvii), translated from the Spanish edition; Nieto-Galan (2012a).
105 Govoni (2002).
106 Shapin (1990: 999).
107 Treatise I, by Thomas Chalmers. *The Adaptation of External Nature to the Moral and Intellectual Constitution of Man.* 2 vols; Treatise II, by John Kidd. *On the Adaptation of External Nature to the Physical Condition of Man*; Treatise III, by William Whewell. *On Astronomy and General Physics*; Treatise IV, by Charles Bell. *The Hand: Its Mechanism and Vital Endowments as Evincing Design*; Treatise V, by Peter Mark Roget. *Animal and Vegetable Physiology Considered with Reference to Natural Theology.* 2 vols; Treatise VI, by William Buckland. *Geology and Mineralogy Considered with Reference to Natural Theology.* 2 vols; Treatise VII, by William Kirby. *On the History Habits and Instincts of Animals.* 2 vols; Treatise VIII, by William Prout. *Chemistry, Meteorology, and the Function of Digestion.* Topham (1992: 398).
108 Topham (1992).
109 Topham (1992: 397–8).
110 Nieto-Galan (2009).
111 Bensaude-Vincent (1989).
112 Bensaude-Vincent, Blondel (2002: 5–17).
113 Bensaude-Vincent, Blondel (2002: 16).
114 Pyenson, Sheets-Pyenson (1999: 226–7).
115 Pohl (2009).
116 Gregory (1977); Kockerbeck (1999).
117 Lightman, Reidy (2014).
118 Pohl (2009).
119 Langlois, Laplanche (1992); Nieto-Galan (2011b).
120 Udías (2003); Herran (2012); Romeiras (2015).

Heterodox science **117**

121 Wessely (2006).
122 Kruger, Mayer, Sommer (2008).
123 Bensaude-Vincent (1987: 72–4). Meyerson was responsible for ensuring that Metzger was never appointed to an academic position in France.
124 Hedfors (2007: 50–1).
125 Bensaude-Vincent (1997: 328–9).
126 Gregory, Miller (1998: 141).
127 Biezunski (1985).
128 Chilvers (2003).
129 Doel, Söderqvist (2006). In particular, for Carl Sagan, see Davidson (1999).
130 Bensaude-Vincent, Van Tiggelen, Schummer (2007).
131 'John Emsley. Welcome to My World of Chemistry', http://www.johnemsley.com/ (accessed 18 June 2015).
132 Dawkins is a classic example of a 'global' populariser of science of our time as can be seen at 'Richard Dawkins Foundation for Reason and Science', https://richarddawk ins.net/ (accessed 18 June 2015).
133 Sterelny (2001); Kelley, Ross, Allmon (2008).
134 Gyerin (1983).

5

CLASSROOM SCIENCE

As Ludwik Fleck stressed decades ago, scientists become experts through a long process of learning in which for years they have been students, laypeople, audiences and active agents in classroom culture, in the exchange of opinions between teachers and students.[1] Equally, outside the official courses and corresponding subject programmes, learning mechanisms are full of hidden intentions, tacit knowledge, unexplained values and rituals and mechanisms for discipline and a critical acceptance of it. Different kinds of science education have taken place at specific places and times which have had a greater influence than we thought in the making of scientific knowledge.[2]

Fleck described the learning process in three stages: experience, sensation and cognition. Experience could never be based on previous suppositions; sensation inevitably required previous learning; and finally, cognition was, in his opinion, a social and group activity – in other words, a further manifestation of the *Denkkollectiv*, in which he adapted his esoteric and exoteric circles to an educational context.[3] Fleck was also convinced that an initiation to scientific knowledge for anyone, including the great figures, was based on the training they received, the central role of science teachers and teaching methods themselves. To what point have the teachers who have marked the intellectual paths of many of the great names in Western science been fundamental in the capacity of their brilliant students to move successfully between the circles? This is a difficult question to answer but there is no doubt that Fleck's model allows the students, so often considered secondary and even irrelevant from an epistemological point of view, to come to the fore.

Perhaps the emerging scientific disciplines, from the university specialities of the nineteenth century to the new bio- and nano-technosciences of the present day, have established themselves and gained ground largely because they were taught, and their teaching is not a simple and logical consequence of their

Classroom science **119**

previous existence. This is a good argument for rethinking the history of science from a teaching perspective, where both teachers and students are active participants in continual negotiation. The following sections of this chapter aim to look further into this question.

5.1. Education and scientific culture

The history of Western knowledge is largely the history of its teaching. Students of philosophy and other disciplines are familiar with the description of the great presuppositions of the ancient civilisations, particularly the Greek philosophers. The aim of this book is not to become bogged down along the difficult path of ancient and medieval history, but it is sometimes worth exploring some of the more distant historical roots of the problems considered here. For instance, the Hippocratic School of the fifth century BC and its contribution to defining the limits of professional medicine throughout history is well known. We have also heard of the Pythagorean School, although little is known about its sociological composition. In Ancient Greece, names like Plato and Aristotle, or Zeno and Epicurus, are impossible to ignore, but very few have questioned what exactly happened in the sites of learning of these four sages in the city of Athens, known respectively as the Academy, the Lyceum, the Stoa and the Garden. Plato's dialogues would be difficult to understand outside the intellectual setting of democratic Athens and fruitful debate among equals, but also between masters and disciples. A case in point is the peripatetic discussions that Aristotle had with his students. The financial independence the ancient philosophers earned from their schools is one explanation for their intellectual freedom and creativity.[4] The intellectual contributions of the Library and Museum of Alexandria are also impossible to contemplate without considering their teaching nature.[5] From the distant past, a clear line between knowledge creation and knowledge diffusion seems questionable.

Similarly, the intellectual history of the Middle Ages cannot be appreciated outside the context of growing urbanisation and the emergence of universities from the thirteenth century onwards, mainly in the context of the ancient Roman tradition of *trivium* and *quadrivium*.[6] The *lectio* and *disputatio*, the famous Paris condemnations of 1277 and other major episodes which are essential to a fundamental understanding of medieval philosophy took place within teaching contexts.[7] So, what if Albertus, Buridan, Ockham and Bacon, among others, had depended more on their students intellectually than we thought? In his attempt to explain Western scientific hegemony over that of China and Islam, sociologist Toby Huff has suggested that only in the medieval Christian universities there was a 'neutral zone'. In that sense, teaching practices enjoyed sufficient freedom to openly discuss diverging natural philosophies which, over time, stimulated the emergence of modern science in the sixteenth and seventeenth centuries.[8]

These glimpses of freedom were not incompatible, however, with a process of homogenisation among the students. In the old guild traditions daily work

120 Classroom science

routines were combined with the progressive training of young apprentices, but they gradually became professional practices with standardised disciplines that subjected students to a set of strict processes for controlling their values and attitudes.[9] Individuals were disciplined in each field through a specific set of objects and rituals: laboratory material, scientific instruments, machinery and experimental procedures, all to the end of teaching young students a set of protocols and knowledge tacitly acquired in scientists' daily lives and closely tied to their material culture.[10] Throughout history, teachers as experts have inculcated in their students the norms, values, discipline, roles and behaviours necessary for their professional future.[11]

As Jerôme Ravetz suggested some years ago, perhaps science is simply one more 'artisan' process, among many others, where scientists do not work directly with nature (if a definition can ever be agreed for it) but with intellectual constructions of indeterminate certainty, keen for public acceptance of their truth. If that were the case, teaching students would basically be a question of finding convincing and credible solutions to certain problems rather than inculcating abstract 'truths' established a priori by a small circle of expert teachers.[12] Rather than a simple institutional history or an acritical approach to course syllabuses, often of questionable erudition and involving an accumulation of quantitative data, perhaps it is more useful to analyse the intentions and values of the teachers and the reactions of the students. Class notes, exams and laboratory notebooks would therefore be as important as textbooks or official syllabuses.[13] If it is accepted that a certain theory or corpus of scientific knowledge can be appropriated differently in varied teaching contexts, then science education should be analysed contingently, in distinct places and periods in history.

There is frequent allusion to philanthropy, to the value of education, the need to extend bridges between experts in different fields to break the isolation of specialist areas. Science education supposedly stimulates new scientific vocations among young people, and provides a better understanding of the rapid scientific changes taking place today. It is even a response to the need for intellectual vigour, which inevitably involves a minimal immersion in contemporary scientific culture. However, behind all this rhetoric, often anchored in the assumptions of the deficit model, are the hidden intentions of the educational process, under permanent dialectical pressure for public legitimation of authority and professionalisation, corporate defence, social control and stability, economic interests and political and ideological struggle.[14] As with other popularisation processes, the act of teaching comes inseparably associated with a strategy for defining disciplines, specialist areas and the legitimation of certain practices. Science teaching is therefore largely a matter of constructing authority in constant struggle with more or less captive audiences. These presuppositions will be explored in more detail in the following sections, taking some of the classical authors as sources of inspiration.

Thomas Kuhn thought that training science students was basically a stable procedure that reflected the consensus of the scientific community through a set of canonical texts or textbooks. It was another expression of 'normal science' of the periods of history when a certain 'paradigm' was accepted by the majority and consequently transmitted to the new generations.[15] Michel Foucault (1926–84), however, approached science teaching and teaching in general as an instrument of power and social control. While Kuhn was more interested in the final product of the education, 'distilled' in normal science texts, Foucault was much more concerned with the learning process: gestures, routines, practices, exams, punishments and spaces. So since the eighteenth century, education would have been another form of coercion (the analogies between schools, factories, prisons and hospitals are clear) where the supervision of disciplinary processes were even more important than the final product itself.[16]

Foucault's emphasis on the learning mechanisms rather than the final outcome of the process leads to a consideration of the student as an active agent in the patrimony of knowledge. Is it possible that the reactions of students at certain historical moments could have influenced the content of scientific knowledge itself? Do teachers ever reconsider their deep-seated convictions – also learned in the classroom and the laboratory – after having to answer unexpected questions from students? In other words, is the status of students or pupils homogeneous and ahistorical, or is it the possible result of a specific context that marks their relationship with the expert in the classroom? To what extent are there clear differences between processes of teaching and popularisation, between a textbook and a popular science book? There is no simple answer to these questions but the critical appropriation of Kuhn and Foucault have contributed in recent years to opening up the debate and reconsidering scientific education from the perspective of active and captive audiences. The following section looks at this new proposal through a series of historical examples.

5.2. Teachers and students

In discussions about the origins of chemistry as a modern science, some historians have considered *Alchemia* (1597) by Andreas Libavius (1550–1616) and *Course de chymie* (1675) by Nicolas Lémery (1645–1715) to be two of the most significant works issued from teaching practices. Consequently, that was where the so-called 'didactic' origins of chemistry lay throughout the seventeenth century. It justified its emergence as a scientific discipline in the sense that it was taught to and enjoyed a relatively stable student audience.[17] In addition to these pioneering courses, in the eighteenth century there were also new public lectures combining oral explanations with experimental demonstrations. They received very varied audiences of doctors, industrialists, tradesmen, aristocrats, women, young people, travellers and sons of important manufacturing families who were sent to these new temples of knowledge to attend a variety of courses and public lectures. The definition of a student was still rather vague and the course teachers and authors of the texts did not end to be associated to a single institution.

122 Classroom science

The organisation of the teaching content was fairly open-ended with the emphasis on rhetorical strategies for attracting potential audiences.[18]

In the Paris of the Enlightenment, the Jardin des apothicaires held regular public chemistry courses. They were advertised on posters all over the city with the name of the teacher appearing alongside those carrying out the demonstrations and experiments. An amphitheatre was built in the Jardin for teaching purposes including a laboratory, which was open to the public and visited frequently by students and *curiosi*, even while the experiments were being set up. The other great garden of teaching was the Jardin du roi, which offered courses in botany as well as chemistry. Its amphitheatre could hold 600 students who witnessed presentations by personalities such as Guillaume-François Rouelle (1703–70), who counted Lavoisier himself among his students.[19] In Britain, and especially at the Scottish universities, chemistry teaching played an important role in the middle of the eighteenth century and featured such illustrious figures as William Cullen (1710–90) and Joseph Black (1728–99) (Figure 5.1).[20]

Yet again, like in other manifestations of the scientific culture of the Enlightenment, the boundaries between public and private were subtly marked. The spectacularity of the demonstrations was often used as a strategy for enabling large numbers to witness the sensibility of a wide range of experts and laypeople.

FIGURE 5.1 Joseph Black in a lesson on heat at the University of Glasgow circa 1760. Louis Figuier, *Les merveilles de la science*, I, p. 77. Reproduced with permission of the Biblioteca de Catalunya (Barcelona).

Jean-Antoine Nollet became an expert in experimental physics and constructed hundreds of apparatus for his courses and demonstrations. His audience was select but varied and his publications focused on the teaching of his physics. As a tutor of young students and a teacher at public talks, Nollet was frequently invited to the aristocratic salons and performed in entertainment spectacles at the Court.[21] In the latter decades of the eighteenth century there is also evidence of numerous public examinations taken by students in a kind of end-of-course open session, an end-of-course celebration, which transcended the traditional audiences of a specific teaching community.[22]

In the case of chemistry, teaching methods had begun to change in the first few decades of the nineteenth century in a move towards giving the students greater importance. Students' notebooks and class notes provide a great and yet little-explored source of information. They show how, for instance, in the chemistry courses taught by French chemist Joseph-Louis Thénard (1777–1857) at the Collège de France in Paris at the beginning of the 1800s, the experiments described did not fit in with the Enlightenment tradition of public demonstration. The young medical and pharmacy students who attended Thénard's courses appeared to be discussing experiments and open problems for which the teacher did not impose a unique solution.[23]

In Germany, the university reforms initiated by Wilhelm von Humboldt (1767–1835) in 1810 with the creation of the University of Berlin gradually included research as an intrinsic part of students' training, and supported academic freedom. This provided a favourable environment for developing new methods for teaching experimental sciences, similar to Thénard's model in Paris and more centred on laboratory work and experiments.[24] During the 1830s an unknown chemistry teacher, Justus von Liebig (1803–73), began to enjoy certain success with a new teaching method that involved the students directly in research projects as a substantial part of their training. Liebig developed a new method of elemental analysis of animal and plant substances measuring the proportion of hydrogen, oxygen, carbon and nitrogen, and he designed and successfully applied a new scientific instrument known as the 'Kaliapparat' for use with alkaline solutions for analytical purposes.[25]

This hitherto unknown teacher also worked at an unknown university in the German town of Giessen. In that relatively provincial setting, Liebig gradually gained acceptance thanks to his new teaching method (Figure 5.2). At the beginning of the course his students were given an unidentified substance of animal or plant origin which they had to analyse in detail over the year. They worked in a laboratory where they were the agents rather than just the spectators of experiments ex cathedra. Daily conversations with Liebig and his more experienced assistants taught students the theory and practice of the new organic chemistry – an emerging speciality in those days – without any clear limits between the regulated education of the young chemistry students and his own research project.[26]

Even though that kind of laboratory organisation is comparable to the way many research teams work today, during the first few decades of the nineteenth

124 Classroom science

FIGURE 5.2 Students in the laboratory of Justus von Liebig in Giessen in the 1840s. Carl Friedrich Wilhelm Trautschold, (1815–77) Bibliothèque nationale, Paris. Archives Charmet. Reproduced with permission of Pictorial Press Ltd / Alamy.

century it was a remarkable innovation, and not just in Giessen. Liebig's disciples came to occupy a significant share of the labour market for academic and industrial chemistry throughout the century. William Henry Perkin (1838–1907) was a young follower of August Wilhelm Hoffmann (1818–92), Director of the Royal College of Chemistry in London and, years earlier, one of the most brilliant students in Liebig's laboratory in Giessen. In 1856, Perkin discovered the first synthetic chemical dye, known as malveine or Perkin's mauve, which revolutionised the organic chemical industry during the second half of the nineteenth century. It would not be possible to explain the chemical structure of certain natural substances and their relationship to dyeing or medical properties during this period without the active participation of thousands of students carrying out small research projects under the supervision of their laboratory teachers.[27]

But it goes even further than that. Some of the main advances in nineteenth-century chemistry were the result of the creativity of young and brilliant doctorate students, which often sat uncomfortably with the academic authorities of the time. Chemists such as Auguste Laurent (1807–53) with his nucleus theory, which was fundamental for the future of structural organic chemistry, or Svante Arrhenius (1859–1927), with the theory of electrolytic dissociation – one of the foundations for the so-called physical chemistry at the end of the century – had serious problems when it came to presenting and obtaining their doctorates, and provoked opposition from many of the 'experts' in the university. Laurent's nucleus theory – a prism made up of a fixed number of carbons and hydrogens – enabled the substitution of the latter by heteroatoms such as chlorine. His theory initially disturbed his teacher, the prestigious French chemist, Jean Baptiste Dumas (1800–84), and directly contradicted the scientific authority of the great Jons Jakob Berzelius (1779–1848) based on his theory of electronegativity. Laurent fell victim to criticism and scorn for his excessive imagination, but his theory explained the release of hydrochloric acid in the industrial bleaching of candles using chlorine (the hydrocarbon in the candle resulted in the substitution of one atom of chlorine for one atom of hydrogen), as well as laying the foundations for animal and plant chemistry (later to become organic chemistry).[28]

Something similar happened with Arrhenius, who was also penalised by the jury who examined his doctoral thesis. His proposal of the real existence of electrically charged atoms which moved through a solution seemed like a completely hare-brained idea to his teachers. In 1884, Arrhenius presented his doctoral thesis on electrolytic conductivity at the University of Uppsala in Sweden. He propounded that salts in solution contained new particles called 'ions', even where there was no electrolytic process involved. He got a very low grade. Arrhenius sent his thesis to a number of prestigious chemists and physicists, including Wilhelm Ostwald (1853–1932) and Jacobus Henricus van 't Hoff (1852–1911), pioneers in the emerging specialist area of physical chemistry, who received his work with great enthusiasm. The controversial student had taken a major step towards eventually receiving the Nobel Prize for Chemistry in 1903. Laurent and Arrhenius's overflowing imagination, which did not always concur with the experimental results and consensus of the time, was relatively easy to criticise or dismiss. However, despite this, their contributions proved to be of great importance in a broader historical context.

Today, for example, we know that the famous periodical table of elements is a cultural phenomenon that goes well beyond the work of Russian chemist Dimitri Mendeleiev (1834–1907). The table is the result of huge efforts in teaching by many chemists throughout the nineteenth century in search of alternative ways of organising the content of courses for the greatest benefit to the students, and they often modified the organisation of the table as a result of their students' reactions. The periodical table is therefore a collective endeavour by scientists such as André-Marie Ampère (1775–1836), Louis-Jacques Thénard (1777–1857), Mateu Orfila (1787–1853), Johann Döbereiner (1780–1848), John Newlands (1837–98), William Olding (1829–1921), Auguste Cahours (1813–91), Lothar Meyer (1830–95), etc., some of whom have been little known until recently.[29]

It is probably no coincidence that between 1859 and 1862 Mendeleiev himself translated some general chemistry lectures by Cahours, written for students at the École centrale des arts et manufactures in Paris to offer a profound discussion of the possibilities for classification of the elements. However, his idea was not fully

126 Classroom science

established until 1869 when he wrote a student textbook in two volumes called called *Principles of Chemistry* (*Osvony khimii*), published between 1868 and 1869.[30] Mendeleiev was therefore not the first to consider the problem of classification, which could ultimately only be understood in a creative classroom context where large numbers of students, lecturers and textbook publishers played an important role in offering a comprehensible presentation of concepts such as affinity, valence, atoms, elements and molecules, which demanded arduous and difficult consensus.[31]

Cases from the field of physics have also shown that student expectations and attitudes established, conditioned and modified class content, textbooks and even the knowledge and priorities of the teachers.[32] In the physics seminars organised by Franz Ernst Neumann (1798–1895) at the University of Königsberg in Prussia, an important culture of exactitude, experimental measure and its mathematical expression, with major applications in state government and public policy, cannot be attributed only to the teacher's talent. Its impact even filtered down to secondary education and influenced the way that physics was taught to young people, some of them future students of Neumann.[33] The seminar began in 1834 and its method not only involved the students directly in mathematical and measurement exercises, it also instilled in them criteria for evaluating the precision of their measurements and theoretical results using different methods of numerical calculus, mainly worked out by the students themselves. This teaching practice needs to be understood in the context of the German tradition of seminars. Whereas initially there were institutions dedicated to the education of the clergy, at the end of the eighteenth century they became places for training secondary school teachers who would soon incorporate the new experimental sciences in their curricula. In the university context, the seminars replaced some of the conventional lectures and became new spaces for dialogue between teachers and students.[34]

During the nineteenth and the beginning of the twentieth centuries, teaching of mathematical physics at Cambridge was mainly concerned with passing the difficult but highly prestigious final exams or Tripos. The change from oral to written examination permitted more demanding papers and more difficult exercises. Given the level of difficulty and the scarcity of official courses at the university, private tutors began to take on a central importance in preparing the students and some very fruitful intellectual relationships were established between them. Problem-solving methods were set up within the dominant teaching model, which was not necessarily transferrable to other, foreign teaching centres.[35] Theoretical work was therefore always linked to specific skills that had to be learned, developed and communicated within a certain teaching context.

At the end of the 1940s, the physicist Richard Feynman drew some diagrams to simplify the tedious calculations involved in some areas of quantum mechanics. The efficiency and capacity of the calculation meant that it was soon applied to other specialist areas in the discipline of physics. The diagrams described in much simpler terms, for example, an electron-electron collision. But the most interesting part of this episode was the relationship that Feynman created with his disciples, between other teachers and students, and even among colleagues at different levels of training and experience. As a result of teaching practices at certain local levels, when Feynman's diagrams as reproduced by students at Cornell University were somewhat different from those produced by students at Columbia, Rochester and Chicago, they were discussed and commented on through a large network of academic contacts. More than 80 per cent of the authors of the diagrams were graduate students. Once again, the students seemed to be conditioning some of the aspects of the lecturers' intellectual pathways and the result of scientific knowledge itself.[36] It is precisely through the actors' accounts and all the historical sources of science education that we can look further, in the following section, into different aspects of the problem.

5.3. Textbooks and notebooks

In 1962, in *The Structure of Scientific Revolutions*, Kuhn talked about textbooks as exponents of accepted theories, agreed works, vehicles in the definition of problems and legitimate methods in a field of research for generations of scientists. Even before textbooks became generally used in nineteenth-century education systems many of the famous science 'classics' by Aristotle, Ptolemy, Newton, Franklin, Lavoisier and Lyell fulfilled a similar function, according to Kuhn.[37] However, recent historical research has called into question this static image of the school textbook, making it a window of rich nuances through which we can reconstruct details of teaching practices in the past that have until now been largely unknown.[38]

Giving the central figures in the learning process a more active role may help us to see that school textbooks or manuals are the result of compilations of student class notes or corrected transcriptions of oral presentations by teachers. It may also show that the different editions of the textbooks are basically the result of student reactions in the classroom, and the possible influences of other audiences (inventors, engineers, amateurs) on modifications introduced by the authors themselves. Also, the supposed stability of the texts, according to Kuhn, was refuted by evidence showing that textbooks sometimes contain scientific controversies and therefore go well beyond the consensuses of normal science.[39]

In recent decades, historians of science have studied the role of textbooks in defining discipline boundaries and specialised fields, in tracing the evolution of scientific ideas, epistemological concerns and priority disputes. Equally they have noticed how the circulation of textbooks and their translations often become a basic element for the international recognition of their authors, and of how textbook regulations shape the image of science for younger generations (as was the case, for instance, in nineteenth-century France or in the US following World War II).[40] A simple historical analysis describing in detail the use of textbooks in specific learning contexts offers sufficient proof of the different intellectual paths

128 Classroom science

set out in the text and allows the mechanisms of demarcation between experts and laypeople to be identified.[41]

Going back to the chemistry courses at the end of the eighteenth and beginning of the nineteenth century it is easy to see that the printed texts often originated from the teachers' lectures, and were subsequently re-elaborated following a series of exchanges of opinions with the students. Oral classroom culture, together with class notes, formed the basis for the printed word in teaching manuals. But by the end of the nineteenth century, textbooks had in many cases become anonymous, homogenised and standardised. They were a genre in their own right that needed no presentation and no justification by the publics they were aimed at. From the literary seduction of potential audiences throughout the eighteenth century, which often included scientific controversy as a stimulus for debate and the motivation of the student or reader, teaching gradually became more rigid and vertical, although in practice the reading of the texts and their resulting influence on the authors was still an important factor.

An example of the new style is the thirtieth edition of a French chemistry course published by J. Langlebert in 1879, in which any sign of a prologue discussing the intellectual path of the author and his interaction with his audience had been removed. It had been replaced by a table of contents together with a cover which specified the origin and production of the text in the following words: 'Elementary course in scientific studies. Published from the official programmes dictated by classical education, special education and the baccalaureate examinations in science . . . including the latest discoveries and most recent progress'.[42]

However, this example does not necessarily mean the conversion of a textbook into a corpus of knowledge isolated from other possible audiences. Textbooks have always been the result of complex negotiations and exchanges of ideas between teachers and students, authors and readers, to the point where their circulation and use transcended the walls of the classroom. Historical research helps to question the preconceived idea of stability and limited creativity of textbooks, supposedly used only by a captive readership of students enrolled on a specific course. In many cases the dialogue of the text, with its corresponding audience, extends beyond the field of teaching in its strict sense.

Jean Marcet's *Conversations in Chemistry* (1806) inspired Michael Faraday as a young scientist, but it was also used more flexibly in several schools as a textbook, and even as an introduction to chemistry for medical students.[43] In 1844, Comte published his *Traité d'astronomie populaire*, which would become the prologue to his *Discourse sur l'esprit positif*, published in the same year. It was the faithful result of 14 years of teaching a public course in astronomy in Paris, where the 24 lessons in the programme became the 24 chapters of the book. Comte addressed the reader in the same spirit as he spoke to his students (who were basically industrial workers and craftsmen), to give them basic knowledge about the stars, the solar system and the universe, without necessarily using a prior mathematical base and with the firm desire of constructing a scientific discourse accessible to everyone.[44]

Adolphe Ganot (1804–87) does not feature among the great names of science, but his textbooks enjoyed great commercial success, were published in numerous editions and translations in other countries, and generally made an important contribution to physics. Ganot did not carry out scientific research and he did not present his work in academic circles or publish in science periodicals or produce any successful invention. He was a textbook author and teacher who prepared a large number of students for the science baccalaureate exam. Ganot's books on physics were obviously read by teachers and students, but also by instrument makers, journalists, amateurs, clerics and theologians, who appropriated them in different ways: popular science, vehicles of entertainment, education or research manuals.[45] From 1851 to 1884 Ganot's *Traité* was published in 18 editions and sold 200,000 copies. It was translated into 13 different languages and in just a few years became one of the main textbooks in physics teaching on every continent. In the *Traité*, Ganot changed the strategies for teaching physics: concise writing, the inclusion of illustrations in the text, the use of new engraving techniques which reflected the realism, the precision and beauty of the instruments and machines. His work was the result of his experience as a teacher but also of his relationship with printers, draughtsmen, engravers and manufacturers of instruments and machines and with his readers, all of them active publics of science.

Ganot's case confirms that, in the field of education, joint initiatives by authors, publishers, printers, book sellers and their customers often went a long way to stimulate the business. Libraries are full of teaching manuals at every level and their circulation and appropriation is varied and complex. However, the materials left behind by students although less numerous are no less valuable. Textbooks together with students' notebooks are two complementary historical sources which are fundamental for reconstructing the circulation of knowledge in classrooms. In between the textbooks and notebooks came oral explanations, reading aloud, accompanied by the gestures, expressions and movements of the teacher, and with the questions, problems and even distractions of the students. Despite the great emphasis placed on the printed text as the depository of 'official' scientific knowledge of the experts (an idea that was reinforced by the traditional view of science popularisation as mentioned in the introduction), orality plays a central role in the complex network of continuous exchange and negotiation that takes place in any classroom.[46] The history of science would not be written in the same way if the information contained in a textbook or the contents of the students' notebooks were the only source, in just the same way as the history of the great scientists cannot be based solely on their academic publications or laboratory notebooks, or those of their collaborators.[47] Students' notebooks allow for an analysis of their competences and the hierarchies of knowledge and disciplines, while class preparation notes by teachers are another excellent source for reconstructing certain aspects of orality and the relationship between the teacher and the student in the classroom.[48]

Some of the original notebooks still preserved explain, for example, the enormous success of Thénard in his chemistry courses at the Collège de France, or

130 Classroom science

the wide acceptance of his *Traité de chimie élémentaire*, which was highly influential during the nineteenth century. The experiments described in the notes are different from previous demonstrations such as those by Nollet or Rouelle and more in the style of Liebig at his famous research school in Giessen. On his arrival at the Collège, Thénard radically changed his teaching method. The nerve centre for his activity was the amphitheatre where he used a large marble table and an oven for heating samples to conduct experiments in the same space as his classes. The adjacent area consisted of a storage room for instruments and chemical products to protect them from the corrosive fumes produced during the experiments. On the other side of the amphitheatre the old laboratory of Thénard's predecessor at the Collège, Jean Darcet (1724–1801), was completely remodelled. There was also an *atelier de chimie* where Thénard and his assistants prepared experiments for the demonstrations. The assistants or *préparateurs* acquired new tasks and responsibilities which were recompensed by higher salaries and as mediators they became another type of scientific audience. Preparing the experiments to be carried out in the amphitheatre formed part of their own education. Thénard recruited assistants from among his students, mainly young pharmacy apprentices who had taken his courses. After completing their studies at the Collège, and taking part in Thénard's original method, they went on to become young chemists with a public image of professionalism and rigour that opened the doors to teaching, research and industry far wider than the limited circles of pharmacy that they had come from.[49]

The case of Thénard's students is just one example among many, and one that remains to be studied, of the mechanisms of appropriating knowledge that can be detected in students if the sources they themselves leave behind are analysed in detail: their grades, exams, notebooks and laboratory notes (Figure 5.3). It is easy to see considerable differences in the historical interpretation not only of the students' sources but also those of the teachers, or experts. The differences between private and public life in the case of Louis Pasteur is one of the best-known examples, but by no means the only one.[50] Consulting only the official textbook or a specialised article published in a periodical of great academic prestige means losing much of the information necessary for reconstructing the different interactions and debates and the positive feedback between teachers and learners.

Despite their flexibility and multiple readerships beyond the classroom, textbooks also played a major role in defining the different scientific disciplines and in the gradual standardisation of teachers and students. New scientific specialities, which became new departments and laboratories, tended to be associated with new research periodicals which gathered experts together, but also with some classic textbooks used by thousands of students which gradually legitimated the new areas of knowledge. So discipline and standardisation in the classroom along with the publishing market were fundamental elements in defining the limits of the authority of old and new experts.[51] In many cases there was, and probably still is, considerable continuity between the specialist journals, textbooks and even popular books, providing a solid package for consolidating a discipline.

FIGURE 5.3 Henri Sainte-Claire Deville (1818–81) in a chemistry class with his colleagues and students circa 1890. Painting by Leon Augustin Lhermitte, (1844–1925). École normale supérieure, Paris. Reproduced with permission of the Wellcome Library, London.

The emergence of physical chemistry at the end of the nineteenth century is normally associated with the publication of a new journal led by Wilhelm Ostwald among others, titled *Zeitschrift für Physikalische Chemie* (*Journal for Physical Chemistry*), but Ostwald's general chemistry textbooks were also canonical and used all over Europe. Its generalist title concealed a new teaching programme for chemistry that included basic questions in the new specialism (ions, conductivity, electrochemistry, thermodynamics), but it was of questionable use for experts in neighbouring specialities. This new area also brought with it a set of new experiments and instruments, a new experimental style and even the use of a new language closer to mathematical physics. It also introduced a new set of problems and new research questions that sought to do away with the old descriptive chemistry which, according to the new physical chemists, had lost sight of the basic questions regarding the whys and wherefores of chemical reactivity. Everything was subtly set out and presented in these new general chemistry textbooks led by Ostwald.[52]

In the early twentieth century quantum mechanics in physics textbooks reflected the tensions between research and pedagogy, and were written for

132 Classroom science

FIGURE 5.4 Linus Pauling teaching chemistry in the 1960s. From the website "Linus Pauling and the Nature of the Chemical Bond: A Documentary History", reproduced with permission of the Oregon State University Special Collections & Archives Research Center.

different purposes: a simple exercise of organising the authors' thoughts, aiming to spread a particular interpretation of the theory, or again a way to reinforce scientific authority and social prestige.[53] Similarly, it would be difficult to appreciate the success of Linus Pauling (1901–94) in applying the new nuclear physics to biochemistry without looking not only at his research articles but also his textbooks and his popularising works (Figure 5.4). Using a similar strategy to Ostwald, Pauling presented a new chemistry in his textbooks that included the new conception of the physical atoms, but which also offered his students a general presentation of chemistry. In his own words:

> Chemistry is a very large subject, which continues to grow, as new elements are discovered or made, new compounds are synthesized, and new principles are formulated. Nevertheless, despite its growth, the science can now be presented to the student more easily and effectively than ever before. In the past the course in general chemistry has necessarily tended to be a patch-work of descriptive chemistry and certain theoretical topics. The progress made in recent decades in the development of unifying

theoretical concepts has been so great, however, that the presentation of general chemistry to the students of the present generation can be made in a more simple, straightforward, and logical way than formerly. For example, every boy now knows about atoms, and accepts them as part of his world – they are split in the atomic bomb and in the comic papers; they stare at him from advertisements. In this book I begin the teaching of chemistry by discussing the properties of substances in terms of atoms and molecules.[54]

Since its first edition in 1947, Pauling's textbook *General Chemistry* has been revised and translated into 13 languages. The manual became one of the main pillars of Pauling's ambitious expository programme: from physical chemistry and chemical bonds to early molecular biology and vitamin C. He was a master at communicating science to laypeople, and published numerous popular science articles and books. Pauling openly discussed heterodox scientific ideas in the public sphere.[55] Again, the legitimisation of a discipline, in this case the new physical chemistry of the twentieth century based on the revolution produced by the conception of the atom and its subsequent applications to different fields of chemistry and biochemistry, was achieved through textbooks. Education and scientific authority again produced mutual feedback.

5.4. Instruction, control and popularisation

From a Foucauldian view of science education, some historical examples can help to re-examine the often simplistic view of objective, neutral science for progress and the welfare of humanity, which has contributed to reinforcing the traditional view of science popularisation being scrutinised in this book.

In the middle of the nineteenth century the British Mechanics' Institutes (MIs) attempted to disseminate the ideals and moral codes of industrial society, and in particular the ruling classes, to the workers.[56] Its educational programme aimed at moulding and disciplining the lower classes using three main strategies: utilitarianism, theological arguments and Baconian empiricism.[57] It remains a controversial topic today, but the history of the MIs is by no means insignificant. Until 1850 there were some 700 MIs in Britain with more than 120,000 students, mainly in the industrial cities. Behind the MI programme, designed by the Victorian elite, was the recurring idea that science education had to influence moral education. Industrial workers who had fallen to alcoholism, promiscuity and the incontrollable exaltation of their passions would be 'disciplined' through habits imposed by scientific knowledge.[58] The strategy also reinforced the social control that already existed through religion. In Britain this was done through the tradition of natural theology, of which the *Bridgewater Treatises*, mentioned in Chapter 4, are a good example.[59]

During that time the controversy was mainly centred on the defenders and detractors of the famous treaty titled *Practical Observations upon the Education of the People*, published in 1825 by statesman Henry Brougham (1778–1868). Brougham defended a certain level of upward social mobility through education,

134 Classroom science

which he considered to be a Christian duty toward the poor and needy and a possible remedy for social discontent. The proposal was quickly opposed by the conservative weekly *Country Gentlemen*, which argued that any kind of change in the base of the social pyramid, in the lower classes, could subvert the social order and end up causing it to topple. Hence the potential danger of science in the MIs in terms of the content and intentions included in the educational plans.[60]

Although apparently generous, Brougham's programme was based on the tacit assumption of the inevitable separation between the intellectual virtues of the upper and lower classes; the former were considered to be profound, abstract, rational, integral and logical while the latter were thought of as superficial, concrete, sensual, fragmented and illogical. The task of the MIs was to harmonise these working-class weaknesses but never to stimulate the 'superior' epistemology of the elite. His syllabuses were therefore focused on specific facts and the presentation of a clear, sharp image of the natural order just as it 'really' was, avoiding abstract speculation or any other sign of a provisional nature. Practical geometry and mathematics were preferable to demonstration or abstraction; the observation and description of specific facts (minerals, machines, chemical substances and diagrams) was preferred over algebraic equations, metaphysical principles or abstract relationships and concepts. In Brougham's words:

> The majority must be content with never going beyond a certain point, and with reaching that point by the most expeditious route . . . Thus, in teaching them geometry, it is not necessary to go through the whole steps of that beautiful system . . . enough will be accomplished, if they are made to perceive the nature of geometrical investigation, and learn the leading properties of figure . . . with their application to practical purposes.[61]

The purpose was therefore to train workers and craftsmen in a pragmatic and supposedly 'neutral' science as an antidote to their revolutionary tendencies, using empirical, utilitarian practices as being preferable to commitment and action. In 1827 Brougham published *Objects, Advantages and Pleasures of Science*, where he explained the reasons why science was particularly appropriate for educating workers. Brougham thought that it instilled in them a regular and constant work ethic, stimulated their philosophical and artistic creativity (including technical skills) and, appealing to natural theology again, provided a better understanding and acceptance of the marvellous divine creation.[62]

Some historians have claimed that, despite the ambitious designs of the elite, the industrial workers never went to these centres, which were finally occupied by the middle classes.[63] But even taking the MIs as a simple project that was doubtfully carried out as originally intended, it offers a reflection on the ultimate objective of science education. It encourages questions about the role of science in the industrial society of which it formed a substantial part. It brings to the fore the strategies of the ruling classes to impose their moral, political and cultural values. It places science as an instrument for the legitimation of power relations.[64]

There is evidence that outside the strict transmission of scientific knowledge in the classroom, much of the science directed at the lower classes aimed to distract them from reading pamphlets and politically marked texts that often subverted the established order. Many social reformers and all kinds of associations promoted popular science publications in the form of books or magazines to increase information for potential readers about nature and prevent them from consuming other 'dangerous' texts.[65] Consequently, access to science by the lower classes had to be cheap, simple, illustrated, using accessible language and a marked experimental and indicative nature, while retaining its entertainment value.[66] Perhaps it is more than a coincidence that in the face of growing concern about social order and stability, the British Association for the Advancement of Science organised its meetings to coincide with bitter debates and riots over laws on the extent of political and social reform in Britain, travelling to the very industrial cities that experienced the greatest social crises during the 1830s and 1840s.[67]

Even though the MIs aimed to distract the lower classes from political ideas of social injustice in Victorian Britain, the culture that they generated at their heart did not necessarily consist of the transmission of bourgeois values to passive workers. For example, evolutionary and socialist ideas developed fairly autonomously in the MIs in the sense that students used part of the education they received to develop their own, authentic projects for social emancipation. The main problem lay in the ability of those groups to freely acquire knowledge of the influence of the hegemonic values of the elite.[68] Although it is accepted that there was a minimum of common elements in the content of most teaching processes, the superficial rhetoric frequently obscured major discrepancies in their ideological bases.[69]

Various reactions to the top-down imposition of certain teaching projects were seen throughout the century. For example, taking a position close to the socialists but removed from the spirit of the MIs was the Escuela Moderna of Catalan pedagogue Francesc Ferrer Guàrdia (1859–1909), who in 1901 expressed his confidence in the extension of scientific knowledge to the whole of society in the following words:

> Science, fortunately, is no longer the patrimony of a small privileged group; its beneficial rays penetrate all social layers with a greater or lesser degree of conscience. Everywhere, traditional mistakes are removed; under the safety of experience and observation it makes all men capable of forming exact doctrine, real criterion, for objects and the laws that rule them, and in the present moments, with indisputable authority, for the good of humanity, to end exclusiveness and privilege once and for all, it becomes the unique director of the life of man, attempting to steep it in a universal, human sentiment.[70]

Within a context of strong hostility to religion, resistance to educational impositions and from a positivist position, Ferrer believed in the emancipating

136 Classroom science

potential of science for his students. However, similar to the design of the British MIs some decades earlier, he also selected his favourite authors (Darwin, Haeckel, Reclus, Kropotkin, etc.) instead of the authors and topics of the elite religious schools. Similarly, in the second half of the nineteenth century, at least in the MIs in northern England, evolutionary ideas were not used to promote individualism, competition and the fight for survival in social terms, but socialist groups developed new organicist discourses of solidarity based on a cooperative view of nature. In socialist circles, belief in the liberating force of science was frequently reflected in popular literature. This was an egalitarian science, without class distinctions in the sense of its universal accessibility and the fact that it offered solid arguments in opposition to religion. Followers of Robert Owen (1771–1858), the Owenites, held their conferences in 'halls of science' which were considered alternative spaces to those of the MIs, which were thought to be too heavily influenced by bourgeois culture. It was not easy for these groups to acquire knowledge that was 'free' from the influence of middle-class values of power.[71]

The favourite scientific topics of the British socialists during the first half of the nineteenth century were geography, because of the interest in environmental factors and cultural relativism, natural history, to understand the position of man in nature, astronomy and chemistry, as powerful, iconic examples to substitute the ancient mythologies and religious foundational myths and strengthen faith in natural laws, human anatomy and geology, to reinforce the anticlerical relativist discourses.[72] Everything was reinforced within the framework of Lamarckian biology and a broad programme of political and social goals: emancipation of women, cooperation, representation in government redistribution of wealth, all in a move against a paternalistic society, the power of the Church and the accumulation of capital.[73]

Consequently, it is impossible to ignore the conceivable view of science education as yet another instrument of propaganda or indoctrination aimed at certain social groups, professionals and experts to legitimate their role in decision making. In fact, the school curriculum inevitably reflected the ideological struggle for cultural hegemony between different social and economic groups.[74] So the advantageous position of professional scientists as a result of many of the educational reform processes that took place in the nineteenth and twentieth centuries meant that they could use education as the grounds for establishing their function as indispensable experts. Others responded with alternative programmes, but these were obviously not exempt from ideologies and values either.[75] This interpretation means reviewing once again the excessively naïve image of scientific progress and science education as an unproblematic appendix to the unarguable progression towards a better world, or as an a posteriori consequence of that supposedly neutral creative act being hatched within the laboratory walls of the experts. It allows a more critical analysis of both the teachers' intentions and the students' reactions.

In other cases, the teachers themselves questioned the authority and capacity for control of the teaching institutions and appeared critical of some of the 'official' objectives. For example, the problems of the Faculty of Medicine in Paris to retain its scientific authority in the mid-nineteenth century are well known. The courses offered there did not always have the approval of the academic authorities, as in the case of Raspail – a controversial character who openly confronted official medicine, as seen in Chapter 4. In 1828, 1830 and 1836, Raspail gave free courses in medicine in the amphitheatres of the faculty from a position opposed to authority and certain complicity with the critical attitudes of the students, who were keen to have more direct participation in the learning process. The boundaries of university education seemed to be getting permeable and frequently questioned.[76]

Raspail's example needs to be extrapolated prudently, but there are still numerous cases of teaching activities that often went beyond the limits set by the official institutional framework. At the end of the nineteenth century natural science textbooks were often unable to match up to the teaching objectives at the time. Even the encyclopaedic view of animals, plants and minerals exhibited in the cabinets, museums and university laboratories seemed to many experts to limit a comprehensive vision of nature by the students. This explained, for example, the sudden boom in educational visits and excursions, a 'science in the field' where the very nature of the meeting place alone considerably changed the relationship between teachers and their students. The old tradition of the scientific journey, usually in the interests of the experts and their alliances with the main institutions of the time, became a new method which revolutionised natural science teaching.[77]

In a similar context, a hands-on nature study movement grew up in the US in the early twentieth century. It was an attempt to introduce nature study to inner-city urban environments, streetcar suburbs, small towns and even rural single-room schools. At a time when zoological and botanical gardens, natural history museums and national parks stressed the link between direct knowledge of nature and its moral and social benefits, hands-on-nature contributed to the introduction of scientific topics into elementary schools. Teachers – mainly women – used nature study to counterbalance the official curricula and bring more creativity to the classroom. They contributed substantially to long-standing debates on science education in the US.[78]

Many professors also took part in the university extension movements. Given the need to open the elitist Oxbridge university model to society, during the second half of the nineteenth century a large number of university extension centres were created in England and they came to form a genuine movement.[79] In France, François-Anatole Thibault (1844–1924), better known as Anatole France, set up the French Université populaire and proclaimed that the aim of creating these new institutions was to contribute to the overall education of the workers. His project defined the spaces that the new institutions should contain with some precision: rooms for courses and talks in secondary, higher and professional education; a museum; a music room and artistic theatre; a library; a laboratory; a discussion room; a medical and legal consulting room; a pharmacy; a restaurant; some rooms for young people from all backgrounds; and a school

138 Classroom science

for popular educators.[80] In other cases there was no specific central building for the movement, which basically consisted of a number of courses taught by university lecturers that travelled all over the country.[81]

The aim was to open the doors of the university and put expert knowledge in touch with the least fortunate classes, in what at first sight looks like a philanthropic gesture. The actual reasons were almost certainly more complex: from the complementary income that was very welcome given the precarious university salaries, especially in countries with a weak university system; a moral and intellectual commitment to positivism, sometimes tinctured with anticlericalism and, in the case of phrenology, a desire to give the lower classes moral alternatives to religion. There were also paternalistic attitudes arising from unresolved academic rivalries, which ended up finding their solution in the lower public echelons.

Little is known about the way the people reacted to these educational courses, talks and excursions. Large numbers seem to have attended them and the activities were carried out with notable frequency. The press tended to cover them in the form of announcements or brief comments a posteriori. The topics chosen and their presentation were not accidental, often attempting to connect with a certain popular epistemology considered by many contemporary actors as different to the scientific discourses of the conservative elite. The discussion of topics such as the theory of evolution, the origin of life or of the universe, and scientific materialism were closely related to the ideological profile of the institution.[82]

During the last few decades of the nineteenth century, workers, cultural societies and popular athenaeums sprang up everywhere with the shared objective, among many others, of educating the working classes. Science courses tended to take the form of evening classes when the workers had free time in an attempt to stamp out their illiteracy and social exclusion. Regular classes were accompanied by frequent talks by distinguished scientists, often university lecturers, who attended assiduously to fulfil their moral obligation to society. The talks were also sometimes combined with botanical or geological excursions and visits to different kinds of industry. From a socialist or anarchist perspective, on which the movement was largely but not exclusively based (consider the Christian workers' societies), popular culture was seen as something nascent in the heart of the people and to which it had to return, bypassing the interests of the elites. This utopian objective was supported by contributions from erudite workers, schoolteachers, writers, artists and university lecturers. New libraries and reading rooms appeared everywhere. A low elementary education underlined the role of the athenaeums and workers' associations as centres for social life, leisure activities and political preaching.[83]

The athenaeums were set up as members' cooperatives and basically maintained through monthly fees. They offered elementary and higher-level education in a wide variety of subjects such as languages, drawing, fine art, women's work, theory and practice of manufacturing, industry, trade and agriculture; in other words, anything that could be of benefit to the workers' sons. The public examinations in these subjects required the presence of university professors and authorities, who awarded prizes to the best students and in doing so acted as legitimating agents for the teaching quality of the centres.

The athenaeums movement, university extension and other contemporary projects helped to create flexible mechanisms for teaching and science popularisation outside the limits of the official educational institutions and regulated teaching syllabuses, and extended a wide network of bridges between experts and laypersons. For example, in Chicago in the 1920s, as a reaction to excessive specialisation and to complement the secondary education taught in schools, a group of engineers offered a new subject. Under the title of 'general science' they presented an image of science closely linked to daily life with an important emphasis on technology. Students learned how to use steel and cement, and how to deal with smoke, dust and organic and industrial waste. In a highly industrialised area such as Chicago, this 'general science' aimed to occupy a new space in scientific culture that was not covered by traditional physics, chemistry and experimental science, which were considered to be too deeply rooted in academic discourse and abstraction and too closely controlled by professional groups in universities.[84]

Some years ago John Rudolph studied how, in 1956, as a reaction against the potential Soviet hegemony in science and technology, a group of top American scientists launched a programme to reform precollege science education in the US, mainly focused on high-school physics and biology. In that Cold War context, the programme was deeply influenced by wartime knowledge about weapons development and defence and permeated official curricula and institutional constraints.[85] Once again, largely informal ways of teaching were taking on different forms.

★ ★ ★

Everyday life at secondary schools, universities and research centres reveals a host of informal mechanisms for transmitting knowledge which lie outside the scope of their missions or official agendas. Informal conversations in the laboratory or corridors, the spontaneity of email and phone calls, master classes, students' questions in seminars, conferences, round tables, coffee breaks and many other examples are simply multiple mechanisms of communication; the tacit transmission of knowledge and the continuous negotiation of authority which goes beyond any official agenda or curriculum. They are oral, informal and reminiscent of the select discussions that took place in the salons of the Enlightenment, or conversations about the lights and shadows of *Vestiges* during Victorian train journeys. They are an intrinsic part of the everyday life of the scientists, as expert and lay actors, teachers and students.[86] Once again, the boundaries between education, entertainment and popularisation seem ambiguous. Among the educational plans of the elite, embodied in projects like those of the Mechanics' Institutes, the educational programmes of the ministries of public instruction in liberal states,

140 Classroom science

or the popular athenaeums and university extension movements, there is a wide range of educational ideas and appropriations of scientific knowledge tailored to the interests and values of each social class, which can explain the plural and often conflicting interpretations of education.

Further exploration in the same direction shows how, in the last few decades of the twentieth century, the scientific knowledge that students were able to acquire through textbooks continues to display an overconventional and rigid approach. Now that scientific information of all kinds is increasingly accessible in the media with highly varied levels of discourse, school curricula should be focusing on reading abilities, comprehension and critical assessment of the avalanche of materials that young students are bombarded with in their daily lives. Only then will they be able to assimilate such a wide variety of genres (from textbook physics problems to televised reports on climate change) and become scientifically educated citizens.[87]

A great deal still remains to be done to recover the fundamental aspects of the culture of classroom science. The historian Kathryn Olesko, an undisputed authority on this issue, points out that scholars have come a long way towards understanding how scientists undertake research. However, much less is known about how they teach, despite the fact that it is through teaching that new researchers are trained. Olesko encourages analysis of science teaching as a creative enterprise, not as an inferior practice but one that is closely tied to the results of the research itself.[88] The closer the details of educational practices are examined, the more information is available to redress the balance of teachers and students in the classroom and in their different spheres of influence throughout history. It does not seem possible for the history of science to exist without the history of science education.

Notes

1 Fleck (1979).
2 Kaiser (2005a: 1–8); Shinn and Whitley (1985).
3 Olesko (1991); Stuckey, Heering (2015).
4 Lloyd (1987).
5 Lindberg (1992); Lloyd (1987).
6 Le Goff (1957).
7 Grant (1996).
8 Huff (1993).
9 Kaiser, Warwick (2005).
10 Latour (1986); Van Helden, Hankins (1994); Bertomeu-Sánchez, García Belmar, Bensaude-Vincent (2002).
11 Kaiser (2005a: 6).
12 Ravetz (1971: 3).
13 Olesko (2006: 12). In 1991 Olesko published a pioneering book on physics teaching in German universities in the nineteenth century in which she reconstructed some of these practices. See also Rudolph (2008).
14 Bensaude, Blondel (1988: 5).
15 Kuhn (1962); Kaiser, Warwick (2005).
16 Foucault (1977).

17 Hannaway (1975); Christie, Golinski (1982).
18 Golinski (1992).
19 Lehmann (2008: 104–6).
20 Donovan (1975).
21 Pyenson, Gauvin (2002); Evans, Marr (2006); Lynn (2006).
22 Nieto-Galan (2011b: 169–70).
23 García Belmar (2006).
24 Holmes (1989a); Geison, Holmes (1993).
25 Holmes (1989a).
26 Brock (2002).
27 Nieto-Galan (2001).
28 Brock (1992).
29 Bertomeu-Sánchez, García Belmar, Bensaude-Vincent (2002).
30 Gordin (2004: 23–4).
31 Bertomeu-Sánchez, García Belmar, Bensaude-Vincent (2002).
32 Lundgren, Bensaude-Vincent (2000); Olesko (1991); Kaiser (2005a).
33 Olesko (1991).
34 Olesko (1991: xiii, 1).
35 Warwick (2003).
36 Kaiser (2005b); Chin, Osborne (2008).
37 Kuhn (1962: 33).
38 Bensaude-Vincent, Bertomeu-Sánchez, García Belmar (2003).
39 Ibid.
40 Vicedo (2012).
41 Rudolph (2008) gives several examples.
42 *Cours élémentaire d'études scientifiques rédigé d'après les programmes officiels prescrits pour l'enseignement classique, l'enseignement spécial et les examens de baccalauréat et sciences. Chimie, par J. Langlebert, professeur de sciences physiques et naturelles, docteur en médecine, officier d'académie. Trentième édition. Tenue au courant des dernières découvertes et des progrès de la science les plus récents.* Langlebert (1879), cover.
43 Lindee (1991: 9).
44 Petit (1989).
45 Simon (2011).
46 Waquet (2003).
47 Latour (1993); Geison (1995).
48 Chartier, A.M. (2009).
49 García Belmar (2006).
50 Geison (1995).
51 Bensaude-Vincent, Bertomeu-Sánchez, García Belmar (2003: 243–51); Gieryn (1983).
52 Servos (1990).
53 Badino, Navarro (2013).
54 Pauling (1947: v). Greatly revised and expanded in 1947, 1953 and 1970. Reprinted by Dover Publications in 1988.
55 'Linus Pauling Institute', http://lpi.oregonstate.edu/linus-pauling-biography (accessed 20 June 2015).
56 Shapin, Barnes (1977: 32).
57 Jacobi, Schiele (1988: 168).
58 Mumford (1934).
59 Topham (1992).
60 Shapin, Barnes (1977).
61 Brougham (1825: 9–10). Thanks to Jaume Sastre for consulting Brougham's original work.
62 Topham (1992: 405).
63 Laurent (1984: 585).
64 Morrell (1986).

142 Classroom science

65 Sheets-Pyenson (1985: 549).
66 Pyenson, Sheets-Pyenson (1999: 226).
67 Morrell, Thackray (1981: 8).
68 Laurent (1984: 585); Fennessy (2005).
69 Bensaude-Vincent, Blondel (1988: 5).
70 Ferrer Guàrdia (2002: 14), translated from the Spanish version; Avilés Farré (2006).
71 'Faith in the socially regenerative properties of materialistic science and a utopian belief in its liberating force were strongly evident in the street literature of the Carlilean, Owenite and Chartists', Desmond (1987: 82).
72 Desmond (1987: 92).
73 Desmond (1987: 104).
74 Nieto-Galan (2011b).
75 Hilgartner (1990).
76 According to his own report: 'The place was packed with people . . . the teachers at the time formed a circle behind me to give them an air of popularity . . . in full view of the multitude of students listening to me . . . You can see that I did more than helping a doctor and dictating prescriptions; I trained doctors and dictated lessons where they didn't miss a single syllable . . . often I also dictated their theses since the thesis is not subject to faculty censorship, thank God; conversely the Faculty, always somewhat old-fashioned, would never have let pass unsanctioned some of the theories that the students were starting to understand better than it did, and which today are being thrown around left, right and centre', Raspail (1876: 36). Translated from the Spanish version.
77 Kuklick, Kohler (1996).
78 Kohlsted (2010).
79 MacKinder, Sadler (1891). Similarly, in Germany the Volkhochschule or schools for the people were becoming widespread.
80 Mercier (1986).
81 Taschwer (1997).
82 The laboratories of Gabriel Lippman (1845–1921), Nobel Prize winner in 1908, were open every Sunday morning to workers of all classes, ages and educational level. Raichvarg (2005: 59).
83 Heward (1980).
84 Rudolf (2005).
85 Rudolph (2002).
86 Waquet (2003).
87 Zimmerman (2001).
88 Olesko (1991).

6
TECHNOLOGICAL SCIENCE

French populariser Louis Figuier described in sumptuous detail the heroic story and tragic ending of the French aeronaut Sophie Blanchard (1778–1819) on 6 July 1819. As she rose above the Tivoli gardens in Paris, the hydrogen balloon carrying her caught fire and the distinguished balloonist free-fell to death.[1] She was the wife of one of the ballooning pioneers, Jean-Pierre Blanchard (1753–1809), who himself followed in the tradition started by brothers Joseph-Michel Montgolfier (1740–1810) and Jacques-Étienne Montgolfier (1745–99) in 1783. Sophie was well known for her numerous ascents and attracted large audiences at events that were often accompanied by firework displays. In that fateful summer of 1819 the fireworks were precisely what set fire to the hydrogen balloon that was carrying her (Figure 6.1).

The tragic report of her death spread throughout Europe and filled the news pages of the daily press. In fact, some years earlier Madame Blanchard had become a tireless traveller and had managed to make more than 60 ascents in different countries. Prestigious writers such as Verne, Dostoyevsky, Dickens and even Figuier himself would tell the tale years later with their own controversial interpretations. Some questioned the ability of women to handle these kinds of apparatus while others discussed the limits of risk in human actions. Yet others highlighted the public spectacle, but all of them reflected on our relationship with inventions and machines.

However, this is quite a rare account in the history of technology, which is generally understood as the history of the great inventions, inventors of machines and contraptions. Sophie Blanchard does not appear in most books on the history of aeronautical navigation, or when she does it is as a simple anecdotal and marginal case which left the progress of aerostatic balloons in the nineteenth century generally unscathed. In 1783 before an audience of 100,000 the Montgolfier brothers gave their first public demonstration of their hot air balloon.

144 Technological science

FIGURE 6.1 The death of Sophie Blanchard in an accident in 1819. Louis Figuier, *Les merveilles de la science*, II, pp. 544, 547. Reproduced with permission of the Biblioteca de Catalunya (Barcelona).

Their invention had a huge public impact which, together with the hydrogen balloon, would enthral the populations of towns and cities for years with their defiance of Newton's laws of gravity. The balloons soon became an icon of the Enlightenment and a common space between experts and laypeople on the question of human ability to conquer the skies. Their invention was considered by many to be one of the great achievements of the century and it inspired profound reflection, feelings and emotions, often far removed from rationality.[2] They influenced pneumatic chemistry, academic debates on the composition of the air and the preparation of other 'airs', hitherto unknown in the laboratories, and the study of their properties. But they also became an attractive commodity through subscriptions and small-scale manufacture and retail. Once in the air they were difficult to control and their path could be unpredictable, but the public spectacle was satisfied.

The Montgolfier brothers, Gay-Lussac, Jean-Baptiste Biot and even Sophie's husband tend to be mentioned as the great heroes, inventors and intrepid navigators of the skies in this kind of story. But writing a history of technology that is different from the traditional ones would involve a large number of Sophie Blanchards. In other words, it would have to include the users of machines that were as necessary for the development of a certain technological culture as for the existence of their inventors. The craftsmen who built these machines and their skills in the use of different materials and mechanics must also be remembered. Also, perceptions about the qualities of air, the imitation of bird flight (the old dream of Leonardo da Vinci) or the ultimate causes of the fact of flying were also in the minds of the thousands of spectators attending these events – people who had seen Sophie making many successful ascents before her accident. Such technological endeavours, deeply entrenched in people's daily lives, requires a detailed analysis of its inventors, engineers, craftsmen and users, all with their own particular importance. This is the main spirit of this chapter. It is a homage to Madame Blanchard and everyone involved in the design, construction, use and observation of her balloon.

6.1. Philosophers and artisans

The undervaluing of manual labour in Western society runs deep. The grand gestures of the Ancient Greek philosophers, Socrates, Plato and Aristotle, have entered the textbooks and even popular wisdom to a certain extent. However, very few people would be able to explain the technological contribution of Greek civilisation. Fifty years ago Marxist historians such as Benjamin Farrington held that low technological creativity in Ancient Greece was the result of an abundance of slaves and available manpower, which did not stimulate creativity or technological invention. Research in recent years has challenged that interpretation but for a long time the history of technology has been a complementary and largely subsidiary sub-discipline in the history of science. For many, thinking has been more important than doing.[3]

Names like Archimedes, Hero, Ctesibius and Vitruvius require closer consideration. Their cogs, mirrors, water clocks, pavements and constructions made up a good part of the technological culture of the ancient period. Medieval inventors such as Villard de Honnecourt (? – c.1250) and Roger Bacon (1220–92), among other creators of machines who remain anonymous, with their mechanical clocks, automata, ploughs and ship's keels also invite a revision

146 Technological science

of the so-called Dark Ages. The profession of engineer as an expert in the construction of machines for princes and kings took on particular importance from the time of the Renaissance. So how can this history be written? Should we reserve an extra chapter after presenting the great thinkers and humanists of antiquity or try to find a way of including these names, little known for the most part, in a single history of natural knowledge and its transformation, and vice versa? That is the challenge.

In the Renaissance, other names like Mariano Taccola (1381–1458), Francesco di Giorgio (1439–1501), or even Leonardo da Vinci (1452–1519) emerged as the great pre-industrial figures and authors of the great war machines, the art of construction and even the imagination of impossible techniques. The so-called Renaissance engineers became experts in building mines, bridges, pavements and water channels. These engineers were also artists and architects, and Leonardo's combination of art, science and technology was nothing less than the culmination of a generation of great creators.[4] Thanks to their notebooks, drawings, notes and codices it has been possible to recreate many of the machines of these engineers, and their reproductions were even the subject of a magnificent travelling exhibition in the 1990s.[5] Their creativity is undeniable and the detail of their designs offers some magnificent examples for reconstructing a large part of pre-industrial technology based on water and animal power, the extensive use of wood and the recovery of machinery such as the famous Archimedes' screw, described in detail in Renaissance treatises, war machines and flying inventions.

It is also impossible to understand the Spanish and Portuguese empires of the sixteenth and seventeenth centuries (curiously, roughly the same period as the Scientific Revolution and the emergence of modern science in Europe) without considering the major technological developments in navigation, mining, metallurgy and agriculture that were also related to a greater or lesser extent to academic subjects such as astronomy, natural history, cartography and mathematics. Metallurgical assayists such as Álvaro Alonso Barba (1569–1662), who trained in the central European mining schools, travelled to colonial America to offer their knowledge for the exploitation of large gold and silver mines. Distillers such as Diego de Santiago, and naturalists like Nicolás Monardes (1854–1915), among other important figures, rethought the ancient medical traditions to include new colonial plants with therapeutic properties in the pharmacopoeia of the metropolis. The art of navigation required new astronomical instruments as well as new construction skills and meteorological and geographical knowledge. From that perspective the material and technological culture of the empire was considerable.[6]

But the history of technology goes beyond some of those more well-known names. Like Menocchio, the simple miller in the sixteenth century (remember the importance of water and windmills in pre-industrial technology), others were leading figures in the construction and daily operation of these machines: artisans, miners, blacksmiths, mechanics, sailors, draughtsmen, printers and instrument makers, among many others.[7] Some decades ago, Alistair Crombie's studies on the intellectual evolution of ideas did not exclude the contribution of artisans and their manual skills in the development of modern science. In his own words:

> It has been often pointed out that science develops best when the speculative reasoning of the philosopher and mathematician is in closest touch with the manual skill of the craftsman. It has been said also that the absence of this association in the Greco-Roman world and in Medieval Christendom was one reason for the supposed backwardness of science in those societies . . . it may be doubted whether even in classical antiquity the separation of technics and science was as complete as has been supposed. In the Middle Ages there is much evidence to show that these two activities were no period totally divorced and that their association became more intimate as time went on.[8]

The frequent obsession with separating science and technology is clearly out of place in a history that is sensitive to the perception of the actors in each period. Following their trail it is relatively easy to see the interchange between thinking and doing, separated by mobile and not always defined boundaries.[9] Details of the remote artisanal, alchemical origins of chemistry are well known, from the pristine capacity for transforming materials using ancient methods such as sublimation, distillation, tanning or dyeing, which have survived in various forms across distant periods and cultures.[10] The different natural philosophies competing since ancient times have coexisted for centuries with oral traditions passed down through the generations about the complex process of mineral and metal transformation, food preparation and conservation and the manufacture of medicines.[11] Some historians in the past described these processes as 'exoteric' alchemy; in other words, they did not fit into certain theoretical (esoteric) explanations about the transmutation of metals or the elixir of longevity. But what is increasingly unclear is that the technological capacity to transform primary materials from nature has nothing to do with the conception of nature itself.[12]

Although there has been reluctance to place any importance on the contribution of technological skills to the emergence of modern science, the spirit of this chapter lies closer to the seminal thesis of Italian philosopher and historian Paolo Rossi (1923–2012). In 1962, Rossi maintained that defending the mechanical arts against accusations of indignity meant ceasing to think of science as a contemplative, disinterested activity or research that is only carried out after satisfying the basic requirements for living.[13] For example, the position of watchmakers, dyers, blacksmiths, weavers and distillers in the Middle Ages is now well known. It was the result of the gradual emergence of a new urban medieval culture.[14] Also, for Crombie, who has been followed by numerous other historians, there is great proof to show that the Middle Ages was a significant period of technological innovation, although most of the progress was probably made by illiterate artisans.[15]

148 Technological science

Looking at the Iberian empires mentioned above it seems quite reasonable that the Scientific Revolution in the sixteenth and seventeenth centuries cannot be properly explained without the hypothesis of a close collaboration between the scholar and the craftsman, between philosophers and machines, between abstract reasoning and the talent of instrument makers or the manufacturers of different types of material.[16] In the Baconian style, a utilitarian and practical view of knowledge leads us to think of the experimental culture of modern science in conjunction with the technological experts: inventors, engineers and artisans.[17] The books of secrets mentioned in Chapter 2 are a good example of this intersection.[18]

Although the concept of technoscience as a complex alliance between modern science, technology and industry has typically been associated with the changes that occurred from the end of the nineteenth century onwards, some historians believe that these kinds of interaction, with their unique characteristics, also took place in previous centuries. So the technical skills needed for the construction and use of instruments and machines (and objects in general) would have been the basis of the experimental culture and the construction of knowledge itself, forged from a subtle magma of shared objects.[19] The case of the instrument makers is especially important.[20] The telescopes of Galileo and Newton, Hooke's microscope and Hooke and Boyle's air pump are well-known examples of iconic objects of the new experimental culture. Their presence at public experiments (Robert Boyle's use of the air pump before the fellows of the Royal Society in London has attracted particular interest) conferred special authority on the expert, the natural philosopher, while the object itself acted as a mediator with the public who watched and endorsed the demonstration.[21] The instrument therefore took on an active role in the face of any possible controversy about the reliability of the experiment, in the same way as the role of telescopes in legitimating the existence of a new infinite universe in the sixteenth and seventeenth centuries.[22]

Scientific instruments would have no sense without their particular publics: aristocrats, travellers, monarchs, courtiers, students, visitors, spectators and workers. Boyle's air pump required a select audience at the Royal Society for its validation, but also other spectacular demonstrations such as that by German natural philosopher Otto von Guericke (1602–86) in 1654, in front of the Holy Roman Emperor Ferdinand III of Habsburg (1608–57). Guericke used the pump to remove most of the air contained in two copper hemispheres 50 centimetres in diameter, hermetically joined so that two groups of eight horses pulling in different directions could not separate them. When a small valve was opened to allow the air to enter the system, and the internal and external pressure to equalise, a child could easily separate the hemispheres to the delight of an admiring distinguished public (Figure 6.2).[23]

During that time instrument makers would announce their collections of telescopes and microscopes and they emerged as new experts, linked to artisanal culture but in fluid dialogue with the academic world, eager to adapt their

FIGURE 6.2 Public demonstration of the power of the air pump by Otto von Guericke (1654). Louis Figuier, *Les merveilles de la science*, I, pp. 40, 41. Reproduced with permission of the Biblioteca de Catalunya (Barcelona).

manual and experimental skills to the requirements of a specific apparatus. In 1683 the English optician John Yarwell (c. 1648–1712) offered a long list of items for sale: 'telescopes of all lengths, microscopes single and double perspectives, great and small, reading glasses of all sizes, magnifying glasses, multiplying glasses, triangular prisms, speaking trumpets, spectacles fitted to all ages, and all other sorts of glasses concave and convex'.[24]

These sophisticated objects were no longer of interest only to natural philosophers or future professional scientists, but they frequently appeared in people's homes and travelled all over the world for public demonstration and education. So some of the key elements of the artisanal world seem to have subtly infiltrated the heart of the academic culture of modern science. This turned out to be a major source of business which expanded dramatically over the coming centuries with a wide-ranging public. Some of the manufacturers of scientific instruments related to astronomy, navigation and topography achieved a great reputation and were even accepted as fellows of scientific societies and invited to publish articles in prestigious scientific journals such as the *Philosophical Transactions*.[25]

In the eighteenth century wealthy aristocrats like Lavoisier were able to commission new and sophisticated instruments for the study of combustion or

150 Technological science

the decomposition of water, the results of which would not have been possible without the manual skills of the manufacturer. Balances, gasometers, aerometers (balances of fluids), calorimeters and concave lenses were made according to Lavoisier's detailed instructions while accepting a certain shift of scientific authority from the Académie des sciences to the manufacturing workshop. Although potential audiences could not use these expensive objects or replicate his experiments, there is no doubt that the instruments played a major role in building up a powerful public image of the new chemistry. Of course, one of the novelties of the *Traité élémentaire de chimie* (1789), the key text on Lavoisier's work, was precisely the detailed presentation of the new instruments illustrated in a beautiful set of engravings.[26] In the nineteenth century, scientific instruments could be found in the laboratory and the classroom, universal exhibitions, science museums, textbooks, the advertising pages of newspapers and magazines or in the homes of the upper and middle classes. They played an important role in science education and in disciplining science students, but also in the public legitimisation of a theory or experiment. Instruments established new common spaces between experts and laypeople, reinforced the philosophy of demonstration and spectacle, and contributed to the material and visual culture of science.[27]

But the skills required to construct and use these instruments were not the only ones that counted. If today the word *manufacture* itself alludes to the carrying out of some kind of activity or the production of some kind of object by hand – connected with the old problem of undervaluing manual skills mentioned above – the word artisan transports us to pre-industrial periods, the guild age. It makes us think of the old meaning of 'art' which was much closer to technology than we might think today. It was a world that is virtually extinct, where technology was fundamentally based on the different manual skills and where, despite the existence of inventors and their legal protection, artisans played a very important role.[28]

Numerous autobiographies of artisans have been preserved: memoirs, personal diaries, family chronicles and travel logs. Their opinions, arguments and writing styles question the subaltern and marginal image that has had such a great influence on our appreciation of contemporary culture. In these texts the dignity of the artisans and their manual skills resists the tragic fate of Icarus, who foolishly tried to fly too high and melted the wax that held the feathers of his wings, made by his father Dedalus.[29] Artisans in workshops, arsenals and apothecary shops thought of their activities as a kind of knowledge in itself that had nothing to do with the individualist obsession of the genius creator, but was more concerned with a sense of lasting perfection in their work thanks to the cooperation and joint efforts of all members.[30]

There are magnificent illustrations of artisan culture from the past. Diderot and D'Alembert's *Encyclopédie* would not be complete without its thick volumes with engravings illustrating manual skills and techniques with great dignity, in other words illustrating the different artisan cultures of the Enlightenment.

Although some historians have highlighted the cold and rational representation of the artisan in the *Encyclopédie*, supposedly far removed from their real daily activity in the workshops, their inclusion is proof of their importance in eighteenth-century French and European society, and a good reminder of the need to highlight their role as significant actors in the history of science. The *Encyclopédie* presented a Baconian-style view of the 'arts', artisans and their skills as an important factor for civilisation which had received little consideration until then. The 11 volumes dedicated to technology became a practical manual for arts and crafts. The compilation and description of this enormous number of technical operations evidently required the active involvement of the artisans themselves (Figure 6.3).[31]

Talking about 'art', Diderot himself spoke of the artisans as people who had not until then had their merits recognised by society. He called for men who were prepared to come out of their scientific academies and visit the workshops, write reports and publish them in a book, in the hope of encouraging artisans to read, philosophers to think more pragmatically and the powerful to reflect on the way they used their authority and wealth.[32] In fact, Diderot sympathised with the

FIGURE 6.3 Artisan dyers in the Manufacture des Gobelins, Paris, 1772. Denis Diderot and Jean D'Alembert, eds. 1751–1780. *Encyclopédie ou dictionnaire raisonné des sciences, des arts et des métiers*. Paris: Briasson, David, Le Breton, Durand; Neuchâtel: Samuel Faulche, Vol X, 1772. Reproduced with permission of the Bridgeman Art Library.

152 Technological science

idea that philosophy was just words, while true knowledge was intimately tied to technological skills. So the blacksmith understood metals, while the metallurgy expert only knew books. Consequently technology (the arts of the time), a kind of science or descriptive knowledge had to be made public.[33]

In numerous scientific societies the artisans, machine inventors and scientific instrument makers were admitted as full members.[34] They had little or no academic training but many thought that their skills should be rewarded. They received special recognition and sometimes even had a special section dedicated to them.[35] However, despite this gradual process of artisan dignification, others were also tussling for the role of the true expert in technology. Throughout the eighteenth century, French engineers consolidated an elitist and military tradition with a solid mathematical base. They were attached to the new technical schools: the École des ponts et chaussées (1747), the École du génie (1748), the École des mines (1783) and finally the École polytechnique (1794).[36] Despite opening the door to a handful of artisans, *de facto* scientific academies played a fundamental role in controlling and legitimating the new machines and inventions.[37] This was the case, for example, in the Académie des sciences in Paris, where artisans and inventors from the provinces sent their inventions in the hope of them being recognised, legitimated and protected from copies and imitations. Powerful experts appeared, closely linked to the reformist monarchies of the enlightened despotism, although they remained in permanent tension with the authority of the artisans in their workshops and *manufactures royales*.[38] Curiously, the Montgolfier brothers came from a family of paper manufacturers and not from one of the prestigious French schools of mines or *ponts et chaussées*, where engineers were trained to serve the monarchy. But that was normal at the time. Until well into the nineteenth century technical education was fundamentally based on tacit knowledge and not so much on academic qualification, in a tradition where the young apprentices would develop their skills throughout their working life.[39]

But the artisan traditions were also firmly rooted in the guild system and since the Middle Ages the spoken word for communicating recipes and methods was essential to their survival. This was especially true in the *manufactures royales*, which attracted a number of different guilds throughout the seventeenth and eighteenth centuries, and tended to strengthen the authority of academics and engineers in frequent confrontation with the guild masters and artisans. The artisans criticised the academics and refused to apply academic knowledge to modify their ancient methods. They rejected the books published on the different arts as they often felt uncomfortable with the language and style.[40] The artisans and some members of the scientific societies shared some common elements but each 'culture' maintained its own identity and autonomy and resisted processes for standardising production.[41]

In the specific case of textile dyeing, the academic works of prestigious figures of the Enlightenment science such as Jean Hellot (1685–1766), Pierre-Joseph Macquer (1718–84) and Claude-Louis Berthollet (1748–1822), who also acted as general inspectors of the workshops, were often rejected by the artisans who refused to accept the rhetoric of academic science. Other books appeared, written in simple language in an attempt to reach the lowest echelons of the artisan world, to very little success. By 1748 Hellot was convinced that academic description of the dyeing processes was incomprehensible to artisans.[42] In 1767 Minister Turgot admitted that many of Hellot and Macquer's works had been completely ignored.[43] Experts made formulae, recipes and methods public through books and pamphlets in the hope of rationalising the tasks in workshops and *manufactures*, but again the results were disappointing.

There are some especially significant cases of artisan resistance such as that by the head of the dyeing workshop at the Gobelins *manufacture* in Paris at the end of the eighteenth century.[44] He was convinced that the intention of visits to his *manufacture* by Paris academics to control and standardise his dyeing processes was a great mistake, at least that is how he described it in 1778, and only responded to the interest of academic promotion of a few. He was particularly critical of Berthollet, who at that time was the general inspector of dyeing and whose job was to theorise on that art. Accustomed as he was to his own particular logic of production, the workshop head of the Gobelins, a man named Homassel, could not see the supposed benefits for his art of changing the names of the dyes, as advised by the experts on the basis of the new chemical nomenclature of Lavoisier, Berthollet and his circle, or the application of new theoretical explanations on the relationship between the dye and the textile fibre when trying to resolve practical problems of fixation. In 1778 Homassel gave a crude description of what, in his view, were the points of conflict:

> At that time, there was only a general complaint about the poor practices used in dyeing, in disregard of Colbert's regulations; and although the inspection of this *manufacture* [at the Gobelins] had long been entrusted to the most famous chemists of Paris, who used up the state's finances more in order to satisfy their cupidity and their chemical ambition by multiplying their experiments without any goal, rather than in improving or correcting the procedures used in dyeing . . . Some scheming chemists, after twisting the words of the famous Hellot to appropriate his ideas for themselves, incessantly appoint and dismiss their lowly and inept protégés at the Gobelins *manufacture* . . . Let us leave the experts of this calibre to grow rich by leading the artists into error, by advising them prematurely to introduce changes in their procedures . . . The career of the arts should receive consideration proportionate to its utility and the knowledge it requires. But when will this fine day dawn in France? When will the reign of the schemers and rogues come to an end?[45]

Scientific academies, Enlightenment monarchies and political reformers took it upon themselves to control and intervene in certain arts. The inertia of the artisans and guilds were often considered to be holding up modernity. The result was visits,

154 Technological science

supervisions and control, which were not always well received, and the guild resistance to its loss of identity in the *manufactures royales*, as spaces where production centred on certain technical skills under a new type of organisation. These are all examples of the strong personality of the artisans as a group and their long-standing tradition of oral communication and tacit knowledge.

As we shall see in the following sections, it is impossible to understand the technological culture of the pre-industrial age – and in all probability later periods as well – without giving the artisans a voice, while merging it with the voices of the other experts.

6.2. The publics of industrial culture

Industrialisation brought new experts in steam, siderurgy, and later on electricity and chemistry, at the service of the new nation-states and private industry. If the metaphor of Icarus and his wings melted by the sun takes us back to the old skills of the artisans, the myth of Prometheus has been used to reflect on the role of academic science in the Industrial Revolution. According to Greek mythology, Prometheus was a highly intelligent titan who stole Zeus's fire to offer it to humans. Zeus punished him for defying divine authority by chaining him to a rock where an eagle devoured his liver bit by bit for eternity. This story has been used as a source of inspiration by some historians to defend the idea that only modern science, in other words, the highest academic and intellectual skills, would have been able to free Prometheus from his chains and return to human beings their capacity to change the world. In some ways the Scientific Revolution of the sixteenth and seventeenth centuries would have determined the subsequent Industrial Revolution.[46]

However, this seems to be an oversimplistic interpretation that lacks rigour. In spite of the Prometheus epic, we know today that until well into the nineteenth century metallurgy, the steam engine and chemistry had all existed in the heart of artisan culture with little intervention by the scientific world. So experts from academia – the emerging professional scientists – would basically have played a legitimating role in offering rhetorical and formal presentations of the skills of the artisans. At most they may have contributed to creating an environment that prioritised some of the more 'scientific' attitudes, such as experimental rigour, quantification and precision, without actually making de facto changes to the technological and industrial processes.[47] A particularly well-known case is that of Nicolas Leblanc (1742–1806) and his industrial production of soda (sodium carbonate) at the end of the eighteenth century. The process was of great use to the chemical industry for almost a century but the theoretical explanations for each of the reactions took much longer to appear.[48]

The tacit knowledge of artisans and workers in workshops and factories took priority over academic discussions of the composition of the matter. That would explain the expansion of the chemical industry of acids and alkalis, with no solid underlying theory to explain the causes for the formation of sodium carbonate or sulphuric acid. Similarly, the success of James Watt's (1736–1819) steam engines at the end of the eighteenth century was not supported by any academic science of thermodynamics to explain the conversion of heat into mechanical power. You did not have to be a great mathematician or physicist, or even a distinguished pupil of a prestigious technical school to develop steam engines, which could easily be connected to weaving and textile machines.[49] This was a flexible technological culture with no clear separation between 'science' and 'technology' or the academy and the workshop, which progressively spread successfully to all corners of Europe (Figure 6.4).

From the perspective of nineteenth-century professional science, figures such as Leblanc and Watt could perfectly well be considered amateurs, but other publics of technology would acquire an important status during this period. That was the case of industrial engineers, an expanding profession in the 1800s, which frequently used an optimistic, technophile rhetoric in accordance with their role as experts of the industrialisation. It was a positivist discourse that could be easily identified in journals and professional publications as well as in the official discourses and commemorative rituals of their associations. With a few exceptions,

FIGURE 6.4 Public launch ceremony for a steam boat near Lyon, in 1783, invention of the marquis Jouffroy d'Abbans. Louis Figuier, *Les merveilles de la science,* I, p. 165. Reproduced with permission of the Biblioteca de Catalunya (Barcelona).

156 Technological science

the new experts of industrial technology, the professionals of the factory system and technical education, tended to display a supposedly neutral ideology, unlike the political classes. The new engineers sometimes combined the epic of the great inventors with the romantic hagiographies of the great names in engineering such as in the works of Samuel Smiles (1812–1904). They projected a public image of talent, responsibility and enthusiasm for technological progress and industrial dynamism, and their public discourse evidently responded to their own corporate interests as experts in the new industrial culture.[50] Their training in technical schools was gradually equated with the syllabuses in the science faculties of the new nineteenth-century universities, so that their professionalisation process was supported not only by private companies but also by public teaching institutions. Their relationship with the artisans and the new industrial workers was remarkably similar to the tension that existed between professionals and amateurs mentioned in Chapter 4.

Throughout the nineteenth century, in their public discourses, engineers tended to create an image of technology as an 'applied' science. To a large extent they justified their academic education and supposedly superior authority when in contact with the technological culture of the factory. Rather than coming closer to the artisan skills mentioned earlier, the 'applied' science concept was used to demonstrate that technological knowledge came from the applications of theories and methods of academic science to the arts, giving it autonomy and a special kind of dignity. Towards the middle of the century the Baconian idea of using natural philosophy for improving the mechanical arts, later reinforced by the Enlightenment philosophers and the French École polythechnique, became ingrained in the teaching of technology as the application of science to the useful arts. This was later for instance one of the rhetorical arguments of the presidents of the American Association for the Advancement of Science.[51]

However, positions were not unanimous and there was significant variation over time. In 1880 Thomas Huxley expressed his unease using this rhetoric in his book *Science and Culture*, in the following words:

> I often wish this phrase, 'applied science,' had never been invented. For it suggests that there is a sort of scientific knowledge of direct practical use, which can be studied apart from another sort of scientific knowledge, which is of no practical utility, and which is termed 'pure science.' But there is no more complete fallacy than this. What people call applied science is nothing but the application of pure science to particular classes of problems.[52]

As the profession gained ground and began to compete for space in the university science faculties, the presidents of the industrial engineers' associations tended to offer public definitions of the clear borders between their knowledge and 'pure science' on the one hand, but also between their own body of knowledge and that of the 'arts' – technology in its supposedly pure form.[53] By the end of the nineteenth century academic scientists and engineers had very different opinions, from those who saw science as a necessary source of knowledge for technological innovation to those convinced that, even at that time, technology evolved independently of academic inertia. Despite the discrepancies one more flexible use of the term 'applied science' enabled groups of experts to find a place of minimum consensus in their public discourses. While the academic scientists defended the need to finance 'pure' science in their universities as a fundamental step feeding into 'applied' science, the engineers tended to present themselves in public as 'applied scientists' to distinguish themselves from other groups of technological experts such as qualified workers, artisans and other specialists.[54] So engineers and scientists used an ambiguous, flexible and changing rhetoric to describe the limits of their authority and competence in their own disciplines.[55] Again, the struggle for scientific authority and the legitimation of the expert entered the public sphere.

Despite the growing power of professional engineers and even the gradual incorporation of academic scientists in industry at the end of the century, there are also other examples where the participation of artisans and workers in the development of certain industrial processes was particularly significant. In 1841, English chemist Lyon Playfair (1818–98) was employed in a calico printing factory in Lancashire having obtained his doctorate in organic chemistry at the University of Giessen, under the supervision of Justus von Liebig. In spite of his high level of academic training, Playfair worked to build bridges with artisan culture and managed to organise occasional informal pub meetings with some 30 people, mainly dyers but also printers, some businessmen and chemists. As in the case of the amateur botanists (see Chapter 4) they would discuss the viability of using new colours or the chemical composition of a certain substance.[56] At each meeting the members of the group described a practical problem related to textile dyeing but they also discussed the more theoretical aspects in an efficient combination of practical knowledge gained in their daily work in the factories and workshops, and academic science. It was a smooth way of exchanging knowledge without the inevitable rigidity of an institution and in close collaboration with a group of artisans open to discussing any kind of question related to the art of colour. Playfair admired the practical knowledge of one of the leading members of the group, John Mercer (1791–1866), who became a member of the prestigious Royal Society in 1852.

But the channels of communication and mutual feedback between technological experts and laypeople were also opening up along other paths. During the final decades of the nineteenth century academic science broke into the heart of industrial culture, especially in Germany.[57] The success of academic chemistry since the middle of the century, in alliance with the powerful chemical industry, headed the manufacture of artificial products on a global scale. In a context of efficient technical education, the German system of patents protected the processes but not the final product. Analysis of the BASF chemical industry in Ludwigshaffen in 1900 shows how academic scientists from the university science faculties and mechanical

158 Technological science

engineers who trained in technical schools played a fundamental role in shaping expert knowledge in the factory. The company had its own basic research laboratories inside the factory. Traders and lawyers ensured the commercial success of the new synthetic products and the new patents. Authority and prestige had shifted from university to industry.[58]

This was the new era of an academic science-based industry (a process that would be more or less repeated with electricity), where the place for tacit knowledge and the autonomy of worker and artisan culture seemed to diminish. However, some aspects of the old world remained, and even the new twentieth-century factories, with their assembly lines and interchangeable parts, did not seem to destroy the old spirit of the guild culture. That was at least one of the great concerns of American mechanical engineer Frederick Winslow Taylor (1856–1915) in his famous book *The Principles of Scientific Management*, published in 1911,[59] where he offered a 'scientific' interpretation of industrial production that would have a profound impact throughout the twentieth century. Taylor proposed improvements to productivity, the standardisation of production processes and an attempt to reduce the tension between workers and managers.[60] New individual relations with each worker were set up in an attempt to destroy the old artisan culture of the small autonomous workshops which, according to Taylor, were micro-cosmoses holding out in the factories and hindering technological progress. All of this had the intention of changing the relations between the workers, whose jobs were manual or systematically mechanised, and the new managers, whose task was 'intellectual', and transform them into something more harmonious and balanced, in contrast to the serious social tensions that the industrial world had seen in the nineteenth century.

But these major changes in the organisation of production were also perceived by others as attacks on the culture of the workers and artisans and their dignity, and were criticised ironically in films like *Modern Times* (1936) with Charles Chaplin (1889–1977). In the film the assembly lines and excessive mechanisation of the production process psychologically affected the victim (Chaplin, who goes from pillar to post between the conveyor belt, the automatic feeding machine, the hospital and the jail, and whose only escape from this world is unemployment, strike, poverty or social conflict). Previously films with Buster Keaton (1895–1966), *The Navigator* (1924) and *The General* (1926), had shown a more positive view of machines, despite their criticism of mechanisation. In these films, perhaps recovering some of the traditional skills of the old artisan cultures, the challenge is not to escape from the assembly line but to try to control the machine and adapt it to new and unexpected needs.[61]

Both of these film makers reflected from different angles on the concerns of a dehumanising industrial culture at the beginning of the twentieth century that had even deeper roots in the nineteenth century. At the heart of the industrial culture of the 1880s the gradual mechanisation of production in the factory system meant that the artisans found it increasingly difficult to maintain their identity.

In 1934 historian Lewis Mumford (1895–1990) explained how artisans had been reduced to competing with the machines in the new industries. He described that: 'the first requirement for the factory system, then, was the castration of skill. The second was the discipline of starvation. The third was the closing up of alternative occupations by means of land-monopoly and dis-education . . . Reduced to the function of a cog, the new worker could not operate without being joined to a machine'.[62]

Perhaps Mumford's view was overpessimistic but it seems fairly clear that growing mechanisation and standardisation led to the gradual disappearance of manual creativity. This situation produced attitudes opposed to the industrial model, defenders of traditional artisan culture of the different 'arts' of making objects, conservation of small-scale identities and resistance to homogenisation. The pre-industrial culture of the guilds had established a profound identification in the figure of the artisans, their skills, their capacity to communicate old manufacturing techniques and their cohesion as a group. Some of the critics of British industrialisation such as William Morris admired the quality of small-scale production in the workshops and hated the industrial production of the factory system. John Ruskin believed that science had separated the common man from daily life. Nostalgia for lost nature, the pain of the disappearance of artisan creativity and the beauty of their work were important factors in these kinds of critical discourse.[63]

Some industrialists demonstrated significant aesthetic sensitivity to the gradual mechanisation and standardisation of products in the face of the crushing victory of quantity over quality. That was the case of English textile industrialist James Thomson (1779–1850), an educated man with his own library and laboratory who had even written some scientific articles as an amateur. Following a trip to France he became aware of the ugliness of British fabrics compared with the French, despite the success of the mass production of the former in the new factories. Opposed to total mechanisation of the colour-printing process, Thomson promoted the role of the designers and the need to retain some of the quality elements of small-scale artisan production. He was a major promoter of design schools and a tireless proponent of the importance of spreading good taste throughout the population.[64]

Opposition to mechanisation resulted in a number of protests, some of them violent. Defending a set of values rooted in artisan culture justified Luddite attitudes of hatred towards machines and the destruction of factories.[65] Anti-machine feelings were also expressed through strikes or repeated complaints to the authority, but in every case they depended on the level of threat to traditional artisan-based values that the introduction of a machine posed. The old-school artisans, now industrial workers, demanded legislation to limit the free introduction of new machines to avoid the appearance of monopolies and protect the model of production by commission off the factory premises. In doing that they thought they could avoid the destruction of the family and moral values entrenched in the artisan tradition. However, machine inventors and industrialists justified the introduction

160 Technological science

of machinery as necessary for economic, technological and industrial progress, the moral virtues of business, the capturing of new markets and the right to free movement of capital. The Luddites, then, were more than just a supposedly irrational movement. They were defending a set of artisan values which in many cases would persist until well into the twentieth century when the factories were in full chain production.[66] This was another example of public expression and discourse interwoven by the hegemony of the machine and its associated values, where the different publics of technology took active positions to defend their own interests in the face of technological change.

Public perception of industrial progress also had other readings. Given the harsh living conditions in the industrial cities, public health played a corrective role, sometimes critical of the price in terms of health and the environment that came with these rapid changes. Faced with the dramatic relationship between poverty and disease, professional scientists were unable to remove themselves from the deterioration in the living conditions of the working classes in industrial cities, and less so when the health of their subjects or citizens was fundamental to the strength of the liberal state. Repeated complaints by workers' movements over inequality and poverty meant that scientists, and doctors in particular, became social and moral mediators, public health agents who required health and social hygiene engineering among other things. The industrial city was in conflict with the industrial interests of certain production processes. Factory activity was often seen as a threat by many of the agricultural landowners on the edges of the cities. As historian of medicine George Rosen stressed in the 1950s:

> Throughout human history, the major problems of health that men have faced have been concerned with community life, for instance, the control of transmissible disease, the control and improvement of the physical environment (sanitation), the provision of water and food of good quality and in sufficient supply, the provision of medical care, and the relief of disability and destitution.[67]

At the beginning of the nineteenth century the struggle against disease increased considerably. It became an organised and preventative strategy to combat the previous resignation in the face of the fatality of the epidemic through medical treatment and the distribution of clean water, treatment of sewage and industrial waste, the study of epidemiological theories, and heightened concern for maternity, nutrition, occupational health and health education. One of the main strategies was the spreading of medical knowledge. All individuals had to play an active part in the fight against illness. Health reforms also implied moral reform. During the 1830s public talks on anatomy, physiology and hygiene became important instruments in the campaign against ignorance. Women and housewives played a new active part in the efficiency of these campaigns in areas of home life such as the kitchen, bathroom, brushing teeth, childcare, child sexuality, cleanliness and household spending. To a large extent these health reforms also represented a counterpoint to the limitations of official medicine in its fight against major epidemics. They contributed to the emergence of a new public medicine prepared to stand up to traditional authority and passive resignation in the face of illness. Throughout the nineteenth century several manuals of hygiene appeared on the market, offering a fluent dialogue between doctors, legislators and the general public.[68]

During the first few decades of the nineteenth century the so-called *Conseil de salubrité* had a meeting of experts at its headquarters (chemists, vets, doctors and pharmacists) who set about inspecting and classifying the industries in Paris as dangerous, unhealthy or nocuous. They also examined the food, rivers, markets, cemeteries, slaughterhouses and public baths.[69] They drew up orders for regulating manufacturing and the use of explosives, food colouring, waste disposal and the cleanliness of wells. As such, new experts emerged in the form of health engineers as a result of the convergence of medical, scientific and technological knowledge who had great authority in the municipal decision concerning drainage, sewers, ventilation systems and cleanliness.[70]

English lawyer Edwin Chadwick (1800–90) developed a health project to supply drinking water, a new system of continuous sewers and general improvements in the health conditions of the British population. His project was published in 1842 under the title *Inquiry into the Sanitary Conditions of the Labouring Population of Great Britain*, and contributed to reducing the mortality rates and increasing life expectancy in England in the middle of the nineteenth century. However, the perception of Chadwick's work in the public sphere was mixed and sometimes controversial. Politicians feared that the cost for the public purse would be too high. Doctors criticised the fact that an intruder in their profession would be in charge of such a big health project. In 1854 they managed to make Chadwick's team resign and replaced it with a team of doctors; this is a dramatic but illustrative example of the struggle for recognition of the experts in the public sphere, beyond any strictly academic decisions.[71]

The treatment of urban waste was also a controversial topic. In fact, in many cities a discontinuous system was used in parallel to the 'water carriage' technique, known in French as 'tout à l'égout'. In 1829, 100 tonnes of excrement was collected daily in the city of New York and used as fertiliser for the neighbouring crop fields. The continual removal of waste required great public investment and supporters of the traditional discontinuous system defended latrines for the use of organic waste as fertiliser. They were opposed to the high public cost of building new pipes.[72] On the other hand, the question of drinking water also came under the microscope. Professional chemists gradually gained public recognition but disagreements among each other over the results of laboratory analyses weakened their authority. Just as the literature of the time reflected the tensions between the doctors and the chemists when it came to deciding upon the correct scientific criteria for certifying the therapeutic properties of springs, publications on water not suitable for drinking did not clearly set out the degree of authority of the chemical analyses.[73]

162 Technological science

Another live source of debate was air pollution. Only the Manchester Association for the Prevention of Smoke and the Noxious Vapours Abatement Association, basically made up of educated elite minorities, developed a critical discourse concerning smoke. In fact, experts saw the main source of air pollution in carbon combustion and the smoke in cities was clear evidence that the industrialisation process had gone too far. It was palpable proof that beauty and health had been sacrificed for economic benefit, causing unnecessary harm to the working classes with social tensions that had to be overcome. The question was how to progress towards eliminating industrial smoke from the urban air without reducing the carbon consumption necessary for locomotives, steam ships, blast furnaces, coke-fired furnaces, heating and domestic cooking. In 1881, two years after the famous London smog, an Exhibition of Smoke-Preventing Technology was organised and displayed all kinds of strategies for reducing urban smoke. This would lead to close cooperation between Britain and the United States in smoke-reduction techniques at the beginning of the twentieth century.[74]

But public perception of pollution was also mixed and sometimes contradictory. Movements against chimney smoke came from certain elite groups, but they were rejected by industrialists and manufacturers, mine owners and even the workers.[75] For the latter group chimney smoke represented wellbeing and economic prosperity which were considered to take priority over the environmental and health price that was paid as a result. Most entrepreneurs and even some humble workers were in favour of the emissions.[76] However, their attitudes did not mean the passiveness of the working classes in terms of the shameful conditions they experienced at work and in the city. The phenomenon of mutualism and the mutual help societies, which were partly joined to the workers' movement throughout the nineteenth century, were iconic examples of active concern by publics that were supposedly well informed about their health.

Faced with the evident moral decline of the working classes in industrial cities, public health policies and the growing medicalisation of society gradually turned the social outcast, sinner and criminal into patients. The 'empirical' medicine of natural and social ills was administered through numerous visits, interviews and dialogues with the new patients, who started to become suppliers of fundamental information for medical research. In psychiatry there is the case of Austrian physician Richard von Kraft-Ebing (1840–1902), and his work with patients locked up for being a danger to the public. In his book *Psychopathia Sexualis (1886)*, he transcribed interviews with patients that enabled him to describe a set of typologies for mental illness, publishing a set of clinical case notes that was enormously useful to potential readers who identified with some of the behaviour or symptoms he described. This contributed to a much more precise definition of each pathology, and the construction of new medical knowledge. In his interviews, Kraft-Ebing explored the behaviours of patients from different social backgrounds and occupations: traders, government workers, teachers, writers, artists, medical students and even doctors themselves.[77]

Technological science **163**

These are some examples of the polyphony of voices in nineteenth-century industrial culture and constant public presence and of the options defended by the different actors. They take us to a past which is closer to a tree with intricate branching than from a single, straight and robust trunk that symbolises a linear and accumulative account. Similarly, the plurality of publics of technology continued throughout the twentieth century, albeit under different parameters which the next section will show.

6.3. Inventors, users and consumers

The heroic image of the inventor was rife in the nineteenth century. Despite technophobic attitudes and the resistance of artisans and workers described in the previous section, the inventors and their hagiographies also reached popular culture. Biographies of the great inventors written by Smiles and in particular his four-volume set on the lives of the great engineers was met with international enthusiasm.[78] The idyllic image and romantic overtones of the genius inventor or the engineer has permeated a good part of our technological culture. However, in recent years some historians have repeatedly criticised how concepts such as invention and innovation have sparked a great deal more interest than the term 'use', to the point where the history of technology has been too closely linked to the history of invention and the big names associated with it: Leonardo, Watt, Stephenson, Marconi and Edison, and to the great machines which, in an exaggeratedly deterministic sense, changed the world for the passive and resigned user.[79] The fact that a certain technology became more widespread is not, however, an absolute measurement of its importance. The alternative options proposed and discussed in society have to be considered as well as the possibility that the user is acting as a guide or stimulus for the invention itself.[80]

As mentioned in the previous section, the great urban reformers of the nineteenth century and the agreements of the new sanitary engineers on the installation of sewers and improvements in public sanitary conditions required public debate and this did not come without controversy. There is constant evidence of how discussions about public works continue to be at the forefront of contemporary societies, where a mass of different reasons and interests as to the construction of a nuclear power station, a high-speed train or an airport are clearer than ever. Understanding these phenomena and their historical roots undoubtedly involves a new, more dynamic reading of users as central figures of technological culture beyond their traditional image of passive consumers.

Research is needed into how, in practice, users consume, modify, domesticate, design, reshape and resist certain technologies; in other words, how do users develop a set of strategies for active appropriation in permanent negotiation between the innovators and the publics of technology? Their arguments for or against certain machines need to be heard. Each group of users could assign different meanings to the same technology in constant discussion with

164 Technological science

the designers.[81] From that perspective we need to place the old above the new, small over big, the mundane over the spectacular, female over male, poverty over wealth and repair and maintenance over design and innovation. In fact, focusing on invention allows us to concentrate on a small group of places which since the modern age have been located in Europe and America. However, the manufacture of objects extends well beyond those boundaries and the map of the users of these objects would be even bigger. Considering the users of technology therefore requires a significant change of focus in viewing the present and the past.[82] As historian David Edgerton suggests, perhaps the history of twentieth-century technology is not, as we thought until recently, the history of aviation, nuclear energy, the contraceptive pill and the internet, but it is much more closely linked to the history of cement, DDT, the condom, rickshaw, horse and bicycle.[83]

Different groups of users contribute to this plural view of technology. Sometimes they have a direct influence on certain changes, while on other occasions they are more distanced from the discourse of the experts, although they may also be affected by it to a greater or lesser extent.[84] Users often become consumers in our societies of mass production so that the consumption of a certain technological object is much more than a simple economic transaction. In the selection process users construct an entire universe of cultural values and social prestige, a fact that is obviously not overlooked by the marketing departments and advertising agencies when trying to identify affinities with potential customers. Production and consumption form another polarity in permanent tension in the face of constant exposure of technology in the public sphere.

Consider, for example, chemical products from a user's perspective. They are quickly associated with practical qualities in the daily lives of millions of consumers. Despite their sometimes negative contemporary public image linked to environmental pollution, their extensive use in the food industry, cosmetics, clothing and medicines cannot be ignored.[85] It cannot be a coincidence that advertising campaigns for the chemical industry place great emphasis on their use in daily life to seduce potential consumers (Figure 6.5). After the negative image of 'chemistry' as a result of their use in World War I, there was a move to bring the industry closer to the general public, as seen for example in Du Pont's slogan in 1935, *Better Things for Better Living, through Chemistry*.[86]

Du Pont launched the campaign in three new science museums: Chicago (1933), Philadelphia (1934) and New York (1936), opening the doors to the chemical industry so that they would present and fund his exhibition projects. In all of those cases the objectives of Du Pont's *Better Things* were threefold: to persuade consumers of the good qualities of the new synthetic products, to change the old image of the industry associated with warfare and the production of explosives and to overcome public unease about the business of the big corporations. Some visitor testimonies seem to indicate that these objectives were largely achieved.[87] However, problems with public reluctance to accept the industry continued for a good part of the twentieth century and continue today. As a result of the discontent that has been a constant theme in this book most of the campaigns aimed at

FIGURE 6.5 'Lab Technician Set for Girls', A.C. Gilbert Co. (1958). Photography by Gregory Tobias. Reproduced with permission of the Chemical Heritage Foundation Collections, Philadelphia, PA.

166 Technological science

convincing the public that chemical products bring health, comfort and well-being have not escaped that sense of hostility from their audiences.[88]

In fact, reactions against artificiality have been and are still frequent among consumers and users. In the mid-twentieth century plastics were often presented as new alternative materials to wood, ceramics, glass and other natural materials, able to offer new artistic possibilities in colours and designs.[89] From 1939 to 1940, the 'Science Service', a non-government organisation dedicated to science popularisation, organised the travelling exhibition 'Fabrics for the Future' showing most of the new synthetic fibres and new polymers including the famous nylon.[90] But despite this kind of discourse and the campaigns of the chemical industry there were groups of users headed by intellectuals who continued to object that plastics were too far removed from nature and could therefore be a health hazard.[91] A New Left manifesto of 1968, together with other widely distributed works, openly criticised the Western model of industrial development in which plastics featured strongly.[92] Current debates about the use of plastic bags, environmental problems and consumer attitudes towards them are a good illustration of the continuing active role of many users.

On the opposite end of the spectrum, journalist John Emsley's book *The Consumer's Good Chemical Guide, Separating Facts from Fiction about Everyday Products* (1994) once again stressed the user satisfaction in daily life of a multitude of chemical products that have made our lives easier.[93] Emsley introduced his work to potential readers as a: 'response to the increasing negative attitudes to anything "chemical". These ignored the fact that modern life would not be feasible without important scientific solutions to the world's problems. All my books have focused on demystifying and explaining chemistry, elements and molecules, and how they have an impact on the processes of life, and death.' Emsley advertised *The Consumer's Good Chemical Guide* as: 'a balanced account of chemicals such as perfumes, sweeteners, alcohol, cholesterol, fats, fibre, painkillers, PVC, dioxins, nitrates and carbon dioxide, which have often been the cause for media alarms and popular concerns, but mainly wrongly so'.[94] However, there is an increasing number of consumer organisations concerned about certain chemicals. The use of phthalates in cosmetics and toys has been regulated recently thanks to pressure by some of those groups in the form of detailed information about the product for consumers and the definition of risk criteria in its different uses.[95]

It is easy to see how at the end of the nineteenth century electricity gradually reached numerous cities and its arrival in homes was met by differing opinions among the growing number of users. Electricity had become a new source of power, a system of urbanisation and distribution never before seen. It was a fascinating phenomenon and at the beginning of the twentieth century an almost endless provider of lighting and new domestic products (fans, irons, radios, vacuum cleaners, refrigerators). In many countries the technophobia surrounding these objects was met by ambitious advertising campaigns and propaganda which aimed to legitimate the new fluid to users and consumers.[96] The universal exhibitions played a very important role in the gradual seduction of visitors (and also users of electricity) and in a process of adaptation to the new current that had initially caused mistrust. These giant showcases of science raised inventors such as Graham Bell, Marconi and Edison to an iconic status but they also tried to make light of the public fear of electrical sparks. With the enthusiastic backing of the electrical companies, future users were gradually tamed by a rhetoric that was closer to entertainment than to a scientific understanding of the phenomenon.

By the end of the nineteenth century potential users were asking for specific explanations for the mysteries of this intangible concept known as electricity. They were paying as consumers for something that they could never see, touch or measure for themselves. All they could do was experience and, in most cases, enjoy its effects. Even the great Edison had trouble giving convincing explanations about the nature of electricity to the people who were using and consuming it in Britain and the United States. So the huge demand for precise and reliable knowledge about electricity provided many individuals with an opportunity to become experts and technical specialists in the middle ground between the world of the professionals and engineers, the amateurs and the users.[97]

Advertising of electricity was especially aimed at housewives but decisions about which particular electrical product or installation fell to the men, as did the comprehension and use of the instruction manuals. Clients as potential users also had the chance to attend demonstrations of the benefits of those goods and installations, either in showrooms or through orders from travelling expert salespeople. Advice also appeared in the daily press, specialised periodicals, satirical publications, illuminated signs, radio and the cinema.[98] In this context of domestic technology, the housewives, maids and male amateur readers of general publications about electricity became active users and publics of technology through which their consumer opinions and attitudes influenced strategies of the corresponding companies. Corporate advertising acted as a key agent for scientific popularisation of electricity but also for nuclear energy and chemistry, and it played on the idea that the more technical information given led to greater acceptance and consumption by users.

Even before the invention of the combustion engine there is sufficient historical evidence of how the bicycle in the mid-nineteenth century provided an opportunity for freedom of movement for women, something which was extremely difficult in the old carriages. Women therefore became active publics who could use technological objects for their own benefit. The addition of motors to bicycles (motorcycles) and the huge success of automobiles at the beginning of the twentieth century was nothing more than a consequence of that growing tendency for materialisation of liberal capitalist individualism in a new transport that continues to fascinate millions of users more than a century later.[99] At the end of the nineteenth century, the automobile became a kind of material extension of the individual as a user and a symbol of individual freedom in the United States. The success of the Ford-T, the first public vehicle to

168 Technological science

be manufactured on an assembly line, was the result of that individualism and a capacity for control in a vast and largely unstructured territory in comparison to the rail networks that had crossed the Old Continent in the nineteenth century. Given young people's enthusiasm for their first motorcycle or their first car or the identification of a technological object with a certain social status for the user, the weight of cultural values is undeniable. The cold image of technology in instruction manuals is overtaken by the active attitudes of its users which influence and condition its design and development.[100]

★ ★ ★

Also from a user perspective, a few years ago historian Arnold Pacey suggested a new way of looking at the problem of technology. In his *people-centred technology* he asked himself what technology would have been like in history if the great inventors had thought more about its potential users and developing technology that was closer to people than about the machines themselves.[101] He proposed a special kind of sensitivity to understand the subtle reactions of the users to their machines, their manual abilities, visual and aesthetic reactions to inventions, and even their mechanical and visual capacity for thought. Some of these main conclusions were largely in keeping with the spirit of this chapter and can be summarised in the following words:

> For too long [according to historian David Nye], 'it has been assumed that the social meaning of a new machine was defined by the inventor'. To counteract that bias, we need to consider the meanings of technology that may be discovered by users of machinery, factory workers, or consumers . . . Some everyday experience of tools and machines is also comparable to more specialized experiences in engineering or industry.[102]

The examples above show how technology today and in the past is deeply rooted in the public sphere and in the daily lives of users, consumers, inventors, artisans, engineers and even spectators. At the end of the eighteenth century, thousands of people were watching balloon flights, which continue to awaken our sense of aesthetics or even adventure today. Machines are a cause for celebration in universal exhibitions, the opening of a new railway line or the public works that have taken so much time and effort. The grand opening ceremony for a new underground train line is usually attended by the politicians and businesspeople involved in its design and development and yet the simple workers who have dug each centimetre of the subsoil and placed their lives at risk remain unseen. Similarly, other official openings such as exhibitions serve as a kind of social balsam where the most invisible publics of technology can feel that they have played their part in a great collective event, even if it is only for one day.[103] Open days for the public in industries, with guided tours and carefully prepared explanations on the (almost always) 'difficult' start for the company and its 'heroic' growth over the years are another strategy. Technological culture is made public for its social legitimation.

Returning to the hot air balloons and poor Madame Blanchard's accident illustrates another important aspect of the public face of technology. The accident was seen as a failure but at the same time it had an enormous impact on public opinion. It meant that technology, with all its lights and shadows, was in everyone's mind. Random attempts to find scientific news items in the daily press from the eighteenth century on will regularly bring up articles about great natural disasters (earthquakes, volcanic eruptions and floods) together with technological accidents (train crashes, boiler explosions and plane crashes).[104] From that more symmetrical perspective the linear, scientist conceptions of innovation are substituted by a more plural and socially interwoven knowledge where unidirectional technological determinism has gradually given way to a broad range of possible itineraries.[105] The old idea of a technology designed by a small group of experts for a precise purpose has been substituted by other conceptions where uncertainty and the active participation of other publics are overriding. So different social groups are able to flexibly appropriate technological objects without any a priori prediction of who will be dominant. Users can therefore acquire a leading position in the multitude of decisions that finally shape technological systems.[106]

Technological experts have a great influence on urban planning, transport, waste management policies, and on our experience as users and consumers. However, their social legitimation depends on critical users, resistance to change, alternative ways of seeing things which serve, according to philosopher Andrew Feenberg, as a counterbalance. They ensure the representativeness of the technology itself and eliminate suspicions of arbitrariness or the existence of hidden interests. If technology lacks this public profile it will inevitably be the object of discontent, mistrust and opposition.[107]

Notes

1 'Elle fit un très-grand nombre de voyages aériens, et finit par acquérir une telle habitude de ces périlleux exercices, qu'il lui arrivait souvent de s'endormir pendant la nuit dans son étroite nacelle, et d'attendre ainsi le lever du jour, pour opérer sa descente. Dans l'ascension qu'elle fit à Turin, en 1812, elle eut à subir un froid si excessif, que les glaçons s'attachaient à ses mains et à son visage', Figuier (1867–70: II, 515).
2 Lynn (2006: 122–4).
3 Farrington (1944, 1947).
4 Gille (1966).
5 Galluzzi (1996).
6 Cañizares-Esguerra (2006); Bleichmar, De Vos, Huffine, Sheehan (2009).
7 Conner (2005).
8 Crombie (1995: 183, 84).
9 Gieryn (1983).
10 Brock (1992).
11 Multhauf (1966); Brock (1992).
12 Holmyard (1957). For an updated interpretation, see Principe (2013).

170 Technological science

13 Rossi (1996). Rupert Hall, one of the indisputable authorities on the Scientific Revolution, rejected, for example, any contribution from the artisan world to the development of modern science. For Hall the appearance of the cannon did not lead to the new Newtonian dynamics and navigation was never behind the correction of the astronomical charts. It was not material need that made Copernicus rearrange the order of the planets and place the sun at the centre of the universe. In his own words: 'It is really of little benefit to an understanding of the Scientific Revolution from Galileo to Newton that quite a lot of men were interested in ships, cabbages and sealing-wax', Hall (1963: 7).
14 Conner (2005); Crombie (1995).
15 Crombie (1995: II, 162).
16 Bennett (1987).
17 Zilsel (1941–2).
18 Eamon (1994: 8).
19 Klein (2005a).
20 Van Helden, Hankins (1994); Bertomeu-Sánchez, García Belmar, Bensaude-Vincent (2002).
21 Shapin, Schaffer (2011); Wise (1988).
22 Van Helden, Hankins (1994).
23 Guericke, Ames (1994).
24 Turner (2005: 128).
25 Bennett (1987); Sorrenson (1993); Roberts, Schaffer, Dear (2007).
26 Holmes (2000).
27 Bertomeu-Sánchez, García Belmar, Bensaude-Vincent (2002); Wise (2006).
28 Berg (1991).
29 Amelang (1998).
30 Rossi (1996: 2–3).
31 Pyenson, Sheets-Pyenson (1999: 415); Gillispie (1959).
32 Gillispie (1959: ix).
33 Gillispie (1959: xix–xx).
34 Nieto-Galan (1997).
35 Sorrenson (1993).
36 Picon (2007).
37 Hilaire-Pérez (2000).
38 Crosland (1992); Nieto-Galan (2001).
39 Donnelly (1994); Fox, Guagnini (1993).
40 Nieto-Galan (2001).
41 Holmes (1989b).
42 Jean Hellot (1750), *L'art de la teinture des laines et des étoffes de laine en grand et petit teint*, Paris: Pissot, Herissant, p. viii; Nieto-Galan (2010).
43 Nieto-Galan (2001).
44 Nieto-Galan (2010).
45 Homassel (1798), *Cours théorique et pratique sur l'art de la teinture en laine, soie, fil, coton*. Paris: Courcier, p. vii, x, xii; Nieto-Galan (2010).
46 Landes (1969).
47 Gillispie (1957).
48 Aftalion (2001).
49 Cardwell (1994).
50 Ahlström (1982).
51 Kline (1995).
52 Thomas H. Huxley, 'Science and Culture' (1880); Kline (1995: 194).
53 Gieryn (1983); Kline (1995: 221).
54 Kline (1995: 198).
55 Gieryn (1983); Bud (2012).
56 Nieto-Galan (1997).
57 Meyer-Thurow (1982).

Technological science **171**

58 Travis (1993); Meyer-Thurow (1982).
59 Cohen (1997).
60 Doray, Macey (1989); Waring (1991).
61 Basalla (1994).
62 Mumford (1934: 173).
63 Levine (1987: 22).
64 Nieto-Galan (2001).
65 Randall (1994).
66 Mumford (1934); Maidment (2001).
67 Rosen (1958: 1).
68 Markell (1997).
69 Fowler La Berge (1975); Le Roux (2011).
70 Le Roux (2011).
71 Hamlin (1998).
72 Tarr (1996).
73 Hamlin (1990).
74 Stradling, Thorsheim (1999).
75 'Hell is a city much like London. A populous and a smoky city', cited by Porter (1994: 257).
76 Mosley (1999).
77 Oosterhuis (2000). I am grateful to Àlvar Martínez-Vidal for this information.
78 Jarvis (1997); Weber, Perkins (1992).
79 Smith, Marx (1994); Bijker, Hughes, Pinch (1987).
80 Edgerton (1999, 2007); Von Hippel (2005).
81 Lie, Sorenson (1996).
82 Edgerton (2007:80).
83 Edgerton (2007: xi).
84 'There is no correct use of a technology . . . Of course, there may be one dominant use . . . or a prescribed use, or a use that confirms the manufacturer's warranty, but there is no one essential use that can be deduced from the artifact itself . . . We . . . follow the research path of studying technologies in their 'context of use' – the society and the web of other artifacts within which technologies are always embedded . . . We are interested in how users consume, modify, domesticate, design, reconfigure and resist technologies', Oudshoorn, Pinch (2003: 1–2).
85 'The Uses of Chemistry (and Alchemy)' was the main topic of the 7th International Conference on History of Chemistry (Sopron, Hungary, 2–5 August 2009).
86 Brock (1992: 656); Rhees (1993).
87 Rhees (1993).
88 Schummer, Bensaude-Vincent, van Tiggelen (2007).
89 Bijker (1995: 106).
90 La Follette (2007).
91 Meikle (1997: 280).
92 Meikle (1997: 285).
93 Gregory, Miller (1998: 137).
94 The Consumer's Good Chemical Guide, http://johnemsley.com/books/consumers_good_chemical_guide.html (accessed 21 June 2015).
95 Iles (2007).
96 Hughes (1983); Schwartz Cowan (1983).
97 Gooday (2008).
98 Nye, D. (1990).
99 Bijker, Hughes, Pinch (1987); Bijker (1995).
100 Volti (1996).
101 Pacey (2001).
102 Pacey (2001: 77).

172 Technological science

103 Nye, D. (1999a, b).
104 Hilaire-Pérez (2008: 37–8).
105 Stirling (2008).
106 Nahuis, Van Lente (2008).
107 Feenberg (1999: 145).

7
MEDIA SCIENCE

In 2000, in a revised re-edition of the famous book *Gaia: A New Look at Life in Earth* (1979), English chemist James Lovelock expressed doubts about the most effective way of reinforcing the authority of his theory, which had been rejected in the previous decades by a large part of the scientific community. He described how: 'Until 1995, it was nearly impossible for a scientist anywhere to publish a paper on Gaia, unless to disprove or disparage it; now at last it is a theory awaiting approval'.[1] Lovelock faced a cruel bifurcation:

> To establish Gaia as a fact I must take the first path, that of science. As a guide on the best way to live with the Earth, it will only be believed if it comes with majority support from the scientific community – politicians and governmental agencies dare not act on myth . . . To keep Gaia as something we all can understand I must take the second path, the one that goes to the postmodern world. Here science itself is questioned . . . Which of these paths should I take?[2]

Gaia provided an elegant metaphor, more or less in agreement with the environmental spirit of the times in which we live. Although most people on the planet have no clear idea about the reliability of the Gaia hypothesis, we are witness to its constant presence in the media. The Gaia case is just one among many others that has caught the attention of historians, sociologists and communication theorists. It invites reflection on the mediatisation of science, which has intensified over the last few decades. Throughout the twentieth century the media probably 'contaminated' science so that today academic knowledge and its media version provide constant and intense feedback. Books, magazines, the daily press, radio, television and, more recently, the internet contain fragments of scientific knowledge whose legitimation is invariable linked to the logic of these

174 Media science

media themselves. As a result, science and its audiences seem to have succumbed to the interests and logic of mass media.[3]

There is extensive evidence to suggest this hypothesis merits serious consideration. The media version of a certain scientific topic sometimes appears before the publication of specialised academic articles, thereby displacing the centre of gravity of the expert discourse towards the public sphere.[4] Controversial topics gain space in the media precisely for their polemical nature and not so much for their 'strict' scientific content. Experts and laypeople are continually negotiating in complex processes where values, interest and convictions that are shared to a greater or lesser extent play a fundamental role.[5] Excessive closeness and intellectual promiscuity between science popularisers, professional scientists and the public at large often provides a distorted perspective. A superficial image of scientists as problem solvers is commonly perceived by audiences that rarely know the details of the expert work. Sound data and information have to fit in the material and formal constraints of each medium. Scientific news diffused in both written and audio-visual media are often associated with caricatures, stereotypes or a simple fascination for alternative and controversial issues.[6]

The media therefore becomes a flexible beast, capable of adapting to the interests of its audience who, caught by this tacit discontent – between admiration and suspicion – demands the 'truth' on the one hand while lapping up the relativism of the accident, risk or public controversy among the experts on the other. That is one possible explanation, for example, for the fascination with 'pseudo-sciences', or non-orthodox sciences, in the public arena. Faced with tragic catastrophes and incurable illnesses the speculations of some popularisers, underpinned by the opinions of certain experts, tend to produce an increase in audience figures.[7] On the other hand, science is often presented in the media as a heroic, apolitical and intrinsically rational enterprise which, from its dominant position, has the effect of legitimising the interests of professional scientists and other groups of power.[8] Most science items appearing in the daily news come from the press offices of private corporations or governments, all of them with their own specific interests when it comes to communicating with the public. In the media, popularisers are often perceived of as simple transmitters of the work of the scientists. Their professional success or failure depends on their ability to explain scientific advances to the public, but not on their critical ability in the face of the dominant discourses of the experts.[9] The old, comfortable image of an objective and neutral science in the hands of experts with clearly defined boundaries of authority – the traditional view of science popularisation – has gradually disappeared with the explosion of new audio-visual media, which has substantially altered the circulation of scientific knowledge in the twentieth century, in both quantitative and qualitative terms.

Experts feel obliged to reveal their research in the media and discuss their discoveries with large sectors of society who, although frequently treated as laypeople, have taken on a significant role when it comes to validating certain policies or lines of research. To an extent, the new media explosion has made science more public, although its constant exposure seems to be a double-edged sword. It offers the experts an authority that they cannot achieve in academic circles (as in the Gaia case) and so the scientists themselves seek a media impact using their own professional strategies, sometimes bypassing the 'peer review' system which is the gold standard of the academic world. On the other hand, those same experts are often seen as vulnerable in the face of fickle audiences, hungry for superficial information, and this can undermine their authority.[10]

In today's media society it seems unlikely for scientists to be able to confine their disagreements to the privacy of their laboratories while opening the doors to offer the public 'truths' and consensus.[11] A large number of recent studies have shown that scientific controversies are increasingly settled in public and that the modern mass media accommodate them as a matter of course. In the light of the shrinking scientific authority of the academy, the media are easily able to capture these 'hot topics' of difficult solution, high controversy and little consensus.

The marked emphasis on specific examples in the twentieth century cannot exclude, however, the possibility of looking at the problem of media science from a broader historical perspective. It is intrinsically related to the mechanisms of popularisation which has become spectacularly intense over the last century. The markets for books of secrets in the eighteenth century, press articles about balloon flights, Faraday's demonstrations at the Royal Institution, the presence of journalists at the sessions of the Académie des sciences during the time of François Arago, the great showcases provided by the universal exhibitions, and many other examples can be considered the 'predecessors' of the gradual mediatisation of scientific knowledge and the increasingly overriding role of the media in validating knowledge in the public sphere at any given time. Despite this, the marked media character of the twentieth century, as well as the density of scientific events 'touched on' by the media, are good reasons to focus in this chapter on examples from the last century.

7.1. Stars and planets

In the 1950s a heterodox theory on the origin of the universe by British astronomer Fred Hoyle (1915–2001) was pushed aside in academic circles but obtained an extraordinary media impact through popularisation and science fiction.[12] Hoyle had studied mathematics at Cambridge and his interest in cosmology arose following World War II, at a time when the active role of science in the Allied victory had profoundly affected British public opinion. His series of astronomy talks on BBC radio were listened to by a large audience. It was there that he began to present his theory of the stationary nature of the universe, which appeared later in book form as *The Nature of the Universe*, in 1950.

Using simple language, Hoyle explained that the earth, the planets of the solar system and the stars had been formed from a primitive dust which condensed billions of years ago. He presented to the media a theory of the origin and evolution of the universe that was contrary to the Big Bang theory, increasingly accepted

176 Media science

by the scientific community. For Hoyle the universe did not have a beginning and an end. Even though the galaxies were moving away from us, new hydrogen atoms are created to fill the void in a process of continual creation.[13] The result was a universe in constant transformation but also stationary in a similar sense to the movement of water molecules flowing through a river which appear to be stable when viewed together from a distance. Although Hoyle popularised the term 'Big Bang' on his radio programme, paradoxically it became one of his main opponents. He also rejected Darwin's theory of evolution in favour of the theory of panspermia, which suggested that life could have been transported from other planets to Earth through interstellar dust particles. Hoyle used his theory as a source of inspiration for numerous science fiction novels. In 1962 he wrote *A for Andromeda*, which quickly became a BBC television series.

Faced with the information provided by new astronomical observations consistent with the Big Bang theory, Hoyle modified his explanation to try to adapt it to the empirical data, but even then it was not accepted in academic circles. In 1957 he became fellow of the prestigious Royal Society in London, but the hostility of the professional astronomers who were against his theory forced Hoyle to accept an invitation from the University of California where he found a more comfortable intellectual atmosphere in which to combine his academic work with his popularisation of science. In 1957 he published the famous science fiction novel *The Black Cloud* and continued to use the media to disseminate his cosmology. The novel told the story of the appearance of a huge gas cloud in the solar system that threatened to destroy all life on the planet by preventing solar radiation from reaching it, and largely reinforced his own theory on the origin of the universe.

In other works of fiction, Hoyle forwarded his hypothesis of the origin of life from space, the result of his continued interest in the study of interstellar dust whose spectral nature he studied for many years, even suggesting some similarities between these dust particles and certain bacteria. Even though Hoyle made several attempts to reinstate himself in the scientific community throughout his life, his academic impact was almost always inversely proportional to his media success. So his popular science and even his science fiction (examples from other historical periods have shown the blurred boundaries between both genres), allowed him to converse with the public, in particular his readers and radio listeners, as well as speculating on the limits of his own theory.

Moving on from Hoyle's interstellar dust to consider the nature of the surface of the earth results in some interesting coincidences. As seen at the beginning of this chapter, in 1961, at the height of his space career, James Lovelock considered the possibility of analysing the planet holistically as an organism that could only be understood globally. Although later on he rectified some aspects, in 1979 he defended the idea that the physical and chemical conditions of the Earth, the atmosphere and the oceans had evolved together and gradually adapted to the presence of life on the planet. This was a self-regulating system by and for life through a complex process of feedback. Despite the controversy and criticism of his theory in academic circles (here we see a parallelism with Hoyle) different references to it can be found in numerous forums and media. Gaia has been on the lips of science popularisers, historians, philosophers, journalists, politicians, science fiction writers and the clergy. Knut Kloster, the Norwegian shipping magnate and President of the World City Corporation, donated £75,000 to Lovelock to cover the cost of the three Gaia conferences that took place in Oxford (1994, 1996 and 1999). In 2002 he even launched a cruise ship named 'Gaia', with a capacity for 1,400 passengers.[14]

On the suggestion of his friend, Nobel Prize-winner William Golding (1911–93), Lovelock named his theory Gaia in honour of the Greek goddess of the earth, nature and life. The name was considered not accurate enough and rejected by many professional scientists. In fact, Lovelock's hypothesis was presented in different forums and in eight specialised articles but it still did not manage to catch the interest of the experts. In 1975 his article 'The Quest for Gaia' had already been published in *New Scientist*, and enjoyed a wide readership which resulted in him being invited by several publishers to write a book about his theory. By 1979 it had become his first best seller and is still being republished and translated today.

Gaia awakened more sympathy in environmental movements than in academic circles. In 1988 Edward Goldsmith, the editor of the *Ecologist*, saw it as the great hope for a new scientific epistemology. The idea also inspired feminist thought which associated our perception of nature with a gendered construction. In his view, Gaia's social, ethical and even spiritual principles explained the enthusiasm with which it was received by environmentalist movements, which lacked scientific recognition due to frequent opposition to official science.[15] The Gaia hypothesis represented for Goldsmith a kind of pristine ecology, pure and not yet perverted by his attempts to approach orthodox science and thereby install himself in the academic world. Gaia was a method, a new way of analysing and understanding nature, which made a fresh claim for the organic, the holistic over the mechanistic. Gaia became a liberation from the heavy slab of modern science that some other critics, such as Carolyn Merchant, had also denounced from a gender perspective. The loss of this organic vision of nature was bemoaned in a wealth of historical detail in Merchant's famous book: *The Death of Nature: Women, Ecology, and the Scientific Revolution.*[16]

However, reactions in the academic world were not slow in coming. In 1981 the biochemist W. Ford Doolittle, in his article 'Is Nature Really Motherly?', criticised Gaia for being too teleological and 'maternal', warning that the content of Lovelock's book could muddle the public. A year later the well-known science populariser Richard Dawkins maintained that Gaia could not remain alive since it had no competitors: at that time the universe would have been full of dead planet systems and Gaia would have to have some form of reproducing. In the face of these initial disagreements, Lovelock decided to drop anchor in the public sphere using new strategies. In 1983 he created the DaisyWorld model: a simulation of a hypothetical world that revolved around a sun whose temperature

178 Media science

increased over time. Like Hoyle, in 1984 Lovelock and Michael Allaby wrote a science fiction work entitled *The Greening of Mars*. The book challenged the scientists who were hemmed in by their own disciplinary barriers and defended the creativity of risky hypotheses such as Gaia.

But Lovelock's media alliances had other dimensions. He worked with US microbiologist Lynn Margulis (1938–2011), whose theory of symbiogenesis (an explanation for cell cooperation) had great weight in the international academic community. Margulis is also the author of around 40 popular science books, far outweighing the number of his research articles in specialised journals. Margulis's academic articles, textbooks and popular science books have become more useful, complementary communication tools than those of Lovelock.

In fact, today Gaia is in the hands of many scientific audiences. The idea of the Earth as a living planet goes beyond a small core of experts and spills over into best sellers, science fiction novels and television documentaries. The Gaia hypothesis is controversial enough to warrant new lines of research while inspiring artists, ecologists and science fiction writers. The problem lies not so much in deciding whether it is a 'good' or a 'bad' theory, but in evaluating the different approaches in recent decades and seeing how they have penetrated the Fleckian circles of experts, but also those of the supposed laypeople. From orthodox and official science the theory has never ceased to be overly speculative, anthromorphic and teleological. Attempts by Margulis and others to normalise it within academic systems have never had much success. Consequently, Gaia has played its cards more on the ground of moral authority (probably closer to the lay public) than scientific authority, where it would seem to lose most of its hands. Despite the controversies, or maybe thanks to its media projection, the Gaia theory has seen spectacular expansion to all corners of our society.

7.2. Media molecules

The public image of molecular biology, one of the stellar disciplines of the twentieth century, is closely linked to the research programme of its experts. In 1968 James Watson (1928–), one of its founding fathers and at the forefront of the structural elucidation of DNA, together with Francis Crick (1916–2004), published *The Double Helix*. Watson used the book to popularise a certain image and a new style of research in biology that would attract young readers to the new specialist area rather than translating a set of complex and, to an extent, esoteric ideas for a large audience.[17] His aggressive style, his autobiographical weight, the elegance of the DNA molecular model and the continual celebrations of the 'annus mirabilis' of 1953, go a long way to explaining the public impact of this molecule and the epic proportions of its discovery. However, something very different – the popularisation that Watson did not carry out – is the understanding of DNA and its functions by the lay public.[18]

Watson did not think about his popularising work while he was occupied with the structural elucidation of DNA – in fact 15 years passed from its discovery in 1953 to the appearance of *The Double Helix* – but the media impact of the book continued to legitimate his work and his leadership at a time when the new scientific discipline of molecular biology was becoming established. Watson visualised a new way of seeing the molecule that would go beyond the walls of the laboratory to become a deep-seated cultural change. It had permeated Western societies in the second half of the twentieth century, to the point where DNA as an icon in the public sphere has become almost as important as Einstein's relativity. Nowadays, an individual's characteristic and identity have a strong genetic component. The description and classification of illnesses has been influenced by the nature of amino-acid sequences. Research in these fields is carried out by large teams using new instruments (ultracentrifuges, electrophoresis techniques, chromotography, x-ray diffraction, and electronic microscopes), new organisms and new experiments, from the new culture that Watson wanted to portray in *The Double Helix*.[19]

One of the icons of the twentieth century is the famous photograph of the DNA molecular model together with its discoverers, Watson and Crick. However, what is less well known is the story behind that image. The picture was taken in May 1953, just two months after the two scientists had constructed their pioneering model, but it was not published. It appeared as an illustration in *The Double Helix* in 1968. To a large extent its initial discovery was 'manufactured' for the public.[20] In the end its presence in the media served to reinforce Watson's and Crick's own scientific authority.

X-ray diffraction to determine the structure of macromolecules and their application in biology also enjoyed major public projection in the media. This was the case of Linus Pauling, Nobel Prize for Chemistry (1954) and Nobel Peace Prize (1962) for his militant pacifism during the Cold War, his tireless popularisation of the new molecular biology and as defender of campaigns supporting vitamin C as an agent for the prevention of numerous illnesses.[21] One of Pauling's great intuitions, which would have important medical applications, was the idea that the size and shape of molecules influenced their interaction with proteins in the cells of the patient, over their actual composition. His study of sickle cell anaemia and the possibility of generic changes in the shape of haemoglobin were at the core of his explanation and caused a great public stir, particularly after the publication of an article in *Science* in 1949, marking the beginning of molecular pathology.[22]

Pauling made a considerable contribution to the application of quantum mechanics to chemistry, as shown in his book *The Nature of the Chemical Bond*, published in 1939 and in a popular version entitled *The Architecture of Molecules* in 1964, as well as in his textbooks (see Chapter 5). Although his media popularity is not comparable with Einstein's, his campaigns and public appearances also resulted in that complex intersection between academic knowledge and popular wisdom. They raised the moral stature of the scientist and therefore reinforced his scientific authority.

180 Media science

In an interview at the National Film Board of Canada in 1960, Pauling explained how:

> The human body contains many other kinds of proteins. Perhaps each human being has as many as 100,000 different kinds of proteins inside of him . . . Now the hemoglobin molecule contains about 10,000 atoms. Nobody knows, even yet, how these atoms are attached together in space. Nobody knows the complete structure. Yet, during the last twenty-five years, many pieces of information about the hemoglobin molecule have been gathered together and I have been especially interested in this.[23]

But the media battle in the field of genetics also had another dimension. At the end of the 1960s a study was carried out on the XYY syndrome – the chromosome supposedly responsible for our criminal instincts – and it caused quite a stir in the media. A number of sensationalist articles appeared on the subject (the biological basis of our behaviour is a topic of great interest for journalists) and these had a negative effect on the academic research being carried out, to the point where scientists accused journalists of having distorted the information. A more detailed look at this case, however, suggests that the scientists took an active part in the popularisation of their research in the media, even giving it a sensationalist tinge. In 1967 the editor of the *British Journal of Psychiatry*, Eliot Slater, wrote in *World Medicine* (an 'intermediate' publication that is neither too popular nor too expert) that:

> It is possible that here might be some biological basis for the remarkable fact, which has puzzled criminologists for decades that the male is many times more prone to delinquent behaviour than the female. If two Y chromosomes put their possessor in serious danger of antisocial behaviour, perhaps a single one can contribute some of the risk.[24]

Consequently, although scientists tried to restore the image of the isolated genius working away in a closed room until they reached their 'eureka' moment, the fact was that scientific knowledge about the XYY chromosome was determined by the context and conditions of its public exposure.

During the last part of the twentieth century there is also evidence of the close relationship between the development of a specific local scientific community and its public image in the press. A recent study of articles on genetics published in the Spanish daily *El País* from its establishment in 1976 to date shows how the newspaper generated a somewhat neutral image of this emerging discipline, without looking too deeply into the social consequences and ideological implications, and contributed to its establishment and professionalisation in Spain. However, when dealing with projects from outside Spain, such as the human genome, the *El País* journalists had no hesitation in discussing their ethical, political and economic aspects.

In articles about the genetic origins of certain illnesses or instruments of genetic diagnosis (subjects developed by Spanish scientists), the journalists adopted a 'technical' stance, including information that appeared in the international press acritically. However, articles related to human genome sequencing not only gave information about the latest breakthroughs but also about their possible consequences for society. This difference is particularly important given that in the case of the human genome the style of the article coincided with what the newspaper's style guide considered to be a good science popularisation text, a style that was not applied to the articles published on the relationship between genes and illnesses.[25] These strategies largely coincide with other attempts to legitimate certain emerging disciplines in the public sphere. In the context of growing competition to obtain funding and under pressure from public and media opinion, human genetics experts made great effort to improve their image, to the extent that they even constructed a new language for the discipline, adapted (sometimes too much) to the interests of the media.[26]

But the media exposure for some individual molecules has gone beyond even genetics itself. In 1996 newspapers around the world announced that Professors Harold Kroto, Robert Curl and Richard Smalley had been awarded the Nobel Prize for Chemistry for synthesising a molecule of 60 carbon atoms, the so-called fullerene or 'buckyball', in honour of architect Richard Buckminster Fuller (1895–1983), who had built a geodesic dome with a similar structure for the Universal Exhibition of Montreal in 1967. The symmetry and even the aesthetic beauty of the C_{60} soon reached the media. Several books were published in quick succession to promote it,[27] and the new compound featured on BBC television, radio and videos. In fact C_{60} had already been described in 1985 in an article in *Nature*, but its structure remained open to some speculation in the absence of a pure sample, experimentally isolated in the laboratory to finally confirm it. C_{60} generated suspicion and enthusiasm in equal measure. The popular book by Hugh Aldersey-Williams, *The Most Beautiful Molecule: The Discovery of the Buckyball*, published in 1995, promoted it in comments such as the following:

> Ten years ago, the discovery of buckminsterfullerene . . . stunned the scientific community . . . This unusual molecule – also known as the buckyball – is composed of 60 carbon atoms arranged in a hollow sphere, with hexagonal and pentagonal configurations similar to those found on a soccer ball. Its near-perfect symmetry is just one reason why scientists have since dubbed it 'the most beautiful molecule' . . . the actual discovery was merely the beginning of an intense – and ongoing – quest to master this newest form of the most basic of elements. Confirmation would take five years and launch an unprecedented flood of investigation and investment. Backed by such giants as AT&T, DuPont, Exxon, and IBM, a highly competitive search for practical applications began – and continues.[28]

182 Media science

No physicist or chemist expected that the carbon atoms would arrange themselves in such symmetry and, in fact, Curl, Kroto and Smalley continued with their work until 1990 in the search for new evidence that the structure they had proposed needed to be corrected. In 1990 the physicists identified other C_{60} structures that confirmed their initial hypothesis. This opened the way for studying even more complex molecules such as C_{70}, C_{76}, C_{78} and C_{84}. The hitherto unpublished properties of the new substances contributed to the growing interest in a new area of study in chemistry and major consequences in disciplines such as astrophysics, superconductivity and new materials. The initial 'existence' of the fullerene was largely due, however, to its media impact and media interest in this epic story that combined scientific research with aesthetic beauty.[29] It is perhaps no coincidence that the *Encyclopaedia Britannica* presents the fullerenes, especially the highly symmetrical C_{60}, as molecules of a beauty and elegance capable of stimulating the imagination of both experts and laypeople, building bridges between science, architecture, mathematics, engineering and the visual arts and for opening a new chapter in the history of nanotechnology.[30]

7.3. Our ancestors

Palaeoanthropology, the science of the origins of man and of *Homo sapiens* in their current status, is full of controversy. Fossils of hominins are very rare and difficult to date and interpret since they are usually fragmented, deformed and of uncertain date. New findings such as the *Homo floresiensis* in Indonesia in 2004 or some of the more recent specimens seem to put human genealogy under constant debate. The discipline is constantly being reviewed and there are major discrepancies among the experts. Also, as the paleoanthropologists themselves admit, their interpretations are inevitably influenced by different ideologies and worldviews.[31]

Palaeoanthropology is also a profoundly 'public' science. Since Darwin's time there has been a long tradition of direct communication with the public of the latest finds, even where these have not been sufficiently discussed with other experts beforehand. The image of paleoanthropologists as adventurers and fossil hunters on every continent is complemented by the description of their excavations in popular magazines, public talks and museums. All these spaces provide a forum for the continual negotiation of questions about the human race. Who are we? Where do we come from? What makes us different from other living beings? These are the eternal questions that guarantee public interest.

In 1974, when paleoanthropologists discovered the AL–288-1 fossil in the Afar Depression in Ethiopia, they christened it 'Lucy'. It is mainly famous for being relatively complete, unlike most other fossil finds (30 per cent of the skeleton is preserved). In Ethiopia the 80 bones of the *Australopithecus afarensis* are thought of as a national treasure. Indeed, 'Lucy' has become a key reference point for palaeoanthropology, with a constant presence in the media and in museums. Many popular books include 'her' name in the title and 3-D reconstructions have been produced for use in museums.[32] However, 'Lucy' has been the subject of considerable controversy among experts in palaeoanthropology in terms of gender, locomotion and even the species to which she belongs. In 2006 an interesting debate arose about the appropriateness of sending the remains of 'Lucy' to the United States for an exhibition tour. 'Lucy' has also become an example of the debate about postcolonial science. It is clear that this is an African finding that has been made profitable through Western science and propaganda, and in that sense it can be considered a kind of boundary object lying between academic circles of experts and the public sphere (Figure 7.1).[33]

Lucy's media impact can be extended to many other cases. Paleoanthropologists often write popular books to reinforce their authority and obtain sufficient funding for their research. These books also act as a kind of battlefield that goes beyond academic circles to keep certain controversies alive. They also provide a kind of meta-narrative for the discipline, keeping questions open about human prehistory that could not be discussed in academic articles. Donald Johanson and Richard Leakey, for instance, owe their fame to the popularisation of their respective epic fossil hunts in East Africa.

From the end of the 1970s to the present day finds of human fossil remains in Spain, and the site at Atapuerca (Burgos) in particular, have had a great impact

FIGURE 7.1 Richard Leakey in 1977 with two skulls: *Australopithecus* in his right hand and *Homo habilis* in his left hand. Reproduced with permission of Marion Kaplan/Alamy.

184 Media science

on debates about the arrival of our ancestors in Europe. Atapuerca has been an inexhaustible source of discoveries. For example, the Gran Dolina cave contains 11 stratigraphic layers containing fossil remains of vertebrates and utensils produced by hominids, alongside giant deer and rhinoceroses, among other mammals. At the Sima del Elefante excavation site, tools have been found that demonstrate that hominids were already exploring the caves in the Atapuerca mountain range more than a million years ago. One of the project leaders described the site in 1999 as the only place in the world for precise documentation of climate change, ecosystems, human groups, their techniques and behaviour over time; the best Palaeolithic and archaeological site in the world – a 'magic mountain'.[34] Specifically, the discovery of the remains of *Homo antecessor* in Atapuerca has had a large public impact in the media and has appeared in numerous books and popularisation publications. According to the discoverers, *Homo antecessor* could be a common ancestor of *Homo neanderthalensis* and *Homo sapiens*. It is a species of similar proportions to modern man with a slightly larger corporal volume, a broader trunk and a somewhat smaller cranial capacity. Its place on the genealogical tree of human evolution is still being argued, however, by the international community of experts.

Despite that, and similar to the case of 'Lucy', Atapuerca has given Spanish paleoanthropologists a spectacular presence in the media and helped them to broaden their sphere of public influence. The project leaders are working in an activity that amply transcends small circles of academic debates. They have written almost 30 popular science books dedicated specifically to the Atapuerca project and their own particular intellectual adventure, and in general have spread the bigger international debate about the origins of man. They have also been surprising in their capacity to produce different genres of popular science materials, writing novels about the excavation site (another example of the complex intersection between science and literature) and a children's book as well as books about the role of diet in human evolution and another about Darwin. They published a book in the form of a conversation between them as well as texts of a clearly philosophical ilk that reflect on the nature of the humanisation process. This enormous popularisation activity is completed with the publication of articles in journals and magazines, guided visits to the site, television documentaries, exhibitions, web pages and blogs as well as the publication of academic articles in prestigious journals.

So a dense network of communicative strategies was built up to try to consolidate scientific authority on a national and international scale. The result was mainly generous financing from public and private sources for the Atapuerca project, while other excavations with similar potential remain in second place and are virtually unknown. It seems clear then that the great success of the Atapuerca site cannot only be explained by the quantity and quality of the fossils found there; since the beginning of the project the bones have always been accompanied by frenetic popularisation activity in the media. Despite its controversial position in the tree of human evolution for the international community, there are frequent references to 'our ancestors' with no critical statements to the *Homo antecessor* in the Spanish local context, in a similar way to the geneticists mentioned before.[35]

The Atapuerca case clearly demonstrates how scientists often subordinate their work to the logic of the media. The team members generally refer to the journalists as 'our friends'. Headlines such as 'The First Hominid in Europe', which appeared in *Nature* in 2008, take nothing away from the media benefits of presenting certain finds.[36] In their media and popular versions, experts send subtle messages not only to the general readership but also to their colleagues, with whom they have major disagreements about the tree of human evolution. Palaeoanthropology experts in general, and specifically the Atapuerca group, have enjoyed a greater freedom to express certain hypotheses or possible reconstructions of specific fossils, which, in the more restricted academic journals, would require a specialised language. So a process comparable with the so-called 'pasteurisation' in France, where the problem of spontaneous generation and microbiological theories reached the far corners of the world through the public science of Louis Pasteur,[37] the epic of Atapuerca has been taken up by all of the media which have contributed to legitimate the scientific authority of the experts and even strengthen national identity, in the sense of a fairly explicit message heralding that these were the bones of the 'first Spaniard'.

Questions about the origin and evolution of our species have also opened up other important discussions in the media. Evolutionary psychology emerged in the 1980s in a large part of the United States in groups that were initially concerned with socio-biology. They sought new explanations for certain types of human behaviour such as monogamy, adultery, rape or sexual attraction. Their focus on the biological bases and not on the cultural or social explanations caused frequent conflicts in related disciplines. The controversy involved experts in life sciences but also social scientists and humanists. Evolutionary psychology also covered important everyday problems with a deep political background.

In the 1990s, these topics had a wide media impact of debate in Britain.[38] A quantitative approach to the news that appeared in the press showed the constant presence of academic experts together with their popular books aimed at the general public (some 25 books between 1990 and 2000). As in the case of palaeoanthropology, this media strategy allowed them to achieve legitimacy and academic authority, as well as strengthening the disciplinary boundaries of their field compared with other related and potentially invasive disciplines. One of the key texts in their public projection was *The Moral Animal* (1994) by Robert Wright, another was *How the Mind Works* (1998) by Steven Pinker; they both became best sellers and widely commented in the media, but also in some specialised journals.

In this case, the boundary between expert and lay opinions seems especially fragile. The specific topic, the discussion of the roles that evolution has played in our gender and sexual behaviour, is of great interest to the general public. This new science was quick to make a connection with public concerns, especially in

186 Media science

a decade when traditional gender roles and the fixed and conservative notions of family were clearly in trouble. Also, the high political content of the study of individual human behaviour in relation to group situations enabled the more liberal and progressive media to take them on in new debates where an alliance between Darwinism and feminism opened up the public debate on the role of human nature in society.[39] Evolutionary psychology was closely followed by the media, almost always in terms of controversy, with public statements by academic experts from various disciplines, journalists and even writers, which usually went beyond specific areas of knowledge to become debates about science, politics, religion, society, gender and sexuality. In this media frenzy evolutionary psychology gained public recognition and academic authority as an emerging discipline.

This example even paves the way for the generalisation of the idea that discrepancies among the so-called experts are often resolved in the media, with frequent appearances on radio and television debates as well as popular lectures and books. In practice, journalists, popularisers and other 'communicators' with an influence in the media act as experts with a status that is similar if not the same as academics. In fact, the academics themselves become important readers of these popular works and the publics of their own science, with all the epistemological consequences that this brings.[40]

7.4. Cold fusion

On 8 May 1989 *Time* magazine published an article entitled 'Science: Fusion or Illusion', which began with the following paragraph:

> Little more than a month ago, they were just two chemists, toiling in virtual anonymity. But B. Stanley Pons and Martin Fleischmann came last week to Washington as heroes, visionaries and scientific superstars. With a mob of reporters following along, the thermodynamic duo marched onto Capitol Hill to tell Congress how their simple table top experiment had generated fusion, the nuclear reaction that powers the sun. Displaying slides filled with complex equations, wielding electronic pointers and pulling a mock-up of their apparatus from a plastic shopping bag, the bespectacled researchers mesmerized the members of the House Committee on Science, Space and Technology with an account of how their device produced more energy, in the form of heat, than it consumed. The politicians may have been baffled by the chemistry, but they had no trouble grasping the implications. It seemed that Pons, a professor at the University of Utah, and Fleischmann, of Britain's University of Southampton, might have pulled off a trick that has eluded some of the best minds in physics for nearly four decades. More important, they might have found a way to solve the world's energy problems for all time.[41]

To understand the scope of that news item, readers should first know the background of the question. In the 1950s, at the height of the nuclear race, after the Manhattan project and the bombings of Hiroshima and Nagasaki at the end of the Second World War, nuclear fusion was detected in tests of hydrogen bombs. The next step was obviously to try to control the enormous quantity of energy produced, trap the deuterium (hydrogen isotope) in a kind of magnetic container and heat it to millions of degrees centigrade so that the nucleus of the atoms fused and produced energy. Later on there were other attempts using high-power laser beams, but none were able to initiate the reaction. The physicists knew, however, that in theory fusion could take place at room temperature if the electrons of the deuterium were replaced by heavier particles called 'muons'. But fusion catalysed by muons never produced significant amounts of energy. And so it was with little initial optimism that the news of cold fusion spread rapidly around the world in the spring of 1989.

Some weeks before the appearance of the article in *Time*, on 23 March 1989 Fleischmann and Pons called a press conference to announce that they had obtained some spectacular results (Figure 7.2). Electrolysis of heavy water (D_2O) using palladium electrodes had unexpectedly produced a release of heat in the system and they had identified tritium, gamma rays and neutrons. These results seemed compatible with nuclear fusion. Laboratories in Utah had achieved a similar process, but in this case at low temperatures – cold fusion – making it

FIGURE 7.2 Stanley Pons and Martin Fleischmann announcing their results on cold fusion in the 23 March 1989 press conference. Reproduced with permission of Bettmann/CORBIS.

188 Media science

a much more accessible process that could revolutionise energy policies and reliance on fossil fuels not only in the United States but the world over. Media interest in the news was clear.[42] The topic contained all the ingredients needed for the media science: fascination for anything nuclear, the energy problem, the trustworthiness of certain experts and their experiments, an interest in the physics and chemistry of the sun, and even some arguments about the priority of the experiment. The result was problematic in both theoretical and practical terms. Experts in nuclear physics thought it impossible to produce energy through fusion at room temperature in the laboratory. But more than a hundred research groups from around the world immediately set to work to reproduce the experiment.

Among the criticisms of Fleischmann and Pons was the idea that they had jumped the gun in organising the press conference in March, encouraged largely by the governing authorities of the University of Utah who saw the experiment as a golden opportunity to promote the university and even obtain a patent that could change world energy policy. In fact, some of the conclusions of the experiment were presented to the press before being peer reviewed by academics and so alienating the expert authority. Taking scientific practice from the laboratory straight to the press room made many scientists uneasy. Said Moshe Gai, a physicist from Yale, was disappointed in his colleagues for their excessive haste. Charles C. Baker, Director of the Argon National Laboratory, considered that organising a press conference and presenting results without previously having prepared a rigorous technical report was no way forward for a good professional scientist. John Maddox, the editor of *Nature*, thought that Fleischmann and Pons's results were not based on sufficient experimental evidence and that their conclusions had been published before the discovery could be confirmed and verified.[43]

However, other scientists seemed to take the side of the heroes. Robert Huggins in Stanford confirmed that he had also obtained an excessive heat emission during his reproduction of the experiment. In fact, the responsibility did not only fall on Fleischmann and Pons and the University of Utah. Groups trying to reproduce the experiment used information that had been spread by the media and this had a decisive influence on the scientific decisions they made in their own laboratories. So the press conference had taken on an extraordinary importance, maybe in this case as a result of the novelty of the results which represented a clear threat to the established paradigms of nuclear physics.[44] The apparent hurry to make their results public and the controversy that followed involved a complex set of factors. The pioneering experiment in supposed cold fusion, a subject of major importance for the physicists, was curiously carried out by two average chemists in a second-rate university and this raised questions of the difficulty in marking out the authority of professional physicists and chemists.[45] The speed at which the experimental results reached the public was a golden opportunity to obtain major research funding for a large-scale project for a new source of energy that a priori was capable of changing the technological systems of Western societies at the end of the twentieth century. There was also the question of personal vanities and institutional rivalries inherent in any scientific controversy.

As well as revolutionising the scientific community of the time, this episode, which lasted only a few months, resulted in reams of paper produced from different perspectives to try to learn from the events. Bruce Lewenstein suggested in an excellent article published in 1995 that the case of cold fusion and its consequences for scientific research could be analysed in four very different periods.[46] The first would be precisely the two months of chaos, from the press conference to the first decisions to cut funding for this kind of investigation. Just two months after the famous press conference, in May 1989, the scientific community had split into followers and sceptics. It was not until the annual meeting of the American Physical Society publically announced its rejection of Fleischmann and Pons's work that the media began to lost interest in the subject. Finally, in the autumn of the same year, the Department of Energy withdrew its subsidy for any new project related to cold fusion. This was the first period of great confusion where contradictory reports were appearing every day in the press and on radio and television. However, in the second step during the summer and autumn of 1989 the atmosphere of chaos died down and some of the ideas were reorganised. Rigorous reports on cold fusion were commissioned to different groups of experts and the problem gradually disappeared from the media.

During the third period, in 1990, the division between the sceptics and the enthusiasts became wider. *Nature*, which had taken a neutral stance from the start, published a devastating article on the anniversary of the Fleischmann and Pons press conference,[47] while the defenders of cold fusion met during the same week at a conference subsidised by the University of Utah. *Science* magazine published an article a few months later which practically accused the defenders of fraud. As was the case in other fields of the media science analysed in this chapter, in 1991 the division between the sides was reflected in the popular books. One that was very critical of Fleischmann and Pons by Frank Close was titled *Too Hot to Handle* (1991), and another in defence of cold fusion by Eugene Mallove was *Fire from Ice* (1991). Lewenstein defines a final fourth period for the problem, in which, curiously, while the critics had gradually abandoned their campaign of hostility in both the specialised journals and the media, the defenders of cold fusion continued to organise conferences to support their cause (which is now absent from the media) and, despite the harsh controversy, their continued activity had brought about the emergence of a new speciality.

From the calmer reflections of people like Lewenstein and some of the others who analysed the scientific controversy with a sense of depth and perspective, some interesting conclusions have emerged.[48] Just like in the first two months of confusion, the overexposure of a new theory or scientific experiment to the media seems to be detrimental to its development, and may even disturb the calm needed for the research. As already seen, in their obsession to reinforce their authority and increase their social legitimation, scientists often use the media as an instrument in their favour, like an extended battlefield outside the strict academic circles to settle their own disagreements. However, the problem for them begins when their own expert knowledge that is not accepted by their peers is exposed

190 Media science

to the public eye.[49] That is where they enter a risky game which may provide some benefits (cold fusion has become a de facto new scientific sub-speciality), but can also see their public credibility eroded, producing a boomerang effect by which discontent with scientific culture is bolstered rather than calmed. This is probably more worrying, since there is no impermeable membrane to actually isolate the academic world from the media activity of the scientists.

7.5. Climate change

There is probably no other scientific topic that has occupied so much space in the mass media in recent years than the study of the causes and consequences of climate change, its gravity and the possible means of overcoming it. Although scientific evidence of global warming and its relation to the increase in carbon dioxide emissions has been known for several decades, one of the key events was the publication in 2006 of the book and later the film *An Inconvenient Truth*. Former Vice President of the United States Al Gore wrote the book, at a time when climate change was becoming a serious issue on the agendas of the political leaders. Its impact was also strengthened by the fact that Gore received the Nobel Peace Prize the following year.

In the introduction to his book Gore recognised the influence that the 1962 best seller *Silent Spring* by the famous marine biologist Rachel Carson (1907–64) had on his interest in environmental issues. *Silent Spring* criticised the contamination of plants and animals (humans included) by chemical pesticides, in particular DDT, and over time it has become a reference text for environmental movements. Despite the fact that academic debates about DDT have been present in the scientific community since the 1940s (in 1942 Paul Müller was awarded the Nobel Prize for Medicine for his study on its effects on human health), *Silent Spring* sold 100,000 copies in just three months and is still being republished today as an iconic text on the environmental turn that occurred in the last decades of the twentieth century.[50] It is another good example of how a scientific controversy (in this case, the negative effects of pesticides on health and the ecosystem) go beyond the strict sphere of expert science to be strongly exposed through the media to public opinion and to influence certain policies and collective actions in both the long and short term. Carson spoke of an idea which was pioneering at the time, but which has since been adopted to a large extent today. She stressed the global dimension and inter-relational nature of environmental problems, which require complex, (often failed) negotiations by different interest groups and varied concerned audiences, where a new global public opinion has acquired a particularly important role.

Gore took *Silent Spring* as yet another symptom of the discontent of scientific culture, extrapolating it to global warming, the analysis of its causes, consequences and possible solutions. He presented himself to the media as a staunch environmentalist, a defender of the Democrat programme and a strong critic of the Republican party that ignored the problems of climate change during the eight-year mandate of President George W. Bush. But Gore is not a scientist and in his communicative strategy he appeals to the authority of the scientists to strengthen his position. In his own words: '2000 scientists, in a hundred countries, working for more than 20 years in the most elaborate and well organized scientific collaboration in the history of mankind have forged an exceptionally strong consensus that all the nations in the Earth must work together to solve the crisis of global warming'.[51]

Using experts to legitimise certain ideas in public, Gore paid homage in his book to Professor Roger Revelle (1909–91), who he considered to be one of the pioneers in the measurement of CO_2 concentration in the atmosphere half a century ago. This strategy, which applied in both the book and the film, was presented with great educational sensitivity using impressive graphics and images (another example of the intersection of documentary cinema and science as discussed in Chapter 3). It was also a reaction to what Gore considered to be the politicisation of global warming. In his view, climate change was an uncomfortable, inconvenient truth for many political and economic interests so some of the big corporations aimed to create confusion on that matter in public opinion. They would even have commissioned reports from certain experts to discredit the supposed scientific consensus.

This is undoubtedly a controversial issue with a strong media factor. Although the consensus is practically general about the increase in carbon dioxide emissions and the consequent increase in the temperature of the planet, discrepancies arise when it comes to blaming only human causes for this. It could be due to natural climate swings which have occurred throughout history without any human intervention. The controversy also extends to the degree to which the problem of climate change should be given priority over other problems that are currently being experienced by humanity. So the more conservative sectors are also cultivating their own experts to weaken the scientific consensus but also to legitimate unlimited economic growth as a source of progress and wealth, even at the cost of climate change which is considered to be of relative importance.

In 2010, in their book *Merchants of Doubt*, Naomi Oreskes and Erik Conway denounced: 'how a handful of scientists', many of them with strong links with industry and politics, 'obscured the truth on issues from tobacco smoke to global warming'.[52] They emphasised the vulnerability of expertise when spreading scientific doubts and uncertainties into the public sphere to avoid paying the environmental cost. They concluded that:

> Scientists have no special purchase on moral and ethical decisions; a climate scientist is no more qualified to comment on health care reform than a physicist to judge the causes of bee colony collapse. The very features that create expertise in a specialized domain lead to ignorance in many others.[53]

For experts from this camp, such as Danish Bjørn Lomborg, Gore's media discourse is nothing more than a pessimistic and apocalyptic litany that makes

192 Media science

us invest thousands of millions in a problem that is not thought of as a priority over more pressing demands such as improvements in education, health, infrastructure and increasing living standards for people in the developing world. For Lomborg, Gore's inconvenient truth was linked to an ancient tradition of cultural pessimism that has travelled through the centuries from literature to film, from the *Frankenstein* of Mary Shelley (1797–1851) to that of Boris Karloff (1887–1969), to the *Jurassic Park* of Crichton or Spielberg. In his controversial but best-selling book, *The Skeptical Environmentalist*,[54] Lomborg had tried to show, using a mass of statistical data and indicators that we live in a better world than our ancestors, a discussion that lacks rigour among the historians and one that would take us back to old speculations about the same problem. Even some of the data were criticised by experts from several fields for their lack of rigour in what became known as the 'Lomborg affair'.

The book appeared in 2001 with the subtitle 'Measuring the Real State of the World', but was criticised for distorting data from organisations like the United Nations, the World Bank and the World Forum. Despite rectifying some of the figures a large number of experts reported Lomborg to the Danish Committee of Scientific Dishonesty, for selective or misuse of statistics, plagiarism and incorrect interpretation of some of the results. The somewhat ambiguous ruling of the Committee (the charges having been lifted) did not close the debate, however, and Lomborg has been regularly invited to argue against the more or less moderate ecologist discourses that continue to occupy an important place in our contemporary societies. In 2001 the World Economic Forum considered him one of the global leaders for tomorrow. In 2004 *Time* magazine nominated him one of the 100 most influential people in the world. In 2008, the *Guardian* described him as one of the 50 people who could save the planet.[55] The public controversy around climate change and in particular the media circus of Gore and Lomborg seems to have dramatically reduced the room available for the supposed scientific authority of the experts.

Some in more conservative positions have called victory on the lack of specific agreements at the 2009 Copenhagen Climate Change Conference. Republican senator James Sensenbrenner recently reported the existence of a major group of scientists interested in silencing evidence contrary to the theory of climate change. A representative of powerful lobbies for the oil and automobile industries in the United States, Sensenbrenner, together with other Republican leaders, has tried to use the media to spread the idea that, despite the huge areas of consensus that already exist among thousands of scientists, the scientific community does not have sufficient credibility regarding this problem.[56] Once again, just like in the cold fusion case, media coverage and the different voices have weakened the authority of the expert.

In recent decades global warming and climate change have evolved from strictly scientific questions discussed in small circles to a social problem with wide-ranging, divergent perceptions on risk, welfare and technological progress, including political, economic, cultural and ethical factors, all interconnected through the mass media. As Mike Hulme stated recently in his book about the causes of current disagreement on climate change, it is only through rigorous analysis of the different public discourses that we can make progress towards a possible solution to the problem. The minimal agreements reached by the experts do not seem to go far enough. Hulme describes in a wealth of detail the plurality of perceptions on climate change as a fundamental cause of the difficulty in reaching an agreement. In the first place, the experts themselves use it to resolve their own differences and discrepancies about the conclusions or methodology used. Others justify the commercialisation of carbon dioxide as a business strategy. However, from the perspective of the environmental activist, climate change is playing a similar role to nuclear energy in the 1960s. In other words, it is a source of inspiration and cohesion for movements critical of industrial development and opposed to the environmental price that we are paying for our present lifestyle.[57]

In the midst of this polyphony, Hulme thinks that the experts have reached a basic agreement in two fundamental aspects: that increase in the temperature of the planet is caused by human activity and therefore transcends any natural swings in climate; and that consequently that increase in temperature causes significant short- and medium-term changes in the atmosphere and the climate of the Earth. But the problem is not being managed correctly, starting with Gore's media catastrophism and the international meetings organised by the United Nations whose effectiveness is highly questionable. This is a particularly complex case. Every time a possible solution is found, our perception of the problem changes. It is a kind of vicious circle where the positions of all the different groups involved are chaotically refuelled.

It was precisely after the disappointing results of the 2009 Copenhagen Conference that *Nature* published the journal's opinion in the following terms:

> A crucial challenge for researchers over the next few years will be to ensure that public communication of the results of climate-change research – whether formally or in the blogosphere – is robust in every sense: making the results comprehensible, and even vivid, yet rigorous; doing full justice to the uncertainties; maintaining such standards in the face of misinformation and propaganda; and responding promptly to the unexpected. But governments have the biggest challenge of all. In the face of major threats to their countries' long-term futures, they need to commit to an international treaty. They also need to sustain the bottom-up motivation for change. They must empower their citizens with information: not only about what science is saying, but also about citizens' own contributions to the problem.[58]

★ ★ ★

In view of these reminiscences of discontent even now into the twenty-first century, the traditional recipe of the deficit, even dressed up in its media version, seems insufficient without the rising participation of new audiences when

194 Media science

dealing with problems such as climate change. We shall analyse some of these possible solutions in further detail in Chapter 8, but for now let us examine a few examples more as a conclusion. One sociological survey a few years ago demonstrated that the studies published in the *New England Journal of Medicine* were received more positively or negatively depending on the impact the topic had previously had in non-specialised media like the *New York Times*. Some studies on recent geological controversies related to the problem of natural catastrophes and the extinction of species have also shown the vast influence of the media in the course of the debate among experts themselves.[59] These examples only go to reinforce some of the conclusions that can already be drawn from the cases presented in this chapter. The battle for scientific authority is increasingly being waged in the media with a vast plurality of voices and interests, which can at times project an excessively relativist image of knowledge. There are permeable boundaries between scholarly articles, preprints, correspondence among scientists, teaching handbooks, appearances in printed and audio-visual media and other forums of debate.[60]

Scientific information that appears in the media, which may apparently be considered oversimplified or 'vulgar', can have a varied, subtle influence on the research conducted by the experts themselves. The media can encourage certain authors or theories to be included in or excluded from the public discourse; they can provide a discussion venue for new interpretations freed from the restrictions and conventions of strictly academic debate; or they can confer a different status on the interpretative models that already exist.[61] It seems clear that scientific news items in the media are not just simplifications of experts' work but also contribute to reinforcing or undermining the authority of certain groups and topics of research. They can even constructively generate new consensuses or end certain controversies. Even though an excess of information may sometimes hinder agreement, a scientific controversy does not tend to be resolved merely through experimental evidence. Its cultural (and media) 'baggage' also plays a crucial role.[62] According to media theorist Bart Simon, the media act not only as bridges between experts and laypeople; they also stimulate relationships among experts and epistemologically influence their private work in the laboratory. Scientists involved in a given controversy often use the media, and the media, in turn, end up affecting the scientists' own decision making in the course of their research.[63]

At this point in the book, if the reader is still left with a few arguments in favour of the traditional image of science popularisation as a process of neutral simplification and objective, anonymous content, I hope that the examples presented in this chapter have tipped the scale. Despite the unease that this thesis may prompt, it seems clear that the global media are playing an increasingly important role today in determining scientific authority in any given field of knowledge. So it is up to the expert to set the boundaries of their battlefield using new parameters. This is one of the major challenges in today's new technoscientific society, the key to which we shall attempt to outline in Chapter 8.

Notes

1 Lovelock (2000a: xi).
2 Ibid.
3 Weingart (2001a, b); Bucchi (1998); Rödder, Franzen, Weingart (2012).
4 Nelkin, Lindee (1995).
5 Nikolow, Schirrmacher (2007).
6 Nelkin (1987); Gregory, Miller (1998: 121).
7 Gregory, Miller (1998: 124).
8 Hilgartner (1990).
9 Gregory Miller (1998: 107); Dornan (1988).
10 Collins, Evans (2003, 2007).
11 Cassidy (2006).
12 Gregory (2003); Wallis (1979).
13 Gregory (2005).
14 Lovelock (2000b).
15 Quoted by Hay (2002: 173).
16 Merchant (1980).
17 Yoxen (1985).
18 Nelkin, Lindee (1995).
19 Abir-Am (1992).
20 Chadarevian (2003).
21 Mead, Hager (2001).
22 Strasser (2006b).
23 Linus Pauling and the Structure of Proteins, A Documentary History, http://scarc. library.oregonstate.edu/coll/pauling/proteins/quotes/all.html (accessed 21 June 2015).
24 Quoted by Green (1985: 149).
25 González-Silva (2009).
26 Nelkin (1994).
27 Baggott (1994); Aldersey-Williams (1995).
28 See http://eu.wiley.com/WileyCDA/WileyTitle/productCd-047119333X.html (accessed 9 December 2015).
29 Gregory, Miller (1998: 137–40); http://www.nobelprize.org/nobel_prizes/chemistry/laureates/1996/press.html (accessed 21 June 2015).
30 http://www.britannica.com/science/fullerene (accessed 30 June 2015); Macoubrie (2006).
31 Lewin (1997); Sommer (2007).
32 Hochadel (2010, 2013a, 2013b).
33 Gieryn (1983).
34 Hochadel (2010: 149).
35 Hochadel (2010).
36 Eudald Carbonell et al., 'The First Hominin of Europe', Nature, 452, 7186 (2008): 465–9.
37 Geison (1995); Latour (1988).
38 Cassidy (2005, 2006).
39 Cassidy (2007).
40 Felt (2000).
41 *Time*, 8 May 1989.
42 Simon (2001).
43 *Time*, 23 March 1989 (editorial).
44 Bucchi (1996); Gieryn (1992, 1999); Lewenstein (1995a).
45 Nye (1993).
46 Lewenstein (1995a).
47 Michael H. Salamon, M.E. Wrenn, H.E. Bergeson, H.C. Crawford, W.H. Delaney and C.L. Henderson, 'Limits on the Emission of Neutrons, Gamma-Rays, Electrons and Protons from Pons/Fleischmann Electrolytic Cells', Nature, 344 (29 March 1990), 401–5.

196 Media science

48 Gieryn (1992, 1999).
49 Bertomeu-Sánchez (2009: 376); Collins, Evans (2003, 2007).
50 In fact Gore himself wrote an introduction for later editions of *Silent Spring* as a symbol of his commitment to environmental sensitivities.
51 Al Gore, 'An Inconvenient Truth' (2006).
52 Oreskes, Conway (2010).
53 Oreskes, Conway (2010: 273).
54 Lomborg (2001).
55 http://www.theguardian.com/environment/2008/jan/05/activists.ethicalliving (accessed 21 June 2015).
56 *El País*, 19 December 2009.
57 Hulme (2009).
58 *Nature*, 24 December 2009, 462: 957.
59 Lewenstein (1995a).
60 Ibid.
61 Bucchi (1996: 387).
62 Lewenstein (1992b, 1995b).
63 Simon (2001: 383–4).

8

DEMOCRATIC SCIENCE

In 2007, Massimiano Bucchi and Federico Neresini chose a set of relevant examples, which in their view described very well the

> profound change in terms and conditions under which scientific knowledge is produced, discussed and legitimated . . . A group of activists protest against GMO outside a biotechnology research institute. The citizens of a region vote in a referendum on a new waste disposal facility. A patients association compiles a database of the symptoms and clinical evolution of a rare genetic disease. A group of citizens is invited to discuss the issue of embryo stem cell research and produce a final document to be submitted to policy makers.[1]

In politics and art we have no problem in accepting the existence of the criticism and influence of public opinion. However, can the same be said for science? If political power reinforces the authority of certain experts with the intention of imposing criteria on the rest of the population (technology, health and environmental projects, for example), how far are they weakening the democratic quality of society? Should we accept that expert knowledge is superior to that of the public at large to justify the absence of democratic control?[2] Obviously this is not a question of putting the laws of gravity to a referendum, but perhaps some of the mechanisms of legitimisation should be reconsidered. As many of the historical examples in this book have shown, it is impossible to understand all the factors in a controversy or a struggle to define the boundaries of knowledge without taking into account the public sphere.[3]

Despite the continual presence of experts in courtrooms, the daily press, radio, television, museums, exhibitions and commemorations, their authority seems to have weakened in recent decades.[4] For many observers there has been a serious

198 Democratic science

crisis in the deficit model and the PUS programme, both associated with the traditional view of scientific popularisation.[5] The ambitious PUS programme has not succeeded in removing the discontent of scientific culture that, as we have seen, permeated throughout much of the twentieth century and up to the present. Despite great efforts to popularise science, fear and scepticism of the application of new technologies (nano and bio) or environmental or health scares have increased. The construction by the experts themselves of the supposed stupidity of the lay masses (at the heart of the deficit model) seems more and more difficult to sustain.

To be fair, it is also true that in recent decades PUS has shifted towards new readings and interpretations of the nature of lay knowledge from more flexible and less hegemonic positions. The result has been the upturn in so-called ethno-science or anthropology of knowledge in daily life and the critical analysis of the construction of the public itself by the experts.[6] These new perspectives point in the right direction. At the root of the discontent with our scientific culture there is something more than just a deficit of information. It is probably a deeper cultural problem.

Lay knowledge is formed through value judgements, trust in scientific institutions, and individual perceptions of its applicability. It ends up forming a corpus that is no less sophisticated than that of the expert. There are also important overlaps between expert and lay knowledge in a set of common places, some them explored very little to date. However, in other areas there are discrepancies.[7] Democratic participation, risk and technoscience seem to be the key words in this apparently new age of the publics of science. This chapter will make a critical analysis of the meaning of these terms.

8.1. The participatory turn

Things have changed since 1994 when Levitt and Gross warned of the dangers of democratising science, in a withering attack on sociologists, ecologists, defenders of alternative medicine, feminists, literary critics and against anything that distanced itself from 'orthodox' science and reasoning.[8] That was probably a desperate attempt to rebuild the wall or redig the ditch that separated the experts from the lay public, which had its uses during the Cold War period but was less active towards the turn of the millennium.[9] From the criticism that largely came from the discontent of scientific culture and attacks on the humanistic world of the so-called academic left, the last few decades of the twentieth century saw a move towards other models that attempted to reinstate science in culture. In doing so, there emerged a new model of public participation in science itself which could potentially overtake the old vertical and traditional view of popularisation. Several authors have theorised on what has become known as the 'participatory turn",[10] where scientific research that is increasingly 'encrusted' in society is influenced by increasingly democratic processes of joint decision making.[11] Faced with the obvious shortfalls of the 1980s programme, this gradual move towards a new model, somewhat utopian and not exempt from controversy, conceives of the public as active citizens in the construction of knowledge itself. However, the new model is uncertain and often trapped in the rhetoric of political correctness that has inundated our times.[12]

Although a large number of experts are still anchored more or less explicitly in the postulates of PUS (we are talking about slight changes in tendencies and not major revolutions), there has been a gradual trend for opening up new debates and balancing them with different and sometimes contentious opinions. The public, which until recently has been considered as ignorant in matters of science, is increasingly interested in the political, social and moral consequences of scientific research in itself and openly questions the experts in these terms. It has therefore achieved a protagonism that would have been unimaginable until recently and one that still causes discomfort in the professional scientists, highly educated and used to move easily within the deficit model. That marked the beginning of a renegotiation process of the relationship between science and society, a new phase of 'hybrid forums' where expert and lay knowledge is not produced in separate watertight containers but in new spaces where specialists and non-specialists can actively interact.[13] The new publics of science include representatives of non-government organisations, local communities, groups of activists, cultural associations, small companies and large corporations and also individual citizens from their own perspective as consumers, users, patients and clients.[14] Professional scientists, company executives and lovers of progress tend to be in favour of transgenic foods, cloning, new nano-materials and artificial life while ecologists, alter-globalists or just defenders of principles of precaution tend to be detractors. The new engineers are involved in live debates on technological changes (as seen in Chapter 6) with new and better informed users, some of them even radical activists (Figure 8.1).[15]

There are also indications to show that the golden age of public investment in scientific research has come to an end – if it ever in fact existed. Food, health and environmental scandals have broken down public confidence in the scientific academy and steered the subtle discontent of scientific culture.[16] Initially focused on questions of health and the gradual involvement of patients, the new participatory model has extended to telecommunications (internet and Wikipedia),[17] genetics research, climate change and nanotechnology. The old tradition of neutral science therefore loses strength as an oversimplistic view of the expert. The 'peer review' system is also insufficient if it is not accompanied by social and ethical considerations, which tend to be discussed in the media, as seen in Chapter 7. Users of free software, movements in defence of the environment, patients' associations discussing research into stem cells, citizens protesting against the installation of a waste treatment plant, consumers demanding a clearer, more rigorous labelling system for food and medicine, activists opposed to transgenic foodstuffs and the users of new and old technologies, all become 'co-producers' of knowledge.[18]

From that point of view the mechanisms for defining science as a normative activity are significantly modified by complex interactions between experts and

FIGURE 8.1 Anti-GMO activists protesting in December 2005 in Hong Kong. Reproduced with permission of Islemount Images/Alamy.

laypeople, whose opinions about science form an intrinsic part of society. And that is where a large part of the core of the new paradigm can be found. The new knowledge regime of technoscience is understood not just as feedback between science and technology, or as a subordination of abstract knowledge to practical and economic interests, but as a new historical process that indistinctly creates changes in nature and society as such science becomes an integral part of society and politics and an irreversible matter of public interest.[19] It is precisely through the connection between the natural world and the modifications that occur around it that modern politics has defined the meaning of citizenship and civil responsibility, the solidarity between nations and interest groups, the boundaries between public and private, concerns for freedom and the need for control.[20]

We have gone from a regime of knowledge based on the primacy of academic research and centred on cognitive ends to another which sketches out the difference between basic and applied research and where the frontline role of the public is increasingly important.[21] ICT, bio and nano, respectively, are the examples of these new powers which escape sovereign spaces and the traditional schemes of classical politics.[22] Perhaps a significant symptom of times to come is the project for a new temporary exhibition in the Science Museum in London to celebrate its centenary. It has been planned according to themes such as 'belief', 'power' and 'trust' as well as offering a broad coverage of non-Western science in a renewed attempt to promote a new 'scientific citizenship'.[23]

But there is also talk of science democratisation movements capable of dealing with a large number of topics in our societies today: the impact of nanotechnology on health, the incongruence of urban plans, the reduction of pollution, climate change, ecological disasters and epidemics, among others.[24] These groups control and defy the opinions of the experts, as well as reorient scientific research itself, to the point where some government try to co-opt them to avoid direct confrontation.[25] Some even talk of 'neo-Luddites' in recollection of the heroic resistance to technological changes and industrial mechanisation in the nineteenth century. Some of the critics were so vehemently opposed to the new information technology they even resorted to violence, as in the case of Californian mathematician Theodor Kaczynski; activists opposed to the production of transgenic foods and in particular those against the Montsanto company; and the eco-warriors such as Dave Foreman, co-founder of 'Earth First', who defend some of the violent action from a radical 'deep ecology' stance to defend nature where everyone has equal rights.[26] Obviously, the defenders of unidirectional and non-negotiable progress, lovers of an inevitable technological determinism, are opposed to these new movements, but they compete with them for the authority and legitimation of their positions in the public sphere.

However, these types of movement should not be idealised and the processes of participation need to be looked at critically. It is not enough simply to count on the presence of new actors in the decision-making process; they must be analysed in terms of how far the participatory process really does take place in practice, beyond a certain empty rhetoric. Simply signing up to certain groups and more or less formal participation in debates does not mean that the relationship with the experts will be symmetrical and balanced enough for laypeople to be considered epistemologically active. Evidently relations of power and scientific authority do not disappear easily. However, despite the limitations, participation mechanisms which have changed the relationship between experts and laypeople considerably over the last few decades can be identified. One of these is local, or even sometimes national, referendums, for example on the course of a new highway or the nature of a certain public work; public gatherings where a small number of citizens are asked for their opinion on a certain matter; surveys and consensus conferences where governments or private companies consult a panel of laypeople on certain topics. The varied mechanisms for participation depend on the different levels of involvement of certain publics, but also on the institutional or corporate initiatives of experts to create new channels for dialogue with sectors that have until recently been largely ignored within the deficit model.[27]

Take the construction of a tunnel, for example. It is not obvious that all the neighbours in a street have anything really substantial to say from a 'technological' point of view. But in recent years many observers in our scientific culture are increasingly supportive of the idea that laypeople and the public in general can understand basic aspects of apparently difficult and inaccessible scientific concepts and methods (remember the debate about the public's capacity for understanding Einstein's theory of relativity a century ago). Some of the obstacles to a true democratic science may come from the corporate reactions of the experts

202 Democratic science

themselves who are still tied to the deficit model, but they are better explained by social and economic inequalities which often bring with them excessive public submissiveness to authority. Debate about the democratic nature of scientific knowledge is inevitably linked to the discussion of the nature of democracy itself, with all its lights and shadows, in contemporary societies.[28]

Reactions to the use of nuclear energy for military and civil purposes, especially during the Cold War, contributed largely to the emergence of ecology movements, defenders of the environment and critical of Western technological growth. The historical roots of that participatory turn probably date back to the decades previous to the dawning of PUS. In the 1970s pioneering movements related to these new trends had already appeared. In view of the growing opposition to the scaling up of nuclear energy and the Cold War other projects emerged, such as 'Science for the People', 'Science Workers for Social Action', 'Aerospaced', 'Computer Professionals for Peace', 'National Coalition for Responsible Genetic Research', while new environmental organisations were springing up everywhere. Many professional scientists became activists for peace, disarmament and the pacific use of science (think of the iconic examples of Einstein and Pauling).

In the 1970s in Holland, 'science shops' were created as a pioneering initiative by groups of chemistry students who decided to offer not-for-profit science knowledge to the public. The phenomenon later spread to other countries. These were local organisations offering the public free access to scientific knowledge, especially concerning the environment, health and education. Later on these first initiatives were taken over by universities, research centres and NGOs in a move to redirect scientific research towards social needs. The success or failure of the science shops depended largely on the generosity of the volunteers and their ability to connect big contemporary scientific topics with the interests of the public and also with their desire to gain access to scientific knowledge outside the media and the education system. In any case, the science shops were a sign of the new 'citizenship' dimension that science and scientific culture had been acquiring since the beginning of the new millennium. The ideal process for the science shops would be to produce interesting feedback and knowledge to back up a more participatory trend far removed from the inertia of the deficit model: receiving proposals and questions from members of the local community; analysing specific problems; keeping communication open with civil society during the process; disseminating the results; helping the local community to apply them; designing follow-up actions; evaluating the results.[29]

Also in the 1970s there were the first talks attempting to obtain new consensuses in the field of biotechnology and gradually incorporate the opinions of lay groups in its development.[30] The new capacity of molecular biology to cut and recombine the DNA of different species opened up an enormous range of possibilities for therapy, but also great concern for public health and ethical limits, especially if genetic engineering was applied to humans. In the United States, the National Academy of Sciences commissioned Nobel Prize-winner Paul Berg to organise the First International Congress on Recombinant DNA Molecules which took place in February 1975 at the Asilomar Conference Grounds in Pacific Grove, California. Some 140 delegates, mostly molecular biologists and physicists, but also some lawyers and journalists, first decided to discuss questions of safety, leaving the ethical issues for later. It was agreed that in research using recombinant DNA only the bacteria that could not survive outside the laboratory would be used.[31]

The nuclear power plant accident at Chernobyl in April 1986 became a paradigmatic case for the detractors of nuclear energy, but continual crises in the mass use of fossil fuels, the problems of climate change and the need for new, clean and renewable sources of power have meant that the nuclear question is still at the centre of debate. Consumers have acquired an increasingly important role in energy decisions taken by public and private agents at both the local and global levels. A good example is the case of the apparently lay knowledge of English farmers in Cumbria regarding the contamination of agricultural land following the Chernobyl accident. Despite expert assurance that the pollution would be short lived, the Geiger counters were still measuring levels of radiation that prevented the crops from being sold.[32] In terms of the new participatory model, this example shows how the public does not assimilate the academic science of the experts separately from other kinds of knowledge, judgements or advice. In practice, the validation of scientific knowledge almost always requires supplementary data, and this effectively strengthens the position of the individual citizen.[33]

Other projects have also proliferated in recent years, such as the Participatory Approaches in Science and Technology (PATH), which aims to work jointly with professional scientists, users, members of government and representatives of private companies. It has been covering three main areas that are particularly controversial for contemporary public opinion: transgenic food production, the preservation of biodiversity and nanotechnology. The exchange of ideas among the different interest groups should produce different directions for pure and applied research, as well as a broad diffusion of the results of these working groups among the general public.[34]

In the year 2000, 10 per cent of the research budget for nanotechnology was invested in studies on its impact on health, the environment and society as a response to public technophobic attitudes. In 2004, following a rigorous and extensive public consultation that included the participation of some environmentalist organisations, the Royal Society issued a report that detailed nano-opportunities but also nano-uncertainties.[35] The report insisted on the fact that if it was already difficult to predict the direction of nanotechnology in the future or the timescale required for carrying out certain developments, it is even more difficult to forecast the kind of social and ethical reactions that it will provoke:

> Nanotechnologies have the potential to impact on a wide range of applications in many industries in the medium and long term. However, some

204 Democratic science

> people exaggerate potential benefits whereas others exaggerate the risks. Overstated claims about benefits and risks, neither of them based on sound science, are doing a disservice to these emerging fields. In this report we have tried to separate hype from realistic hopes and concerns. For example, significant benefits to the environment are being claimed from the application of nanotechnologies. We recommend that a life cycle approach be taken to evaluate these claims and to ensure that savings in resource consumption during the use of the product are not offset by increased consumption during other stages.[36]

But in the short and medium term the main concerns centred on two basic questions: who controls the use of nanotechnology? And, who will benefit from its use?[37] Small groups of users met to identify the positive aspects (its application to medicine and new materials) but also the negative side (long-term secondary effects, unreliability of the new applications, their financing and control). As a result of its potential convergence with other state-of-the-art technologies such as robotics, artificial intelligence, biotechnology and neuroscience, public debate about the light and shadows of nanotechnology and related decision-making mechanisms seems more necessary than ever. This is not just a process of marketing or of the acceptance or rejection of the final product by the public, client, consumer or user, but one where the participation of a number of different actors in the actual design of a new line of research or in the consequent decisions that are taken could have epistemological consequences.[38]

In fact, the public debate on so-called 'technoscience' began in the period from 1980 to 1990 at a time of crisis (nuclear catastrophes, mad cow disease, transgenic, etc.). The decision-making mechanisms of the experts gradually began to enter the public sphere. Evaluation processes for new technologies, ethics committees, the precautionary principle and risk analyses became the instruments of regulation and control in an attempt to adapt technological innovations to the values and ideals of the people. In doing so it made at least a partial contribution to the creation of a much more favourable opinion towards the idea that science belongs to society, that it is 'ours', and that topics of such importance cannot be left in the hands of small groups of experts. However, if it is to be efficient in the long term it requires a calmer evaluation and one made with a greater historical perspective.

In terms of environmental thought, some of the theorists have suggested that we are experiencing a change from the old social questions with shades of dominance and authoritarianism that give preference to hierarchy, efficiency, markets, competition, materialism and rapid changes in lifestyles, toward a new environmental paradigm that is more open, participatory, sensitive to the public sphere and based on cooperation, simplicity and a certain post-materialism.[39] For theorists of this radical ecological thinking such as Murray Bookchin, the word 'people' today does not mean either the dehumanised proletariat of the Marxist tradition, or the consumers manipulated and homogenised by the capitalist market, but it has become a community of responsible individuals, autonomous in their decisions and socially active.[40] These perceptions are almost certainly excessively utopian and require deeper discussion which goes beyond the objectives of this book. However, civil society can no longer be considered an unmoveable agent that guarantees democracy and is devoid of scientific rationality. The very definition of citizenship can be modified by the scientific rules that subtly permeate all individuals. It is no longer necessary to lay down rules from a supposed political authority since the very mechanisms of technoscience tacitly regulate in practice the behaviour and social order.[41]

In recent decades, not only the laypeople in a broad sense, but also large groups of experts have been concerned about technoscience. The demand for public participation in scientific matters can be seen as yet another sign of criticism of the traditional democracies when it comes to channelling public concerns about new global challenges. Science would be part of a democratic deficit, and would play an increasingly important role in processes that include or exclude citizens in taking certain decisions.[42] Although the so-called participatory turn continues to be controversial, the rigid separation between experts and laypeople, inherited from the traditional view of science popularisation and largely adopted by PUS, is being replaced by unstable and heterogeneous assemblies of experts, citizens, patients, clients and users.[43]

Dorothy Nelkin has theorised in recent years about the considerable increase in scientific controversies that have been resolved in the public sphere, in which values, ideas, power and authority are all at stake. They therefore become a political question where the democratic factor cannot be put aside in favour of the supposed technocratic objectivity of the expert. The examples that Nelkin uses are a good complement to those presented at the beginning of this chapter and enable a greater understanding of the nature of the participatory turn in constant turmoil. In 1976, animal rights activists held a demonstration in front of the American Museum of Natural History in New York to try to stop experiments that caused unnecessary suffering to animals. A decade later the same activists went around laboratories snatching all the animals they could and calling for an end to that kind of experimentation. American anti-abortion groups managed to stop the financing of research using human foetuses from 1981 to 1994. The following section will show how homosexual activists have discussed and influenced the protocols of AIDS detection tests. Agriculture and livestock farmers and other interested parties have mobilised at different levels to stop the use of biotechnological products. Environmental groups have protested against certain decisions on the exploitation of natural resources by large corporations, while the latter have often questioned committees of academic experts on their decisions concerning the dangers of imposing certain regulations (for example, the anti-climate change lobbies mentioned in Chapter 7 [Figure 8.2]). For Nelkin, this set of conflicts among many others shows the vigour of the new participatory turn, but it also reveals a new symptom of social discontent about the hegemonic values of official science.[44]

FIGURE 8.2 Environmental activists at the 'I Count Stop Climate Chaos' Rally, Trafalgar Square, London, 4 November 2006. Reproduced with permission of deadlyphoto.com/ Alamy.

8.2. Health, resistance and appropriation

Health has been one of the biggest fields in recent years to experience the participatory turn and therefore merits a special section in this chapter. From a more traditional approach, closer to the deficit model, it would be easy to see how doctors, their agents and health programmes in the media bombard the public with information and health education, while the ordinary citizen is an avid consumer of the advice and instructions of the professionals. Every parent has invested in domestic health manuals or practical books on childcare; newspapers and magazines often publish articles featuring a doctor, an expert, willing to answer readers' questions; television and radio contain health advice programmes where they explain the latest advances in medicine and they frequently include the participation of patients, listeners and viewers.[45]

But this is obviously not a one-way track. We know that there is significant resistance and appropriation of certain kinds of treatment. In the 1920s, in the US, a heterogeneous group of individuals delivered a scientific, political and philosophical discourse against vaccines. They confronted the medical elite to control the public sphere in what was a harsh media battle for publicity. In a country of strong initiatives from civil society, some considered the vaccination campaigns to be state interference in the care of their children. As a result of the active participation of activists, the anti-vaccine league had a significant influence on public opinion up until the end of the decade. Many of the members were laypeople in the world of medicine (lawyers, businessmen, curers), but before attributing an anti-scientific irrationality to the group (as was the case of the Luddites in the nineteenth century) it is interesting to see how their arguments managed to persuade large sectors of the American public of the time. They used published 'scientific' data on the safety and effectiveness of vaccinations together with critical arguments questioning the legitimacy of some forms of knowledge over others, and finally of the legitimacy of science when making decisions about one's own body. In 1912 one of the pamphlets gave its message as follows:

> This pamphlet is a special appeal to you to repeal all compulsory vaccination as a needless legal and medical barbarism very dangerous to public health and human life, and based on gross deception of the public mind as to the true facts about smallpox and vaccination. It also urgently suggests to you the necessity of a new Law which will compel the record and publication in our vital statistics of all deaths caused directly or indirectly by vaccination or other inoculations.[46]

The strength of certain publics in medicine to take on scientific authority intensified throughout the twentieth century as a reaction against the reinforcement of the deficit model and the processes of medicalisation. During the 1970s a study was carried out in Canada to evaluate the levels of communication between doctors and patients. A survey was handed to each patient to evaluate their medical culture while the doctors were asked for their opinions about the patients' knowledge. The results were rather surprising. Most patients seemed to have a reasonable knowledge of the details of their illness, but fewer than half of the doctors were able to correctly estimate their patients' knowledge. Notwithstanding, they did not modify their communication strategies with patients. So, tacitly they had taken on the thesis of the deficit model to a large degree and assumed the ignorance of their lay patients.[47]

However, that tendency began to change in the last decades of the twentieth century. The crisis of the hegemonic hospital model and the strengthening of the welfare state, at least in Western Europe, gave patients a stronger position. In the same way as consumers and users, patients have also associated to call for their own rights. Students have protested against changes in official medical degrees, women's activism has increased as well as other groups who have until now been discriminated against in their search for treatments that meet their needs, and new patients' associations have been formed. The American Academy for Communication in Healthcare (AACH) states, for example, that better communication results in better clinical results, greater satisfaction for patients and healthcare staff and fewer cases of bad practice. It recommends that doctors take the Doc.com online course to improve their relations with patients and their ability to offer the most appropriate and sensitive treatment.[48]

208 Democratic science

Along similar lines, the AACH publishes the *Patient Education and Counseling* magazine, with the aim of improving treatments, trying to promote health education, research and medical practice in permanent communication with patients, their families and healthcare staff (another major public of medicine). The *Journal of American Medical Association* gave an increasing amount of space to the voice of the patients and, in recent years, has progressed towards a more 'narrative' medicine which has recovered some of the positive values of the old oral tradition. This is also a more 'reflexive' medicine where the professionals try to be self-critical in their practice and involve the opinions of other publics when taking certain decisions. Weekly health supplements and the new 2.0 websites where patients share experiences openly and dynamically are some of the manifestations of this new active participation by publics of medicine (and science in general) that we are witnessing today.[49] A new spirit of 'biological citizenship', which calls for each individual to take responsibility for their own health is a good example of the reaction to the so-called 'bio-power' (a term coined by philosopher Michel Foucault in the 1970s) resulting from the medicalisation process and hierarchical control of patients. So individual patients, ethics committees, the patients' associations and insurance companies gain more influence as publics of medicine.[50]

There is also widespread evidence of the active participation of patients' groups, not just in the application of certain therapies but also in the process of designing and researching new drugs or treatments.[51] In the US AIDS activist groups even questioned some of the criteria of the researchers as well as government public health policies. They also managed to influence modifications in clinical tests carried out in the 1990s.[52] During the 1980s AIDS patients took part in AZT testing, a drug which was considered at the time to be the most useful in combatting the disease, and they gave their opinions on the development of the experimental study.[53] That is how the tendency has grown to demand from the medical professionals a set of attitudes that are more harmonious with a democratic society together with a greater responsibility from patients when evaluating their own health risks and acting in consequence.[54] The activism of concerned patients' groups could result in the modification of public health policies or even important decisions about which lines of research have greatest priority. It is very probable that academic experts and company groups (especially the big pharmaceutical corporations) have more power than activists, but things start to change when the activists are able to influence public opinion and decide, if only partially, aspects of patient behaviour.

Interviews with patients and health professionals by the *British Committee on the Safety of Medicines and the Medicines Commission* have shown that both groups have different perceptions and do not always agree about illness and pain. If the testimonies of the patients and their families are listened to carefully by the medical classes, new information emerges that could be of great importance in the scientific study of specific illnesses: symptoms, photographs, active participation in clinical tests and collection of genetic data. Expert biomedics therefore develop a closer relationship with the patient in a collective learning process that has the potential to enrich both parties. The success of many of these processes evidently relies on the high organisational capacity of the patients' associations or other groups concerned about a certain health problem.

Until the 1980s, breast cancer, one of the most common illnesses among women, was surrounded by secrecy and patients suffered in silence, sometimes even hiding their diagnosis from friends and family. The gradual organisation and mobilisation of patients has enabled the gradual and more open emergence of statistics and details of the illness for the general public. During the 1990s it also stimulated legislative and political changes for prevention and has gradually managed to involve experts, governments and public and private companies in the problem.[55]

In the same vein in the US, the *Environmental Breast Cancer Movement* (EBCM) has worked over the last few decades on the identification and prevention of environmental risks associated with breast cancer. Contrary to the objectives of other movements in favour of the fight against cancer and which are mainly concerned with collecting funds to invest in its cure, the EBCM has focused on prevention and the need to identify the contaminating agents that are potential causes of the illness. But its campaign is not just one of agitation and protest. In fact it is quite the opposite, with prominent members of the EBCM working jointly with experts in universities to influence both the lines of research and the specific policies for prevention that need to be in place.[56]

The French Muscular Dystrophy Association is an excellent example of coordination in the interests of patients, the capacity to influence the content of biomedical research and social recognition of the patients themselves. The Association was established in 1958 at a time when this type of illness was considered to be a genetic rarity and of little interest to specialists. The aim was to store the maximum possible amount of clinical information, with all the available patient data. The Association even built up a genetic data bank for use by experts interested in researching the disease, but also so that the information reached the general public.[57]

Some of the bioethics committees carry out studies that show how their value judgements and stances do not always coincide with certain public perceptions of the problem. They run the risk of acting as new experts from a middle position between doctors and patients which largely impede the true participation of the public in certain health decisions. The committees are actually stable but flexible bodies where experts along with laypeople with a specific medical interest (such as abortion, euthanasia, stem cell research and in vitro fertilisation) fight for hegemony. Their success is based on their ability to include plural perceptions of the different publics with regard to a specific health problem.[58]

In terms of the participatory turn, there has been a gradual move away from a view that was fairly insensitive to the opinion of the patients themselves towards another in which the inevitable discrepancies between experts and laypeople are

210 Democratic science

openly discussed when administering certain drugs. These discrepancies are often based more on the different values and beliefs of the groups in question than, as may have seemed the case at first glance, on the deficit of technological information about the drug itself. We are all readers of the package inserts for different drugs, yet we approach them in very different ways according to factors that go beyond the strict field of pharmacology.[59]

8.3. Technoscience, risk and uncertainty

In line with the analyses of German sociologist Ulrich Beck (1944–2015) a few decades ago, science can be described as intimately associated with risk and chance, factors which until relatively recently have not been submitted to rigorous consideration. The lurking dangers have no time limit and can equally affect us as they can future generations (for example, transgenic foods, the concentration of DDT in the blood or radioactivity). Neither can they be restricted spatially in an ever globalised world where risks such as rising temperatures as a result of carbon dioxide emissions affect cities, states and entire continents. But the quantification and standardisation of these risks raise difficulties and further controversies. They depend largely on the interests and position of each individual or institution in society. The question here, and possibly the most interesting in Beck's analysis, is in the growing importance of the general public in the face of this enormous new problem. If one of the main characteristics of industrial society is the distribution of consumer goods, the risk society distributes 'dangers' to the entire population.[60] From that perspective, the risk society has substituted admiration for productivity and progress with scepticism in the face of the supposed benefits of science (discontent) and the permanent stress caused by its consequences.[61]

We live in a society with multiple risks that need to be rationalised using a range of strategies. Without the institutionalisation of an expert discourse about environmental, nutritional or technological perils, life would be very hard to bear. So the experts and dangers seem to be two inextricably linked concepts, basic pillars for social stability, although their function is not removed from their audiences. In fact, risk perception and assessment can easily become a common ground for the different protagonists, although they do not necessarily share the same discourse.[62] Controversial topics such as mad cow disease (BSE), genetically modified foodstuffs, food additives or bird flu tend to generate major discrepancies and different perceptions of risk, and these need to be analysed according to the social identity of each group.

Experts tend to minimise the risk of certain activities that laypeople see as being dangerous, while the latter question the authority and legitimacy of the experts. This is a serious problem and one that cannot easily be overcome from the traditional positions associated with the deficit model, without a more 'humble' attitude and open dialogue.[63] From a traditional perspective, when the risk potential of our civilisation is discussed, scientific and social rationality tend to take different paths. Lay groups with active and participative attitudes tend to ask questions that are never properly answered by risk experts and when they are it tends to be in terms that do not address the original questions and true concerns of the public.[64]

Consequently there is no consensus over the best solutions for environmental problems, from how to deal with an emergency oil slick to the necessary speed limits for reducing atmospheric pollution in big cities. Representatives of local and national political power, prestigious university professors and researchers, professional associations, nature protection groups, rural property owners, local governments and cultural organisations tend to form a polyphony of voices that dilutes the supposed 'truths' of the problem. On the other hand, environmental activists are often accused of spreading overzealous criticism of the science of experts and their responsibility for the destruction of the planet. In the 1990s, for example, defenders of the green revolution such as John Young spread ideas poisoned with discontent. Young considered that science had undermined democracy and that knowledge in the hands of a minority of experts had become an instrument of power without public participation. He also reported the immorality of the scientific objectivity with which experts frequently presented themselves in order to appear politically neutral.[65]

There are also other problems stemming from this. As mentioned in Chapter 7, risk becomes an appealing topic for the media when it comes to attracting audience figures in the face of some imminent danger or the pain and consternation of a natural disaster or accident. However, despite the reports and recommendations of the supposed experts, the public takes its own decisions about situations of risk that do not necessarily coincide with theirs, further complicating the so-called scientific 'objectivity'. Where the scientists are unable to display sufficient sensitivity to the public, communication in situations of risk and the subsequent recommendations for avoiding them fall on fallow ground.

When analysing environmental problems such as toxic spillages, industrial accidents or confrontations of interest, it is easy to see how the supposed authority and independence of the experts is questioned in the way they present the problem to the public. Emphasis on controversy, emotions and fascination about the limits of knowledge often seem to take priority over objectivity.[66] A relatively in-depth study of public attitudes towards a certain technological or environmental challenge will show a degree of mistrust in the expert, or the scientific or political authority. Perhaps this is not openly expressed and often a discreet silence is maintained which hides feelings of resentment and mistrust.[67] The noise made by environmentalist groups or movements defending a highway route remain in the background.

Some years ago Steven Yearley theorised about the influence of environmental problems in the gradual erosion of scientific authority. From his point of view problems such as global warming, the shrinking of the ozone layer, the use of pesticides and genetically modified organisms are some clear examples of the degree of crisis that expertise is experiencing. They also become instruments

212 Democratic science

of criticism against major aspects of industrial society and official or institutionalised science.[68] Even Beck thought that many of the public protests against environmental problems formed an intrinsic part of a new modernity in which discrepancies involving risks are already an integral part of the model. Ecology as an academic discipline or its more heterodox versions such as the Gaia theory mentioned previously or the feminist interpretation of nature put forward alternative scientific methodologies that also become sources of tension. Their capacity for interdisciplinarity in the context of the new technoscience also questions the traditional disciplinary organisations of academic science, which is largely a result of the university model of the nineteenth century, and is currently undergoing profound changes.

Despite attempts by the oil industry to legitimate its contribution to progress through the manufacture of household goods, food additives, medicines and pesticides, the public impact of the famous *Silent Spring* by Rachel Carson in 1962 contributed to the construction of a mistrustful and critical image of artificiality that had presumably been provided by the chemical industry. In response to these claims of environmental pollution the chemical industry tends to counterattack using public discourse and media advertising to socially legitimate its products.[69] These risk generators try to seek a certain 'counterscience' (in Beck's terms); in other words, a set of arguments and explanations formally presented with academic rigour to compete in the public sphere with other arguments that are considered over-pessimistic by the laypeople. This is where access to the media becomes crucial and the arguments to persuade the general public (including advertising and marketing) become almost essential to the success of a company or enterprise.[70]

A list of terms that cause anxiety among the public (nuclear waste, transgenics, asbestos, tobacco, genetic therapies, bird flu or mobile phone aerials) provides a paradigmatic example of how the traditional division between experts and laypeople has become outdated. In an age of risk and uncertainty, these new problems require fresh spaces for discussion and debate where technocratic and often authoritarian decisions on traditional political practices tend no longer to be the case. From traditional representative democracy, with all its limitations (especially when it comes to scientific issues), we need to move on to a democracy of dialogue where the new hybrid forums can give a voice to many who have until now been silenced. The examples are many and forceful: the treatment of nuclear waste in France, deformations in newborn babies in Japan, child leukaemia in Massachusetts or mad cow disease in the United Kingdom.[71]

The opinions of a group of electrical workers on the risks of radiation from the Sellafield nuclear reprocessing plant in England are well known. From a sceptical position the workers considered that any information about nuclear radiation that the experts could give them in talks or pamphlets would inevitably lead to confusion. They rejected the rhetoric of risk assessment or calculations of probability which they did not consider to form part of their own values but rather the discourse of the experts to whom they delegated much of the decision

Democratic science **213**

making concerning their own safety. Even though the resistance of the electrical workers could be seen as anchored in ignorance, it is interesting to see how in this case, as in many others, there was a clash of different technological cultures, both of them relevant.[72]

There is, then, a need to learn to share vulnerabilities in the public sphere. Even accepting the most traditional procedures for risk control and assessment, it is impossible to eliminate a certain degree of uncertainty in the medicines we take, the air we breathe or the means of transport we choose. In the complex technoscientific systems of the present there is an unavoidable need to live with that sense of vulnerability, which could even make the system and its actors more flexible and creative. There are, for example, many uncertainties about climate change, but there is a minimum international consensus that the temperature of the planet will increase by around 2.5 degrees by the end of the twenty-first century. That warming will have a series of effects on human activity and could be catastrophic for certain plants and animals. As seen in Chapter 7, the problem is not restricted to a merely scientific question but to major political, ethical and social challenges with respect to the values that we will share in the future.[73] Experts in a certain process no longer have a central role. The notion of risk is often defined in practice by specific economic activities and political stances.[74] Risk, then, is not so much a problem of probability which can be calculated objectively and rationally in a cold cost–benefit analysis, but is intimately linked to the modern human condition, to our societies where we have to assume all manner of coexistence with uncertainty.[75] In that sense the new participatory model gains strength daily over the deficit model and common places, intersections and shared spaces for discussion take on a new protagonism.

* * *

In a now canonical text by sociologist Thomas F. Gieryn from 1983, he referred precisely to the moveable boundaries between scientific disciplines and between experts and laypeople. Chapter 4 showed that those boundaries are not unmovable or timeless but are constructed by the protagonists themselves in a certain historical time and space.[76] That model can be extended to a large number of the problems presented in this book, and the historical actors that constructed the complex limits between scientific, professional and amateur disciplines, academic and popular science, orthodox and heterodox science, expert knowledge and science popularisation or regulated education and informal learning. Similarly, the participatory turn and technoscience require a joint approach to science in coevolution with society in order to gain a better understanding of the complex, unpredictable, volatile and irregular facets of the present, where the academic and cognitive authority of an apparently unproblematic science anchored in the deficit model seems to be coming to an end.[77]

In recent years some authors have tried to describe the breadth and nature of these changes. Sociologist Michel Callon has proposed, for example, a theoretical framework which basically attempts to describe on three levels the relationship

214 Democratic science

between experts and laypeople that largely co-exist today and have manifested themselves throughout history.[78] Model 1, which Callon calls 'the public education', is quite similar to that described in the introduction to this book when trying to diagnose some of the causes of the discontent of scientific culture. Again, it is based on the irreducible opposition between expert and lay knowledge. Here, the basic objective of the experts, protected by their institutions, is to eradicate all lay knowledge, considered to be inferior and disposable, and ignore any kind of participation by its holders. However, in order to bring about that eradication it is necessary to create a relationship of trust, which presumably can only come about through education and information, hence the crucial role of science popularisers.

Alternatively, or as a complement – the coexistence of aspects of these different models cannot be ignored when analysing certain historical cases (or current problems) – there is model 2, or the 'public debate' model, where the relation between experts and laypeople is somewhat more enriching. Here, the experts are aware of the need to define and differentiate their potential audiences according to their profession, location, age, sex, etc., assigning competences and knowledge to each group, like in a marketing study. Experts recognise here that their capacity for influencing ethical, economic or any other kind of problem outside their specialist area is no greater than that of the laypeople. Therefore there arises the need to listen to the other side in problems of waste treatment, industrial risks, water management and environmental problems; to encourage forums for debate, talks and meetings to try to find a minimum consensus between the different interest groups. The crucial problem is deciding who to include in this kind of debate. Once again it is the experts from a position that can be considered somewhat more generous and open who decide on the profile and nature of their publics.

Closer to the spirit of democratic science presented in this chapter, the third model, the 'coproduction of knowledge' model, is probably the most controversial, but at the same time the most intriguing. It involves including the laypeople not only in more or less open debates, which normally are not exempt from the rhetoric of a certain kind of 'enlightenment despotism' by the experts, but also in the process of constructing knowledge itself. Experts and laypeople therefore work closely from the start of a health, environmental or technological project. At the end they reach a supposedly and reasonably balanced consensus where both parties feel that they have been treated with dignity and respect in the expression of other ideas, over and above the strict interests of each group. For Callon, in our present society there is not a confidence crisis in science but a crisis in the participation mechanisms by laypeople, the general public, in specific projects. For him this underlines the main cause of discontent in our scientific culture. If we maintain the basic elements of models 1 and 2 the experts will retain their hegemony without too many problems. In model 3, which would seem to be the model for the future, there is a change in the dominant epistemic-cognitive regime.

As in any historical turning point, today it is difficult to analyse the key factors of these radical changes, and others will have to fine-tune the arguments presented here. However, even with a sceptical view of terms that are relatively new in the history of science, such as risk, vulnerability, participatory turn and coproduction, we will probably not be able to educate future generations with a solid scientific culture using the traditional academic disciplines of the nineteenth century. Perhaps this is because, among other reasons, the two cultures of Snow – the humanistic and the scientific – have become outdated for us. They are a response to intellectual schemes more than 50 years old, which have been the source of inspiration for addressing many problems, but which now need a profound revision in this new age of technoscience and the almost inevitable democratisation of knowledge and renewed protagonism of the public.

Notes

1 Bucchi, Neresini (2007: 449).
2 Turner (2001).
3 Gieryn (1999).
4 Burnett (2007).
5 Bucchi, Neresini (2007: 450).
6 Wynne (1995).
7 Bucchi, Neresini (2007: 451).
8 Levitt, Gross (1994); Kleinman (2000: 1–2).
9 Kleinman (2000: 5).
10 Jasanoff (2003a).
11 Nowotny, Scott, Gibbons (2001, 2003); Jasanoff (2003a: 14).
12 Lengwiler (2008).
13 Callon, Lascoumes, Barthe (2009).
14 Joss (1999).
15 Bensaude-Vincent (2009a).
16 Brown, Mikkelsen (1990); Collins (2014).
17 Nielsen (2011).
18 Jasanoff (2004).
19 Jasanoff (2004); Bensaude-Vincent (2009b).
20 Jasanoff (2004: 14).
21 Bensaude-Vincent (2009b: 34).
22 Bensaude-Vincent (2009b: 15); Bucchi, Neresini (2002).
23 Morris (2007: 324).
24 McCormick (2007).
25 Lengwiler (2008).
26 Devall (2001).
27 Rowe, Frewer (2000).
28 Kleinman (2000).
29 Wachelder (2003); Leydesdorff, Ward (2005).
30 Joss (1999).
31 Hindmarsh, Gottweis (2005).
32 Wynne (1991).
33 Wynne (1995: 114).
34 For specific examples of PATH projects, see http://www.macaulay.ac.uk/economics/research/path/PATH-Poster1.pdf (accessed 17 December 2015). In the last five years the

216 Democratic science

European Union has also organised a series of debates and publications on the concept of the 'Public Engagement of Science'.

35 Nanoscience and nanotechnologies: Opportunities and Uncertainties (2004), https://royalsociety.org/~/media/Royal_Society_Content/policy/publications/2004/9693.pdf (accessed 21 June 2015).

36 Nanoscience and Nanotechnologies: Opportunities and Uncertainties (2004: 79).

37 Bensaude-Vincent (2009b); Drexler (1986).

38 Bensaude-Vincent (2009b); Cacciatore, Scheufele, Corley (2011).

39 Hay (2002: 278).

40 Hay (2002: 290).

41 Bensaude-Vincent (2009b: 183).

42 Bucchi, Neresini (2007: 465).

43 Irwin, Michael (2003), cited by Bucchi, Neresini (2007: 467).

44 Nelkin (1995: 444–5).

45 Porter (1992: 1).

46 Cited by Colgrove (2005: 176).

47 Segall, Roberts (1980), cited by Bucchi, Neresini (2007: 452).

48 http://www.aachonline.org/ (accessed 21 June 2015).

49 Bucchi, Neresini (2007).

50 Bensaude-Vincent (2009b: 181).

51 Lengwiler (2008); Epstein (1996, 2007).

52 Epstein (1996, 2007).

53 Epstein (1995).

54 Abraham, Sheppard (1997).

55 Braun (2003).

56 McCormick (2007: 612).

57 Rabeharisoa, Callon (1999, 2004).

58 Kelly (2003).

59 Callon (1999); Abraham, Sheppard (1997).

60 Beck (2008: 2–3).

61 Hay (2002: 309).

62 Gregory, Miller (1998: 187–95).

63 Blok, Jensen, Kaltoft (2008).

64 Beck (2008: 30).

65 Hay (2002: 128).

66 Boudia, Jas (2014).

67 Beck (2008: 6).

68 Yearley (1995).

69 Dunlap (2008).

70 Beck (2008: 32).

71 'Acting in an Uncertain World' was the attractive title of a book published by French sociologist Michel Callon and his collaborators in 2003. Callon, Lascoumes, Barthe (2009). Sociologist Wiebe Bijker has worked on some aspects of this problem under the concept of 'technological vulnerability'. Hommels, Mesman, Bijker (2014).

72 Michael (1992).

73 Jamieson (1992).

74 Boudia, Jas (2007).

75 Jasanoff (2003a).

76 Gieryn (1983).

77 Nowotny, Scott, Gibbons (2001).

78 Callon (1999).

9

CONCLUSION

In 1985, sociologist Richard Whitley stressed the fact that science popularisation has become: 'a means of claiming legitimacy for many social movements and interest groups, and also part of scientists' claims for social support and legitimacy as a separate group of autonomous intellectuals'.[1] He added that: 'by successfully combining claims to universal validity and social utility through popularisation, they laid the foundation for the present domination and expansion of the sciences'.[2] Whitley's point offers a highly critical view of the legacy of the deficit model, in which any signs of philanthropy, generosity or charitable interpretation seem to have no place. This book concurs to a large extent with Whitley's thesis, inviting a critical approach to popularisation as a complex mechanism of communication in a given historical context and integrating the reasons and interests of the different actors. However, Whitley's forceful words, which match many of the main ideas in the preceding chapters, could be criticised for introducing elements that are too relativist and critical of the experts, and for giving excessive centre stage to society in general and to the laypeople in particular. It is an understandable reaction. Until recently our scientific culture has given preference to an elitist view of the great ideas and figures that legitimised the status quo of present-day science. It has been an instrument for analysis and selection of elements of the past, subtly anchored in Hilgartner's 'dominant view', in itself not far from that of Whitley.

In an excellent book on orality and knowledge, French historian Françoise Waquet has identified several historical examples that show how certain public academic acts 'disturb' or 'corrupt' the expert. That was seen in Chapter 4, in the Arago–Biot debate on press access to the sessions at the Académie des sciences in Paris in the nineteenth century, but it can also be extended to the public rituals of presenting doctoral theses or applying for access to the public institutions. Academics such as Georges Duby, Michel Foucault and Roland Barthes have all

218 Conclusion

borne witness to the difficulties of presenting their thinking before audiences that are either too large or too inexpert and the fear of a certain rebellion of the masses. Consequently, they defended the need to armour their authority in closer circles with previously established limits.[3] The objections are reasonable enough. Even some of my students do not share the main thesis of this book and defend a more 'traditional' view of the circulation of knowledge. They are not prepared to give up the authority and autonomy of the expert as a creator of knowledge while seeing the role of popularisation as subsidiary. They are concerned about the supposed danger of open negotiation; a kind of bazaar where knowledge is bought and sold to the highest bidder, with no experts to act as intermediaries and set the rules of the game.[4] So my authority as an expert (and this is where the interesting question of reflexivity comes in) may be questioned by my own audience: students, readers and colleagues.

However, in practice, there is a kind of continuum for methods and practices with the aim of transferring scientific information, whether it be the results of basic research, a teaching programme or reflections on their social and economic implications.[5] The strict boundary between science and pseudo-science is diluted and any postulates advocating the existence of different epistemologies between the content of communicative discourses and those of science proper fade into the distance.[6] Through a complex feedback process, the stability of the paradigms goes well beyond the strict consensus of the experts. While for Kuhn in the 1960s their stability depended basically on agreement between a small community of experts, now the door is open to a complex set of practices where both experts and laypeople can play an important role, and thereby form an intrinsic part of the construction of scientific knowledge in a specific historical context. From that perspective it is easier to understand the role of the audiences in legitimising one theory or another. It is simpler to categorise the amateurs or popularisers according to their power of influence in the esoteric circles of academic science, or the contribution of students or patients in producing different consensuses. It is easier to apply the thesis of the continuum of genres to manuals, popular science books, science fiction stories and novels. Common places of science, often associated with their material and visual cultures, become vehicles for interpenetration of different Fleckian circles.

The idea of the circulation of scientific knowledge between esoteric and exoteric circles is intriguing yet still controversial, and one that bears some similarity to Habermas's developments in the 1960s on the concept of the public sphere: as such it has been a very useful analytical tool for many of the historical examples that appear throughout this book. As mentioned previously, Habermas agreed that expert knowledge should be contrasted in new spaces of sociability that transcended the strict controls of circles of experts. Later on, towards the end of the 1970s (and perhaps it was no coincidence that this was when Fleck entered the English-speaking academy), sociologists began to criticise the consideration of science as a normative activity. They questioned whether it was capable of generating a genuine and privileged type of knowledge that was different from the rest. From the reconstruction of scientists' daily practice, the idea that the creation and diffusion of scientific knowledge belonged to separate spheres came into serious question.

A few years later, a closer interpretation of Fleck's proposal (although one that was reworded in the intellectual milieu of the new sociology of science) was Richard Whitley's book, written in collaboration with science historian Terry Shinn, *Expository Science: Forms and Functions of Popularization* (1985). As Whitley saw it, scientific knowledge does not exist in an abstract form, but it only takes shape when presented or expounded in a specific context and before a certain kind of audience. This 'expository science' explains why a specialised article resulting from first-class research and presented before a conference of specialists is no more 'science' than an adventure film with scientific content aimed at the public at large. They are both discourses about the natural world aimed at different audiences.[7] Based on that presupposition, experts can learn about the attitudes and opinions of laypeople and the attitudes of the latter can influence the content and values of science. Scientists express their thought and the results of their research in many different ways, including letters, seminars, specialised articles, essays, textbooks, popularisation conferences, industrial reports, technical advice, government consultancy, safety reports, legal reports, membership of scientific committees, press conferences, interviews with journalists, press releases, popularisation articles, radio and TV programmes.[8] And each of these communicative activities is directed at a different audience whose reactions influence their intellectual pathway and the long- and short-term decisions they make. Criticism by colleagues at a conference, applause in a popularisation meeting, student indifference or their enthusiastic questions, the rejection of an article for publication in a prestigious academic journal, obtaining funding for a research project, among many other things, are nothing more than complex journeys through Fleck's esoteric and exoteric circles, and central components of the collective dimension of scientific knowledge that this book has tried to defend.

But all that circulation of knowledge has other political dimensions. Opposed to the dominant view of science popularisation and obsessed with constructing a counterhegemony, Gramsci and other Marxist-inspired thinkers, such as E. P. Thompson (1924–93) and his 'history from below', possibly took the glorification of a popular culture, supposedly autonomous and independent of the attempts at domination by the elites, a little too far. In recent decades as a reaction to some of these positions cultural historians such as Roger Chartier and Robert Darnton have criticised precisely the possible existence of an autonomous, popular (lay) culture, independent of the 'expert' culture. For Chartier the study of cultural organisations, which until now have been considered socially pure, should be replaced with a new approach which analyses them as a mixture of different elements, both popular and elite. There is a need for a history of ordinary people taken from their active position and their capacity to adapt,

220 Conclusion

transmit and subvert all the knowledge that is directed at them.[9] That way, the supposed essence of what is 'popular' will not be found in a set of finished texts which only require identification and cataloguing as a kind of library of popular culture, but rather the 'popular' will refer to a certain type of relationship and a way of actively appropriating knowledge or culture in general and an original way of using cultural produces and legitimating ideas and attitudes.

So, popular does not refer to a culture created from above for the people below – although we have seen that history is full of strategies for cultural hegemony by the dominant elites – and neither is culture rooted in the people. It is simply a certain type of dynamic relation between certain cultural objects.[10] In his works, Darnton repeatedly insisted on the importance of analysing how ordinary people manage to make sense of the world, with their particular way of thinking and their cosmology or attitudes. In his famous publication about the great slaughter of cats in eighteenth-century France and other episodes in French history, Darnton thought that in treating Diderot and D'Alembert, the editors of the *Encyclopédie* and distinguished *philosophes*, together with the 'peasant tellers of tales and the plebeian killers of cats', he was abandoning the traditional distinction between popular and elite culture, and showing that the intellectuals and the ordinary people shared the same problems.[11]

'Popular science' – as a part of 'popular culture' – has been a contested area in academic life for decades. As historian of science Jon Topham summed up, overcoming the dichotomy between 'popular science' and 'proper science' has not been an easy task, at least for historians of science. This is probably one of the reasons why the history of science popularisation has for a long time occupied a marginal place in mainstream historiography. It was usually trapped within a diffusion model which took for granted that scientific knowledge was first of all created and later spread to the ignorant public in two separate steps and spheres of expert and lay knowledge.[12]

To oppose the former thesis, Topham drew heavily on James Secord's emphasis on the history of science conceived as the history of science communication: the history of 'knowledge in transit'.[13] Both authors endorse a more dynamic approach to science as a cultural phenomenon, in which the distinction between creating and spreading, between making and communicating progressively fades away. They have also convincingly shown how this approach borrows ideas and methods from cultural history, and how this 'knowledge in transit' can reinforce recent and even future research into the history of science popularisation, scientific education and international scientific communication, among other fields.[14]

In the 2009 *Isis Focus* on 'Historicizing "popular science"', Topham even suggested abandoning the term 'popular science' as an analytical concept, becoming simply an actors' category.[15] Both Topham and Secord have proposed using the term 'popular science' only in the particular cultural traditions and languages which specific actors used in specific historical contexts.[16] Particularly throughout the nineteenth and twentieth centuries popular science became a marketing label designed to help science sell, and a useful device for communicating between widely separated and too often isolated scientific disciplines and degrees of scientific expertise.[17]

In addition, the Secordian 'circulation of knowledge' has often been set in an urban market in which science could be bought and sold as a commodity. In fact, as discussed in Chapter 2 of this book, Secord's masterpiece *Victorian Sensation* brilliantly combines elements of the cultural history of the book with the history of the circulation of evolutionary ideas in the context of Victorian Britain.[18] In a similar way, Bernard Lightman and Aileen Fyfe have added other nuances to that circulation. In their *Science in the Marketplace* (2007), they emphasised that during the nineteenth century, and particularly in urban contexts, ordinary people actually did 'participate' in science by way of education and entertainment, by way of exhibitions, galleries, museums and popular lectures, as new marketable strategies.[19] They also added that popular shows often influenced the way in which experts and showmen constructed their own public addresses for their audiences and potential customers.[20]

In this framework of a continuous circulation of knowledge among different actors, Topham briefly mentioned the fact that elite and popular culture are inevitably caught up in complex mechanisms of *domination*, *appropriation* and *resistance*,[21] but not going further in a potentially sharper analysis. This is therefore a good reason to have used our Fleck–Gramsci–Habermas framework as the main source of inspiration for this book, as a way to build up a stronger political dimension when analysing processes of knowledge in transit and science popularisation, when describing the enormous tensions between expert and lay actors in history in their struggle for power and social prestige.

It is perhaps time now to return to Stephen Hilgartner's canonical paper, 'The Dominant View of Popularization' (1990).[22] Hilgartner criticised the way science popularisation was used in the past and is still often used today by scientists and experts to ensure that they themselves decide how science should be interpreted by laypeople, and thus maintain their powerful, privileged social status. Even where experts were able to demonstrate that the popularisers had made mistakes when disseminating certain aspects of science to the public, this would similarly reinforce their authority as the exclusive repositories of knowledge.

As emphasised by historians Roger Cooter and Stephen Pumphrey, knowledge is not simply transferred as if it were a material commodity; it is always transformed in unexpected and sometimes startling ways by different groups and actors. *Appropriation* processes should include strategies of legitimisation and legitimating spaces which often lie outside the borders and the function of established institutions, and they are always close to processes involving the construction of different counterhegemonies. Appropriation also involves eclecticism between ongoing, hegemonic programmes and existing traditions.[23] Moreover, the *resistance* of different groups to elite knowledge is particularly relevant. Every group struggles for its own organic interests and agendas, for its cultural hegemony.

222 Conclusion

It is worth remembering that, in Gramscian terms, political stability had to be explained by other factors, further physical coercion and repression. Therefore, hegemony brought to the fore how the so-called civil society, with its institutions ranging from education, religion and family to the microstructures of everyday practices, contributed to the production of meaning and values, which direct and maintain the spontaneous consent of the various strata of society. Hegemony was a ruling tool for any class or group, an instrument for cultural, moral, ideological leadership over subordinated groups, a prestige language, for example, that reinforced cultural influence and control over weaker linguistic (and scientific, why not?) communities. It was conceived as a dynamic force, a continuous process of formation.

In the ongoing battle for hegemony and scientific authority, the need to recover an enormous number of primary sources of testimonies which have been largely unheard so far in the history of science is not unrealistic. Although they are integrated in their relationship with the more usual protagonists of historical narration (teachers, inventors, scientists – experts in the broad sense), subaltern actors such as readers, visitors, spectators, amateurs, students, artisans, workers, users, patients, etc. have all appeared in the previous chapters and undoubtedly deserve greater attention in future research. Gramsci's hegemony and intellectuals therefore help to retain a certain sensitivity towards the weaker testimonies in the history of science.

According to Cooter, whose work on phrenology in nineteenth-century England was influenced some decades ago by Gramsci's thinking, 'popular' scientific knowledge contains its own perception of nature. Despite the complex communication and feedback processes discussed earlier, *layness* is at least partly opposed to expertness so it never really exactly coincides with the knowledge of the elites.[24] From that perspective, and one that some other thinkers also subscribe to, lay knowledge is not a watered down or quantitatively inferior version of expert knowledge, but it is qualitatively different.[25] So, for Cooter, the impact of science popularisation on the publics of science has not yet been measured with sufficient precision and, as seen in Chapter 8, this is a good reason to strengthen a participative model and appeals to the democratisation of science in our societies of global citizenship.

Based on the previous sources of inspiration and the entire set of historical examples examined, we should now be poised to reassess the deficit model legacy set forth at the beginning of this book. In doing so, we will be providing at least partial solutions to palliate the discontent of scientific culture as developed and exemplified throughout these pages.[26] The idea of the exclusivity of a natural knowledge among scientists, or experts in general, is relatively recent and the separation between the experimental natural sciences and other fields of knowledge mainly occurred in the nineteenth and twentieth centuries. Even in that period of rising professionalisation, it is clear that knowledge boundaries are still subtle and in constant negotiation, and can only be understood in certain specific spaces and times.[27] Different disciplines, practices, actors or subjects can make the esoteric and exoteric circles of knowledge more or less permeable. Therefore, a more dynamic and flexible image of the mechanisms through which scientific knowledge is transmitted arises; one that is more in line with the different historical contingencies and plurality of actors.[28]

Another clear conclusion is that scientific knowledge is and has generally been throughout history more horizontal and flexible than it may seem at first glance. Experts often become laypeople when they find themselves outside their speciality, so both categories are ever-shifting. Also, beyond texts, the material culture of science has built numerous bridges, common places and intersections throughout history. Once the deficit model and the main features of PUS have been criticised, it also seems reasonable to accept that the publics are never totally passive, while admitting that as soon as the audiences question the expert's authority, the public tends to have little power. Science popularisation is never neutral and science is never ideologically neutral.

The days of vertical, textual and ahistorical science popularisation in two discontinuous stages, first in the privacy of the laboratory and later popularised in society, seem numbered. This book has precisely striven to break down barriers, or at least to grasp the terms under which these barriers are erected by the actors in each historical period, and to further show an array of spaces of intersection, between Copernicus and Menocchio, Darwin and Chambers, Verne and Flammarion, Fontenelle and his distinguished lady, Aldrovandi and his visitors, the juries and award winners at fairs, naturalists and their audiences, Faraday and the young students around a candle, Crichton, Spielberg and film viewers.

In that sense, the voices of amateurs, students, readers, visitors, viewers, artisans and activists have risen in status compared to the traditional actors who have been more deeply studied from the prevailing view of popularisation: doctors, engineers, writers, collection owners, organisers of world fairs, scientists, university professors, researchers, civil servants, teachers, advisers, popularisers and many more. The role of the latter as organic intellectuals, in Gramsci's words, is fairly well known, although one of the goals of this book has obviously been to survey the mechanisms of their scientific authority at different points in time. The history of the former, of the organic intellectuals associated with the majority of audiences of science, has still largely yet to be written, and other historians of science must revive new authors and actors that have fallen into the oblivion of the past. Much remains to be done to construct a historical ethnography of 'popular science', not in itself isolated but in constant interaction and struggle with the elites of each period.

New actors emerge, but so do new ways for knowledge to circulate. This is also a history of verbs, of scientific practices such as writing, reading, printing, collecting, displaying, representing, teaching, learning, experimenting, demonstrating, controlling, doing, organising, constructing, measuring, popularising, appropriating, protesting, resisting and criticising.[29] It is a dynamic view of scientific knowledge, an approach to the constant permeability of Fleck's

224 Conclusion

esoteric and exoteric circles, membranes of variable osmotic pressures capable of letting codified information pass through in both directions. It is a contribution to historical symmetry, to reviving voices from above and from below, the voices of the orthodox and the voices of the heterodox.

Perhaps like the problem of climate change itself, this is a somewhat 'wicked' book. Once immersed in this symmetry of diverse actors, spaces of intersection and scientific authorities with varied geometry, the truths of objective, neutral science vanish both in the past – think, for example, of the books from the Scientific Revolution, or the natural philosophers from the Enlightenment and their audiences – and in the present, with the media impact of technoscience, the vulnerability of expert authority in public controversies, and activist and patient groups capable of influencing certain medical or technical decisions. As we saw in Chapter 8, in the Habermasian public sphere, the scientific, the political and the social cannot be clearly disentwined from each other, much to the dismay of the defenders of traditional popularisation and to the pleasure of its critics. There are clearly conflicting positions, and the academic and public debates on these issues seem hard to avoid in the forthcoming decades.

Finally, this book encourages a kind of reflexivity. I mentioned at the beginning of this chapter that some of my students feel uncomfortable with this new approach to scientific culture and prefer to take refuge in a more traditional vision. The powerful idea that knowledge is created first in private and only later becomes public remains virtually intact in the younger generation. But just like any other result of research, this book is the outcome of my own intellectual pathway. In his *Orientalism* (1978), Edward Said upheld the need for the historian or humanist in general to explain their own pathway in order to understand their work. So this book is the outcome of my own processes of expository science with my students, yet also with my teachers, colleagues and the supposed laypeople who have enabled me to enter and leave Fleck's circles countless times.

Perhaps only a deep, individual and collective immersion in this new magma of knowledge will contribute to at least assuaging the old discontent and thus, from a new perspective, dignifying all the publics of science indistinctly.

Notes

1 Shinn, Whitley (1985: 25).
2 Ibid.
3 Waquet (2003: 350–7).
4 Collins, Evans (2003, 2007).
5 Shinn, Whitley (1985: vii–viii).
6 Ibid., 31.
7 Shinn, Whitley (1985); Lewenstein (1995b).
8 McElheny (1985).
9 Chartier (1984: 13).
10 Chartier (1984: 233–5).

Conclusion **225**

11 'By including them with the peasant tellers of tales and the plebeian killers of cats, I have abandoned the usual distinction between elite and popular culture, and have tried to show how intellectuals and common people coped with the same sort of problems', Darnton (1985: 6).
12 Topham (2009b).
13 Secord (2004).
14 Topham (2009a).
15 Ibid.
16 In the same *Focus* section, however, Ralph O'Connor was in favour of using the term 'popular science' as an 'umbrella-label', useful for communicating with other disciplines. O'Connor (2009).
17 Topham (2009a, 2004); Rudwick (1982).
18 Secord (2000).
19 Fyfe, Lightman (2007).
20 For the active role of audiences in the construction of scientific knowledge, see Shinn, Whitley (1985).
21 Topham (2009a: 13).
22 Hilgartner (1990).
23 For the concept of appropriation, see Gavroglu et al. (2008).
24 Cooter and Pumphrey (1994).
25 Bucchi, Neresini (2007: 450).
26 Myers (2003).
27 Gieryn (1999).
28 Bensaude-Vincent, Bertomeu-Sánchez and García Belmar (2003: 243–51).
29 Pyenson, Sheets-Pyenson (1999).

BIBLIOGRAPHY

This bibliography is an updated version of the one that appeared in the Spanish edition (Marcial Pons, 2011). It is not intended to be exhaustive but rather to reflect my own intellectual journey in the writing of this book. It includes in alphabetical order the primary and secondary sources consulted and cited in the footnotes throughout the chapters as well as some works of reference to complete the information for the reader. As a general criterion the works cited are those that were consulted. In some cases there are references to previous or other language editions, depending on their interest in terms of the problem of science in the public sphere.

Abir-Am, Pnina G. (1992) 'The Politics of Macromolecules: Molecules, Biologists, Biochemists and Rhetoric', *Osiris*, 7, 164–91.

Abir-Am, Pnina G. and Elliot, Clark A. (eds) (1999) 'Commemorative Practices in Science', *Osiris*, 14.

Abraham, John and Sheppard, Julie (1997) 'Democracy, Technocracy and the Secret State of Medicines Control: Expert and Non-Expert Perspectives', *Science, Technology and Human Values*, 22(2), 139–67.

Adorno, Theodor and Horkheimer, Max (2002) *Dialectic of Enlightenment*, Stanford, CA: Stanford University Press (1st German edition, 1947).

Aftalion, F. (2001) *A History of the International Chemical Industry: From the 'Early Days' to 2000*, Philadelphia, PA: Chemical Heritage Press.

Agar, Jon and Smith, Crosbie (1998) *Making Space for Science: Territorial Themes in the Shaping of Knowledge*, London: Macmillan.

Agassi, Joseph (2003) *Science and Culture*, Dordrecht: Kluwer.

Ahlström, Göran (1982) *Engineers and Industrial Growth: Higher Technical Education and the Engineering Profession during the 19th and Early 20th Centuries: France, Germany, Sweden, and England*, London: Croom Helm.

Alberti, Samuel J.M.M. (2005) 'Objects and the Museum', *Isis*, 96, 559–71.

228 Bibliography

Alberti, Samuel J.M.M. (2007) 'The Museum Affect: Visiting Collections of Anatomy and Natural History', in A. Fyfe and B. Lightman (eds), *Science in the Marketplace*, Chicago, IL: Chicago University Press, 371–403.

Alberti, Samuel J.M.M. (2011) *Morbid Curiosities: Medical Museums in Nineteenth-Century Britain*, Oxford: Oxford University Press.

Aldersey-Williams, Hugh (1995) *The Most Beautiful Molecule: The Discovery of the Buckyball*, New York: John Wiley and Sons.

Alkon, Paul K. (1994) *Science Fiction before 1990: Imagination Discovers Technology*, New York: Twayne.

Amelang, James (1998) *The Flight of Icarus: Artisan Autobiography in Early Modern Europe*, Stanford, CA: Stanford University Press.

Anderson, Robert G.W. (1992) 'What Is Technology? Education through Museums in the Mid-Nineteenth Century', *The British Journal for the History of Science*, 25, 169–84.

Andrews, James T. (2003) *Science for the Masses: The Bolshevik State and the Popular Imagination in Soviet Russia, 1917–1934*, College Station, TX: Texas A&M University Press.

Andrews, James T. and Siddiqi, Asif A. (2011) *Into the Cosmos: Space Exploration and Soviet Culture*, Pittsburgh, PA: University of Pittsburgh Press.

Andries, Lise (1992) 'Médecine populaire et littérature de colportage au XIXème siècle', in J. Poirier and C. Langlois (eds), *Raspail et la vulgarisation médicale*, Paris: J. Vrin, 11–26.

Anon (1857) *Cuatro métodos curativos (Los), o sea Manual de higiene y de medicina popular que comprende los sistemas de Raspail, Leroy, Morrison y Holloway, acompañados de un resumen de homeopatía*, Barcelona: Luis Tasso.

Apple, Rima D. and Apple, Michael W. (1993) 'Screening Science', *Isis*, 84, 750–4.

Apple, Rima D., Downey, Gregory J. and Vaughn, Stephen L. (eds) (2012) *Science in Print: Essays on the History of Science and the Culture of Print*, Madison, WI: University of Wisconsin Press.

Arago, François (1836) *Leçons d'astronomie professées a l'Observatoire Royal par . . . membre de l'Institut. Nouvelle édition, augmentée de ses dernières leçons, avec des nouvelles vues sur les comètes, les aérolites, et accompagnée de 5 planches gravées*, Paris: Just Rouvier et E. Le Bouvier.

Arago, François (1858) *Astronomie populaire par . . . Secrétaire perpétuel de l'Académies des Sciences. Publié d'après son ordre sous la direction de M.J.A. Barral, ancien élève de l'École polytechnique, Livre XVII. Les Comètes. Oeuvre Posthume*, Paris: Gide (Facsimile edition. Blanchard. Paris 1986).

Arago, François (1867) *Astronomie populaire. Nouvelle édition mise au courant des progrès de la science par M.J.A. Barral. Oeuvre posthume. 4 vols.* Paris: L. Guérin.

Ashmore, Malcolm and Evelleen Richards (1996) (eds) 'The Politics of SSK: Neutrality, Commitment and Beyond', *Social Studies of Science*, 26(2).

Aubin, David, Bigg, Charlotte and Sibum, Heinz Otto (2010) *The Heavens on Earth: Observatories and Astronomy in Nineteenth-Century Science and Culture*, Durham, NC: Duke University Press.

Auerbach, Jeffrey A. (1999) *The Great Exhibition of 1851: A Nation on Display*, New Haven, CT: Yale University Press.

Avilés Farré, Juan (2006) *Francisco Ferrer y Guardia: pedagogo, anarquista y mártir*, Madrid: Marcial Pons.

Badino, Massimiliano and Navarro, Jaume (2013) *Research and Pedagogy: A History of Quantum Physics and Its Early Textbooks*, Berlin: Max Planck Research Library for the History and Development of Knowledge.

Baggott, Jim (1994) *Perfect Symmetry: The Accidental Discovery of Buckminsterfullerene*, Oxford: Oxford University Press.

Baigrie, Brian S. (ed.) (1996) *Picturing Knowledge: Historical and Philosophical Problems Concerning the Use of Art and Science*, Toronto: University of Toronto Press.

Barber, Benjamin. R. (1984) *Strong Democracy: Participatory Politics for a New Age*, Berkeley, CA: University of California Press.

Basalla, Georges (1994) 'Keaton and Chaplin: The Silent Film's Response to Technology', in C. W. Pursell, Jr. (ed.), *Technology in America. A History of Individuals and Ideas*, Cambridge, MA: MIT Press, 227–36.

Bauer, Martin (ed.) (1994) *Resistance to New Technology: Nuclear Power, Information Technology and Biotechnology*, Cambridge: Cambridge University Press.

Bayertz, Kurt (1985) 'Spreading the Spirit of Science: Social Determinants of the Popularization of Science in Nineteenth-Century Germany', in T. Shinn and R. Whitley (eds), *Expository Science*, Dordrecht: Reidel, 209–27.

Beck, Ulrich (2008) *Risk Society: Towards a New Modernity*, London: SAGE (1st edition in German, 1986; 1st edition in English, 1992).

Bédéï, Patricia and Bédéï, Jean-Pierre (2005) *François-Vincent Raspail*, Paris: Alvik.

Bedini, Silvio (1965) 'The Evolution of Science Museums', *Technology and Culture*, 1–23.

Beer, Gillian (1990) 'Science and Literature', in R. C. Olby, G. N. Cantor, J. R. R. Christie, M. J. S. Hodge (eds), *Companion of the History of Modern Science*, London: Routledge, 783–98.

Béguet, Bruno (ed.) (1990) *La science pour tous. Sur la vulgarisation scientifique en France de 1850 à 1914*, Paris: Conservatoire national des arts et métiers.

Béguet, B., Cantor, M. and Le Men, S. (eds) (1994) *La science pour tous*, Paris: Réunion des musées nationaux.

Benedic, Catherine (1994) 'Le Mondes des vulgarisateurs', in Bruno Béguet (ed.), *La Science pour tous*, Paris: Conservatoire National des Arts et Métiers, 30–49.

Benedict, Barbara. M. (2001) *Curiosity: A Cultural History of Early Modern Europe*, Chicago, IL: Chicago University Press.

Benjamin, Walter (1969) 'The Work of Art in the Age of Mechanical Reproduction', in H. Arendt (ed.), *Illuminations*, New York: Schocken, 217–52.

Bennett, Jim A. (1987) *The Divided Circle: A History of Instruments for Astronomy, Navigation and Surveying*, Oxford: Phaidon-Christie's.

Bennett, Jim A. (1995) 'Can Science Museums Take History Seriously?', *Science as Culture*, 5(1), 124–37.

Bennett, Jim (2005) 'Museums and the History of Science', *Isis*, 96(4), 559–608.

Bennett, Tony (1995) *The Birth of the Museum: History, Theory and Politics*, London: Routledge.

Bennett, Tony (2007) *Critical trajectories: Culture, Society, Intellectuals*, Oxford: Blackwell.

Bensaude-Vincent, Bernadette (1987) 'Hélène Metzger's *La chimie*: A Popular Treatise', *History of Science*, 25, 71–84.

Bensaude-Vincent, Bernadette (1989) 'Camile Flammarion: Prestige de la science populaire', *Romantisme*, 65, 93–104.

Bensaude-Vincent, Bernadette (1991) 'L'astronomie populaire, priorité philosophique et projet politique', *Revue de synthèse*, 112, 49–60.

Bensaude-Vincent, Bernadette (1993) 'Un public pour la science: l'essor de la vulgarisation au XIXe siècle', *Réseaux*, 58, 47–66.

Bensaude-Vincent, Bernadette (1995) 'Les savants et les autres', *Diogène*, 169, 136–55.

Bensaude-Vincent, Bernadette (1997) 'In the Name of Science', in J. Krige and D. Pestre (eds), *Science in the Twentieth Century*, Amsterdam: Harwood Academic, 319–38.

Bensaude-Vincent, Bernadette (2000) *L'opinion publique et la science. A chacun son ignorance*, Paris: Institut d'édition Scenofi-Synthélabo.

230 Bibliography

Bensaude-Vincent, Bernadette (2001) 'A Genealogy of the Increasing Gap between Science and the Public', *Public Understanding of Science*, 10, 99–113.

Bensaude-Vincent, Bernadette (2009a) 'A Historical Perspective on Science and Its "Others"', *Isis*, 100, 359–68.

Bensaude-Vincent, Bernadette (2009b) *Les vertiges de la technoscience. Façoner le monde atome par atome*, Paris: Editions de la Découverte.

Bensaude-Vincent, Bernadette and Blondel, Christine (1986) *Les scientifiques français et la vulgarisation dans l'entre-deux-guerres*, Paris: CNRS.

Bensaude-Vincent, Bernadette and Blondel, Christine (eds) (1988) 'Vulgariser les sciences (1919–1939): Acteurs, projets, enjeux', *Cahiers d'histoire et de philosophie des sciences*, 24.

Bensaude-Vincent, Bernadette and Blondel, Christine (2002) *Des savants face à l'occulte, 1870–1940*, Paris: La Découverte.

Bensaude-Vincent, Bernadette and Blondel, Christine (eds) (2008) *Science and Spectacle in the European Enlightenment*, Aldershot: Ashgate.

Bensaude-Vincent, Bernadette and Rasmussen, Anne (eds) (1997) *La science populaire dans la presse et l'édition. XIXe et XXe siècles*, Paris: CNRS.

Bensaude-Vincent, Bernadette, Bertomeu-Sánchez, José Ramón and García Belmar, Antonio (2003) *L'émergence d'une science des manuels. Les livres de chimie en France (1782–1852)*, Paris: Éditions des archives contemporaines.

Bensaude-Vincent, Bernadette, Van Tiggelen, Brigitte and Schummer, Joachim (eds) (2007) *The Public Image of Chemistry*, Singapore: World Scientific.

Berg, Maxine (1991) *Markets and Manufactures in Early Industrial Europe*, London: Routledge.

Berman, Morris (1975) '"Hegemony" and the Amateur Tradition in British Science', *Journal of Social History*, 8(3), 30–50.

Berman, Morris (1978) *Social Change and Scientific Organisation: The Royal Institution, 1799–1844*, London: Heinemann.

Bertomeu-Sánchez, José Ramón (2009) 'Popularizing Controversial Science: A Popular Treatise on Poisons by Mateu Orfila (1818)', *Medical History*, 53, 351–78.

Bertomeu-Sánchez, José Ramón (2013) 'Managing Uncertainty in the Academy and the Courtroom: Normal Arsenic and Nineteenth-Century Toxicology', *Isis*, 104(2), 197–225.

Bertomeu-Sánchez, José Ramón (2014) 'Classrooms, Salons, Academies, and Courts: Mateu Orfila (1787–1853) and Nineteenth-Century French Toxicology, *Ambix*, 61 (2), 162–86.

Bertomeu-Sánchez, José Ramón and Nieto-Galan, Agustí (eds) (2006) *Chemistry, Medicine, and Crime: Mateu J. B. Orfila (1787–1853) and His Times*, Sagamore Beach, MA: Science History Publications.

Bertomeu-Sánchez, José Ramón, García Belmar, Antonio and Bensaude-Vincent, Bernadette (2002) 'Looking for an Order of Things: Textbooks and Chemical Classifications in Nineteenth Century France', *Ambix*, 49 (2), 227–51.

Bertucci, Paola (2008) 'Domestic Spectacles: Electrical Instruments between Business and Conversation', in B. Bensaude-Vincent and C. Blondel (eds), *Science and Spectacle in the European Enlightenment*, Aldershot: Ashgate, 75–87.

Biezunski, Michel (1985) 'Popularization and Scientific Controversy: The Case of the Theory of Relativity in France', in T. Shinn and R. Whitley (eds), *Expository Science*, Dordrecht: Reidel, 183–94.

Bigg, Charlotte (2010) 'Staging the Heavens: Astrophysics and Popular Astronomy in the Late Nineteenth Century', in D. Aubin, C. Bigg and H. O. Sibum (eds),

The Heavens on Earth: Observatories and Astronomy in Nineteenth-Century Science and Culture, Durham, NC: Duke University Press, 305–24.

Bijker, Wiebe E. (1995) *Of Bicycles, Bakelites, and Bulbs: Toward a Theory of Sociotechnical Change*, Cambridge, MA: MIT Press.

Bijker, Wiebe E. (2009) *The Paradox of Scientific Authority: The Role of Scientific Advice in Democracies*, Cambridge, MA: MIT Press.

Bijker, Wiebe, Hughes, Thomas and Pinch, Trevor (eds) (1987, 2012) *The Social Construction of Technological Systems*, Cambridge, MA: MIT Press.

Blake, John B. (1977) 'From Buchan to Fishbein: The Literature of Domestic Medicine', in G. Risse, R. L. Numbers and J. W. Leavitt (eds), *Medicine without Doctors*, New York: Science History, 11–30.

Bleichmar, Daniela, De Vos, Paula, Huffine, Kristin and Sheehan, Kevin (eds) (2009) *Science in the Spanish and Portuguese Empires, 1500–1800*, Stanford, CA: Stanford General.

Blok, Anders, Jensen, Mette and Kaltoft, Pernille (2008) 'Social Identities and Risk: Expert and Lay Imaginations on Pesticide Use', *Public Understanding of Science*, 17, 189–209.

Blondel, Christine and Dörries, Matthias (eds) (1994) *Restaging Coulomb. Usages, controverses et réplications autour de la balance de torsion*, Florence: Leo S. Olschki.

Boon, Timothy (2008) *Films of Fact: A History of Science in Documentary Films and Television*, London: Wallflower Press.

Boon, Timothy (2015) '"The Televising of Science Is a Process of Television": Establishing *Horizon*, 1962–1967', *The British Journal for the History of Science*, 48(1), 87–121.

Boudia, Soraya and Jas, Nathalie (2007) 'Introduction: Risk and "Risk Society" in Historical Perspective', *History and Technology*, 23(4), 317–31.

Boudia, Soraya and Jas, Nathalie (eds) (2014) *Powerless Science? Science and Politics in a Toxic World*, London: Berghahn Books.

Bourdelais, Patrice (ed.) (2001) *Les hygiénistes. Enjeux, modèles et pratiques*, Paris: Belin.

Bowler, Peter J. (1993) *Biology and Social Thought, 1850–1914*, Berkeley, CA: University of California Press.

Bowler, Peter J. (2009) *Science for All: The Popularization of Science in Early Twentieth-Century Britain*, Chicago, IL: Chicago University Press.

Bowler, Peter J. and Morus, Iwan Rhys (2005) *Making Modern Science: A Historical Survey*, Chicago, IL and London: University of Chicago Press.

Brain, Robert (1993) *Going to the Fair: Readings in the Culture of Nineteenth-Century Exhibitions*, Cambridge: Whipple Museum of the History and Science.

Braun, Susan (2003) 'The History of Breast Cancer Advocacy', *Breast Cancer Journal*, 9(2), 101–3.

Bret, Patrice (2004) 'Un batailleur de la science: Le "machiniste-physicien" François Bienvenue et la diffusion de Franklin and Lavoisier', *Annales historiques de la Révolution Française*, 338, 95–127.

Briggs, Asa (1985) *The BBC: The First Fifty Years*, Oxford: Oxford University Press.

Brock, William H. (1992) *The Fontana History of Chemistry*, London: Fontana Press.

Brock, William H. (2002) *Justus von Liebig: The Chemical Gatekeeper*, Cambridge: Cambridge University Press.

Broks, Peter (1996) *Media Science before the Great War*, London: MacMillan.

Broks, Peter (2006) *Understanding Popular Science*, Maidenhead: Open University Press.

Broman, Thomas (1998) 'The Habermasian Public Sphere and Science in the Enlightenment', *History of Science*, 26, 123–49.

Broman, Thomas (2002) 'Introduction: Some Preliminary Considerations on Science and Civil Society', *Osiris*, 17, 1–21.

232 Bibliography

Broughman, Henry (1825) *Practical Observations upon the Education of the People Addressed to the Working Class and Their Employers*, 5th edition. London: Richard Taylor.

Brown, Phil and Mikkelsen, Edwin (1990) *No Safe Place: Toxic Waste, Leukemia and Community Action*, Berkeley, CA: University of California Press.

Browne, Janet (1992) 'Squibs and Snobs: Science in Humorous British Undergraduate Magazines around 1830', *History of Science*, 30, 165–97.

Browne, Janet (2010) 'Making Darwin: Biography and the Changing Representations of Charles Darwin', *Journal of Interdisciplinary History*, 40, 347–73.

Bucchi, Massimiano (1996) 'When Scientists Turn to the Public: Alternative Routes in Science Communication', *Public Understanding of Science*, 5, 375–94.

Bucchi, Massimiano (1998) *Science and the Media. Alternative Routes to Scientific Communication*. Abingdon: Routledge.

Bucchi, Massimiano (2009) *Beyond Technocracy: Science, Politics and Citizens*, Dortdrecht: Springer.

Bucchi, Massimiano and Neresini, Federico (2002) 'Biotechs Remains Unloved by the More Informed', *Nature*, 416, 261.

Bucchi Massimiano and Neresini, Federico (2007) 'Science and Public Participation', in E. Hackett, O. Amsterdamska and M. Lynch (eds), *Handbook of Science and Technology Studies*. Cambridge, MA: MIT Press, 449–73.

Bucchi, Massimiano and Trench, Brian (eds) (2008) *Handbook of Public Communication of Science and Technology*, Abingdon: Routledge.

Bud, Robert (1995) 'Science, Meaning and Myth in the Museum', *Public Understanding of Science*, 4(1), 1–16.

Bud, Robert (2012) '"Applied Science": A Phrase in Search of a Meaning, *Isis*, 103(3), 537–45.

Burke, Peter (2000) *A Social History of Knowledge*, Cambridge: Polity Press.

Burke, Peter (2005) *History and Social Theory*, Cambridge: Polity Press.

Burnett, Graham (ed.) (2007) *Focus: Science and the Law, Isis*, 98 (2), 310–51.

Burnham, John C. (1987) *How Superstition Won and Science Lost: Popularizing Science and Health in the U.S.*, New Brunswick, NJ: Rutgers University Press.

Burton, Ruth (1990) 'An Influential Set of Chaps: The X-Club and Royal Society Politics, 1864–85', *British Journal for the History of Science*, 23, 53–81.

Butler, Stella (1992) *Science and Technology Museums*. Leicester: Leicester University Press.

Butterfield, Herbert (1949) *The Origins of Modern Science, 1300–1800*, London: Bell.

Cacciatore, Michael A., Scheufele, Dietram A. and Corley, Elizabeth A. (2011) 'From Enabling Technology to Applications: The Evolution of Risk Perceptions about Nanotechnology', *Public Understanding of Science*, 20, 385–404.

Calhoun, Craig (ed.) (1992) *Habermas and the Public Sphere*. Cambridge, MA: MIT Press.

Callon, Michel (ed.) (1989) *La science et ses réseaux. Genèse et circulation des faits scientifiques*, Paris: La Découverte.

Callon, Michel (1999) 'The Role of Lay People in the Production and Dissemination of Scientific Knowledge', *Science, Technology and Society*, 4(1), 81–94.

Callon, Michel and Rabeharisoa,Vololona (2008) 'The Growing Engagement of Emergent Concerned Groups in Political and Economic Life: Lessons from the French Association of Neuromuscular Disease Patients', *Science, Technology and Human Values*, 33 (2), 230–61.

Callon, Michel, Lascoumes, Pierre and Barthe, Yannick (2009) *Acting in an Uncertain World: An Essay on Technical Democracy*, Cambridge, MA: MIT Press (1st French edition, 2001).

Bibliography 233

Cañizares-Esguerra, Jorge (2006) *Nature, Empire, and Nation: Explorations of the History of Science in the Iberian World*, Stanford, CA: Stanford University Press.

Cardot, Fabienne (1989) 'Le théâtre scientifique de Louis Figuier', *Romantisme*, 65, 59–67.

Cardwell, Donald (1994) *The Fontana History of Technology*, London: Fontana Press.

Carre, Patrice A. (1989) 'Expositions et modernité: Electricité et communication dans les expositions parisiennes de 1867 à 1900', *Romantisme*, 65, 37–48.

Carson, Rachel (1962) *Silent Spring*, London: Hamish Hamilton.

Cassedy, James H. (1977) 'Why Self-Help? Americans Alone with Their Diseases, 1800–1850', in G. Risse, R. L. Numbers and J. W. Leavitt (eds), *Medicine without Doctors*, New York: Science History, 31–48.

Cassidy, Angela (2005) 'Popular Evolutionary Biology in the UK: An Unusual Case of Science in the Media?', *Public Understanding of Science*, 14, 115–41.

Cassidy, Angela (2006) 'Evolutionary Psychology as Public Science and Boundary Work', *Public Understanding of Science*, 15, 175–205.

Cassidy, Angela (2007) 'The (Sexual) Politics of Evolution: Popular Controversy in the Late 20th-Century United Kingdom', *History of Psychology*, 10(2), 199–226.

Cavallo, Guglieimo and Chartier, Roger (eds) (1995) *Histoire de la lecture dans le monde occidental*, Paris: Seuil.

Chadarevian, Soraya de (2003) 'Portrait of a Discovery: Watson, Crick and the Double Helix', *Isis*, 94(1), 90–105.

Chambers, Robert (1994) *Vestiges of the Natural History of Creation and Other Evolutionary Writings*, Chicago, IL: University of Chicago Press (1st original edition, 1844).

Chapman, Allan (1998) *The Victorian Amateur Astronomer: Independent Astronomical Research in Britain, 1820–1920*, New York: Wiley; Chichester: Praxis.

Chapple, J. A. V. (1986) *Science and Literature in the Nineteenth Century*, London: Macmillan.

Chartier, Anne-Marie (2009) 'Los cuadernos escolares: Ordenar los saberes escribiéndolos', *Cultura Escrita y Sociedad*, 6, 163–82.

Chartier, Roger (1984) 'Culture as Appropriation: Popular Cultural Uses in Early Modern France', in S. Kaplan (ed.), *Understanding Popular Culture: Europe from the Middle Ages to the Nineteenth Century*, Amsterdam: Mouton Publications, 229–53.

Chartier, Roger (1987a) *Lectures et lecteurs dans la France d'Ancien Régime*, Paris: Seuil.

Chartier, Roger (1987b) *The Cultural Uses of Print in Early Modern Europe*, Princeton, NJ: Princeton University Press.

Chartier, Roger (1994) *The Order of Books: Authors and Libraries in Europe between the 14th and 18th Centuries*, Cambridge: Polity Press.

Chartier, Roger (1995) 'Lecteurs et lectures "populaires": De la Renaissance à l'âge classique', in G. Cavallo and R. Chartier (eds), *Histoire de la lecture dans le monde occidental*, Paris: Seuil, 315–30.

Chartier, Roger and Corsi, Pietro (eds) (1996) *Sciences et langues en Europe*, Paris: EHESS.

Chesneaux, Jean (1982) *Jules Verne. Une lecture politique*, Paris: François Maspero.

Chilvers, Chris A. J. (2003) 'The Dilemmas of Seditious Men: The Crowther-Hessen Correspondence in the 1930s', *The British Journal for the History of Science*, 36, 417–35.

Chin, Christine and Osborne, Jonathan (2008) 'Students' Questions: A Potential Resource for Teaching and Learning Science', *Studies in Science Education*, 44(1), 1–39.

Chittenden, David, Farmelo, Graham and Lewenstein, Bruce V. (eds) (2004) *Creating Connections: Museums and the Public Understanding of Current Research*. Walnut Creek, CA: Altamira Press.

Christie, John R. R. and Golinski, Jan V. (1982) 'The Spreading of the Word: New Directions in the Historiography of Chemistry, 1600–1800', *History of Science*, 20, 235–66.

234 Bibliography

Clark, William, Golinski, Jan and Schaffer, Simon (eds) (1999) *The Sciences in Enlightened Europe*, Chicago, IL: University of Chicago Press.

Coen, Deborah R. (2013) *The Earthquake Observers: Disaster Science from Lisbon to Richter*, Chicago, IL: University of Chicago Press.

Cohen, Floris H. (1994) *The Scientific Revolution: A Historiographical Inquiry*, Chicago, IL: University of Chicago Press.

Cohen, I. Bernard (1980) 'The Fear and Distrust of Science in Historical Perspective: Some First Thoughts', in A. S. Markovits and K. W. Deutsch (eds), *Fear of Science – Trust in Science: Conditions for Change in the Climate of Opinion*, Cambridge, MA: Oelschlager, Gunn and Hein.

Cohen, Robert S. and Schnelle, Thomas (eds) (1986) *Cognition and Fact: Material on Ludwik Fleck*, Dordrecht: Kluwer/Reidel.

Cohen, Yves (1997) 'Scientific Management and the Production Process', in J. Krige and D. Pestre (eds), *Science in the Twentieth Century*, Amsterdam: Harwood Academic, 111–24.

Cohen, Yves and Drouin, Jean-Marc (eds) (1989) 'Les amateurs de sciences et de techniques', *Cahiers d'histoire et de philosophie des sciences*, 27.

Colgrove, James (2005) '"Science in a Democracy": The Contested Status of Vaccination in the Progressive Era and the 1920s', *Isis*, 96, 167–91.

Collins, Harry M. and Pinch, Trevor J. (1998) *The Golem: What You Should Know about Science* (2nd edition), Cambridge: Cambridge University Press.

Collins, Harry (2014) *Are We All Scientific Experts?* Cambridge: Polity Press.

Collins, Harry and Evans, Robert (2003) 'The Third Wave of Science Studies: Studies of Expertise and Experience', *Social Studies of Science*, 32 (2), 235–96.

Collins, Harry and Evans, Robert (2007) *Rethinking Expertise*, Chicago, IL: Chicago University Press.

Conner, Clifford D. (2005) *A People's History of Science: Miners, Midwives and 'Low Mechanics'*, New York: Nation Books.

Cooter, Roger (1984) *The Cultural Meaning of Popular Science: Phrenology and the Organization of Consent in Nineteenth-Century Britain*, Cambridge: Cambridge University Press.

Cooter, Roger (1988) *Studies in the History of Alternative Medicine*, London: Macmillan.

Cooter, Roger (ed.) (2001) *Phrenology in Europe and America*, London. Routledge.

Cooter, Roger and Pumphrey, Stephen (1994) 'Separate Spheres and Public Places: Reflections on the History of Science Popularization and Science in Popular Culture', *History of Science*, 32, 237–67.

Cooter, Roger and Stein, Claudia (2013) *Writing History in the Age of Biomedicine*, New Haven, CT: Yale University Press.

Cotardière, Philippe de la and Fuentes, Patrick (1994) *Camille Flammarion*, Paris: Flammarion.

Craveri, Benedetta (2005) *The Age of Conversation*, New York: New York Review Books (1st Italian edition, 2001).

Crombie, Alistair (1952, 1995) *The History of Science: From Augustine to Galileo*, New York: Dover.

Crosland, Maurice (1992) *Science under Control: The French Academy of Science, 1795–1914*, Cambridge: Cambridge University Press.

Cunningham, Andrew (1996) 'The Culture of Gardens', in N. Jardine, J. Secord and E. Spary (eds), *Cultures of Natural History*, Cambridge: Cambridge University Press, 38–56.

Darnton, Robert (1968) *La fin des lumières. Le mesmérisme et la Révolution*, Paris: Odile Jacob (1st English edition, 1995).

Darnton, Robert (1979) *The Business of Enlightenment: A Publishing History of the Encyclopédie 1775–1800*, Cambridge, MA: Harvard University Press.

Darnton, Robert (1982) 'What Is the History of Books?', *Daedalus*, summer, 65–83.

Darnton, Robert (1985) *The Great Cat Massacre and Other Episodes in French Cultural History*, New York: Vintage Books.

Daston, Lorraine (1991) 'Marvelous Facts and Miraculous Evidences in Early Modern Europe', *Critical Inquiry*, 18, 93–124.

Daston, Lorraine (ed.) (2004) *Things that Talk: Object Lessons from Art and Science*, New York: Zone Books.

Daston, L. and Galison, P. *Objectivity*, New York: Zone Books.

Daum, Andreas W. (1998) *Wissenschaftspopularisierung im 19 Jahrhundert. Bürgerliche Kultur, naturwissentschaftliche Bildung und die deutsche Öffentlichkeit, 1848–1914*, Munich: R. Oldenburg.

Daum, Andreas W. (2002) 'Science, Politics and Religion: Humboldtian Thinking and the Transformations of Civil Society in Germany', *Osiris*, 17, 107–40.

Daum, Andreas W. (2009) 'Varieties of Popular Science and the Transformations of Public Knowledge: Some Historical Reflections', *Isis*, 100, 319–32.

Davidson, Keay (1999) *Carl Sagan: A Life*, New York: Wiley.

Dawkins, Richard (1989) *The Selfish Gene*, 2nd edition, Oxford: Oxford University Press.

De Blecourt, William and Usborne, Cornelie (1999) 'Alternative Medicine in Europe since 1800', *Medical History*, 43, 283–393.

De Buen, Odón (1896) *Historia Natural (edición popular, con profusión de grabados)*, 2 vols, Barcelona: Manuel Soler.

Debus, Allen G. (1987) 'Science versus Pseudo-Science: A Persistent Debate', in A.G. Debus, *Chemistry, Alchemy and the New Philosophy, 1550–1700*, Aldershot: Ashgate, 1–18.

Della Porta, Donatella and Tarrow, Sidney (2004) (eds) *Transnational Protest and Global Activism*, New York: Roman and Littlefield.

Dennis, Michael Aaron (1989) 'Graphic Understanding: Instruments and Interpretation in Robert Hooke's *Micrographia*', *Science in Context*, 3, 309–64.

Desmond, Adrian (1987) 'Artisan Resistence and Evolution in Britain, 1819–1848', *Osiris*, 2nd series, 3, 77–110.

Desmond, Adrian (2001) 'Redefining the X Axis: "Professionals", "Amateurs" and the Making of Mid-Victorian Biology', *Journal of the History of Biology*, 34, 3–50.

Devall, Bill (2001) 'The Deep, Long-Range Ecology Movement 1960–2000: A Review', *Ethics and the Environment*, 6(1), 18–41.

Dickson, David (1986) 'From Strangelove to Star Wars: The New Politics of Science', *Metascience*, 4, 35–45.

Dickson, David (1988) *The New Politics of Science*, Chicago, IL: Chicago University Press.

Dickson, David (2000) 'Science and Its Public: The Need for a "Third Way"', *Social Studies of Science*, 30(6), 917–23.

Dierkes, Meinolf and Von Grote, Claudia (eds) (2000) *Between Understanding and Trust: The Public, Science and Technology*, Amsterdam: Harwood.

Dinges, Martin (ed.) (2002) *Patients in the History of Homeopathy*, Sheffield: EAHMH.

Doel, Ronald E. and Söderqvist, Thomas (2006) *The Historiography of Contemporary Science, Technology, and Medicine: Writing Recent Science*, London: Routledge.

Donnelly, James (1994) 'Consultants, Managers, Testing Slaves: Changing Roles for Chemists in the British Alkali Industry, 1850–1920', *Technology and Culture*, 35, 100–28.

236 Bibliography

Donovan, Arthur L. (1975) *Philosophical Chemistry in the Scottish Enlightenment: The Doctrines and Discoveries of William Cullen and Joseph Black*, Edinburgh: Edinburgh University Press.

Doray, Bernard and Macey, David (1989) *From Taylorism to Fordism: A Rational Madness*, London: Free Association.

Dornan, Christopher (1988) 'The Problem of Science and the Media: A Few Seminal Texts in Their Context, 1956–1965', *Journal of Communication Inquiry*, 12, 43–70.

Dornan, Christopher (1990) 'Some Problems in Conceptualizing the Issue of Science and the Media', *Critical Studies in Mass Communication*, 7, 48–71.

Dörries, Mathias (2000) 'The Public Face of Science: François Arago', in J. Batlló et al. (eds), *V Trobades d'Història de la Ciència i de la Tècnica*, Barcelona: SCHCT, 43–54.

Drexler, Eric (1986) *Engines of Creation: The Coming Era of Nanotechnology*, New York: Anchor Book.

Drouin, Jean-Marc and Bensaude-Vincent, Bernadette (1996) 'Nature for the People', in N. Jardine, J. Secord and E. Spary (eds), *Cultures of Natural History*, Cambridge: Cambridge University Press, 408–25.

Dunlap, Thomas R. (ed.) (2008) *DDT, Silent Spring, and the Rise of Environmentalism: Classic Texts*, Washington, DC: University of Washington Press.

Durant, John R. and Gregory, Jane (eds) (1993) *Science and Culture in Europe*, London: Science Museum.

Durant, John R., Evans, Geoffrey A. and Thomas, Geoffrey P. (1989) 'The Public Understanding of Science', *Nature*, 340, 11–14.

Eamon, William (1984) 'Arcana Disclosed: The Advent of Printing, the Books of Secrets Tradition and the Development of Experimental Science in the Sixteenth Century', *History of Science*, 22(2), 111–50.

Eamon, William (1994) *Science and the Secrets of Nature*, Princeton, NJ: Princeton University Press.

Edgerton, David (1999) 'From Innovation to Use: Ten Eclectic Theses on the Historiography of Technology', *History and Technology*, 16, 1–26.

Edgerton, David (2007) *The Shock of the Old: Technology and Global History since 1900*, Oxford: Oxford University Press.

Eidelman, Jacqueline (1985) 'The Cathedral of French Science: The Early Years of the 'Palais de la Découverte', in T. Shinn, R. Whitley (eds), *Expository Science*, Dordrecht: Reidel, 195–207.

Eidelman, Jacqueline (1992) 'La création du Palais de la découverte', in B. Schröder-Gudehus (ed.), *La société industrielle et ses muses*, Paris: EAC, 161–70.

Eisenstein, Elizabeth (1979) *The Printing Press as an Agent of Change: Communications and Cultural Transformations in Early-Modern Europe*, Cambridge: Cambridge University Press.

Elkins, James (2008) *Six Stories from the End of Representation: Images in Painting, Photography, Astronomy, Microscopy, Particle Physics, and Quantum Mechanics, 1980–2000*, Stanford, CA: Stanford University Press.

Epstein, Steven (1995) 'The Construction of Lay Expertise: AIDS Activism and the Forging of Credibility in the Reform of Clinical Trials', *Science, Technology and Human Values*, 20, 408–37.

Epstein, Steven (1996) *Impure Science: AIDS, Activism, and the Politics of Knowledge*, Berkeley, CA: University of California Press.

Epstein, Steven (2007) *Inclusion: The Politics of Difference in Medical Research*, Chicago, IL: Chicago University Press.

Evans, Francis T. (1997) 'Roads, Railways and Canals: Technical Choices in 19th-Century Britain', in T. S. Reynolds and S. H. Cutcliffe (eds), *Technology and the West:*

A Historical Anthology from Technology and Culture, Chicago, IL: University of Chicago Press, 99–234.

Evans, Robert, Weston, John and Marr, Alexander (2006) *Curiosity and Wonder from the Renaissance to the Enlightenment*, Aldershot: Ashgate.

Evelyn, John (1901) *The Diary of John Evelyn*, New York, London: Walter Dunn.

Fara, Patricia (1995) 'Fit for a King? The George III Gallery at the Science Museum', *History of Science*, 33, 359–67.

Fara, Patricia (2009) *Science: A Four Thousand Year History*, Oxford: Oxford University Press.

Faraday, Michael (1865) *A Course of Six Lectures on the Chemical History of a Candle; to Which Is Added a Lecture on Platinum . . . Delivered during the Christmas Holidays of 1860–1*, edited by W. Crookes, London: Charles Griffin and Company.

Faraday, Michael (2011) *The Chemical History of a Candle*, edited and introduced by Frank A.J.L. James, Oxford: Oxford University Press.

Farrington, Benjamin (1944) *Greek Science: Its Meaning for Us (Thales to Aristotle)*, London: Penguin.

Farrington, Benjamin (1947) *Head and Hand in Ancient Greece: Four Studies in the Social Relations of Thought*, London: Watts.

Farry, James and Kirby, David A. (2012) 'The Universe Will Be Televised: Space, Science, Satellites and British Television Production, 1946–1969', *History and Technology*, 28(3), 311–33.

Felt, Ulrike (2000) 'Why Should the Public "Understand" Science? A Historical Perspective on Aspects of the Public Understanding of Science', in M. Dierkes and C. Von Grote (eds), *Between Understanding and Trust*, Amsterdam: Harwood, 7–38.

Feenberg, Andrew (1999) *Questioning Technology*, London: Routledge.

Fennessy, Kathleen M. (2005) '"Industrial Instruction" for the "Industrious Classes": Founding the Industrial and Technological Museum, Melbourne', *Historical Records of Australian Science*, 16, 45–64.

Ferguson, Eugene S. (1965) 'Technical Museums and International Exhibitions', *Technology and Culture*, 6, 30–46.

Ferrer Guàrdia, Francesc (2002) *La Escuela Moderna*, Barcelona: Tusquets (original edition, 1913).

Figuier, Louis (1867–70) *Les merveilles de la science, ou, description populaire des inventions modernes*, 4 vols, Paris: Furne, Jouvet et Cie.

Figuier, Louis (1879) *Connais-toi toi même: Notions de physiologie à l'usage de la jeunesse . . . Ouvrage illustré, etc.*, Paris: Hachette.

Findlen, Paola (1994) *Possessing Nature: Museum Collecting and Scientific Culture in Early Modern Italy*, Berkeley, CA: University of California Press.

Findling, John E. and Pell, Kimberley D. (eds) (1990) *Historical Dictionary of World's Fairs and Expositions, 1851–1989*, London: Greenwood Press.

Fiorino, D.J. (1990) 'Citizen Participation and Environmental Risk: A Survey of Institutional Mechanisms', *Science, Technology and Human Values*, 15(2), 226–43.

Flammarion, Camille (1865) *La pluralité des mondes habités*, 5th edition, Paris: Didier.

Flammarion, Camille (1869) *Dieu dans la nature*, 5th edition, Paris: Didier.

Flammarion, Camille (1880) *Astronomie populaire*, Paris: Marpon et E. Flammarion.

Flammarion, Camille (1890) *Urania, illustrated by de Bieler, Myrbach and Gambard, translated by Augusta Rice Stetson,* Boston, MA: Estes and Lauriat (1st French edition, 1889).

Flammarion, Camille (1912) *Mémoires historiques et philosophiques d'un astronome*, Paris: Ernest Flammarion.

Fleck, Ludwik (1979) *Genesis and Development of a Scientific Fact*, Chicago, IL: University of Chicago Press (1st German edition, 1935).

238 Bibliography

Florensa, Clara, Hochadel, Oliver and Tabernero, Carlos (eds) (2014) *Science on Television (special issue), Actes d'Història de la Ciència i de la Tècnica*, 7.

Fontenelle, Bernard de (1724) *Entretiens sur la pluralité des mondes*, 7th edition, Paris: M. Brunet (1st French edition, 1686).

Fontenelle, Bernard de (1803) *Conversations on the Plurality of Worlds . . . with Notes, and a Critical Account of the Author's Writings, by Jerome de La Lande*, translated from a late Paris edition by Miss Elizabeth Gunning, London: T. Hurst.

Forgacs, David (ed.) (2000) *The Antonio Gramsci Reader: Selected Writings 1916–1935*, New York: New York University Press.

Forgan, Sophie (2003) 'Atoms in Wonderland', *History and Technology*, 19(3), 177–96.

Forgan, Sophie (2005) 'Building the Museum: Knowledge, Conflict and the Power of Place', *Isis*, 96(4), 572–85.

Forgan, Sophie and Gooday, Graeme (1996) 'Constructing South Kensington: The Buildings and Politics of T. H. Huxley's Working Environments', *British Journal for the History of Science, 29*, 435–68.

Foucault, Michel (1977) *Discipline and Punish: The Birth of the Prison*, London: Allen Lane (1st French edition 1975).

Foucault, Michel (2001) *The Order of Things: An Archaeology of the Human Sciences*, London: Routledge (1st French edition 1966).

Fowler La Berge, Ann (1975) 'The Paris Health Council, 1802–1848', *Bulletin of the History of Medicine*, 49, 339–52.

Fox, Nicholas J. (1988) 'Scientific Theory Choice and Social Structure: The Case of Joseph Lister's Antisepsis, Humoral Theory and Asepsis', *History of Science*, 26, 367–97.

Fox, Robert (1989) 'Les conférences mondaines sous le Second Empire', *Romantisme*, 65, 49–57.

Fox, Robert (1995) *Science, Industry and Social Order in Post-Revolutionary France*, Aldershot: Ashgate.

Fox, Robert (2006) 'History and the Public Understanding of Science: Problems, Practices, and Perspectives', in M. Kokowski (ed.), *The Global and the Local: The History of Science and the Cultural Integration of Europe: Proceedings of the 2nd ICESHS* (Krakow, 6–9 September 2006).

Fox, Robert (2012) *The Savant and the State: Science and Cultural Politics in Nineteenth-Century France*, Baltimore, MD: Johns Hopkins University Press.

Fox, Robert and Guagnini, Anna (1993) *Education, Technology and Industrial Performance in Europe, 1850–1939*, Cambridge: Cambridge University Press.

Fox, Robert and Nieto-Galan, Agustí (eds) (1999) *Natural Dyestuffs and Industrial Culture in Europe, 1750–1880*, Canton, MA: Science History Publications.

Frasca-Spada, Marina and Jardine, Nick (eds) (2000) *Books and the Sciences in History*, Cambridge: Cambridge University Press.

Fraser, Nancy (1990) 'Rethinking the Public Sphere: A Contribution to the Critique of Actually Existing Democracy', *Social Text*, 25–6, 56–80.

Freenberg, David (1989) *The Power of Images: Studies in the History and Theory of Response*, Chicago, IL: Chicago University Press.

Freud, Sigmund (1930) *Civilization and Its Discontents*, London: Hogarth Press (German original edition, *Das Unbehagen in der Kultur*, Vienna: Internationaler Psychoanalytisher Verlag).

Friedman, Alan J. (1995) 'Exhibits and Expectations', *Public Understanding of Science*, 4, 305–13.

Friedman, Lester D. (ed.) (2004) *Cultural Sutures: Medicine* and *Media*, Durham, NC: Duke University Press.

Friedman, Sharon M., Dunwoody, Sharon and Rogers, Carol L. (1986) *Scientists and Journalists: Reporting Science as News*, New York: Free Press.

Furhnam, Adrian (1992) 'Lay Understanding of Science: Young People and Adults' Ideas of Scientific Concepts', *Studies in Science Education*, 20, 29–64.

Fyfe, Aileen (2004) *Science and Salvation: Evangelical Popular Science Publishing in Victorian Britain*, Chicago, IL: Chicago University Press.

Fyfe, Aileen (2005) 'Conscientous Workmen of Booksellers' Hacks? The Professional Identities of Science Writers in the Mid-Nineteenth Century', *Isis*, 96, 192–223.

Fyfe, Aileen and Lightman, Bernard (2007) *Science in the Marketplace: Nineteenth-Century Sites and Experiences*, Chicago, IL: Chicago University Press.

Galluzzi, Paolo (1996) *Renaissance Engineers from Brunelleschi to Leonardo da Vinci*, Giunti: Istituto e Museo di Storia della Scienza.

García Belmar, Antonio (2006) 'The Didactic Uses of Experiment: Louis-Jacques Thénard's Lectures at the Collège de France', in J. R. Bertomeu-Sánchez and A. Nieto-Galan (eds), *Chemistry, Medicine and Crime*, Sagamore Beach, MA: Science History Publications, 25–54.

Gaudillière, Jean-Paul and Hess, Volker (eds) (2013) *Ways of Regulating Drugs in the 19th and 20th Centuries*, Basingstoke: Palgrave Macmillan.

Gavroglu, Kostas et al. (2008) 'Science and Technology in the European Periphery: Some Historiographical Reflections', *History of Science* 46, 153–75.

Geison, Gerald (1995) *The Private Science of Louis Pasteur*, Princeton, NJ: Princeton University Press.

Geison, Gerald and Holmes, Frederic L. (eds) (1993) 'Research Schools: Historical Reappraisals', *Osiris*, 8.

Gibbons, Michael, Limoges, Camille, Nowotny, Helge, Schwartzman, Simon, Scott, Peter and Trow, Martin (1994) *The New Production of Knowledge: The Dynamics of Science and Research in Contemporary Societies*. London: SAGE.

Gieryn, Thomas F. (1983) 'Boundary-Work and the Demarcation of Science from Non-Science: Strains and Interests in Professional Interests of Scientists', *American Sociological Review*, 47, 781–95.

Gieryn, Thomas F. (1992) 'The Ballad of Pons and Fleischmann: Experiment and Narrative in the (Un)Making of Cold Fusion', in E. McMullin (ed.), *The Social Dimensions of Science*, Notre Dame, IN: University of Notre Dame Press, 217–43.

Gieryn, Thomas F. (1998) 'Balancing Acts: Science, "Enola Gay" and History Wars at the Smithsonian', in S. MacDonald (ed.), *Politics of Display: Museums, Science, Culture*, London: Routledge, 197–228.

Gieryn, Thomas F. (1999) *Cultural Boundaries of Science: Credibility on the Line*, Chicago, IL: University of Chicago Press.

Gille, Bertrand (1966) *Engineers of the Renaissance*, Cambridge, MA: MIT Press (French edition, Hermann, Paris, 1964).

Gillispie, Charles C. (1957) 'The Natural History of Industry', *Isis*, 48, 398–407.

Gillispie, Charles C. (ed.) (1959) *A Diderot Pictorial Encyclopedia of Trades and Industry: Manufacturing and the Technical Arts in Plates. Selected from 'L'Encyclopedie, ou Dictionnaire raisoné des sciences, des arts et des metiers' of Denis Diderot*, 2 vols, New York: Dover.

Gillispie, Charles C. (1980) *Science and Polity in France at the End of the Old Regime*, Princeton, NJ: Princeton University Press.

240 Bibliography

Ginzburg, Carlo (1980) *The Cheese and the Worms: The Cosmos of a Sixteenth-Century Miller*, translated by John and Anne Tedeschi, London: Routledge and Kegan Paul (Italian edition, 1976).

Glaser, Catherine (1989) 'Journalisme et critique scientifiques: L'exemple de Victor Meunier', *Romantisme*, 65, 27–48.

Goldberg, Stanley (1999) 'The Enola Gay Affair: What Evidence Counts When We Commemorate Historical Events?', *Osiris*, 14, 176–86.

Goldman, Lawrence (2005) *From Art to Politics: John Ruskin and William Morris*, London: William Morris Society.

Goldsmith, Maurice (1986) *The Science Critic: A Critical Analysis of the Popular Presentation of Science*, London: Routledge and Kegan Paul.

Golinski, Jan (1992) *Science as Public Culture: Chemistry and Enlightenment in Britain, 1760–1820*, Cambridge: Cambridge University Press.

Golinski, Jan (1998, 2005) *Making Natural Knowledge: Constructivism and the History of Science*, Cambridge: Cambridge University Press.

Golinski, Jan (1999) 'Barometers of Change: Meteorological Instruments as Machines of Enlightenment', in W. Clark, J. Golinski and S. Schaffer (eds), *The Sciences in Enlightened Europe*, Chicago, IL: Chicago University Press, 69–93.

Golinski, Jan (2008) 'Joseph Priestley and the Chemical Sublime in British Public Science', in B. Bensaude-Vincent and C. Blondel (eds), *Science and Spectacle in the European Enlightenment*, Aldershot: Ashgate, 117–28.

Gomis, Cels (1884) *La lluna segons lo poble*, Barcelona: Biblioteca de l'Avens.

Gomis, Cels (1987) *La bruixa catalana*, Barcelona: Altafulla (biographical note by Llorenç Prats, 5–31).

González-Silva, Matiana (2009) 'With or without Scientists: Reporting on Human Genetics in the Spanish Newspaper *El País* (1976–2006)', in F. Papanelopoulou, A. Nieto-Galan and E. Perdiguero (eds), *Popularizing Science and Technology in the European Periphery, 1800–2000*, Aldershot: Ashgate, 217–36.

González-Silva, Matiana and Herran, Néstor (2009) 'Ideology, Elitism and Social Commitment: Alternative Images of Science in Two Fin-de-Siècle Barcelona Newspapers', *Centaurus*, 51(2), 97–115.

Gooday, Graeme (2008) *Domesticating Electricity: Technology, Uncertainty and Gender, 1880–1914*, London: Pickering and Chatto.

Gordin, Michael, A. (2004) *A Well-Ordered Thing: Dmitrii Mendeleev and the Shadow of the Periodic Table*, New York: Basic Books.

Gore, Al (2006) *An Inconvenient Truth: The Planetary Emergency of Global Warming and What We Can Do about It*, New York: Rodale.

Goschler, Constantin (eds) (2000) *Wissenschaft und Öffentlichkeit in Berlin, 1870–1930*, Sttutgart: Franz Steiner.

Gouyon, Jean-Baptiste, (2011) 'From Kearton to Attenborough: Fashioning the Telenaturalist's Identity', *History of Science*, 49, 25–60.

Govoni, Paola (2002) *Un pubblico per la scienza. La divulgazione scientifica nell'Italia in formazione*, Rome: Carozzi.

Grant, Edward (1996) *The Foundations of Modern Science in the Middle Ages: Their Religious, Institutional and Intellectual Contexts*, Cambridge: Cambridge University Press.

Green, Jeremy (1985) 'Media Sensationalism and Science: The Case of the Criminal Chromosome', in T. Shinn and R. Whitley (eds), *Expository Science*, Dordrecht: Reidel, 139–62.

Greenberg, Mark L. and Schachterle, Lance (eds) (1992) *Literature and Technology*, Bethlehem: Lehigh University Press.

Greenhalgh, Paul (1988) *Ephemeral Vistas: The Expositions Universelles, Great Exhibitions and World's Fairs, 1851–1939*, Manchester: Manchester University Press.

Grégoire, Henri (1794) *Convention nationale. Instruction publique. Rapport sur l'établissement d'un conservatoire des arts et métiers, par Grégoire. Séance du 8 vendémiaire l'an III*, Paris: Imprimérie nationale.

Gregory, Frederick (1977) *Scientific Materialism in Nineteenth-Century Germany*, Dordrecht: Reidel.

Gregory, Jane (2003) 'The Popularization and Excommunication of Fred Hoyle's "Life-from-Space" Theory', *Public Understanding of Science*, 12, 25–46.

Gregory, Jane (2005) *Fred Hoyle's Universe*, Oxford: Oxford University Press.

Gregory, Jane and Miller, Steve (1998) *Science in Public Communication, Culture and Credibility*, New York: Basic Books.

Grollier de Servière, Nicholas (1719) *Recueil d'ouvrages curieux de mathématique et de mécanique, ou Description du cabinet de Monsieur Grollier de Servière*, Lyon: David Forey.

Gross, Paul and Levitt, Norman (1994) *Higher Superstition: The Academic Left and Its Quarrels with Science*, Baltimore, MD: Johns Hopkins University Press.

Grundmann, Reiner and Cavaillé, Jean-Pierre (2000) 'Simplicity in Science and Its Publics', *Science as Culture*, 9, 353–89.

Guericke, Otto von and Ames, Margaret Glover Foley (1994) *The New (So-Called) Magdeburg Experiments of Otto von Guericke*, Dordrecht: Kluwer.

Gurney, Peter (2001) 'An Appropriated Space: The Great Exhibition, the Crystal Palace and the Working Class', in L. Purbrick (ed.), *The Great Exhibition of 1851*, Manchester: Manchester University Press, 114–45.

Habermas, Jürgen (1962) *Structurwandel der Öffentlichkeit: Untersuchungen zu einer Kategorie der bürgerlichen Gesellschaft*, Neuwied: Luchterhand (English edition (1989) *The Structual Transformation of the Public Sphere: An Inquiry into the Category of Bourgeois Society*, Cambridge, MA: MIT Press).

Habermas, Jürgen (1968) *Technik und Wissenschaft as Ideologie*, Frankfurt am Main: Surkhamp.

Habermas, Jürgen (1984) *The Theory of Communicative Action (I): Reason and the Rationalization of Society*, Boston, MA: Beacon Press.

Habermas, Jürgen (1987) *The Theory of Communicative Action (II): Lifeworld and System*, Boston, MA: Beacon Press.

Hall, A. Rupert (1954) *The Scientific Revolution 1500–1800: The Formation of the Modern Scientific Attitude*, London: Longmans, Green.

Hall, A. Rupert (1963) 'Merton Revisited or Science and Society in the Seventeenth Century', *History of Science*, 2, 1–16.

Hall, David (1986) 'The History of the Book: New Questions, New Answers', *Journal of Library History*, 21, 27–36.

Haller, John S. (2009) *The History of American Homeopathy: From Rational Medicine to Holistic Health Care*, New Brunswick, NJ: Rutgers University Press.

Hamlin, Christopher (1990) *A Science of Impurity: Water Analysis in Nineteenth-Century Britain*, Bristol: Adam Hilger.

Hamlin, Christopher (1992) 'Predisposing Causes and Public Health in Early 19th Century Medical Thought', *Social History of Medicine*, 5, 43–70.

Hamlin, Christopher (1998) *Public Health and Social Justice in the Age of Chadwick: Britain 1800–1854*, Cambridge: Cambridge University Press.

Handlin, Oscar (1965) 'Science and Technology in Popular Culture', in G. Holton (ed.), *Science and Culture: A Study of Cohesive and Disjunctive Forces*, Cambridge: Riverside Press, 184–98.

Hankins, Thomas (1985) *Science and the Enlightenment*, Cambridge: Cambridge University Press.

242 Bibliography

Hankins, Thomas (1995) *Instruments and the Imagination*, Princeton, NJ: Princeton University Press.

Hannaway, Owen (1975) *The Chemist and the Word: The Didactic Origins of Chemistry*, Baltimore, MD: Johns Hopkins University Press.

Harwood, Jonathan (1986) 'Ludwik Fleck and the Sociology of Knowledge', *Social Studies of Science*, 16, 173–87.

Hay, Peter (2002) *Main Currents in Western Environmental Thought*, Bloomington, IN: Indiana University Press.

Haynes, Roslynn (1994) *From Faust to Strangelove: Representations of the Scientist in Western Literature*, Baltimore, MD: Johns Hopkins University Press.

Hedfors, Eva (2007) 'Fleck in Context', *Perspectives on Science*, 15, 49–86.

Herran, Néstor (2012) '"Science to the Glory of God": The Popular Science Magazine *Ibérica* and Its Coverage of Radioactivity, 1914–1936', *Science and Education*, 21(3), 335–53.

Hessenbruch, Arne (2000) 'Science as Public Sphere: X-Rays between Spiritualism and Liberalism in Fin-de-Siècle Berlin', in C. Goschler (ed.), *Wissenschaft und Öffentlichkeit in Berlin, 1870–1930*, Stuttgart: Franz Steiner, 127–54.

Heward, Christine M. (1980) 'Industry, Cleanliness and Godliness: Sources for and Problems in the History of Scientific and Technical Education and the Working Classes, 1850–1910', *Studies in Science Education*, 7, 87–128.

Higgitt, Rebekah and Withers, Charles W.J. (2008) 'Science and Sociability: Women as Audience at the British Association for the Advancement of Science, 1831–1901', *Isis*, 99, 1–27.

Hilaire-Pérez, Liliane (2000) *L'invention technique au siècle des Lumières*, Paris: Albin Michel.

Hilaire-Pérez, Liliane (2008) 'Technology, Curiosity and Utility in France and England in the 18th Century', B. Bensaude-Vincent and C. Blondel (eds), *Science and Spectacle in the European Enlightenment*, Aldershot: Ashgate, 25–42.

Hilgartner, Stephen (1990) 'The Dominant View of Popularisation: Conceptual Problems, Political Issues', *Social Studies of Science*, 20, 519–39.

Hilgartner, Stephen (1997) 'The Sokal Affair in Context', *Science, Technology and Human Values*, 22(4), 506–22.

Hilgartner, Stephen (2000) *Science on Stage: Expert Advice as Public Drama*, Stanford, CA: Stanford University Press.

Hilgartner, Stephen (2004) 'The Credibility of Science on Stage', *Social Studies of Science*, 34(3), 443–52.

Hindmarsh, Richard and Gottweis, Herbert (2005) 'Recombinant Regulation: The Asilomar Legacy 30 Years on', *Science as Culture*, 14, 299–307.

Hobsbawn, Eric (1994) *Age of Extremes: The Short Twentieth Century, 1914–1991*, London: Michael Joseph.

Hochadel, Oliver (2003) *Öffentliche Wissenschaft. Elektrizität in der deutschen Aufklärung*, Göttingen: Wallstein.

Hochadel, Oliver (2008) 'The Sale of Shocks and Sparks: Itinerant Electricians in the German Enlightenment', in B. Bensaude-Vincent and C. Blondel (eds), *Science and Spectacle in the European Enlightenment*, Aldershot: Ashgate, 89–101.

Hochadel, Oliver (2010) 'Darwin in the Monkey Cage: The Zoological Garden as a Medium of Evolutionary Theory', in D. Brantz (ed.), *Beastly Natures: Animals, Humans, and the Study of History*, Charlottesville, VA: University of Virginia Press, 81–107.

Hochadel, Oliver (2013a) *El mito de Atapuerca. Orígenes, ciencia, divulgación*, Bellaterra: Servei de Publicacions UAB.

Bibliography **243**

Hochadel, Oliver (2013b) 'A Boom of Bones and Books: The "Popularization Industry" of Atapuerca and Human-Origins Research in Contemporary Spain', *Public Understanding of Science*, 22, 530–7.

Holmes, Frederic L. (1989a) 'The Complementary of Teaching and Research in Liebig's Laboratory', *Osiris*, 5, 121–64.

Holmes, Frederic L. (1989b) *Eighteenth-Century Chemistry as an Investigative Enterprise*, Berkeley, CA: University of California Press.

Holmes, Frederic L. (2000) 'The Evolution of Lavoisier's Chemical Apparatus', in F.L. Holmes and T. Levere (eds), *Instruments and Experimentation in the History of Chemistry*, Cambridge, MA: MIT Press, 137–52.

Holmes, Frederic L. and Levere, Trevor H. (eds) (2000) *Instruments and Experimentation in the History of Chemistry*, Cambridge, MA: MIT Press.

Holmyard, Eric John (1957, 1990) *Alchemy*, New York: Dover Publications.

Holton, Gerald (1992) 'How to Think about the Anti-Science Phenomenon', *Public Understanding of Science*, 1, 103–28.

Holton, Gerald (1993) *Science and Anti-Science*, Cambridge, MA: Harvard University Press.

Holton, Gerald and Blanpied, William A. (eds) (1976) *Science and Its Public: The Changing Relationship*, Dordrecht: Reidel.

Holub, Renate (1992) *Antonio Gramsci: Beyond Marxism and Postmodernism*, London: Routledge.

Hommels, Anique, Mesman, Jessica and Bijker, Wiebe (2014) *Vulnerability in Technological Cultures: New Directions in Research and Governance*, Cambridge, MA: MIT Press.

Hoskin, Michael (1997) *The Cambridge Illustrated History of Astronomy*, Cambridge: Cambridge University Press.

Huff, Tobby E. (1993) *The Rise of Early Modern Science: Islam, China, and the West*, Cambridge: Cambridge University Press.

Hug, Tamara and Cunningham, Andrew (1994) *Focus on the Frontispiece of the Fabrica of Vesalius, 1543*, Cambridge: Cambridge Wellcome Unit for the History of Medicine.

Hughes, Thomas P. (1983) *Networks of Power: Electrification in Western Society, 1880–1930*, Baltimore, MD: Johns Hopkins University Press.

Hulme, Mike (2009) *Why We Disagree about Climate Change: Understanding Controversy, Inaction and Opportunity*, Cambridge: Cambridge Universty Press.

Iles, Alastair (2007) 'Identifying Environmental Health Risks in Consumer Products: Non-Governmental Organizations and Civic Epistemologies', *Public Understanding of Science*, 16(4), 371–91.

Impey, Oliver and MacGregor, Arthur (eds) (1985) *The Origins of Museums: The Cabinet of Curiosities in 16th and 17th Century Europe*, Oxford: Clarendon Press.

Inge, Thomas M. (ed.) (1981) *American Popular Culture*, 3 vols, London: Greenwood Press.

Irving, Alan and Michael, Mike (2003) *Science, Technology and Public Knowledge*, Maidenhead: Open University Press.

Irving, Alan and Wynne, Brian (eds) (1996) *Misunderstanding Science? The Public Reconstruction of Science and Technology*, Cambridge: Cambridge University Press.

Jacobi, Daniel (1999) *La communication scientifique. Discours, figures, modèles*, Grenoble: Presses Universitaires de Grenoble.

Jacobi, Daniel and Schiele, B. (eds) (1988) *Vulgariser la science. Le procès de l'ignorance*, Seysell: Champ Vallon.

244 Bibliography

James, Frank A.J.L. (2002) 'Never Talk about Science, Show It to Them: The Lecture Theatre of the Royal Institution', *Interdisciplinary Science Reviews*, 27(3), 225–8.

Jamieson, Dale (1992) 'Ethics, Public Policy, and Global Warming', *Science, Technology and Human Values*, 17(2), 139–53.

Jardine, Nick, Secord, James and Spary, Emma (eds) (1996) *Cultures of Natural History*, Cambridge: Cambridge University Press.

Jarrell, Richard A. (1998) 'Visionary or Bureaucrat? T.H. Huxley, the Science and Art Department and Science Teaching for the Working Class', *Annals of Science*, 55(3), 219–40.

Jarvis, Adrian (1997) *Samuel Smiles and the Construction of Victorian Values*, Stroud: Sutton.

Jasanoff, Sheila (2003a) 'Technologies of Humility: Citizens' Participation in Governing Science', *Minerva*, 41(3), 223–44.

Jasanoff, Sheila (2003b) 'Breaking the Waves in Science Studies: Comment on H.M. Collins and Robert Evans', *Social Studies of Science*, 33(3), 389–400.

Jasanoff, Sheila (ed.) (2004) *States of Knowledge: The Coproduction of Science and Social Order*, London: Routledge.

Jasanoff, Sheila (2005) *Designs on Nature: Science and Democracy in Europe and the United States*, Princeton, NJ: Princeton University Press.

Jasanoff, Sheila, Markle, Gerald E., Petersen, James C. and Pinch, Trevor (eds) (1995) *Handbook of Science and Technology Studies*, London: Sage.

Jeanneret, Yves (1994) *Écrire la science: Formes et enjeux de la vulgarisation*, Paris: Presses universitaires de France.

Johns, Adrian (1998) *The Nature of the Book: Print and Knowledge in the Making*, Chicago, IL: University of Chicago Press.

Jones, Caroline and Galison, Peter (eds) (1998) *Picturing Science, Producing Art*, London, New York: Routledge.

Jordanova, Ludmila (ed.) (1986) *Languages of Nature: Critical Essays on Science and Literature*, London: Free Association Books.

Joss, Simon (ed.) (1999) *Public Participation in Science and Technology*, special issue, *Science and Public Policy*, 26(5).

Jütte, Robert, Risse, Guenter B. and Woodward, John (eds) (1998) *Culture, Knowledge and Healing: Historical Perspectives of Homeopathic Medicine in Europe and North America*, Sheffield: EAHMH.

Kafker, Frank A. (ed.) (1981) *Notable Encyclopedias of the 17th and 18th Centuries: Nine Predecessors of the* Encyclopédie, Oxford: Voltaire Foundation.

Kafker, Frank A. (ed.) (1994) *Notable Encyclopedias of the Late 18th Century: Eleven Successors of the* Encyclopédie, Oxford: Voltaire Foundation.

Kaiser, David (ed.) (2005a) *Pedagogy and the Practice of Science: Historical and Contemporary Perspectives*, Cambridge, MA: MIT Press.

Kaiser, David (2005b) *Drawing Theories Apart: The Dispersion of Feynman Diagrams in Postwar Physics*, Chicago, IL: University of Chicago Press.

Kaiser, David and Warwick, Andrew (2005) 'Conclusion: Kuhn, Foucault, and the Power of Pedagogy', in D. Kaiser (ed.), *Pedagogy and the Practice of Science*, Cambridge, MA: MIT Press, pp. 393–404.

Kaplan, Steven L. (ed.) (1984) *Understanding Popular Culture: Europe from the Middle Ages to the Nineteenth Century*, Amsterdam: Mouton Publications.

Kargon, Robert (1977) *Science in Victorian Manchester: Enterprise and Expertise*, Manchester: Manchester University Press.

Keene, Melanie (2015) *Science in Wonderland: The Scientific Fairy Tales of Victorian Britain*, Oxford: Oxford University Press.

Kelley, Patricia D., Ross, Robert M. and Allmon, Warren D. (2008) *Stephen Jay Gould: Reflections on His View of Life*, Oxford: Oxford University Press.

Kelly, S.E. (2003) 'Public Bioethics and Publics: Consensus, Boundaries and Participation in Biomedical Science Policy', *Science, Technology and Human Values*, 28(3), 339–64.

Kent, Julie (2003) 'Lay Experts and the Politics of Breast Implants', *Public Understanding of Science* 12(4), 403–22.

Kirby, David A. (2008) 'Cinematic Science', in M. Bucchi and B. Trench (eds), *Handbook of Public Communication of Science and Technology*, Abingdon: Routledge, 41–56.

Kirby, David A. (2011) *Lab Coats in Hollywood: Science, Scientists, and Cinema*, Cambridge, MA: MIT Press.

Klein, Ursula (2005a) 'Introduction: Technoscientific Production', *Perspectives on Science*, 13, 139–41.

Klein, Ursula (2005b) 'Technoscience avant la lettre', *Perspectives on Science*, 13, 226–66.

Kleinman, Daniel Lee (2000) *Science, Technology and Democracy*, Albany, NY: State University of New York Press.

Kline, Ronald (1995) 'Construing "Technology" as "Applied Science": Public Rhetoric of Scientists and Engineers in the United States, 1880–1945', *Isis*, 86, 194–221.

Knight, David (2002) 'Scientific Lectures: A History of Performance', *Interdisciplinary Science Reviews*, 27(3), 217–24.

Knight, David (2006) *Public Understanding of Science: A History of Communicating Scientific Ideas*, London: Routledge.

Kockerbeck, Christoph (1999) *Carl Vogt, Jacob Moleschott, Ludwig Büchner, Ernst Haeckel: Briefwechsel*, Marburg: Basilisken-Presse.

Kohler, Robert (2007) 'Finders/Keepers: Collecting Science and Collecting Practice', *History of Science*, 45, 1–27.

Kohlsted, Sally Gregory (2010) *Teaching Children Science: Hands-on Nature Study in North America, 1890–1930*, Chicago, IL: University of Chicago Press.

Krige, John and Pestre, Dominique (eds) (1997) *Science in the Twentieth Century*, Amsterdam: Harwood Academic.

Krige, John and Pestre, Dominique (eds) (2003) *Companion to Science in the Twentieth Century*, London: Routledge, 2003.

Kruger, Gesine, Mayer, Ruth, Sommer, Marianne (eds) (2008) *'Ich Tarzan': Affenmenschen und Menschenaffen zwischen Science und Fiction*, Bielefeld: Science Studies.

Kuhn, Thomas S. (1962, 2012) *The Structure of Scientific Revolutions*, 50th anniversary, 4th edn, Chicago, IL: University of Chicago Press.

Kuklick, Henrika and Kohler, Robert E. (eds) (1996) 'Science in the Field', *Osiris*, 11.

Kusukawa, Sachiko (2012) *Picturing the Book of Nature: Image, Text, and Argument in Sixteenth-Century Human Anatomy and Medical Botany*, Chicago, IL: University of Chicago Press.

Kusukawa, Sachiko and Maclean, Ian (eds) (2006) *Transmitting Knowledge: Words, Images, and Instruments in Early Modern Europe*, Oxford: Oxford University Press.

La Follette, Marcel (1990) *Making Science Our Own: Public Images of Science, 1910–1955*, Chicago, IL: University of Chicago Press.

La Follette, Marcel (2007) 'Taking Science to the Marketplace: Examples of Science Service's Presentation of Chemistry during the 1930s', in J. Schummer, B. Bensaude-Vincent and B. Van Tiggelen (eds), *The Public Image of Chemistry*, Singapore, London: World Scientific, 259–98.

La Follette, Marcel (2008) *Science on the Air: Popularizers and Personalities on Radio and Early Television*, Chicago, IL: University of Chicago Press.

246 Bibliography

La Follette, Marcel (2012) *Science on American Television: A History*, Chicago, IL: University of Chicago Press.

Landes, David S. (1969) *The Unbound Prometheus*, Cambridge: Cambridge University Press.

Landon, Brooks (2002) *Science Fiction after 1900: From the Steam Man to the Stars*, New York, London: Routledge.

Langlebert, Edmond-Jean-Joseph (1879) *Chimie. Cours élémentaire d'études scientifiques . . . Chimie*, 30th edition, Paris: Imprimérie et Librairie classiques.

Langlois, Claude and Laplanche, François (eds) (1992) *La science catholique. L'Encyclopédie théologique de Migne (1844–1873) entre apologétique et vulgarisation*, Paris: CERF.

Lankford, John (1981a) 'Amateurs and Astrophysics: A Neglected Aspect in the Development of a Scientific Specialty', *Social Studies of Science*, 11(3), 275–303.

Lankford, John (1981b) 'Amateurs versus Professionals: The Controversy over Telescope Size in Late Victorian Science', *Isis*, 72, 11–28.

Latour, Bruno (1986) *Laboratory Life: The Construction of Scientific Facts*, Princeton, NJ: Princeton University Press.

Latour, Bruno (1988) *The Pasteurization of France*, Cambridge, MA: Harvard University Press.

Latour, Bruno (2004) *Politics of Nature: How to Bring the Sciences into Democracy*, Cambridge, MA: Harvard University Press.

Latour, Bruno and Weibel, Peter (2005) *Making Things Public: Atmospheres of Democracy*. Cambridge, MA: MIT Press.

Laurent, John (1984) 'Science, Society and Politics in Late Nineteenth-Century England: A Further Look at Mechanics' Institutes', *Social Studies of Science*, 14, 585–619.

Law, John (ed.) (1991) *A Sociology of Monsters: Essays on Power, Technology and Domination*, London: Routledge.

Lay, Mary, Gurak, Laura, Gravon, Clare and Myntti, Cynthia (eds) (2000) *Body Talk: Rethoric, Technology, Reproduction*, Madison, WI: University of Wisconsin Press.

Le Goff, Jacques (1957, 1993) *Intellectuals in the Middle Ages*, Cambridge, MA: Blackwell (1st French edition, 1957).

Le Roux, Thomas (2011) *Le laboratoire des pollutions industrielles Paris, 1770–1830*, Paris: A. Michel.

Lehman, Christine (2008) 'Between Commerce and Philanthropy: Chemistry Courses in Eighteenth-Century Paris', in B. Bensaude-Vincent and C. Blondel (eds), *Science and Spectacle in the European Enlightenment*, Aldershot: Ashgate, 103–16.

Lengwiler, Martin (2004) 'Shifting Boundaries between Science and Politics: New Insights into the Participatory Question in Science Studies', *Technoscience*, 20(3), 2–5.

Lengwiler, Martin (2008) 'Participatory Approaches in Science and Technology', *Science, Technology and Human Values*, 33(2), 186–200.

Lenoir, Timothy (1997) *Instituting Science: The Cultural Production of Scientific Disciplines*, Stanford, CA: Stanford University Press.

Lenoir, Timothy (1998) *Inscribing Science: Scientific Texts and the Materiality of Communication*, Stanford, CA: Stanford University Press.

Levine, George (ed.) (1987) *One Culture: Essays in Science and Literature*, Madison, WI: University of Wisconsin Press.

Levitt, Norman and Gross, Paul (1994) 'The Perils of Democratizing Science', *Chronicle of Higher Education*, 5 October, B1, B2.

Lewenstein, Bruce V. (1992a) 'Cold Fusion and Hot History', *Osiris*, 7, 135–63.

Lewenstein, Bruce V. (1992b) *When Science Meets the Public*, Washington, DC: American Association for the Advancement of Science.

Bibliography **247**

Lewenstein, Bruce V. (1995a) 'From Fax to Facts: Communication in the Cold Fusion Saga', *Social Studies of Science*, 25, 408–24.

Lewenstein, Bruce V. (1995b) 'Science and the Media', in S. Jasanoff et al. (eds), *Handbook of Science and Technology Studies*, London: Sage, 343–60.

Lewenstein, Bruce V. (2000) 'Popularization', in A. Hessenbruch (ed.), *Reader's Guide to the History of Science*, London: Fitzroy, 586–8.

Lewin, Roger (1997) *Bones of Contention: Controversies in the Search for Human Origins*, 2nd edn, Chicago, IL: University of Chicago Press.

Leydesdorff, Loet and Ward, Janelle (2005) 'Science Shops: A Kaleidoscope of Science: Society Collaborations in Europe', *Public Understanding of Science*, 14, 353–72.

Lie, M. and Sorenson, K.H. (eds) (1996) *Making Technology Our Own? Domesticating Technology into Everyday Life*, Oslo: Scandinavian University Press.

Lightman, Bernard (ed.) (1997) *Victorian Science in Context*, Chicago, IL: University of Chicago Press.

Lightman, Bernard (2000) 'The Visual Theology of Victorian Popularizers of Science: From Reverent Eye to Chemical Retina', *Isis*, 91, 651–80.

Lightman, Bernard (2007a) *Victorian Popularizers of Science: Designing Nature for New Audiences*, Chicago, IL: Chicago University Press.

Lightman, Bernard (2007b) 'Lecturing in the Spatial Economy of Science', in A. Fyfe and B. Lightman (eds), *Science in the Marketplace*, Chicago, IL: Chicago University Press, 97–132.

Lightman, Bernard and Reidy, Michael S. (eds) (2014) *The Age of Scientific Naturalism: Tyndall and His Contemporaries*, London: Pickering and Chatto.

Lindberg, David (2007) *The Beginnings of Western Science: The European Scientific Tradition in Philosophical, Religious, and Institutional Context, Prehistory to A.D. 1450*, Chicago, IL: University of Chicago Press.

Lindee, Susan M. (1991) 'The American Career of Jean Marcet's *Conversations on Chemistry*, 1806–1853', *Isis*, 82, 9–23.

Livingstone, David N. (2003) *Putting Science in Its Place: Geographies of Scientific Knowledge*, Chicago, IL: University of Chicago Press.

Livingstone, David N. and Withers, Charles W.J. (eds) (2011) *Geographies of Nineteenth-Century Science*, Chicago, IL: University of Chicago Press.

Lloyd, Geoffrey E.R. (1987) *The Revolutions of Wisdom: Studies in the Claims and Practice of Ancient Greek Science*, Berkeley, CA: University of California Press.

Locke, S. (2002) 'The Public Understanding of Science: A Rhetorical Invention', *Science, Technology and Human Values*, 27, 87–111.

Lomborg, Björn (2001) *The Skeptical Environmentalist: Measuring the Real State of the World*, Cambridge: Cambridge University Press.

Long, Pamela O. (1991) 'The Openness of Knowledge: An Ideal and Its Context in 16th-Century Writings on Mining and Metallurgy', *Technology and Culture*, 32, 318–55.

Lovelock, James (1979; 2nd edn 2000a) *Gaia. A New Look at Life on Earth*, reissued with a new preface and corrections, Oxford: Oxford University Press.

Lovelock, James (2000b) *Homage to Gaia: The Life of an Independent Scientist*, Oxford: Oxford University Press.

Lundgren, Anders and Bensaude-Vincent, Bernadette (2000) *Communicating Chemistry: Textbooks and Their Audiences, 1789–1939*, Canton, MA: Science History Publications.

Lynn, Michael R. (2006) *Popular Science and Public Opinion in Eighteenth-Century France*, Manchester: Manchester University Press.

Lyotard, Jean-François (1984) *The Postmodern Condition*, Manchester: Manchester University Press (French edition 1979).

248 Bibliography

MacDonald, Sharon (1996) 'Authorising Science: Public Understanding of Science in Museums', in A. Irving and B. Wynne (eds), *Misunderstanding Science? The Public Reconstruction of Science and Technology*, Cambridge: Cambridge University Press.

MacDonald, Sharon (2002) *Behind the Scenes at the Science Museum*, Oxford: Berg.

MacDonald, Sharon (2005) 'Accessing Audiences: Visiting Visitor Books', *Museums and Society*, 3, 119–36.

MacDonald, Sharon and Silverstone, Roger (1992) 'Science on Display: The Representations of Scientific Controversy in Museum Exhibitions', *Public Understanding of Science*, 1, 69–87.

MacKenzie, John M. (1984) *Propaganda and Empire: The Manipulation of British Public Opinion, 1880–1960*, Manchester: Manchester University Press.

MacKenzie, John M. (1986) *Imperialism and Popular Culture*, Manchester: Manchester University Press.

Mackinder, Halford John and Sadler, Michael Ernest (1891) *University Extension: Past, Present and Future*, London: Cassell.

Macoubrie, Jane (2006) 'Nanotechnology: Public Concerns, Reasoning and Trust in Government', *Public Understanding of Science*, 15, 221–41.

Mah, Harold (2000) 'Phantasies of the Public Sphere: Rethinking the Habermas of Historians', *Journal of Modern History*, 72, 153–82.

Maidment, Brian (2001) 'Entrepreneurship and the Artisans: John Cassell, the Great Exhibition and the Periodical Idea', in L. Purbrick (ed.), *The Great Exhibition of 1851*, Manchester: Manchester University Press, 97–113.

Markell Morantz, Regina (1997) 'Nineteenth Century Health Reform and Women: A Program of "Self-Help", in G. Risse, R. L. Numbers and J. W. Leavitt (eds), *Medicine without Doctors*, New York: Science History, 73–93.

Markovits, Andrei S. and Deutsch, Karl W. (eds) (1980) *Fear of Science – Trust in Science: Conditions for Change in the Climate of Opinion*, Cambridge, MA: Oelgeschlager, Gunn and Hain.

Marx, Leo (1964, 2000) *The Machine in the Garden: Technology and the Pastoral Ideal in America*, Oxford: Oxford University Press.

Marx, Leo (1992) 'Environamental Degradation and the Ambiguous Social Role of Science and Technology', *Journal of the History of Biology*, 25, 449–68.

Matthews, Michael R. (ed.) (2014) *International Handbook of Research in History, Philosophy and Science Teaching*, Dortdrecht: Springer.

Mayhew, Henry (1851) *1851, or the Adventures of Mr. and Mrs. Sandboys and Family Who Came up to London to "Enjoy Themselves," and to See the Great Exhibition*, London: D. Boque.

Mazzolini, Renato G. (1993) (ed.) *Non-Verbal Communication in Science Prior to 1900*, Firenze: Olschki.

McCormick, Sabrina (2007) 'Democratizing Science Movements: A New Framework for Mobilization and Contestation', *Social Studies of Science*, 37(4), 609–23.

McCray, W. Patrick (2006) 'Amateur Scientists, the International Geophysical Year, and the Ambitions of Fred Whipple', *Isis*, 97, 634–58.

McElheny, Victor K. (1985) 'Impacts of Present-Day Popularization', in T. Shinn and R. Whitley (eds), *Expository Science*, Dordrecht: Reidel, 277–88.

Mead, Clifford and Hager, Thomas (eds) (2001) *Linus Pauling: Scientist and Peacemaker*, Corvallis, OR: Oregon State University Press.

Medina-Domènech, Rosa María and Menéndez Navarro, Alfredo (2005) 'Cinematic Representations of Medical Technologies in the Spanish Official Newsreel, 1943–1970', *Public Understanding of Science*, 14, 393–408.

Meikle, Jeffrey L. (1997) 'Material Doubts: The Consequences of Plastic', *Environmental History* 2(3), 278–300.

Mellor, Felicity (2003) 'Between Fact and Fiction: Demarcating Science from Non-Science in Popular Physics Books', *Social Studies of Science*, 33, 509–38.

Merchant, Carolyn (1980) *The Death of Nature: Women Ecology and the Scientific Revolution*, San Francisco, CA: Harper.

Mercier, Lucien (1986) *Les universities populaires, 1899–1914*, Paris: Les éditions ouvrières.

Mertens, Joost (2000) 'Technology as the Science of Industrial Arts: Louis-Sébastien Lenormand (1757–1837) and the Popularization of Technology', *History and Technology*, 18(3), 203–31.

Meunier, Victor (1857–9) *Essais scientifiques*, 3 vols, Paris: Bureau de l'ami des sciences.

Meunier, Victor (1865) *Science et démocratie*, Paris: Baillière.

Meyer-Thurow, Georg (1982) 'The Industrialization of Invention: A Case Study from the German Chemical Industry', *Isis*, 73, 363–81.

Michael, Mike (1992) 'Lay Discourses in Science: Science-in-General, Science-in-Particular, and the Self', *Science, Technology and Human Values*, 17, 313–33.

Michalczyk, John J. (ed.) (1994) *Medicine, Ethics, and the Third Reich: Historical and Contemporary Issues*, Kansas City, MO: Sheed and Ward.

Millar, Robin (1994) 'School Student's Understanding of Key Ideas about Radioactivity and Ionizing Radiation', *Public Understanding of Science*, 3, 53–70.

Mitman, Gregg (1993) 'Cinematic Nature: Hollywood Technology, Popular Culture, and the American Museum of Natural History', *Isis*, 84, 637–61.

Moranta, Alessandro, Guggenheim, Michael, Gisler, Priska and Pohl, Christian (2003) 'The Reality of Experts and the Imagined Lay Person', *Acta Sociologica*, 46, 150–65.

Morrell, Jack (1986) 'Brains of Britain', *Social Studies of Science*, 16, 735–45.

Morrell, Jack (1995) 'Wissenschaft in Worstedpolis: Public Science in Bradford, 1800–1850', *British Journal for the History of Science*, 18, 1–23.

Morrell, Jack and Thackray, Arnold (1981) *Gentlemen of Science: Early Years of the British Association for the Advancement of Science*, Oxford: Oxford University Press.

Morris, Peter (2007) 'The Image of Chemistry Presented in the Science Museum, London in the 20th Century: An international Perspective', in J. Schummer, B. Bensaude-Vincent and B. Van Tiggelen (eds), *The Public Image of Chemistry*, Singapore, London: World Scientific, 297–328.

Morris, Peter (ed.) (2010) *Science for the Nation: Perspectives on the History of the Science Museum*, New York: Palgrave Macmillan; London: Science Museum, 2010.

Morton, Alan Q. (1995) *Science Lecturing in the Eighteenth Century*, special issue, *The British Journal for the History of Science*, 28.

Morus, Iwan Rhys (1996) 'Manufacturing Nature: Science, Technology and Victorian Consumer Culture', *British Journal for the History of Science*, 29, 403–34.

Morus, Iwan Rhys (1998) *Frankenstein's Children: Electricity, Exhibition, and Experiment in Early-Nineteenth-Century London*, Princeton, NJ: Princeton University Press.

Morus, Iwan Rhys (2006) 'Seeing and Believing Science', *Isis*, 97, 101–10.

Morus, Iwan Rhys (2007) '"More the Aspect of Magic than Anything Neutral": The Philosophy of Demonstration', in A. Fyfe and B. Lightman (eds), *Science in the Marketplace*, Chicago, IL: Chicago University Press, 336–70.

Moscoso, Javier (2012) *Pain: A Cultural History*, Basingstoke: Palgrave Macmillan.

Mosley, Stephen (1999) 'Public Perceptions of Smoke Pollution in Victorian Manchester', in D. E. Nye (ed.), *Technologies of Landscape*, Cambridge, MA: MIT Press, 161–86.

Multhauf, Robert P. (1966) *The Origins of Chemistry*, London: Oldbourne.

Mumford, Lewis (1934) *Technics and Civilization*, London: G. Routledge and Sons.

250 Bibliography

Myers, Greg (1985) 'Nineteenth-Century Popularizations of Thermodynamics and the Rhetoric of Social Prophecy', *Victorian Studies*, 29, 35–66.

Myers, Greg (2003) 'Discourse Studies of Scientific Popularisation: Questioning the Boundaries', *Discourse studies*, 5(2), 265–79.

Nahuis, Roel and Van Lente, Harro (2008) 'Where Are the Politics? Perspective on Democracy and Technology', *Science, Technology and Human Values*, 33, 559–81.

Naumann, Barbara (2005) *Science and Literature*, special issue, *Science in Context*, 18(2).

Navarro Brotons, Víctor and Eamon, William (eds) (2007) *Más allá de la Leyenda Negra: España y la Revolución Científica/Beyond the Black Legend: Spain and the Scientific Revolution*, Valencia: Universitat de València – CSIC.

Nelkin, Dorothy (1978) 'Scientists in an Adversary Culture: The 1930s', *Science, Technology and Human Values*, 24, 33–9.

Nelkin, Dorothy (1987) *Selling Science: How the Press Covers Science and Technology*, New York: Freeman and Co.

Nelkin, Dorothy (1994) 'Promotional Metaphors and Their Popular Appeal', *Public Understanding of Science*, 3(1), 25–31.

Nelkin, Dorothy (1995) 'Science Controversies: The Dynamics of Public Disputes in the United States', in S. Jasanoff et al. (eds), *Handbook of Science and Technology Studies*, 444–56.

Nelkin, Dorothy and Lindee, Susan M, (1995) *The DNA Mystique: The Gene as a Cultural Icon*, New York: Freeman.

Nelson, Adam R. and Rudolph, John L. (eds) (2010) *Education and the Culture of Print in Modern America*, Madison, WI: University of Wisconsin Press.

Nicholls, Phillip A. (1988) *Homeopathy and the Medical Profession*, London: Croom Helm.

Nicholls, Phillip A. (2001) 'The Social Construction and Organisation of Medical Marginality: The Case of Homoeopathy in Mid-Nineteenth-Century Britain', in R. Jutte, M. Eklof and M.C. Nelson (eds), *Historical Aspects of Unconventional Medicine: Approaches, Concepts, Case Studies, EAHMH Network Series*, vol. 4, Sheffield: European Association for the History of Medicine and Health Publications, 163–81.

Nicolson, Majorie H. (1956) *Science and Imagination*, Ithaca, NY: Cornell University Press.

Nicolson, Majorie H. (1960) *Voyages to the Moon*, New York: MacMillan.

Niderst, Alain (ed.) (1991) 'La diffusion des sciences au XVIIIe siècle', *Revue d'histoire des sciences*, 44(3/4).

Nielsen, M. (2011) *Reinventing Discovery: The New Era of Networked Science*, Princeton, NJ: Princeton University Press.

Nieto-Galan, Agustí (1997) 'Calico Printing and Chemical Knowledge in Lancashire in the Early 19th Century: The Life and "Colours" of John Mercer', *Annals of Science*, 54, 1–28.

Nieto-Galan, Agustí (2001) *Colouring Textiles: A History of Natural Dyestuffs in Industrial Europe*, Dordrecht: Kluwer.

Nieto-Galan, Agustí (2009) '. . . Not Fundamental in a State of Full "Civilization": The *Sociedad Astronómica de Barcelona* (1910–1921) and Its Popularization Programme', *Annals of Science*, 66(4), 497–528.

Nieto-Galan, Agustí (2010) 'Between Craft Routines and Academic Rules: Natural Dyestuffs and the "Art" of Dyeing in the Eighteenth Century', in U. Klein and E. Spary (eds), *Materials and Expertise in Early Modern Europe: Between Market and Laboratory*, Chicago, IL: Chicago University Press, 321–54.

Nieto-Galan, Agustí (2011a) 'Antonio Gramsci Revisited: Historians of Science, Intellectuals, and the Struggle for Hegemony', *History of Science*, 49, 453–78.

Nieto-Galan, Agustí (2011b) *Los públicos de la ciencia. Expertos y profanos a través de la historia*, Madrid: Marcial Pons.

Nieto-Galan, Agustí (2012a) 'The Cultures of Natural History in Spain around 1900: Odón de Buen (1863–1945) and His Audiences', *Historical Studies in the Natural Sciences*, 42(3), 159–89.

Nieto-Galan, Agustí (2012b) 'Historicitat i heterodòxia. La divulgació científica de Louis Figuier (1819–1894)', *Quaderns de Filologia: Estudis Lingüístics*, 17, 81–94.

Nikolow, Sybilla and Schirrmacher, Arne (eds) (2007) *Wissenschaft und Öffentlichkeit als Ressourcen füreinander. Studien zur Wissenschaftsgeschichte im 20. Jahrhundert*, Frankfurt: Campus.

Nowotny, Helga, Scott, Peter and Gibbons, Michael (2001) *Re-Thinking Science: Knowledge and the Public in an Age of Uncertainty*, Cambridge: Polity Press.

Nowotny, Helga, Scott, Peter and Gibbons, Michael (2003) '"Mode 2" Revisited: The New Production of Knowledge', *Minerva*, 41(3), 179–94.

Nowotny, Helga, Pestre, Dominique, Schmidt-Assmann, Eberhard, Schulze-Fielitz, Helmuth and Trute, Hans-Heinrich (2005) *The Public Nature of Science under Assault: Politics, Markets, Science and the Law*, Berlin: Springer.

Numbers, Ronald L. (1977) 'Do-It-Yourself the Sectarian Way', in G. Risse, R. L. Numbers and J. W. Leavitt (eds), *Medicine without Doctors*, New York: Science History, 49–72.

Nye, David E. (1990) *Electrifying America: Social Meanings of a New Technology*, Cambridge MA: MIT Press.

Nye, David E. (1999a) *American Technological Sublime*, Cambridge, MA: MIT Press.

Nye, David E. (ed.) (1999b) *Technologies of Landscape*, Cambridge, MA: MIT Press.

Nye, Mary Jo (1975) 'Science and Socialism: The Case of Jean Perrin in the Third Republic', *French Historical Studies*, 9(1), 141–69.

Nye, Mary Jo (1993) *From Chemical Philosophy to Theoretical Chemistry: Dynamics of Matter and Dynamics of Disciplines, 1800–1950*, Berkeley, CA: University of California Press.

Nyhart, Lynn K. (1995) *Biology Takes Form: Animal Morphology and the German Universities, 1800–1900*, Chicago, IL; London: University of Chicago Press.

Nyhart, Lynn K. (2009) *Modern Nature: The Rise of the Biological Perspective in Germany*, Chicago, IL: University of Chicago Press.

Nyhart, Lynn K. and Broman, Thomas H. (eds) (2002) *Science and Civil Society*, Osiris, 17.

O'Connor, Ralph (2007) *The Earth on Show: Fossils and the Poetics of Popular Science, 1802–1856*, Chicago, IL: University of Chicago Press.

O'Connor, Ralph (2009) 'Reflections on Popular Science in Britain: Genres, Categories and Historians', *Isis*, 100, 333–45.

O'Connor, Ralph (ed.) (2012) *Science as Romance*, London: Pickering and Chatto.

Olesko, Kathryn M. (1989) 'Physics Instruction in Prussian Secondary Schools before 1859', *Osiris*, 5, 94–120.

Olesko, Kathryn M. (1991) *Physics as a Calling: Discipline and Practice in the Königsberg Seminar for Physics*, Ithaca, NY: Cornell University Press.

Olesko, Kathryn M. (1993) 'Tacit Knowledge and School Formation', *Osiris*, 8, 16–29.

Olesko, Kathryn M. (2006) 'Science Pedagogy as a Category of Historical Analysis: Past, Present, and Future', *Science and Education*, 15, 863–80.

Olmi, Giuseppe (1992) *L'inventario del mondo. Catalogazione della natura e luoghi del sapere nella prima eta moderna*, Bologna: Il Mulino.

Olson, Richard (2008) *Science and Scientism in Nineteenth-Century Europe*, Urbana, IL: University of Illinois Press.

Oosterhuis, Harry (2000) *Step-Children of Nature: Richard von Krafft-Ebing's Psychiatry, and the Making of Sexual Identity*, Chicago, IL: Chicago University Press.

Oreskes, Naomi and Conway, Erik M. (2010) *Merchants of Doubt: How a Handful of Scientists Obscured the Truth on Issues from Tobacco Smoke to Global Warming*, New York: Bloomsbury Press.

252 Bibliography

Oreskes, Naomi and Conway, Erik M. (2014) *The Collpapse of Western Civilization: A View from the Future*, New York: Columbia University Press.

Osborne, Michael A. (1994) *Nature, the Exotic, and the Science of French Colonialism*, Bloomington, IN: Indiana University Press.

Oudshoorn, Nelly and Pinch, Trevor (eds) (2003) *How Users Matter: The Co-Construction of Users and Technologies*, Cambridge, MA: MIT Press.

Pacey, Arnold (1999, 2001) *Meaning in Technology*, Cambridge, MA: MIT Press.

Pandora, Katherine and Rader, Karen A. (2008) 'Science in the Evereyday World: Why Perspectives from the History of Science Matter', *Isis*, 99, 350–64.

Papanelopoulou, Faidra and Kjærgaard, Peter C. (2009) 'Making the Paper: Science and Technology in Spanish, Greek and Danish Newspapers around 1900', *Centaurus*, 51(2), 89–96.

Papanelopoulou, Faidra, Nieto-Galan, Agustí and Perdiguero, Enrique (eds) (2009) *Popularizing Science and Technology in the European Periphery, 1800–2000*, Aldershot: Ashgate.

Pardo-Tomás, José (2003–4) 'Censura inquisitorial y lectura de libros científicos. Una propuesta de replanteamiento', *Tiempos Modernos*, 9, 1–18.

Pardo-Tomás, José (2014) *Salvadoriana: The Cabinet of Curiosities of Barcelona*, Barcelona: Museu de Ciències Naturals de Barcelona, Institut Botànic de Barcelona.

Pardo-Tomás, José and Martínez-Vidal, Àlvar (2000) 'Victims and Experts: Medical Practitioners and the Spanish Inquisition', in J. Woodward and R. Jütte (eds), *Coping with Sickness: Medicine, Law and Human Rights: Historical Perspectives*, Birmingham: European Association for the History of Medicine and Health Publications, 11–27.

Pardo-Tomás, José and Martínez-Vidal, Àlvar (2005) 'Anatomical Theatres and the Teaching of Anatomy in Early Modern Spain', *Medical History*, 49, 251–80.

Pardo-Tomás, José and Martínez-Vidal, Àlvar (2008) 'Stories of Disease Written by Patients and Lay Mediators in the Spanish Republic of Letters (1680–1720)', *Journal of Medieval and Early Modern Studies*, 38(3), 467–91.

Parry, Linda (ed.) (1996) *William Morris*, London: Phillip Wilson Publishers; Victoria and Albert Museum.

Pauling, Linus (1947) *General Chemistry: An Introduction to Descriptive Chemistry and Modern Chemical Theory*, San Francisco, CA: W. H. Freeman and Company.

Perdiguero, Enrique (1992) 'The Popularization of Medicine during the Spanish Enlightenment', in R. Porter (ed.), *The Popularization of Medicine, 1650–1850*, London: Routledge, 160–93.

Pestre, Dominique (2003a) 'Regimes of Knowledge Production in Society: Towards a More Political and Social Reading', *Minerva*, 41(3), 245–61.

Pestre, Dominique (2003b) *Science, argent et politique*, Paris: INRA.

Pestre, Dominique (2013) *À contre-science. Politiques et savoirs des sociétés contemporaines*, Paris: Seuil.

Petit, Annie (1989) 'La diffusion des savoirs comme devoir positive', *Romantisme*, 65, 7–25.

Pickstone, John (2000) *Ways of Knowing: A New History of Science, Technology and Medicine*, Manchester: Manchester University Press.

Picon, Antoine (2007) 'French Engineers and Social Thought, 18th–20th Centuries: An Archeology of Technocratic Ideals', *History and Technology*, 23, 197–208.

Pluche, Antoine-Nöel (1733) *Spectacle de la Nature; or, Nature Display'd. Being Discourses on Such Particulars of Natural History as Were Thought Most Proper to Excite the Curiosity, and Form the Minds of Youth*, London: R. Francklin, etc.

Pohl, Stefan (2009) 'The Circulation of Energy: Thermodynamics, National Culture and Social Progress in Spain, 1868–1890', in F. Papanelopoulou, A. Nieto-Galan and E. Perdiguero (eds), *Popularizing Science and Technology in the European Periphery, 1800–2000*, Aldershot: Ashgate, 115–34.

Poirier, Jacques and Langlois, Claude (eds) (1992) *Raspail et la vulgarisation médicale*, Paris: J. Vrin.

Porter, Roy (1983) 'The Patient's View: Doing Medical History from Below', *Theory and Society*, 14, 175–98.

Porter, Roy (ed.) (1985a) *Patients and Practitioners: Lay Perceptions of Medicine in Pre-Industrial Society*, Cambridge: Cambridge University Press.

Porter, Roy (1985b) 'Lay Medical Knowledge in the Eighteenth Century: The *Gentleman's Magazine*', *Medical History*, 29, 138–68.

Porter, Roy (ed.) (1992) *The Popularization of Medicine, 1650–1850*, London: Routledge.

Porter, Roy (1994) *London: A Social History*, London: Penguin Books.

Principe, Lawrence (2013) *The Secrets of Alchemy*, Chicago, IL: University of Chicago Press.

Purbrick, Louise (ed.) (2001) *The Great Exhibition of 1851: New Interdisciplinary Essays*, Manchester: Manchester University Press.

Pursell, C.W., Jr. (ed.) (1994) *Technology in America: A History of Individuals and Ideas*, Cambridge, MA: MIT Press.

Pyenson, Lewis and Gauvin, Jean-François (eds) (2002) *The Art of Teaching Physics: The Eighteenth-Century Demonstration Apparatus of Jean Antoine Nollet*, Sillery: Editions du Septentrion.

Pyenson, Lewis and Sheets-Pyenson, Susan (1999) *Servants of Nature: A History of Scientific Institutions, Enterprises and Sensibilities*, London: Norton.

Rabeharisoa, Vololona and Callon, Michel (1999) *Le pouvoir des malades. L'Association française contre les myopathies et la recherche*, Paris: Les Presses de l'École des mines.

Rabeharisoa, Vololona and Callon, Michel (2004) 'Patients and Scientists in French Muscular Dystrophy Research', in S. Jasanoff (ed.), *States of Knowledge*, London: Routledge, 142–60.

Raichvarg, Daniel (1993) *Science et spectacle. Figures d'une rencontre*, Nice: Z Editions.

Raichvarg, Daniel (2005) *Sciences pour tous?* Paris: Découvertes Gallimard.

Raichvarg, Daniel and Jacques, Jean (1991) *Savants et ignorants: Une histoire de la vulgarisation des sciences*, Paris: Seuil.

Ramsey, Matthew (1999) 'Alternative Medicine in Modern France', *Medical History*, 43(3), 286–322.

Randall, Adrian J. (1994) 'Reinterpreting "Luddism": Resistance to New Technology in the British Industrial Revolution', in M. Bauer (ed.), *Resistance to New Technology*, Cambridge: Cambridge University Press, 57–80.

Raspail, François-Vincent (1847) *Manual de la salud, o medicina y farmacia domésticas*, Barcelona: Imprenta de la Sra. Viuda e Hijos de Mayol.

Raspail, François-Vincent (1853) *Domestic Medicine: Or, Plain Instructions in the Art of Preserving and Restoring Health by Simple and Efficient Means*, translated from 'Manuel annuaire de la santé', London: G.L. Strauss.

Raspail, François-Vincent (1876) *Biblioteca de Raspail, . . . Causas y defensas. Manual de la salud. Farmacopea y casos prácticos*, Barcelona: Luis Tasso.

Ravetz, Jerôme R. (1971) *Scientific Knowledge and Its Social Problems*, Oxford: Clarendon Press.

Ravetz, Jerôme R. (1990) *The Merger of Knowledge and Power: Essays in Critical Science*, London and New York: Mansell Publishing.

Reingold, Nathan (1985) 'Metro-Goldwyn-Mayer Meets the Atom Bomb', in T. Shinn and R. Whitley (eds), *Expository Science*, Dordrecht: Reidel, 229–45.

254 Bibliography

Rey, Roselyne (1991) 'La vulgarisation médicale au XVIIIè siècle: Le cas des dictionnaires portatifs de santé', *Revue d'histoire des sciences*, 44(3/4), 413–33.

Rhees, David J. (1993) 'Corporate Advertising, Public Relations and Popular Exhibits: The Case of Du Pont', *History and Technology*, 10, 65–75.

Rippa Bonati, Maurizio and Pardo-Tomás, José (eds) (2004) *Il teatro dei corpi. Le pitture colorate d'anatomia di Girolamo Fabrici d'Acquapendente*, Milan: Mediamed.

Risse, Gunter B., Numbers, Ronald L. and Leavitt, Judith W. (eds) (1977) *Medicine without Doctors: Home Health Care in American History*, New York: Science History.

Rivers, Isabel (ed.) (1982) *Books and Their Readers in Eighteenth-Century England*, Leicester: Leicester University Press.

Roberts, Lissa, Schaffer, Simon and Dear, Peter (eds) (2007) *The Mindful Hand: Inquiry and Invention from the Late Renaissance to Early Industrialisation*, Amsterdam: Konikliijke Nederlandse Akademie van Wetenschappen.

Roberts, Marie Mulrey and Porter, Roy (eds) (1993) *Literature and Medicine during the Eighteenth Century*, London: Routledge.

Rödder, Simone, Franzen, Martina and Weingart, Peter (eds) (2012) *The Sciences' Media Connection: Public Communication and Its Repercusions*, Dordrecht: Springer.

Romeiras, Francisco (2015) *Ciência, Prestígio e Devoção – Os Jesuítas e a Ciência em Portugal (sécs. XIX e XX)*, Cascais: Lucerna.

Rosen, George (1958, 1993) *A History of Public Health*, Baltimore, MD: Johns Hopkins University Press.

Rossi, Paolo (1996) *Les philosophes et les machines 1400–1700*, Paris: Presses universitaires de France (1st Italian edition, 1962).

Rousseau, Georges S. (1982) 'Science Books and Their Readers in the Eighteenth Century', in I. Rivers (ed.), *Books and Their Readers in Eighteenth-Century England*, Leicester: Leicester University Press, 197–237.

Rowe, Gene and Frewer, Lynn J. (2000) 'Public Participation Methods: A Framework for Evaluation', *Science, Technology and Human Values*, 25(1), 3–29.

Royal Society of London (1985) *The Public Understanding of Science*, London: Royal Society.

Rudolph, John L. (2002) *Scientists in the Classroom: The Cold War Reconstruction of American Science Education*, New York: Palgrave Macmillan.

Rudolph, John L. (2005) 'Turning Science to Account: Chicago and the General Science Movement', *Isis*, 96, 353–89.

Rudolph, John L. (2008) 'Historical Writing on Science Education: A View of the Landscape', *Studies in Science Education*, 44(1), 63–82.

Rudwick, Martin, 'Charles Darwin in London: The Integration of Public and Private Science', *Isis*, 73, 1982, 186–206.

Ruiz-Castell, Pedro (2008) *Astronomy and Astrophysics in Spain (1850–1914)*, Newcastle: Cambridge Scholar Press.

Rydell, Robert W. (1984) *All the World's a Fair: Visions of Empire at American International Expositions, 1876–1916*, Chicago, IL: University of Chicago Press.

Sastre-Juan, Jaume (2013) 'Un laboratori de divulgació tecnològica: El New York Museum of Science and Industry i la política de la museïtzació de la tecnologia als Estats Units (1912–1951)', unpublished thesis, Universitat Autònoma de Barcelona.

Schaffer, Simon (1983) 'Natural Philosophy and Public Spectacle in the Eighteenth-Century', *History of Science*, 21, 1–43.

Schaffer, Simon (1999) 'Enlightened Automata' in William Clark, Jan Golinski and S. Schaffer (eds), *The Sciences in Enlightened Europe*, Chicago, IL: Chicago University Press, 126–68.

Schiele, Bernard (2008) 'Science Museums and Science Centres', in M. Bucchi and B. Trench (eds), *Handbook of Public Communication of Science and Technology*, Abingdon: Routledge, 27–40.

Schirrmacher, Arne (ed.) (2013) *Communicating Science: National Approaches in Twentieth-Century Europe*, special issue, *Science in Context*, 26(3).

Schroeder-Gudehus, Brigitte and Rasmussen, Anne (1992) *Les fastes du progrès. Le guide des expositions universelles 1851–1992*, Paris: Flammarion.

Schroeder-Gudehus, Brigitte, Rasmussen, Anne and Bolenz, E. (eds) (1992) *La Société industrielle et ses musées: Demande sociale et choix politiques*, Paris: EAC.

Schummer, Joachim, Bensaude-Vincent, Bernadette and Van Tiggelen, Brigitte (eds) (2007) *The Public Image of Chemistry*, Singapore, London: World Scientific.

Schwartz Cowan, Ruth (1983) *More Work for Mother: The Ironies of Household Technology from the Open Hearth to the Microwave*, New York: Basic Books.

Scott, Monique (2005) 'Writing the History of Humanity: The Role of Museums in Defining Origins and Ancestors in a Transnational World', *Curator*, 48(1), 74–89.

Scott, Monique and Giusti, Ellen (2006) 'Designing Human Evolution Exhibitions: Insights from Exhibitions and Audiences', *Museums and Social Issues*, 1, 49–68.

Secord, Anne (1994) 'Science in the Pub', *History of Science*, 32(3), 269–315.

Secord, Anne (1996) 'Artisan Botany', in N. Jardine, J. Secord and E. Spary (eds), *Cultures of Natural History*, Cambridge: Cambridge University Press, 378–93.

Secord, James (1985) 'Newton in the Nursery: Tom Telescope and the Philosophy of Tops and Balls, 1761–1838', *History of Science*, 23, 127–51.

Secord, James (2000) *Victorian Sensation: The Extraordinary Publication, Reception and Secret Authorship of* Vestiges of the Natural History of Creation, Chicago, IL: University of Chicago Press.

Secord, James (2002) 'Botany on a Plate: Pleasure and the Power of Pictures in Promoting Early Nineteenth-Century Scientific Knowledge', *Isis*, 93(1), 28–57.

Secord, James (2004) 'Knowledge in Transit', *Isis*, 95, 654–72.

Secord, James (2007) 'How Scientific Conversation Became Shop Talk', in A. Fyfe and B. Lightman (eds), *Science in the Marketplace*, Chicago, IL: Chicago University Press, 23–59.

Secord, James (2014) *Visions of Science: Books and Readers at the Dawn of the Victorian Age*, Chicago, IL: University of Chicago Press.

Seed, David (2005) *A Companion to Science Fiction*, Oxford: Blackwell.

Segall, Alexander and Roberts, Lance W. (1980) 'A Comparative Analysis of Physician Estimates and Levels of Medical Knowledge among Patients', *Sociology of Health and Illness*, 2(3), 317–34.

Serrano, Elena (2012) 'The Spectacle de la nature in Eighteenth-Century Spain: From French Households to Spanish Workshops', *Annals of Science*, 69(2), 257–82.

Serrano, Elena (2013) 'Chemistry in the City: The Scientific Role of Female Societies in Late Eighteenth-Century Madrid', *Ambix*, 60(2), 139–59.

Servos, John W. (1990) *Physical Chemistry from Ostwald to Pauling: The Making of a Science in America*, Princeton, NJ: Princeton University Press.

Shapin, Steven (1990) 'Science and the Public', in R. C. Olby, G. N. Cantor, J. R. R. Christie and M. J. S. Hodge (eds), *Companion of the History of Modern Science*, 990–1007.

Shapin, Steven (1991) '"A Scholar and a Gentleman": The Problematic Identity of the Scientific Practitioner in Early Modern England', *History of Science*, 29, 279–327.

Shapin, Steven (1994) *A Social History of Truth, Civility and Science in Seventeenth-Century England*, Chicago, IL: University of Chicago Press.

256 Bibliography

Shapin, Steven (1996) *The Scientific Revolution*, Chicago, IL: University of Chicago Press.

Shapin, Steven (2010) *Never Pure: Historical Studies of Science as if It Was Produced by People with Bodies, Situated in Time, Space, Culture, and Society, and Struggling for Credibility and Authority*, Baltimore, MD: Johns Hopkins University Press.

Shapin, Steven and Barnes, Barry (1977) 'Science, Nature and Control: Interpreting Mechanics' Institutes', *Social Studies of Science*, 7, 31–74.

Shapin, Steven and Schaffer, Simon (1985, 2011) *Leviathan and the Air-Pump: Hobbes, Boyle, and the Experimental Life*, Princeton, NJ: Princeton University Press.

Sheets-Pyenson, Susan (1985) 'Popular Science Periodicals in Paris and London: The Emergence of a Low Scientific Culture, 1820–1875', *Annals of Science*, 42, 549–72.

Sheets-Pyenson, Susan (1986) 'Cathedrals of Science: The Development of Colonial Natural History Museums during the Late Nineteenth Century', *History of Science*, 25, 279–300.

Shelley, Mary Wollstonecraft (1818) *Frankenstein; or, the Modern Prometheus*, London: Lackington.

Shiele, Bernard and Koster, Emlyn (eds) (1998) *La révolution de la muséologie des sciences: Vers les musées du XXIe siècle*, Lyon: Presses universitaires de Lyon.

Shinn, Terry and Whitley, Richard (eds) (1985) *Expository Science: Forms and Functions of Popularization*, Dordrecht: Reidel.

Shorter, Edward (1985) *Beside Manners: The Troubled History of Doctors and Patients*, New York: Simon and Schuster.

Shortland, Michael (1987) 'Screen Memories: Towards a History of Psychiatry and Psychoanalysis in the Movies', *The British Journal for the History of Science*, 20(4), 421–52.

Shteir, Anne B. (1996) *Cultivating Women, Cultivating Science: Flora's Daughters and Botany in England, 1760 to 1860*, Baltimore, MD: Johns Hopkins University Press.

Shteir, Anne B. (1997) 'Gender and "Modern" Botany in Victorian England', *Osiris*, 12, 29–38.

Shuttleworth, S. (2010) *The Mind of the Child: Child Development in Literature, Science and Medicine, 1840–1900*, Oxford: Oxford University Press.

Sleigh, Charlotte (2011) *Literature and Science*, Basingstoke: Palgrave Macmillan.

Simon, Bart (2001) 'Public Science: Media Configuration and Closure in the Cold Fusion Controversy', *Public Understanding of Science*, 10, 383–402.

Simon, Josep (2011) *Communicating Physics: The Production, Circulation and Appropriation of Ganot's Textbooks in France and England, 1851–1887*, London: Pickering and Chatto.

Smith, Merritt Roe and Marx, Leo (eds) (1994) *Does Technology Drive History? The Dilemma of Technological Determinism*, Cambridge, MA: MIT Press.

Smith, Pamela H. (2006) 'Art, Science, and Visual Culture in Early Modern Europe', *Isis*, 97, 83–100.

Smith, Pamela H. and Findlen, Paula (eds) (2002) *Merchants of Marvels: Commerce, Science, and Art in Early Modern Europe*, London: Routledge.

Snow, Charles Pearce (1959) *The Two Cultures and the Scientific Revolution*, Cambridge: Cambridge University Press.

Sokal, Alan (1996a) 'Transgressing the Boundaries: Towards a Transformative Hermeneutics of Quantum Gravity', *Social Text*, 46/47, 217–52.

Sokal, Alan (1996b) 'A Physicist Experiment with Cultural Studies', *Lingua Franca*, May/June, 62–4.

Sokal, Alan and Bricmont, Jean (1999) *Intellectual Impostures*, London: Profile Books.

Sommer, Marianne (2007) *Bones and Ochre: The Curious Afterlife of the Red Lady of Paviland*, Cambridge, MA: Harvard University Press.

Sorenson, Knut H., Aune, Margrethe and Halting, Marten (2012) 'Against Linearity: On the Cultural Appropriation of Science and Technology', in M. Diekers and C. van Grote (eds), *Between Understanding and Trust*, London: Harwood.

Sorrenson, Richard J. (1993) 'Scientific Instrument Makers at the Royal Society of London, 1720–1780', unpublished thesis, Princeton University.

Spary, Emma C. (2004) 'Scientific Symmetries', *History of Science*, 42(1), 1–46.

Spurgeon, David (ed.) (1986) *La vulgarisation scientifique: Son histoire, ses succès, ses échecs*, special issue, *Impact, Science et Société*, 36(4).

Star, Susan L. and Griesemer, James R. (1989) 'Institutional Ecology, "Translations" and Boundary Objects: Amateurs and Professionals in Berkeley's Museum of Vertebrate Zoology, 1907–39', *Social Studies of Science*, 19, 387–420.

Steinmüller, Karlheinz (1997) 'Science Fiction and Science in the 20th Century', in J. Krige and D. Pestre (eds), *Science in the 20th Century*, Amsterdam: Harwood Academic, 339–60.

Sterelny, Kim (2001) *Dawkins vs. Gould: Survival of the Fittest*, Cambridge: Cambridge University Press.

Stern, M. (2004) '*Jurassic Park* and the Movable Feast of Science', *Science as Culture*, 13, 347–72.

Stewart, Larry (1992) *The Rise of Public Science: Rhetoric, Technology and Natural Philosophy in Newtonian Britain, 1660–1750*, Cambridge: Cambridge University Press.

Stirling, Andy (2008) '"Opening up" and "Closing down" Power, participation, and pluralism in the social appraisal of technology', *Science, Technology and Human Values*, 33(2), 262–92.

Stradling, David and Thorsheim, Peter (1999) 'The Smoke of Great Cities: British and American Efforts to Control Air Pollution, 1860–1914', *Environmental History*, 4(1), 6–31.

Strasser, Bruno J. (2006a) *La fabrique d'une nouvelle science: La biologie moléculaire à l'âge atomique (1945–1964)*, Florence: Leo S. Olschki.

Strasser, Bruno J. (2006b) 'A World in One Dimension: Linus Pauling, Francis Crick and the Central Dogma of Molecular Biology', *History and Philosophy of the Life Sciences*, 28, 491–512.

Stuckey, Marc and Heering, Peter (2015) 'The Philosophical Works of Ludwik Fleck and Their Potential Meaning for Teaching and Learning Science', *Science and Education*, 24, 381–98.

Suton, Geoffrey (1985) *Science for a Polite Society: Gender, Culture and the Demonstration of Enlightenment*, Boulder, CO: Westview Press.

Suvin, Darko (1979) *Metamorphoses of Science Fiction: On the Poetics and History of a Literary Genre*, New Haven, CT: Yale University Press.

Tarr, Joel A. (1996) *The Search for the Ultimate Sink: Urban Pollution in Historical Perspective*, Akron, OH: University of Akron Press.

Taschwer, Klaus (1997) 'People's Universities in a Former Metropolis: Interfaces between the Social and Spatial Organization of Popular Adult Education in Vienna, 1890–1930', in B.J. Hake, T. Steele (eds), *Intellectuals, Activists and Reformers: Studies of Cultural, Social and Educational Reform Movements in Europe, 1890–1930*, Leeds: Leeds Studies in Continuing Education, 175–202.

Taub, Liba (1998) 'On the Role of Museums in History of Science, Technology and Medicine', *Endeavour*, 22, 41–3.

Taylor, Katie (2009) 'Learning with Dissectable Paper Globe Kits', *Explore Whipple Collections*, Cambridge: Whipple Museum of the History of Science.

258 Bibliography

Terral, Mary (2000) 'Fashionable Readers of Natural Philosophy', in Nick Jardine and Marina Frasca-Spada (eds), *Books and the Sciences in History*, Cambridge: Cambridge University Press.

Teysseire, Daniel (1995) *La médecine du peuple de Tissot à Raspail: 1750–1850*, Créteil: Conseil général du Val de Marne.

Thomas, Geoffrey and Durant, John (1987) 'Why Should We Promote the Public Understanding of Science?', *Scientific Literary Papers*, 1, 1–14.

Thurk, Jessica and Fine, Gary Alan (2003) 'The Problem of Tools: Technology and the Sharing of Knowledge', *Acta Sociologica*, 46(2), 107–17.

Timmermann, Carsten (2001) 'Rationalizing "Folk Medicine" in Interwar Germany: Faith, Business, and Science at "Dr. Madaus & Co."', *Social History of Medicine*, 14(3), 459–82.

Tissandier, Gaston (1883) *Popular Scientific Recreations in Natural Phylosophy, Astronomy, Geology, Physics, Chemistry, etc., Translated and Enlarged from 'Les récreations scientifiques' of Gaston Tissandier (Editor of 'La Nature'). Profusely Illustrated*, London, New York: Ward, Lock, and Co., Warwick House (French edition, 1877).

Topham, Jonathan (1992) 'Science and Popular Education in the 1930s: The Role of Bridgewater Treatises', *British Journal for the History of Science*, 25, 397–430.

Topham, Jonathan (2000) 'Scientific Publishing and the Reading of Science in Nineteenth-Century Britain', *Studies in the History and Philosophy of Science*, 1(4), 559–612.

Topham, Jonathan (2004) '*The Mirror of Literature, Amusement and Instruction* and Cheap Miscellanies in Early Nineteenth-Century Britain', in Geoffrey Cantor et al. (eds), *Science in the Nineteenth-Century Periodicals*, Cambridge: Cambridge University Press, 37–66.

Topham, Jonathan (2009a) 'Introduction: Historicizing "Popular Science"', *Isis*, 100, 310–18.

Topham, Jonathan (2009b) 'Rethinking the History of Science Popularization/Popular Science', in Faidra Papanelopoulou, Agustí Nieto-Galan and Enrique Perdiguero (eds), *Popularizing Science and Technology in the European Periphery, 1800–2000*, Aldershot: Ashgate, 1–10.

Travis, Anthony S. (1993) *The Rainbow Makers: The Origins of the Synthetic Dyestuffs Industry in Western Europe*, London and Toronto: Lehigh Associated University Press.

Treitel, Corinna (2000) 'The Culture of Knowledge in the Metropolis of Science: Spiritualism and Liberalism in Fin-de-Siècle Berlin', in Constantin Goschler (ed.), *Wissenschaft und Öffentlichkeit in Berlin, 1870–1930/Science for the Public in Berlin, 1870–1930*, Wiesbaden: Franz Steiner Verlag.

Tucker, Jeniffer (2006) 'The Historian, the Picture and the Archive', *Isis*, 97, 111–20.

Turner, Frank Miller (1974) *Between Science and Religion: The Reaction to Scientific Naturalism in Late Victorian Britain*, New Haven, CT: Yale University Press.

Turner, Frank Miller (1980) 'Public Science in Britain, 1880–1919', *Isis*, 71, 589–608.

Turner, Gerard L.E. (2005) 'The Impact of Hooke's *Micrographia* and Its Influence on Microscopy', in P. Kent and A. Chapman (eds), *Robert Hooke and the English Renaissance*, Leominster, MA: Gracewing Press, 124–45.

Turner, Stephen (2001) 'What Is the Problem with Experts?', *Social Studies of Science*, 31(1), 123–49.

Udías, Agustín (2003) *Searching the Heavens and the Earth: The History of Jesuit Observatories*, Dordrecht, Boston: Kluwer.

Van Helden, Albert and Hankins, Thomas (eds) (1994) 'Instruments', *Osiris*, 9.

Van Wyhe, John (2002) 'The Authority of Human Nature: The *Schädellehre* of Franz Joseph Gall', *British Journal for the History of Science*, 35, 17–42.

Van Wyhe, John (2004a) *Phrenology and the Origins of Victorian Naturalism*, Ashgate: Aldershot.

Van Wyhe, John (2004b) 'Was Phrenology a Reform Science? Towards a New Generalization for Phrenology', *History of Science*, 42(3), 313–31.

Van Wyhe, John (2007) 'The Diffusion of Phrenology through Public Lecturing', in A. Fyfe and B. Lightman (eds), *Science in the Marketplace*, Chicago, IL: Chicago University Press, 60–96.

Verne, Jules (1867) *From the Earth to the Moon*, London: Sampson Low and Co. (1st French edition, 1865).

Verne, Jules (1871) *A Journey to the Centre of the Earth*, London: Griffith and Farran (1st French edition, 1864).

Vicedo, Marga (2012) 'Introduction: The Secret Lives of Textbooks', *Isis*, 103, 83–7.

Vincent, Levinus (1719) *Description abrégé des planches qui représentent les cabinets et quelques-unes des curiosités contenues dans le théâtre des merveilles de la nature*, Harlem: Aux dépens de l'auteur.

Volti, Rudi (1996) 'A Century of Automobility', *Technology and Culture*, 37, 663–85.

Von Hippel, Eric (2005) *Democratizing Innovation*, Cambridge, MA: MIT Press.

Wachelder, Joseph (2003) 'Democratizing Science: Various Routes and Visions of Dutch Science Shops', *Science, Technology and Human Values*, 28(2), 244–73.

Wallis, Roy (ed.) (1979) *On the Margins of Science: The Social Construction of Rejected Knowledge*, Keele: University of Keele.

Waquet, Françoise (2003) *Parler comme un livre. L'oralité et le savoir (XVIe–XXe siècle)*, Paris: Albin Michel.

Waring, Stephen P. (1991) *Taylorism Transformed: Scientific Management Theory since 1945*, Chapel Hill, NC: University of North Carolina Press.

Warner, Michael (2002a) *Publics and Counterpublics*, New York: Zone Books.

Warner, Michael (2002b) 'Publics and Counterpublics', *Public Culture*, 14(1), 49–90.

Warwick, Andrew (2003) *Masters of Theory: Cambridge and the Rise of Mathematical Physics*, Chicago, IL: University of Chicago Press.

Weber, Robert J. and Perkins, David N. (eds) (1992) *Inventive Minds: Creativity in Technology*, Oxford: Oxford University Press.

Weiner, Dora Bierer (1968) *Raspail, Scientist and Reformer*, New York, London: Columbia University Press, 1968.

Weingart, Peter (1999) 'Scientific Expertise and Political Accountability: Paradoxes of Science in Politics', *Science and Public Policy*, 26(3), 151–61.

Weingart, Peter (2001a) *Die Studen der Wahrheit? Vom Verhältnis der Wissenschaft und Medien in der Wissensgesellschaft*, Weilerwist: Velbrück.

Weingart, Peter (2001b) *Die Wissenschaft der Öffentlichkeit. Essays zum Verhältnis von Wissenschaft, Medien und Öffentlichkeit*, Weilerwist: Velbrück.

Weingart, Peter (2007) 'Chemists and Their Craft in Fiction Films', in J. Schummer, B. Bensaude-Vincent and B. Van Tiggelen (eds), *The Public Image of Chemistry*, Singapore, London: World Scientific, 81–96.

Wessely, Christina (2006) 'Karriere einer Weltanschauung. Die Welteislehre 1894–1945', *Zeitgeschichte*, 6, 3–22.

Wessely, Christina (2008) *'Künstliche Tiere'. Zoologische Gärten und urbane Moderne. Wien und Berlin 1840–1910*, Berlin: Kadmos.

Westfall, Richard (1980) *Never at Rest: A Biography of Isaac Newton*, Cambridge: Cambridge University Press.

Westfall, Richard (1993) *The Life of Issac Newton*, Cambridge: Cambridge University Press.

260 Bibliography

Whitaker, Katie (1996) 'The Culture of Curiosity', in N. Jardine, J. Secord and E. Spary (eds), *Cultures of Natural History*, Cambridge: Cambridge University Press, 75–90.

White, Stephen K. (ed.) (1995) *The Cambridge Companion to Habermas*, Cambridge: Cambridge University Press.

Williams, Raymond (1977) *Marxism and Literature*, Oxford: Oxford University Press.

Willis, Martin (ed.) (2014) *Literature and Science*, Basingstoke: Palgrave Macmillan.

Winter, Alison (1991) 'Etheral Epidemic: Mesmerism and the Introduction of Inhalation Anaesthesia in Early Victorian London', *Social History of Medicine*, 4, 1–27.

Winter, Alison (1994) 'Mesmerism and Popular Culture', *History of Science*, 32(3), 317–43.

Wise, Norton (1988) 'Mediating Machines', *Science in Context*, 2(1), 77–113.

Wise, Norton (2006) 'Making Visible', *Isis*, 97, 75–82.

Withers, Charles W.J. (1998) 'Towards a History of Geography in the Public Sphere', *History of Science*, 36, 45–78.

Wynne, Brian (1987) *Risk Management and Hazardous Wastes: Implementation and the Dialectics of Credibility*, Dortdrecht: Springer.

Wynne, Brian (1991) 'Knowledges in Context', *Science, Technology and Human Values*, 16(1), 111–21.

Wynne, Brian (1995) 'Public Understanding of Science', in S. Jasanoff, G. E. Markle, J. C. Petersen and T. Pinch (eds), *Handbook of Science and Technology Studies*, London: SAGE, 361–88.

Yanni, Carla (1996) 'Divine Display or Secular Science: Defining Nature at the Natural History Museum in London', *Journal of the Society of Architectural Historians*, 55, 276–99.

Yearley, Steven (1995) 'The Environmental Challenge to Science Studies', in S. Jasanoff, G. E. Markle, J. C. Petersen and T. Pinch (eds), *Handbook of Science and Technology Studies*, London: SAGE, 457–79.

Yeo, Eileen and Yeo, Stephen (eds) (1981) *Popular Culture and Class Conflict 1590–1914: Explorations in the History of Labour and Leisure*, Chichester: Harvester Press.

Yeo, Richard (1991) 'Reading Encyclopaedias: Science and the Organization of Knowledge in British Dictionaries of Arts and Sciences, 1730–1850', *Isis*, 82, 24–49.

Yeo, Richard (2001) *Encyclopaedic Visions: Scientific Dictionaries and Enlightenment Culture*, Cambridge: Cambridge University Press.

Yoxen, Edward (1985) 'Speaking out about Competition. An Essay on "the Double Helix" as Popularisation', in T. Shinn and R. Whitley (eds), *Expository Science*, Dordrecht: Reidel, 163–81.

Zilsel, Edgar (1941–2) 'The Sociological Roots of Science', *American Journal of Sociology*, 47, 544–62.

Ziman, John (1968) *Public Knowledge: An Essay Concerning the Social Dimension of Science*, Cambridge: Cambridge University Press.

Zimmerman, Corinne, Bisanz, Gay L., Bisanz, Jeffrey, Klein, Juliette S. and Klein, Peter (2001) 'Science at the Supermarket: A Comparison on What Appears in the Popular Press, Experts' Advice to Readers, and What Students Want to Know', *Public Understanding of Science*, 10, 37–58.

Zola, Émile (1893) *The Experimental Novel, and Other Essays,* New York: Cassell Publishing, Paris: Charpentier (French edition, 1881).

INDEX

A for Andromeda (Hoyle) 176
AACH (American Academy for Communication in Healthcare) 207–8
AAAS (American Association for the Advancement of Science) 156
ACS (American Chemical Society) 5–6
academics: artisan resistance to 152–3; in industry 154–8
Académie des sciences 71, 81, 83, 100, 150, 152, 175, 217
activists: AIDS 208; anti-GMO 199, *200*, 201; environmental 205, *206*; examples of 205; for peace 202
Adorno, Theodor 2, 11, 15, 77
Les affiches de Paris (newspaper) 71
Agassi, Joseph 1
Agricola, Georgius (George Bauer) 26–7
air pollution 162
air pump, Boyle's 148, *149*
AL-288-1 fossil (Lucy) 182–3, *183*
Alchemia (Libavius) 121
alchemical books 26–7
alchemy, 15, 26–7, 85, 147
Aldersey-Williams, Hugh 181
Aldrovandi, Ulisse 53, 223
Algarotti, Francesco 30
Allaby, Michael 178
Ampère, André-Marie 125
alternative medicine: development of 89–91; Raspail system 87–8; varieties of 86–7
amateurs: astronomy and 92–3, 95, *95*; botany and 95–6; meteorology and 93–4;

recreation and 98; as science popularisers 91–2; status of 96–7
American Academy for Communication in Healthcare (AACH) 207–8
American Chemical Society 5–6
anaesthetics *89*, 89
anatomical illustrations 27–8, *29*
anatomy theatres 68–70, *69*
ancien régime 14, 34, 63, 96
Ancient Greece 145
animal magnetism 81–4, *82*
L'Année scientifique et industrielle (Figuier) 74
anti-GMO activists 199, *200*, 201
appropriation, of scientific knowledge 221
Arago, François 100–2, *101*, 104–5, 175, 217
Archimedes 146
The Architecture of Molecules (Pauling) 179
Aristotle 119, 127, 145
Arrhenius, Svante 124–5
Artificial Intelligence: A.I. (film) 76
artificialia 54, 55
artisans: in industrial culture 158–9; role of 150–4, *151*
Asilomar Conference 203
Asimov, Isaac 4, 45, 47
Astronomical Dialogues between a Gentleman and a Lady (Harris) 28
Astronomie populaire (Flammarion) 40
astronomy: amateurs and 92–5, *95*; bridging science/religion 106; Carl Sagan and 111; media science about 175–8
Atapuerca archaeological site 184–5

262 Index

athenaeums movement 19, 138–40
Australopithecus afarensis 182–3, *183*
automata xvi, 52, 56, 145
automobiles 167–8
AZT testing 208

BAAS (British Association for the Advancement of Science) 96, 135
Bachelard, Gaston xvi, 110
Baker, Charles C. 188
Barba, Álvaro Alonso 146
Barker, Joseph 36
Barthes, Roland 217
BASF 157
Beck, Ulrich 210, 212
Bell, Graham 58, 167
Benedetti, Alessandro 68
Berg, Paul 202–3
Bernard, Claude 43, 87, 102
Berthollet, Claude-Louis 152
Berzelius, Jons Jakob 125
Better Things for Better Living, through Chemistry (Du Pont) 164
Bibliothèque des merveilles 40
Bienvenue, François 71
Big Bang theory 175–6
Biochemistry 19, 45, 107, 132–3
Biot, Jean-Baptiste 100–1
Biringuccio, Vannoccio 26–7
Black, Joseph *122*, 122
The Black Cloud (Hoyle) 176
Blanchard, Jean-Pierre 143
Blanchard, Sophie 143–5, *144*
Blum, Léon 65
Bookchin, Murray 204
books: chemistry textbooks 128–33; cycle of 24–5; of secrets 26; *see also* printed science
Borel, Pierre 55
botanical gardens 63, 66–7, 69, 137
botany 94–7, 107, 122
Bowler, Peter 41
Boyle, Robert 10, 148
Brahe, Tycho 25–6
Brande, Thomas 72
breast cancer treatments 209
Bricmont, Jean 6–7
Bridgewater Treatises 105, 133
British Association for the Advancement of Science (BAAS) 96, 135
British Broadcasting Corporation (BBC) 75, 175–6, 181
British Committee on the Safety of Medicines 208

British Journal of Psychiatry 180
British Mechanics' Institutes (MIs) 133–4
Broglie, Louis de 110
Broman, Thomas 16
Brotéria 107
Brougham, Henry 133–4
Bucchi, Massimiano 197
Buchan, William 32–3
Büchner, Ludwig 106
buckyball molecule 181–2
Buen, Odón de 105
Burroughs, Edgar Rice 109
Buscaren, Juliette 74
Bush, President George W. 191
Buxton, Richard 96

cabinets de curiosités 17, 53–5, *54*, 60–1, 94, 137
Callon, Michel 213–14
calorimeter 71, 150
Calzolari, Francesco 53
carbon dioxide emissions 191
Carson, Rachel 5, 190, 212
Cercle de la presse scientifique 99
Chadwick, Edwin 161
Chambers, Ephraim 33
Chambers, Robert 36
Chaplin, Charles 158
Châtelet, Émile du 30
charitable handbooks 27
Chartier, Roger 219
The Cheese and the Worms (Ginzburg) 23
chemistry: applied to industry 157–8; public experiments in 71; quantum mechanics applied to 179; science shops 202; teaching practices of 122–6; textbooks 128–33; user's perspective of 164–6, *165*
Chernobyl 203
children, scientific literature for 47–8
cinema, theatrical science in 74–7
circulation of knowledge 219, 221 (see 'knowledge in transit')
Cité des sciences et de l'industrie 65
Civilization and Its Discontents (Freud) 1, 2
classroom science: education/scientific culture 119–21; learning process and 118–19; overview of 18–19; social control/popularisation in 133–9; teachers/students 121–7; textbooks for 127–33
climate change: activists 205, *206*; media coverage of 190–3
Close, Frank 189
cognition, in learning process 118

Index **263**

cold fusion 186–90, *187*
collective thought (*Denkkollectiv*) 11–13
Collins, Harry 3
Combe, Georges 37–8, 84
commonality, of literature and science 41, 43–8
communication: patient-doctor 207–9; regarding risk potential 210–11; of science 219–20
Comte, Auguste 92–3, 100, 128
Condorcet, marquis de 83
Conseil de salubrité 161
Conservatoire nationale des arts et métiers 60
Constitution of Man Considered in Relation to External Objects (Combe) 37–8, 85
consumers, of technology 163–9
The Consumer's Good Chemical Guide (Emsley) 112, 166
continuum of genres 218
Conversations in Chemistry (Marcet) 128
Conway, Erik 191
Cooter, Roger xi, 221, 222
Copenhagen Climate Change Conference 192–3
Copernicus 9, 23, 24, 25, 27, 30, 48, 223
coproduction of knowledge model 214
cosmology 23, 41, 175–6, 220
Così fan tutte (opera) 83
Cospiano Museum 56
Coulomb, Charles-Augustin 71
counterhegemony 14, 94, 219
Cours de philosophie positive (Comte) 92
Course de Chymie (Lémery) 121
Crichton, Michael 76, 192, 223
Crick, Francis 178–9
Crombie, Alistair 146–7
Crowther, James Gerald 111
Crystal Palace xi, 56, 58
Cullen, William 122
cultural hegemony i, xii, 10, 14, 18, 67, 94, 104–8, 113, 136, 220–1
curiosities, collection of 53–5, *54*
Curl, Robert 181–2

da Vinci, Leonardo 146
D'Alembert, Jean 33–4, 82
dangers, of scientific development 210–13
Darcet, Jean 130
Darnton, Robert 24, 34, 48, 219–20
Darwin, Charles xi, 9, 24, 34–6, 38–9, 43–4, 48, 91, 97, 105, 112–3, 136, 176, 182–4, 223
Darwinism 17, 61, 104–5, 186

Das Unbehagen in der Kultur/ see Civilization and Its Discontents
Davy, Humphrey 72
Dawkins, Richard 112, 177
DDT 5, 164, 190, 210
De Humani Corporis Fabrica (Vesalius) 25, 28, 68
De Revolutionibus Orbium Celestium (Copernicus) 25
The Death of Nature: Women, Ecology, and the Scientific Revolution (Merchant) 177
deficit model legacy: crisis in 197–8; criticism of 217; in medical profession 207; PUS movement and 3–10
della Porta, Giambattista 26
democratic science: health issues and 206–10; overview of 20, 197–8; participatory turn and 198–205, *200*, *206*; risk/uncertainty and 210–13
The Demon-Haunted World (Sagan) 111
Denkkollectiv see collective thought
Desaguliers, John-Théophile 30
Descartes, René 65
Deville, Henri Sainte-Claire *131*
Dialectic of Enlightenment (Adorno and Horkeimer) 2
Dickens, Charles 47, 72, 143
Dickson, David 10
dictionaries 33–4
Dictionnaire universel des arts et sciences (Furetière) 33
Diderot, Denis 33–4, 81, 151–2
Die Natur 39
Discourse de la méthode (Descartes) 65
Discourse sur l'esprit positif (Comte) 128
distillation 26–7, 147
distortion, in popularisation 108–13
DNA (deoxyribonucleic acid) molecules: ethics of recombinant 202–3; media coverage of 179
documentaries, science popularisation via 75–6
Domestic Medicine (Buchan) 33
'The Dominant View of Popularization' (Hilgartner) 9, 221
Doolittle, W. Ford 177
Dostoyevsky, Fiodor 59
The Double Helix (Watson and Crick) 178–9
Duby, Georges 217
Dumas, Jean Baptiste 125
Du Pont chemical company 164, 166
Dyson, Frank 110

264 Index

Eamon, William 26
EBCM (Environmental Breast Cancer Movement) 209
Echegaray, José 106
École centrale des arts et manufactures 125
École des mines 152
École des ponts et chaussées 152
École du génie 152
École polytechnique 152
Edgerton, David 164
Edison, Thomas A. 58, 163, 167
education, scientific culture and 119–21
Einstein, Albert 109–11
electricity 41, 44, 52, 58, 70–1, 81–2, 100–1, 106, 127, 154, 158, 166–7
The Elements (Emsley) 112
elite culture 219–20
Emsley, John 111–12, 166
encyclopaedias 33–4
Encyclopédie française 109
Encyclopédie méthodique 34
Encyclopédie ou dictionnaire raisonné des sciences, arts et métiers (Diderot and D'Alembert) 33–4, 82, 150–1, *151*
Encyclopédie theólogique (Migne) 107
Entretiens sur la pluralité des mondes (Fontenelle) 30, *31*, 32
Entstehung und Entwicklung einer wissenschaftlichen Tatsache (Fleck) 11
Environmental Breast Cancer Movement (EBCM) 209
environmental concerns 190–3, 205, *206*
Epitome (Vesalius) 25
Ercker, Lazarus 26–7
Essais scientifiques (Meunier) 104
ether, anaesthetic use of 89, *89*
Evelyn, John 54–5, 68–9
evolutionary psychology 185–6
evolutionism 34–6, 38, 104
Exhibition of Smoke-Preventing Technology 162
exhibitions, of scientific development 55–9, *57, 66*
experience, in learning process 118
expert-lay relationships: considering scientific risks 210–13; media and 193–4; mediators in 17–20; models of 213–14; science museums and 66–7; scientific progress and 10–17; women and 96
Exploratorium (San Francisco) 65
Expository Science: Forms and Functions of Popularization (Whitley & Shinn) 219

Fabricius, Hieronymus 68
Faraday, Michael 72, *73*, 92, 128

Farrington, Benjamin 145
Fasciculo di Medicina 27–8
Feenberg, Andrew 169
Ferrer Guàrdia, Francesc 135–6
Feuilletons scientifiques (Figuier) 74
Feynman, Richard 126–7
Figuier, Luis *see also Les merveilles de la science* (Figuier) 74, 102, 103, 143
films *see* cinema, theatrical science in First International Congress on Recombinant DNA Molecules 203
Flammarion, Camille: astronomy and 92, 93; as science populariser 40, 47, 102–3, 105–6
Fleck, Ludwik: esoteric/exoteric circles of 10, 218–19, 223–4; on learning process 118; life/work of 10–12
Fleischmann, Martin 186–90, *187*
Flower, William Henry 62
folklore 94
Fontenelle, Louis-Bernard de 30, *31*, 32
Foreman, Dave 201
Foucault, Michel 14, 18, 121, 133, 208, 217
Frankenstein (Shelley) 44
Franklin, Benjamin 56, 74, 81, 127
French Muscular Dystrophy Association 209
Freud, Sigmund 1–2
From the Earth to the Moon (Verne) 45
Fuller, Richard Buckminster 181
fullerene molecule 181–2
Fyfe, Aileen 221

Gai, Moshe 188
Gaia: A New Look at Life in Earth (Lovelock) 173, 177
Gaia hypothesis 173, 177–8
Galilei, Galileo 148
Gall, Franz-Joseph 36–7
Ganot, Adolphe 129
Gazette de santé (journal) 86–7
General Chemistry (Pauling) 133
Genesis and Development of a Scientific Fact (Fleck) 11
gender 16, 67, 143.4, 177, 183–6
genetics: media coverage of 179–81; responsible research in 202
geography 136
Gieryn, Thomas F. 213
Ginzburg, Carlo 23
Glazial-Kosmogonie (Hoerbiger) 108
global warming 190–3, 205, *206*
Gobelins manufacture 153
The God Delusion (Dawkins) 112
Golding, William 177

Goldsmith, Edward 177
Gomis, Cels 94
Gore, Al 76, 190–3
Gould, Stephen Jay 112
Gramsci, Antonio 10–15, 219, 221–3
Gran Dolina cave 184
Great Exhibition of London 56–9, *57*, 60–1
The Greening of Mars (Lovelock and Allaby) 178
Grégoire, Henri 56
Grollier de Servière, Nicholas 55
Gross, Paul 6, 198
The Guardian (newspaper) 192
Guericke, Otto von 148, *149*

Habermas, Jürgen 10–1, 15–17, 218, 221, 224
Hachette, Louis 40
Hahnemann, Samuel 86
Handlin, Oscar 4
hands-on nature study movement 137
Harris, John 28
health books 27–8, 32–3
health issues: dangers of chemicals 166; democratisation in 206–10; reforms of industrial culture 160–3
hegemony, Gramsci and 14–15, 222 (see Gramsci and cultural hegemony)
Hellot, Jean 152–3
Herschell, John 97
heterodox science: alternative medicine 86–91; integrating orthodoxy 104–8; mesmerism 81–4, *82*; overview of 18, 85–6; phrenology 83, *84*, 85; popularisation/distortion/simplification 108–13; popularisers and 99–104; professionals/amateurs 91–9
Hilgartner, Stephen 9–10, 77, 108, 217, 221
Hippocratic School 119
Historia corporis humani, sive Anatomice (Beneditti) 68
Hobhouse, Sir John 35
Hobsbawn, Eric 2
Hoerbiger, Hanns 108–9
Hoffmann, August Wilhelm 124
Holton, Gerald 5
homeopathic medicine 6, 86, 89–90
Homo antecessor 184–5
Homo floresiensis 182
Homo neanderthalensis 184
Homo sapiens 184
Hooke, Robert 28
Horkheimer, Max 2, 15, 77
hot air balloons 143–5
How the Mind Works (Pinker) 185

Hoyle, Fred 175–6
Huff, Toby 119
Huggins, Robert 188
Hulme, Mike 193
human genome sequencing 181
Humboldt, Alexander von 102
Humboldt, Wilhelm von 123
Huxley, Thomas 72, 156
hydropathy 86

Ibérica 107–8
An Inconvenient Truth (Gore) 76, 190
industrial culture: academic science-based 156–8; artisans' role in 158–9; development of 154–5, *155*; health reforms of 160–3; opposition to 159–60
industrial museums 60–1
Inquiry into the Sanitary Conditions of the Labouring Population of Great Britain (Chadwick) 161
intellectuals 4, 34, 106, 166, 217, 120–3; hegemony and 14–15
interactive science museums 65–6
International Exhibitions 57–9, 64, 66, 73
International Year of Geophysics 98
inventors, in technological culture 163–9
Isis (journal) 220

Jardin des apothicaires 122
Jardin du roi 122
Jesuit scientific journals 107–8
Johanson, Donald 183
Journal of American Medical Association 208
Jurassic Park (film) 77

Kaczynski, Theodor 201
Keaton, Buster 158
Kloster, Knut 177
knowledge: power and 14–15; in transit 220–1; tacit 10–1, 26, 93, 118, 152, 157–8; lay 24, 66, 109, 198–9, 203, 214, 220, 222
Kosmos (Humboldt) 102
Kraft-Ebing, Richard von 162
Kroto, Harold 181–2
Kubrick, Stanley 76
Kuhn, Thomas 12, 24, 120–1, 127, 218

laboratory: science 5; medicine 43; university 65, 137; chemistry 97
La lluna segons lo poble (Gomis) 94
The Land That Time Forgot (Burroughs) 109
Langevin, Paul 65
Langlebert, J. 128
Laplace, Pierre-Simon 97
Laurent, Auguste 124–5

266 Index

Lavoisier, Antoine-Laurent 70–1, 83, 149–50
Le Verrier, Urban 102
Leakey, Richard 183, *183*
Leblanc, Nicolas 154–5
Lectures on Diet and Regime (Willich) 33
Lémery, Nicolas 121
Levitt, Norman 6, 198
Lewenstein, Bruce 189
Lexicon Technicum (Harris) 28
Libavius, Andreas 121
Libri, Giuglielmo 100
Liebig, Justus von 123–4, *124*, 157
Lightman, Bernard 221
Linné, Carl von 96
Lister, Joseph 89
literature, science in 41, 43–8
Lomborg, Bjørn 191–2
Lovelock, James 173, 176–8
Lucy (AL-288-1 fossil) 182–3
Luddism 159–60, 20, 207
Ludwik Fleck Prize 13
Lyotard, François 7

Macquer, Pierre-Joseph 152–3
macromolecules 179
Maddox, John 188
Magia naturalis (della Porta) 26
Mallove, Eugene 189
Malveine (Perkin's mauve) 124
Manchester Association for the Prevention of Smoke 162
manufactures *151–4*
Mantegazza, Paolo 105
Manuel annuaire de la santé (Raspail) 87
Marat, Jean-Paul 83
Marcet, Jean 128
Margulis, Lynn 178
Martin, Benjamin 28
Marx, Leo 2
Marxism 13, 15–6, 111, 145, 204, 219
Mechanics' Institutes (MIs) 133, 139
media science: climate change and 190–3; cold fusion and 186–90, *187*; effects/role of 173–5; molecular biology and 178–82; overview of 19–20; palaeoanthropology and 182–6, *183*; scientific authority and 193–4; stars/planets and 175–8
mediator(s) 3, 18, 20, 94, 96, 99–100, 130, 140, 160
medical books 27–8, 32–3
medical issues, democratisation in 206–10
Mendeleiev, Dimitri 125–6
Menocchio (Domenico Scandella) 23–4
Mercer, John 157

Merchant, Carolyn 177
Merchants of Doubt (Oreskes and Conway) 191
Les merveilles de la science (Figuier): anaesthesia in *89*; animal magnetism in *82*; experimental physics in *70*; François Arago in *101*; front cover of *42*; Joseph Black in *122*; power of air pumps in *149*; Sophie Blanchard's death in *144*; steam boats in *155*
Mesmer, Franz Anton 81–4
mesmerism 81–4, *82*, 89
metallurgy 26–7
meteorology 93–4
Metzger, Hélène 109–10
Meunier, Victor 103–4
Meyerson, Émile 110
Micrographia (Hooke) 28
Migne, Jacques-Paul 107
Mind in the Modern World (Trilling) 5
Modern Times (film) 158
molecular biology: ethics in 202–3; media coverage of 178–82
Monardes, Nicolás 146
Monsanto company 201
Montgolfier brothers 143–4, 152
The Moral Animal (Wright) 185
Morris, William 59, 159
The Most Beautiful Molecule: The Discovery of the Buckyball (Aldersey-Williams) 181
motorcycles 167–8
Müller, Paul 190
Mumford, Lewis 159
Musée d'histoire naturelle 61, *62*, 96
Museographia 56
Museum of Science and Industry 64
museums *see* science museums
Mussolini, Benito 13

nanotechnology risks and benefits 203–4
natural history museums 60–4 *62*, 98, 137
The Natural History of Selborne (White) 97
naturalia 55, 61
Nature (journal) 3–4, 10, 188–9, 193
The Nature of the Chemical Bond (Pauling) 179
The Nature of the Universe (Hoyle) 175
Nelkin, Dorothy 205
Neresini, Federico 197
Neumann, Franz Ernst 126
New England Journal of Medicine 194
New Guide of Health or Botanic Family Physician (Thomson) 86
New Scientist (magazine) 10
newspapers, science in 39–40

Newton, Isaac 24, 28, 30, 148
Newtonianism 16–7, 28, 30, 48, 71
Nickelius, Caspar Friedrich 56
Nollet, Jean-Antoine 52, *70*, 70–1, 123
notebooks, role of 127–33
Nowotny, Helga 7
Noxious Vapours Abatement Association 162
nuclear energy: cold fusion vs. 186–90; risks/benefits of 202–3

Objects, Advantages and Pleasures of Science (Brougham) 134
occasionnels 27
Oporinus, Johann 28
Oppenheimer, Franck 65
orality, in classroom science 129
Oreskes, Naomi 191
Orfila, Mateu 87
Orientalism (Said) 224
Origin of Species (Darwin) 34–6, 38
orthodoxy, in public sphere 104–8
Osborn, Henry 109
Ostwald, Wilhelm 125, 131
Owen, Richard 62
Owen, Robert 136

Pacey, Arnold 168
palaeoanthropology 182–6, *183*
Palais de la découverte 64–5
Panckoucke, Charles-Joseph 34
Participatory Approaches in Science and Technology (PATH) 203
participatory turn: in medical/health issues 206–10; risk/uncertainty requiring 210–13; in scientific research 198–205, *200*, *206*
Pasteur, Louis 103, 130
patient(s) xiv, 18, 20, 32–3, 81–90, 162, 179, 199, 205–10, 218, 222, 224
Patient Education and Counseling magazine 208
Pauling, Linus *132*, 132–3, 179–80
The Penny Mechanic (magazine) 105–6
people-centred technology 168–9
Pepper, John H. 73
periodical table of chemical elements 125–6
periodicals, scientific 39
Perkin, William Henry 124
Perkin's mauve (Malveine) 124
Perrin, Jean 65
Pestre, Dominique 7
Philadelphia International Exhibition of 1876 66

philosophers, technological creativity of 145–50
Philosophical Transactions (journal) 149
philosophy of demonstration 52–3
phrenology 36–8, *37*, 83, *84*, 85
physics: public experiments in 70–1; teaching practices of 123, 126–7; textbooks 129, 131–2
Piemontese, Alessio 26
Pinker, Steven 185
planets, media science and 175–8
plastics, attitudes towards 166
Plato 112, 119, 145
Playfair, Lyon 157
Pluche, Antoine-Noël 32
La pluralité des mondes habités (Flammarion) 102
Pons, B. Stanley 186–90, *187*
popular culture 219–20
popularisation: of astronomy 92–5, *95*; changing status of 99–104; cinema for 75–7; distortion/simplification in 108–13; experts' concerns about 217–18; of science 4–10, 39–40
positivism 6, 11, 135, 138
Pouchet, Félix 103
power, knowledge and 14–16
Practical Observations upon the Education of the People (Brougham) 133–4
Priestly, Joseph 71
Principia Mathematica Philosophia Naturalis (Newton) 24, 25, 28, 30
Principles of Chemistry (Mendeleiev) 126
The Principles of Scientific Management (Taylor) 158
printed science: cycle of books and 24–5; encyclopaedias/dictionaries 33–4; historic iconic texts of 24; literature and 41, 43–8; Menocchio and 23–4; Newtonianism and 28, 30–2; overview of 17; popular paradigms 34–8; public accessibility in 25–8; publishing 38–41, *42*; self-help manuals 32–3
The Prison Notebooks (Gramsci) 13–14
Prometheus myth 154
propaganda, science education as 136
pseudoscience 218
Psychopathia Sexualis (Kraft-Ebing) 162
public debate model 214
public education model 214
public health policies 160–2
public lectures 40, 72–3, *73*, 83, 91, 103, 106, 121
public participation in scientific research 198–205, *200*, *206*

268 Index

public sphere: heterodoxy and orthodoxy in 104–8; of industrial culture 154–63; participatory turn and 198–205, *206*; scientific activity and 15–17; technology in 168–9
Public Understanding of Science (PUS) movement 3–10, 15, 65, 197–9, 202, 205
publishing, of printed science 38–41
Pumphrey, Stephen 221
Pythagorean School 119

Quaderni del carcere (Gramsci) 13–14
quantum mechanics 126–7, 131–2, 179

radio xvi, 19, 41, 75, 112, 166–7, 173, 175–6, 181, 186, 189, 197, 219
Raspail, François-Vincent 87–8, 137
Ravetz, Jerôme R. 7, 120
recombinant DNA, ethics and 202–3
Recréations scientifiques (Tissandier) 40
Reinhold, Erasmus 25
relativism 6
religion, science and 104–8
Renaissance: cabinets de curiosités of 53–5, *54*; printed science and 17, 24; technological creativity of 146
resistance, to elite theories/technologies 221
Ress, Abraham 33
Revelle, Roger 191
Revue élémentaire de médecine et de pharmacie domestiques (Raspail) 87
risk 210–13
Le roman experimental (Zola) 43–4
Rosen, George 160
Rossi, Paolo 147
Rouelle, Guillaume-François 122
Rousseau, Jean-Jacques 70
Royal Institution (RI) 72–3, *73*, 92; Christmas Lectures 72
Royal Polytechnic Institution 72–3
Rudolph, John 139
Ruskin, John 59, 159

Sagan, Carl 111
Said, Edward 224
Santiago, Diego de 146
Scandella, Domenico (Menocchio) 23–4
Schaffer, Simon 10
science: literary perspective in 43–8; popular vs. proper 220–1; professionalism of 91; religion and 104–8
Science and Culture (Huxley) 156

Science and Its Public (Holton) 5
Science Centres xvi, 65–7
science communicator 65
Science et démocratie (Meunier) 104science fiction 44–7
'Science: Fusion or Illusion' (magazine article) 186
'Science in American Life' (exhibition) 5–6
Science in the Marketplace (Lightman and Fyfe) 221
science museums: changes in 64–6; controversial aspects of 67–8; development of 60–1, *62*; expert-lay boundaries in 66–7; gardens and parks at 63–4; spatial organisation of 61–2
science popularisation: by amateurs 91; cinema for 75–7; criticism of 217; distortion/simplification of 108–13; experts' concerns of 217–18; printed science and 39–40; role of 18; status of 99–104
Science Service organisation 166
science shops 202
scientific culture, education and 119–21
scientific instruments 148–50
scientific knowledge: appropriation of 221; circulation of 219, 221; creation/diffusion of 218–19; dynamic flexibility of 223–4; expert-lay boundaries in 10–17; lessons from past 17–20; negative image of 1–3; PUS movement and 3–10
scientific materialism 104–7, 138
scientific naturalism 104–6
Scientific Revolution 25–8, 146, 148, 154, 224
Secord, James 35, 36, 220–1
Secreti (Piemontese) 26
Sedgwick, Reverend Adam 35–6
self-help manuals 32–3
The Selfish Gene (Dawkins) 112
seminars 126
sensation, learning and 118
Sensenbrenner, James 192
Servan, A.J.M. 83
Shapin, Steven 9, 10
Shelley, Mary 44
Shinn, Terry 219
Silent Spring (Carson) 5, 190, 212
Sima del Elefante excavation site 184
Simon, Bart 194
simplification, in popularisation 108–13
Les six parties du monde (Figuier) 74
The Skeptical Environmentalist (Lomborg) 192

Slater, Eliot 180
Smalley, Richard 181–2
Smiles, Samuel 156, 163
Smithsonian Institution's Museum of American History 5
Smithsonian National Air and Space Museum 67
Snow, Charles Pierce 5, 215
social control xv, 15, 18, 120–1; in science education 133–5
The Social Relations of Science (Crowther) 111
Social Studies of Science (journal) 9
Social Text (journal) 6
Sokal, Alan 6–7
Somerville, Mary 96–7
South Kensington Museum 60–1
spectacular science: curiosities/exhibitions of 53–9, *54*; demonstration of 52–3; museums and 59; overview of 17–18; theatricality and 68–77
Spurzheim, Johann Kaspar 37
stars, media science and 175–8
steam engines *155*, 155
The Structural Transformation of the Public Sphere: An Inquiry into a Category of Bourgeois Society (Habermas) 15
The Structure of Scientific Revolutions (Kuhn) 127
students 18–19, 121–7

Tarzan 109
taxidermy 97–8
Taylor, Frederick Winslow 158
teaching: of science 121–7; scientific culture and 119–21
technological science: artisans and 150–4; hot air balloons and 143–5, *144*; industrial culture and 154–63; inventors/ users/consumers 163–9; overview of 19; people-centred 168–9; philosophers' role in 145–50; public debate on 204; risk/ uncertainty and 210–13
Technology Review magazine 10
technoscience 118, 148, 198, 200, 204–5, 210–5, 224
television xvi, 19, 74–5, 109, 111–2, 173–8, 181, 184, 186, 189, 197, 206
textbooks, origin/role of 127–33
textile dyeing 152–3
theatrical science: anatomy theatres and 68–70, *69*; experiments/lectures and *70*, 70–3, *73*; Figuier's attempts at 74; visual culture of 74–7

Thénard, Joseph-Louis 123, 129–30
theory of relativity 109–11
Thibault, François-Anatole 137–8
Thompson, E.P. 219
Thomson, Dr. Samuel 86
Thomson, James 159
Time magazine 186, 187, 192
the *Times* 110
Tissandier, Gaston 40–1, 94
Tissot, Samuel-André 32
Topham, Jon 220–1
Traité (Ganot) 129
Traité de chimie élémentaire (Thénard) 130
Traité élémentaire de chimie (Lavoisier) 150
Trilling, Lionel 5
2001: A Space Odyssey (film) 76
Tyndall, John 106

uncertainty, in scientific development 210–13
universe, media science and 175–8
university extension movements 137–8
Urania (Flammarion) 47
Urania theatre 73–4
urban waste disposal 161
users, of technology 163–9, *165*
Utopian themes 44–5

vaccination campaigns 206–7
van 't Hoff, Jacobus Henricus 125
Verne, Jules 45, *46*
Vesalius, Andreas 25, 28, *29*, 68
Vestiges of the Natural History of Creation (Chambers) 34–6, 104
Vicq d'Azyr, Félix 83
Victorian scientific naturalism 104–6
Victorian Sensation (Secord) 221
Vincent, Levinus 53–4, *54*
visual culture, of theatrical science 74–7; turn 17, 53, 74
Les Voyages Extraordinaires (Verne) *46*

Waquet, Françoise 217
Wassermann, August von 11
Water-Cure Journal 86
Watson, James 178–9
Watt, James 155
Webb, T.W. 93
Whewell, William 91
White, Gilbert 97
Whitley, Richard 217, 219

270 Index

Willich, Anthony F.M. 33
Wilson, George 60
Wise, Norton 53
Woodcroft, Bennet 60–1
working classes 138–9, 158–62
World Economic Forum 192
Worm, Ole 53Wormianum Museum 56
Wright, Robert 185

XYY syndrome 180

Yarwell, John 149
Yearley, Steven 211
Young, John 211
The Young Gentleman and Lady's Philosophy
    (Martin) 28

Zeitschrift für Physikalische Chemie (Ostwald)
    131
Zola, Émile 43–4
zoological parks 63–4